Tibet

THE BRADT TRAVEL GUIDE

THE BRADT STORY

The first Bradt travel guide was written by Hilary and George Bradt in 1974 on a river barge floating down a tributary of the Amazon in Bolivia. From their base in Boston, Massachusetts, they went on to write and publish four other backpacking guides to the Americas and one to Africa.

In the 1980s Hilary continued to develop the Bradt list in England, and also established herself as a travel writer and tour leader. The company's publishing emphasis evolved towards broader-based guides to new destinations – usually the first to be published on those countries – complemented by hiking, rail and wildlife guides.

Since winning The Sunday Times Small Publisher of the Year Award in 1997, we have continued to fill the demand for detailed, well-written guides to unusual destinations, while maintaining the company's original ethos of low-impact travel.

Travel guides are by their nature continuously evolving. If you experience anything which you would like to share with us, or if you have any amendments to make to this guide, please write; all your letters are read and passed on to the author. Most importantly, do remember to travel with an open mind and to respect the customs of your hosts – it will add immeasurably to your enjoyment.

Happy travelling!

Hilary Bradt

19 High Street, Chalfont St Peter, Bucks SL9 9QE, England
Tel: 01753 893444 Fax: 01753 892333
Email: info@bradt-travelguides.com
Web: www.bradt-travelguides.com

Tibet

THE BRADT TRAVEL GUIDE

Michael Buckley

Bradt Travel Guides Ltd, UK
The Globe Pequot Press Inc, USA

Published in 2003 by Bradt Travel Guides Ltd
19 High Street, Chalfont St Peter, Bucks SL9 9QE, England
web: www.bradt-travelguides.com
Published in the USA by The Globe Pequot Press Inc, 246 Goose Lane,
PO Box 480, Guilford, Connecticut 06475-0480

ISBN 1 84162 061 0

British Library Cataloguing in Publication Data
A catalogue record for this book is available from the British Library

Library of Congress Cataloging-in-Publication Data applied for

Photographs
Cover Pilgrims throwing "windhorses" on Bompori Hill, just outside Lhasa
(Ian Cumming/Tibet Images)
Text Michael Buckley

Illustrations Carole Vincer
Maps Alan Whitaker

Typeset from the author's disc by Wakewing
Printed and bound in Italy by Legoprint SpA, Trento

Author

Michael Buckley has travelled widely in Tibet, China, central Asia and the Himalaya, visiting many Tibetan enclaves. He is author of *Heartlands: Travels in the Tibetan World* (Summersdale Publishers, UK, 2002), a travel narrative about forays to the far reaches of the Tibetan Plateau. He has also contributed stories to the anthologies *Travelers' Tales Tibet* (Travelers' Tales, USA, 2002) and *Travelers' Tales India* (Travelers' Tales, USA, 1995), and is author of a comprehensive guide to Indo-China, titled *Vietnam, Cambodia and Laos* (Moon Handbooks, USA, 2002). In the course of journeys to Tibet, he has hitchhiked overland from Chengdu to Lhasa, trekked around Mount Kailash, and mountain-biked from Lhasa to Kathmandu.

CONTRIBUTOR

Bradley Rowe, author of the Amdo section, has been visiting Tibet since it first opened to individuals in 1984. He has spent over five years in the region, much of it on foot. His photos appear in many publications under the name 'Stone Routes.' Apart from Amdo, his main concern is to encourage preservation of what is left of the unique eco-systems of the plateau – from the handful of unshaven forested mountains to the Tibetan antelope, harried even to the bleakest highest desert. He lives in the UK with his wife, Wendy Teasdill, and their three daughters.

YOUR INPUT

Guidebooks are like time capsules – 'snapshots' taken when the data was collected. The reader should make allowances for fluctuating rules and regulations in Tibet. A guidebook is a two-way process: your input is invaluable for bringing the next edition up to date. If you notice details that have changed or are inaccurate, drop us a line. Marking up maps is especially useful – feel free to photocopy maps, alter them and send them along to us. I believe a guidebook must do much more than present the facts: it must make sense of them. So I welcome suggestions, comments, beefs, bones of contention, insights, travel tips and travellers' tales. Writers will be acknowledged in the next edition. Drop a postcard or letter to:

Michael Buckley, c/o Bradt Travel Guides Ltd,
19 High St, Chalfont St Peter, Bucks SL9 9QE, UK
Email: buckeroo555@yahoo.com

Contents

LIST OF MAPS

Acknowledgements

INSPIRATION, INSIGHTS AND THANKS

Fellow travellers make a big difference to a project like this: on-the-road inspiration was provided by Gary McCue and Kathy Butler, Terry and James Anstey, Kat, Rene and Kris, Thysje, Johanna, Tess, Barbara, Kozo, Pema, Jorge, Markus, Keith, Tom, John Buchanan, Rocky Dang, Shelley Guardia, Doko, Marion Lahme and all the other great people I met along the way. Special thanks to Tony Williams, and fond memories of Peta on the trip in Konkaling. My gratitude to Jane Garnett and Derek Henson for computer support, to Roland Hardt and Jack Joyce for mapping input, to Pat and Baiba Morrow for mountaineering research, and to Tashi Gyal and Dickyi Dolkar for help with the Tibetan language section. Direct contributions were provided by Bradley Rowe, John Ackerly, Geoff Flack and Brian Harris.

ABBREVIATIONS

ATP	Alien Travel Permit, small cardboard folder
BOC	Bank of China
CAAC	Civil Aviation Administration of China
CITS	China International Travel Service, the official government travel agent
CSWA	China Southwest Airlines, local arm of CAAC, the national carrier
PAP	People's Armed Police (paramilitary group)
PLA	People's Liberation Army
PRC	People's Republic of China
PSB	Public Security Bureau (police)
TAC	Tibetan Autonomous County
TAP	Tibetan Autonomous Prefecture
TAR	Tibet Autonomous Region
TTB	Tibet Tourism Bureau
WWII	World War II

Introduction

A visit to Tibet is a strange experience, with intense emotional highs and lows. It's weird because the real Tibet no longer exists. Since military occupation in 1950, the Chinese have systematically dismantled the Tibetan social fabric, destroyed its great monasteries, persecuted its monks and nuns, and wreaked devastating damage on Tibet's pristine environment. Any description of present-day Tibet and Tibetan culture must be framed in this context of iron-fisted Chinese occupation.

'Intense' is a word that applies to many aspects of Tibet.

It applies to the amazing resilience of the Tibetan people in the face of extreme adversity. Their battle has been largely a pacifist one, of suffering and enduring – a game of ultimate patience and tolerance. 'Intense' captures the feel of the landscape. The intensity of colours at this elevation is extraordinary, with glacial-blue lakes, luminous-yellow fields of mustard, deep reds and browns of barren rock landscapes, and then, up on the horizon, looms an ethereal Himalayan snowcap, backed by piercing blue skies. The colours practically glow: when you show photographs of these landscapes to people who haven't been there, they question the unreal colours – what kind of filter did you use?

Travel in the Land of Snows is a guaranteed adventure, with the wildest, roughest road routes in High Asia. Here are the highest mountains and the highest trekking in the world – and the deepest gorges. Tibetan Buddhist monasteries blend into the landscape, becoming navigation landmarks; imposing fortress ruins cling to sheer hilltops; nomads herd yaks in snow-dusted pastures; pilgrims prostrate their way across the land to reach the sacred city of Lhasa. It is this combination of extraordinary landscape, extraordinary people and high adventure that makes Tibet so special.

There is only one drawback to visiting Tibet: you can easily become addicted to the place. It makes you reluctant to leave, and as you do, you're already plotting your return – a return not necessarily to Tibet itself, but to Tibetan culture. Sadly, real Tibetan culture is more likely to be found outside Tibet, in places where refugees continue their Buddhist practices, festivals and way of life in exile – in India, Nepal and Bhutan. A section of this book briefly introduces these places as well.

Travel to Tibet raises important ethical questions. One of the biggest is: should you go? Should you put money in Chinese coffers, thus indirectly subsidising Chinese military bills in Tibet? Most of the tourist business is in the hands of the Chinese, and some of the travel agencies are run by the military. This raises the thorny question of lending legitimacy to Chinese government operations by visiting, but more important for the Tibetans is the moral support they get from visitors. Your mere presence in Tibet provides a 'buffer zone' in an ugly situation between Chinese and Tibetans.

Tourists love monks. This is one of the great anomalies of tourism in Tibet: the monasteries are kept open and operating because of tourist demand to see them.

Apart from Himalayan landscapes, the main tourist 'attraction' in Tibet is in fact its monks and monasteries, its Buddhist rituals and sutra-chanting. The Chinese really have no difficulty with this – they simply cash in on it. Apart from making a buck out of Buddhism, the Chinese have absolutely no interest in Tibet's rich culture, its religion or its language. If you go, you line the pockets of Chinese travel agents, hoteliers and airline agents, but if you stay away, you isolate the Tibetans.

The position of the Tibetan exile leadership is to encourage tourism. When asked about this ethical dilemma – to go or not to go – Nobel Peace Prize laureate the Dalai Lama responded: 'Yes, go to Tibet and see as much as you can. Then tell the world.' He knows that any Western visitor to Tibet will learn of conditions there and of the aspirations of Tibetans, will not fail to be moved by the experience, and will keep the Tibetan issue alive.

In neighbouring Burma, with its appalling human rights record, fellow Nobel laureate Aung San Suu Kyi has adopted a different stance: she has advised travellers to stay away, imposing a form of economic embargo on Burma. Another Burmese phrased it this way: 'We would like tourists to come and enjoy our country, but not now: the money they spend will simply water the poisonous plant.'

The situation in Tibet is different: there is no organised economic embargo here as there once was against South Africa. The Western tourist trade in Tibet represents a small fraction of the number of visitors going to China. By far the biggest group visiting Tibet is Chinese tourists, flocking to see this exotic corner of the Motherland. Chinese tourist arrivals in Tibet doubled over the period 1997 to 2001. In 2001, of a total of 675,000 visitors to Tibet, around 560,000 were Chinese domestic tourists and 115,000 were foreign tourists. While tourism is a mainstay of the economy in Tibet, in the overall picture of visits to China, it does not have a high profile. Basically, whether you go to Tibet or not comes down to a personal choice, to be weighed by each traveller.

If you can resolve the question of 'should you go?' the next thing to consider is 'can you go?' The Chinese are suspicious – with good reason – of the activities of independent travellers in Tibet, and have attempted to shepherd visitors into monitored, higher-paying group tours. After riots and martial law in the early 1990s, the majority of visitors to Tibet visited on group tours. There are, however, ways around this, which you can uncover in this book.

Part One

General Information

Windhorse

2

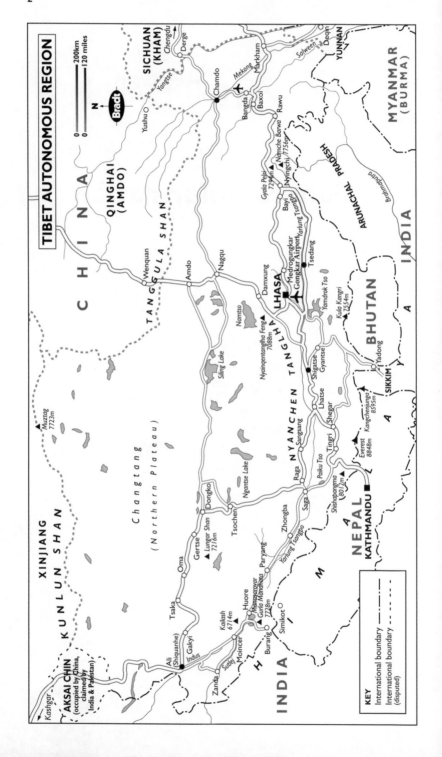

Background Information

GEOGRAPHY AND CLIMATE

The Chinese and the Tibetans refer to different-sized areas when it comes to Tibet. The Tibetans refer to the much larger area of Ethnic Tibet, encompassing the entire Tibetan Plateau, and including the northeastern and eastern areas of Kham and Amdo. Ethnic Tibet or Greater Tibet covers a quarter of China's total area: ethnic Tibet is roughly 2.3 million km², which is almost double the size of what is now called 'Tibet' (Xizang Province) by the Chinese. In 1965, the Chinese created the Tibet Autonomous Region (TAR), having previously carved off much of Kham and Amdo and assimilating them into neighbouring Chinese provinces. Even so, the TAR is huge. With an area of 1.2 million km², the TAR is roughly the size of England, France, Germany and Austria put together. The TAR measures 2,600km from west to east, and 1,300km from north to south.

Superlatives abound when it comes to the subject of physical Tibet: the world's highest peaks and lakes – and the world's deepest gorges – are all located here. The landlocked region of Tibet borders India, Nepal, Bhutan, Burma – and China. Major rivers sourced on the Tibetan Plateau are the Mekong, Yellow, Yangtse, Salween, Yarlung Tsangpo (the source of the Brahmaputra), Indus, Sutlej and Karnali. On their wild journey off the plateau, the rivers carve deep gorges. In the south, bordering Nepal, lie the 8,000m-plus Himalayan giants of Everest, Lhotse, Makalu and Cho Oyu. The world's 14th highest peak, Shishapangma, lies wholly within Tibet. The Himalaya – Tibet's natural mountain border for centuries – have the world's highest snowline, and some 17,000 glaciers. To the north of Tibet are the Kunlun Mountains, while to the west are the Pamirs and the Karakoram Range.

Most of the Tibetan Plateau is over 4,000m high. It was formed millions of years ago by a collision of the Indian and Asian continental plates. A glance at a satellite map will easily delineate this zone, and will show dramatic drop-offs from the edge of the plateau to forested areas. The northern sector of Tibet is the forbidding Changtang, an immensely rocky and arid desert where nomads roam, eking out a tough living. To the northeast, in Amdo, the landscape turns to lush green, with rich grasslands irrigated by the Yellow River. In Kham, semi-monsoonal conditions and lower elevations result in copious forest cover – one of China's greatest sources of timber. The Yarlung Tsangpo River, running from the far west of Tibet to the east, is responsible for the rich pockets of farmland in central Tibet – it's considered the cradle of Tibetan civilisation, with historic Tibetan settlements along the river banks.

Tibet is landlocked: though many Tibetans have not seen the ocean, the pristine turquoise lakes of the plateau are vast – to the eye, the larger ones form their own inland sea. There has been little development at these lakes – Tibetans do not eat fish, and they regard a number of the lakes as sacred places. The largest lakes are Manasarovar (west Tibet), Namtso (north), Yamdrok Tso (central Tibet) and Kokonor (Amdo).

SOLVING THE RIDDLE OF THE TSANGPO GORGES

It seems incredible at the dawn of the 21st century that important new geographic discoveries are still being made. In 1998, and again in 2002, secrets of one of the world's last great uncharted rivers were finally revealed.

The river is the Yarlung Tsangpo. In the 1800s, it was unknown what the course of the river actually was, and whether the Tsangpo (flowing from Tibet) and the Brahmaputra (flowing into India) were the same river, or two different rivers. The reason for the uncertainty lay in the river's dramatic course: for the first half of its 2,900km length, the Yarlung Tsangpo runs east through Tibet. Then it makes an abrupt hairpin turn and flows west into India – where it is called the Brahmaputra – and south again to its mouth in Bangladesh.

This abrupt hairpin turn foxed geographers and adventurers for centuries, but equally mystifying was the river's dramatic drop: on its journey east, the Tsangpo roars into a 4,900m cleft between two mighty peaks – Namche Barwa (elevation 7,756m) and Gyala Pelri (7,294m). In a distance of around 240km, the Tsangpo plummets some 2,700m through what is now known as the Tsangpo Gorge. This is the deepest gorge in the world, and is three times the depth of the Grand Canyon.

Geographers speculated that with such a precipitous drop, there had to be some huge waterfalls within the gorge, but because of its steep, forbidding walls, the gorge was considered inaccessible. In the 1880s, the British sent an Indian pundit by the name of Kinthup into the area to determine if the Tsangpo and the Brahmaputra were indeed one and the same. His task was to launch 500 small, marked logs through the gorge to determine the course of the river. After a series of epic misadventures, Kinthup completed mission impossible, launching all 500 logs (50 a day over a period of ten days), but his message back to headquarters went astray and there were no observers to witness the logs coming through at the other end.

Nobody believed Kinthup's discoveries, including his claim of sighting a fall of 45m in height. In forays to the region in 1911 and 1913, British officer Fred Bailey confirmed Kinthup's exploration, but found only a 9m fall at the site mentioned. (Bailey later tracked Kinthup down in Darjeeling and found that a scribe had confused a thin 45m cascade from a tributary with the 9m fall on the main river, and Kinthup could neither read nor write to check the account.) Bailey conclusively showed that the Tsangpo and Brahmaputra did form the same river, but he did not have the resources to fully explore the region.

Not making matters easier was the local custom of poisoning outsiders as sacrifices to evil spirits, but the British persevered. In 1924, British botanist Frank Kingdon Ward spent 11 harrowing months surveying the gorge and discovered Rainbow Falls, which, observed from a considerable distance, he estimated at nine to 12m high. His reconnaissance was described in his 1926 book, *Riddle of the Tsangpo Gorges*. Ward discovered that the Tsangpo's precipitous descent was probably not due to one or two massive cascades, but rather was the result of a near-continuous succession of violent rapids. But still the secrets remained; Ward's reconnaissance reduced the unexplored part to one raging section about 15km long.

Even satellite imagery could not probe this section, as the gorge is deep and twisted, with overhanging vegetation. In 1987, a Chinese Army photographer claimed to have photographed falls in the region while flying over the Upper Gorge in a military helicopter, but no accurate measurements of the height of the falls could be made from these pictures. In fact, the unexplored section was considered impenetrable until Nepal-based explorers Ian Baker and Ken Storm made persistent attempts in the 1990s. In a 1998 expedition they found a way through – and were able to get near to the falls – by following *takin* tracks. Using climbing ropes, Baker and Storm rappelled down the Tsangpo walls and got up close to Ward's Rainbow Falls, which they recalculated to be 22m high, double Kingdon Ward's original estimate.

Then the team went where none had gone before: they continued their descent deeper into the canyon, and discovered a huge new waterfall, calculated at 32m high, which they christened Hidden Falls. That name probably won't appear on Chinese maps, however. Baker and Storm upstaged a Chinese scientific expedition in the same area at the same time: both teams claimed the prize discovery of the waterfall. Baker and Storm mounted an intense publicity campaign in the US to reinforce their claim, and the Chinese responded by closing the Tsangpo Gorge region to foreigners for a significant period. Among rafters and kayakers, the Yarlung Tsangpo is regarded as the Everest of white water. The river claimed the lives of two kayakers attempting first descents: Yoshitaka Takei, who vanished in 1993, and Doug Gordon, who was lost in a massive rapid while on a *National Geographic*-sponsored expedition in 1998. After Gordon's death, white-water experts wrote the Tsangpo off as un-runnable.

In early February 2002, however, a team of explorers and kayakers from seven nations began a two-month expedition through the Upper Tsangpo Gorge. Their goal was twofold: to chart some of the unvisited parts of the gorge, and to complete its first white-water descent. The 80-man ground crew included Ken Storm, who had discovered Hidden Falls in 1998, and 68 Tibetan porters lugging 1,100kg of supplies.

Expedition leader Scott Lindgren, from California, had had his eyes on the gorge for more than a decade, after pioneering descents of other Himalayan rivers. He scouted the Tsangpo several times and concluded that the flow of water was suicidally high in the spring, but that late winter might work because of the lower flow.

Seven of the world's top kayakers launched into the wild water of the Upper Tsangpo Gorge – the most fearsome they had ever seen – and went where nobody had ever been before. They survived Class V+ rapids, thundering past boiling eddies, great vertical drops, massive lateral waves and huge boulders. Alternately paddling and portaging – and seal-launching from huge boulders – the team paddled about 90% of the Upper Gorge. Then the battered group started an epic winter portage over 3,600m Sechen La, to by-pass the un-runnable Rainbow Falls and Hidden Falls. The expedition members and porters threaded their way up treacherous couloirs and steep snow-slopes, which must have looked a strange spectacle with kayaks in tow. Finally, they rejoined the river, but found that a flash flood had scoured the banks of the Tsangpo to near-vertical rock. At this point, Lindgren prudently decided to end the expedition. The team had covered 70 river kilometres – the first-ever descent of the Upper Tsangpo Gorge – and lived to tell the tale.

Tibet's extreme altitude makes it a special place for hardy high-alpine flora, with secrets yet to be revealed. This rare flora attracted the attention of early 20th-century British plant hunters, who discovered the Himalayan blue poppy and many species of rhododendron (there are estimated to be over 400 in Tibet). Over 2000 species of medicinal plants have been documented by the Tibetans themselves. Herbal remedies lie at the core of Tibetan medicinal practices.

Climate

The climate of Tibet is cool, high and dry. With an average elevation of 4,500m, the weather in Tibet can best be described as 'extreme', oscillating from searing heat to freezing cold – sometimes in the course of a single day. It is possible to be simultaneously hot and cold, if a person's head is in the shade, but his or her legs are in the sun. Climatic conditions vary with elevation and exposure: there is little moisture in the atmosphere and intense UV rays can be problematic.

There is no best time to visit Tibet: the weather is unpredictable and no matter which season, there are extreme conditions to deal with. Few travellers visit during the winter, however, because of treacherous road conditions, and because access flights often close down for this period.

Spring March to May. Strong winds are possible and can whip up dust storms and sandstorms. However, this is one of the better trekking seasons, when conditions are not too hot.

Summer June to August. In this period are higher temperatures, which are conducive to staging festivals like horse-racing fairs. Most of Tibet's rainfall occurs during July and August. In southern and eastern Tibet, the Himalaya form a barrier against the rain-bearing monsoons, so Tibet does not experience heavy monsoons like Nepal, Sikkim or Bhutan. However, in Tibet rainwater build-up combined with glacial meltwater can result in rampaging rivers and flooding in the autumn.

Autumn September to November. As a result of the aforementioned rampaging rivers, travel in autumn is prone to delays due to mudslides, washouts, flooding and bridges that have been swept away. Otherwise, it's not a bad time to travel, and it can be sunny.

Winter December to early March. Severely cold conditions and snowfalls can shut down high passes to traffic. The Tibetans call the plateau *Kangjong* (Land of Snows), but the sun is quick to melt off snowfalls in the central Tibetan region. February and March are good festival months: *Losar* (Tibetan new year) falls in this period and during this time there are many nomads in Lhasa.

ECOLOGY

Though they had no sewage systems or concept of garbage disposal, in the realm of conservation the Tibetans were light years ahead of the West (at a time when the Tibetans were still in control of their environment). The Buddhist compassion for all life – human, animal or insect – protected Tibet's wildlife, and in a sense made Tibet one great wildlife preserve. Because Tibet was isolated from the rest of the world for so long, it sheltered rare species: even in the 1990s, species thought long-extinct were discovered in Tibet (a breed of small forest pony was found in Kham, and the Tibetan red deer was found in the Shannan district). Huge herds of wild gazelles, antelopes, wild asses and yaks used to graze the grasslands of Central Tibet. If animals were culled, the Tibetans only took what they needed, so impact on the wildlife was minimal.

HIGH-ALTITUDE WILDLIFE

Adapting to the harsh conditions of the Tibetan Plateau is some remarkable wildlife. Some animals, like the wild yak (*drong* in Tibetan), are so well-adapted to the altitude that they cannot live at lower elevations. Wild yaks are enormous creatures: an adult male can weigh 800kg – double the weight of a domestic yak. The biggest wild yaks stand two metres high at the shoulder.

Unique in its camouflage – a greyish spotted coat, blending in with its terrain – is the snow leopard (*gangzig*), which stalks blue sheep. Your chances of sighting the snow leopard are slim, as during the day it sleeps in caves or on rocky ledges: it is a nocturnal hunter, mostly active at dusk and dawn. Equally reclusive is the takin (*bamen*), a hairy, hoofed herbivore with a bulbous nose and backward-facing horns. It is a strange mix of horse, moose and musk-ox, and can weigh up to 200kg, with a body two metres long. The takin favours the forested slopes of the plateau, particularly in eastern Tibet and in Bhutan, where it inhabits dense forest. By contrast, the swift Tibetan antelope (*chiru*) is partial to high, treeless desert zones – particularly the remote Changtang region of northern Tibet.

There are reckoned to be over 480 species of birds in the TAR, with rare species like the black-necked crane seasonally migrating. Among the birds are some real high-fliers. For many years it was believed that no birds flew over the high peaks of the Himalaya. However, griffon vultures have been sighted flying at 9,000m, over the summit of Everest, and yellow-billed choughs are often seen at Everest base camps at around 7,000m. Snow pigeons and bar-headed geese have also been sighted flying over peaks at 8,300m.

In the 1940s, American adventurer Leonard Clark reported: 'Every few minutes we would spot a bear, a hunting wolf, herds of musk deer, *kiang* (wild ass), gazelles, big horned sheep, or foxes. This must be one of the last unspoiled big game paradises.' His words were in some ways prophetic: with the coming of the Chinese in the 1950s, everything changed rapidly. Chinese soldiers machine-gunned wildlife not only for food, but for export to China – and for sport. Some of Tibet's once-plentiful wildlife now faces extinction: in the last 40 years, large mammals have gone the way of the bison in North America. Apart from supplying China with meat, there is a demand for rare animals in Chinese restaurants and for Chinese traditional medicine. This has decimated numbers of the snow leopard, for instance.

Tibetan Buddhists have a sense of sacred landscape. Larger lakes and mountains were sacred and were left untouched, and mining was not practised. With its harsh environment, Tibet has a delicate ecological balance – one with which the Chinese are interfering. Such interference can have disastrous consequences, leading – for example - to increased desertification at Qinghai Lake, or destruction of an entire ecosystem. This may be happening with the building of a hydroelectric project at Lake Yamdrok Tso – a highly controversial project that the Chinese have rushed, with uncertain results. Another large dam is being constructed in Kham and more are planned. The Chinese have made a priority of exploiting Tibet's untapped oil and mineral wealth. Oil fields in Amdo produce over a million tons of crude oil a year. In 2001, Chinese scientists announced the discovery of billions of tons of oil and gas in the remote Changtang region of northern Tibet.

The Dalai Lama once said that he could understand Chinese anger with Tibetan 'separatists', but what did they have against the trees? It is estimated that over 50 percent of Tibet's forests have been cut down since 1959 – mostly in eastern, northeastern and southeastern Tibet. If massive clear-cutting takes place on the slopes of the Tibetan Plateau, there will be nothing to stop landslides and mudslides cascading down during monsoon season into neighbouring nations like Burma or India. There could be unbridled erosion and flooding in these areas; the monsoon patterns themselves could be affected by changes in the ecological balance in Tibet. Severe flooding of the Yangtse in the late 1990s is, according to Chinese sources, directly attributable to deforestation at the edge of the Tibetan Plateau. The situation became so critical that in 1998 Chinese authorities issued a ban on logging in the upper reaches of the Yangtse and Yellow rivers.

Apart from exploitation of natural resources comes the threat of pollution. Although Chinese officials have shied away from the topic, there is evidence that remote parts of Tibet have been used for the dumping of nuclear waste. China is intent on using Tibet as a missile-launching site, targeting Indian cities. There are a number of missile bases and military airfields scattered around Tibet. Far more progressive is the Dalai Lama's vision. He calls for complete demilitarisation of the region of Tibet, to serve as a buffer between the nations of India and China. He envisages the transformation of Tibet into a sanctuary, a zone of peace – as it once used to be.

On paper, there have been attempts by Chinese officials to set up nature reserves, but in effect there is little protection or policing going on, and these are largely cosmetic. The reserve with the highest profile is Qomolangma Nature Preserve, in the Everest region, with a 34,000km^2 zone said to be under protection (although it is a mixed-use zone, with herders living within the boundaries). Under the guidance of renowned naturalist George Schaller, the mega Changtang Nature Reserve (around 247,000km^2) was established in 1993, but poaching of Tibetan antelope proceeds at a brisk pace within its confines.

HISTORY AND POLITICS

To do justice to the subject, an account of history and politics in Tibet really requires a separate 800-page book. Even the modern era could easily provide enough content for a 500-page book. Two hefty tomes to consult are Melvyn Goldstein's *A History of Modern Tibet 1913–1951*, and Tsering Shakya's *The Dragon in the Land of Snows*, covering the period since 1947. The following is a very brief introduction, but one that should be read in combination with the section on 'Tibetan Buddhism' because in Tibet you cannot separate religion from politics.

Tibetan recorded history dates back over 2,000 years. The emergence of Tibet as a geopolitical entity dates to the 7th century AD, when warrior-king Songtsen Gampo unified the clans of Tibet. At this time, Tibet was a great military power that expanded its boundaries south into India and east into China.

King Songtsen Gampo (circa 618–649) is regarded as a great 'religious king' – he actively spread the teachings of Buddhism in regions under his control. The king had three Tibetan queens. As Tibet's power grew, neighbouring countries sought alliances through marriage: Princess Wencheng from China was sent to marry Songtsen Gampo, and Nepal sent a royal princess as a bride.

In the 8th century, King Trisong Detsen adopted Buddhism as the official religion of Tibet, bringing Buddhism into conflict with the ancient Bon shaman religion of Tibet. Tibet waged war on China, occupying the Tang dynasty capital of Xian. In the 9th century, war broke out again between the Tibetans and the Chinese, with the Tibetans emerging victorious. At the centre of Lhasa, outside the Jokhang Temple, stands a stone obelisk that affirms in Tibetan and Chinese the terms of a peace treaty concluded between King Ralpachen and Chinese Emperor Wangti in the year 823. It is written in stone: 'Tibet and China shall abide by the

SAVING THE CHIRU

In March 2002, police in New Delhi intercepted two Kashmiri traders with 80 *shahtoosh* shawls. It takes the underwool of three antelopes to make a single *shahtoosh* shawl, so that haul represented at least 240 dead Tibetan antelopes. And on the international market, at US$5,000 a shawl (the average price for a fine shawl), the cache was worth US$400,000.

Renowned naturalist George Schaller has conducted extensive research on the chiru (Tibetan antelope) in their main habitat of Changtang in remote northern Tibet. Schaller says upwards of 20,000 *chiru* are poached each year for their underwool, from which *shahtoosh* shawls are made. This is pushing the chiru to the brink of extinction. The demand for shahtoosh shawls in the fashion centres of Western countries has boosted the trade. The wool of the chiru is the finest animal fibre in the world – finer than that of cashmere goats. This also makes it the most expensive fibre. Although the sale of shahtoosh shawls is supposedly banned around the world, they can be bought at haute couture boutiques, with clients paying up to US$20,000 for a single shawl.

The main centre for *shahtoosh* spinning is Kashmir, even though the trade was outlawed there in mid-2000. Kashmir is of course a renowned centre for spinning cashmere wool, also from Tibet. Poachers from Tibet trade chiru wool for tiger parts from India. The Kashmiris need the chiru wool, and the tiger parts are highly valued in Chinese traditional medicine. So here's a vicious circle involving two highly endangered species: poachers are using automatic weapons to gun down chiru so that Kashmiris can weave *shahtoosh* shawls to sell to high-fashion divas in the west. And Indian traders are poaching tigers, which the Kashmiris sell to the poachers in Tibet in exchange for chiru wool: the tiger parts are divided up for sale in Chinese traditional medicine potions which are mostly directed at boosting a flagging male libido.

frontiers of which they are now in occupation. All to the east is the country of Great China; and all to the west is, without question, the country of Great Tibet.'

In 826, Ralpachen was assassinated by his elder brother Langdarma, who succeeded him and changed tack completely: he attempted to snuff out Buddhism under pressure from Bon priests. In 842, he was killed by a monk, and Tibet dissolved into chaotic factions. A hundred years later, Buddhism was introduced again in western Tibet, in the Guge Kingdom. By the 12th century, three Buddhist lineages or schools had emerged in Tibet: Nyingmapa, Kagyupa, and Sakyapa. The fierce rivalry between them was not so much religious as political.

The snowcapped peaks and high deserts of the Tibetan Plateau served as natural defenses and increased Tibet's isolation. But in the 13th century, Tibet fell under Mongol domination. The Mongol Khans ruled an empire that stretched as far as Europe and encompassed all of China. The Mongols took a great interest in Tibetan Buddhism. In 1350, Tibet resumed its independent ways, but enjoyed a special patron-priest relationship with Mongolia over the next few centuries; invited to educate the Mongols in spiritual matters, the Tibetans in turn accepted Mongolian guarantees to stave off would-be invaders.

It was the Mongolian leader Altan Khan who bestowed the title 'Dalai Lama' (Great Ocean, or Ocean of Wisdom) on Sonam Gyatso, the 16th century leader of the Geluk or Yellow Hat sect. This reformist school had been established in the

14th century: Sonam Gyatso is regarded as the third Dalai Lama (the title was conferred posthumously on his predecessors). The Geluk sect gradually assumed a dominant role in politics and from 1642 onwards they effectively ruled Tibet through their leader, the 5th Dalai Lama. The 'Great Fifth' (Lobsang Gyatso) managed to reunify Tibet and extended his authority to the fringes of Tibetan territory. During his reign, Tibetan culture flourished – many monasteries were erected and the Potala was rebuilt. By this time, Tibet operated under one of the most unusual forms of government in the world: a theocracy, or a Buddhocracy (a system whereby the spiritual leader is also a king figure – sometimes referred to as 'god-king' – combining religious and political responsibilities). The system lasted over 300 years, up until the Chinese invasion in 1950.

By the 17th century, Mongol power was waning, and another set of invaders stormed the Great Wall to occupy China: the Manchus. By this time, Tibet had largely demilitarised – perhaps the first nation in history ever to do so. The national priorities lay in spiritual matters. The Manchus recognised Tibet as an independent nation under the authority of the Dalai Lama, and agreed to protect the peace of the demilitarised nation. Over the next 300 years, Tibet's fortunes fluctuated, with various incursions across its borders by the forces of Nepal and China. One of the stranger chapters in Tibetan history was an invasion in 1903 by the British colonial forces, intent on opening Tibet to trade and convinced that arch-rival Russia was influencing Tibet. After blasting their way through to Lhasa, the British stayed for two months. Failing to find anyone of real authority (the Dalai Lama had fled), the British concluded a useless treaty with some head lamas, and then withdrew, leaving a telegraph line and a few trade links in place.

In 1911, with China weakened by civil war, the Tibetans seized the opportunity to formally announce Tibetan independence, expelling all Chinese from Tibetan soil. Between 1913 and 1950, Tibet asserted its independent status by controlling its own affairs, signing treaties with neighbouring nations, patrolling its own borders, bearing its own flag, and by issuing its own currency, passports and stamps. In this regard, it was ahead of its neighbours: India and China shook off the yoke of colonial rule only after World War II.

Curiously, the main Chinese claim to Tibet goes back to an era when China itself was occupied by a foreign power – the Mongols. If Tibet really were part of China, it's odd that the Chinese would wait over a thousand years before staking their claim. A better explanation would be that the Tibetans successfully defended themselves against the Chinese for more than a thousand years. Over the last two thousand years, Tibet has nurtured a culture that is very different from that of China, with a separate language and literature, separate form of religion, separate economy and central government, and distinct forms of art and architecture. Out of this rare society – based on the tenets of Tibetan Buddhism – emerged a distinct 'Tibetan-ness'. It is this Tibetan-ness that forms the basis for their claim to independence. Pre-Chinese-occupied Tibet was not a paradise. It was a mediaeval society that was out of synch with the rest of the world, and which paid dearly for its isolationist policy and its failure to keep abreast of the times.

Post-1950 Tibet

After their victory in the long-running civil war in 1949, the forces of Mao Zedong wasted little time in announcing their next target would be the 'return of Tibet to the embrace of the Motherland'. The Chinese invaded Tibet from the east in 1950. Their justification for invasion was to liberate the Tibetans from 'feudalism'. However, it is dubious whether this came to pass: Tibetan nobility and clergy were simply replaced with harsher Chinese masters.

COMMUNISM AND BUDDHISM

Can Communism and Buddhism co-exist? They are both rational, non-theistic (no belief in a superior god) and altruistic philosophies. So in theory they should be able to get along with each other. The problem is communist intolerance of Buddhism, not the reverse. In the early years after the Chinese invasion, the Dalai Lama claimed that he liked some of Mao Zedong's ideas, even going so far as saying he considered himself half-Marxist, half-Buddhist. And Buddhism had long been practiced in China itself. But Mao Zedong told the Dalai Lama 'religion is poison'.

One of the main reasons the Chinese claimed they set out to 'liberate' Tibet was to free it from 'feudalism,' which, it transpired, meant not only Tibetan aristocrats but also the entire monastic system. The communists lumped Tibetan Buddhism in with the old 'feudal' ways of Tibet. The monks, claimed the Chinese, did nothing: they just sat around the monasteries and exploited the people, which prevented Tibet from modernising. The question remains: what would've happened if the Chinese had not invaded in 1950? The Dalai Lama – not old enough to rule at the time – was most certainly a progressive person who intended to introduce modern ways. He was – and is – fascinated by the West and by modern inventions.

Communist countries have historically replaced Buddhist teachings with communist ideology, weakening the power of the monasteries, eliminating the privileges of monks and discrediting the monastic leadership. Persecution of Buddhists in Russia and Mongolia nearly wiped them out. So what does the Chinese communist leadership do about a region that is overwhelmingly Tibetan Buddhist in faith? Well, they set up the Chinese Religious Affairs Bureau to oversee what is happening in the monasteries, to introduce Marxism into the curriculum and to demand allegiance to Beijing. During the Cultural Revolution, statuary at main altars in some Lhasa temples was replaced with portraits of Mao Zedong. Karl Marx believed religion to be the opiate of the masses, employed by repressive regimes to divert the attention of the people from their true enemies. In a true communist society, religion does not exist – it is replaced by loyalty to the Party. A modified version of this is that religious practices that do not harm political rule can be tolerated. In Tibet, however, monks and nuns often spearhead political protest.

Under a document called the 17-Point Agreement – dictated by the Chinese in 1951 – the Dalai Lama would remain at the head of the Tibetan government, but China would be in charge of military matters and other key facets. The 17-Point Agreement quickly turned into a sham: monastic lands were confiscated, tribal lands were collectivised, and it soon became apparent that the Chinese idea of schooling was very different from the Tibetan idea. Tibetans had little empathy for the zeal of Maoism, and alongside the construction of hydro-electric stations, experimental farms and roads, armed resistance took place at various points (particularly in eastern Tibet) from 1954–59. Concerned for his safety, those close to the Dalai Lama engineered his escape on horseback to India. In 1959, he crossed the border into northeast India and into exile. Behind him, Lhasa fell into chaotic fighting – tens of thousands of Tibetans were killed in the subsqent uprising.

In India, meanwhile, the Dalai Lama renounced the 17-Point Agreement and set up his government-in-exile.

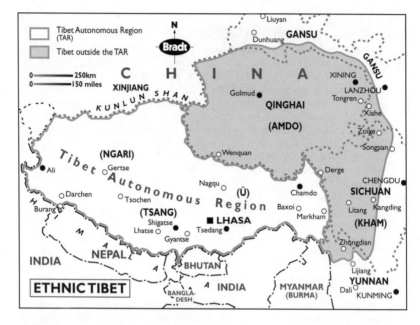

Barely recovering from the vicious reprisals of 1959, Tibet was hurled headlong into the madness of the Cultural Revolution (1966–76), which hit Tibet harder than any other part of China.

Chinese officials would later blame destruction of monasteries on this period, when in fact many buildings were blown up or dismantled before the onset of the Cultural Revolution. With the flight of the Dalai Lama, the Chinese dissolved the remnants of the Tibetan Government, and set up the Tibet Autonomous Region (1965), splitting the area of Ethnic Tibet in half. All forms of Tibetan customs and worship – public and private – were banned, including barter. Large numbers of Tibetans died in labour camps and prisons.

Since the 1960s, Chinese policy in Tibet has see-sawed – sometimes harsh and repressive, other times loosening up. China's human rights record in Tibet, meanwhile, has been appalling, constituting one of history's worst cases of cultural genocide.

In 1987 major rioting took place in Lhasa: this was followed by intermittent demonstrations which were brutally put down by Chinese troops. Martial law was imposed in 1989 and not lifted for over a year. Since 1996, it has been forbidden to own or display any image of the Dalai Lama in Tibet: this followed in the wake of a major falling-out over the choice of the 11th Panchen Lama. Little dialogue has taken place between the Chinese and the Tibetan government-in-exile over the issue of Tibet. China has tightened its grip on the region, ruling what is today the largest colony in the world.

In mid-2001, Chinese authorities in Lhasa staged 'celebrations' to mark 'the 50th anniversary of the peaceful liberation of Tibet'. Looking back on those 50 years, the Chinese see Tibet as a great success story – the socialist transformation for Tibetans from primitive feudalism to a much higher standard of living. From the Tibetan point-of-view, those 50 years have been a complete catastrophe, a sad story of pillage, rape, torture, dislocation and destruction – a deliberate attempt to obliterate their culture, their religion and their values.

ETHNIC TIBET

The map opposite shows the shifting political boundaries of Tibet, old and new. The wider area encompasses 'Ethnic Tibet' – the area recognised as Tibet by the British in the Simla Treaty of 1914 (which the Chinese did not ratify). Starting in the 1920s, the area bordering China to the east was slowly encroached upon. In the 1950s, the Amdo and Kham regions were carved up and incorporated into Chinese provinces, mostly as a collection of Tibetan Autonomous Prefectures (TAPs). In 1965, the Chinese administration created the Tibet Autonomous Region (TAR), reducing the area designated as 'Tibet' to half its former size. When the Chinese refer to 'Tibet', they mean Xizang or the TAR, which embraces the former Tibetan regions of Ü, Tsang and Ngari. When Tibetans talk about 'Tibet', however, they mean the much wider Ethnic Tibet region, embracing not only central and western Tibet, but also the former regions of Amdo and Kham.

ECONOMY

The chief crops in Tibet are barley, wheat, millet and buckwheat. Animal husbandry is the major activity in Tibet's great pasturelands, with the raising of yaks, sheep and goats, as well as horses and mules. Yaks, the 'ships of the plateau', are the mainstay of the traditional Tibetan economy. In larger towns, the main traditional industry is craft production – the making of carpets, Tibetan boots, *tankas* and religious items.

Before the 1950s, industry in Lhasa was really only present in the form of a mint and an ammunition factory. Since then, light industry around Lhasa has ballooned to the point where pollution is a concern: industry includes power plants, machinery plants, printing shops, chemical factories, woollen textile plants, leather processing factories, grain processing factories, carpet factories, a concrete factory and a brewery.

A key factor in the Chinese 'development' of Tibet is finding or creating sources of energy. Hydro-electric projects are under way in parts of the plateau to tap the enormous power generated by rivers originating in Tibet. A number of these projects show little concern for the surrounding environment. The high altitude in Tibet results in intense solar radiation, which has successfully been utilised through solar panels and solar cookers. There is also great potential for harnessing wind energy.

THE FORBIDDEN FLAG

The Chinese flag shows five bright yellow stars on a deep red background. Red is the colour of revolution: the large yellow star is said to indicate the Party, while the four smaller stars represent the classes that uphold it – workers, peasants, soldiers and intellectuals. Interpretation of the star symbolism varies: another version has it that the big star is the Han majority, and the smaller stars indicate the key minorities – Tibetans, Uighurs, Mongols and Hui. The pre-1950 Tibetan flag shows two snow lions (white with turquoise manes and tails) upholding the three precious jewels of Buddhism, framed by a snow-covered mountain and a rising sun motif with red and blue rays. The flag is outlawed in Tibet: possessing one is cause for a lengthy jail sentence; displaying one in public has led to summary execution.

Before 1950, Tibet was self-sufficient in food, with barley as the staple. In the 1960s and 1970s, the Chinese ordered wheat to be planted instead of barley, banned barter, and formed communes – a disastrous policy that led to Tibet's first-ever famines. Now Beijing claims that it has to heavily subsidise the ailing economy in Tibet, but officials fail to mention several key factors, such as how much money is drained by propping up Chinese settlers and the military in Tibet. Estimates put the number of PLA (People's Liberation Army) troops in Tibet at between 200,000 and half a million. Long convoys of military trucks are a common sight, as are military garrisons, particularly in border areas. There are at least nine military airfields in Tibet, a number of radar stations and several missile bases. Tibet has become one of China's largest missile-launching bases, capable of targeting India and other areas near the Indian Ocean.

Although officially the Tibetan economy appears to be running at a loss, a factor not mentioned is how much of Tibet's natural wealth is being taken out. Since 1959, over half of Tibet's forests have been cut down. Tibet's mineral resources were largely untouched before 1950: the Chinese have identified reserves of gold, radium, titanium, lithium, iron, lead, bauxite and other minerals, including major deposits of uranium. For religious reasons, Tibetans did not mine – disturbing the earth was considered a bad omen. Today, it is rumoured that mining accounts for a third of Tibet's industrial output, with dozens of mining sites opening up. Large deposits of oil and gas have been discovered in Tibet's northern Changtang region. This raises the essential issue of what the Chinese are doing in Tibet in the first place. The answer is: they're doing what every colonial power has done throughout recorded history – they are exploiting the colony's resources. They are cutting down all the trees because China proper has run out of trees.

Railway on the rooftop

A poster put out by China Mobile and China Construction Bank shows Lhasa as a futuristic land of high-rise buildings, telecom towers and fly-over highways, with a train running through it all. There are two Tibetan buildings depicted in the poster: Tibet Museum, and the Potala Palace (perhaps some type of elaborate railway station? Lhasa Grand Central?). This is Lhasa in the 21st century – a Chinese clone. The blueprint is to modernise, go high-rise, and bring in entrepreneurs to stimulate the market. The train in the poster has sleek aerodynamic lines like the Japanese Bullet Train or the French TGV (the high-speed train that runs across France).

And all this may yet come to pass. Under construction from Golmud to Lhasa is the world's highest railway line. Like most large Chinese projects in Tibet, this is highly controversial. The line, with a budget of US$2.4 billion, may be completed by 2007. The projected line is a formidable engineering challenge, covering a distance of 1,130km, crossing the Kunlun mountain range, boring through 30km of tunnels, cresting two 5,000-metre passes, and running past 29 stations before heading for Lhasa. Along the way, the railway is bound to disrupt Tibet's fragile eco-system and impact on its rare wildlife. About 550km, or half, of the line would be built on permafrost, which is unstable: any construction is bound to damage this environment. In warm weather, the frozen ground can thaw, causing rail track to buckle and sink. The Chinese claim to have made a technological breakthrough for dealing with this: the plan is to build a refrigeration system that captures wintry air and circulates it year-round through underground pipes to keep the earth frozen. Once the line is in place, it is projected to run 16 trains a day from Golmud to Lhasa – eight each way – and move eight million tons of cargo annually. For passengers, the railroad would offer railcars pressurised like jetliners: 'oxygen bars' would be available to first-class passengers. The Golmud-Lhasa run would take 15 hours by train, knocking at least ten hours off the current best time by bus.

The Chinese claim that the TAR is the only part of China not connected by rail, and that a railway would accelerate economic and social development of Tibet. Those same two factors – viewed from a Tibetan perspective – amount to a nightmare. 'Economic development' could mean Chinese mining companies using the rail line as a way of extracting precious metals and other resources and freighting them back to China. 'Social development' could obliquely mean a massive influx of Chinese settlers, drawn by financial incentives and tax breaks. There are precedents here: you do not have to look any further than Golmud itself. Fifty years ago, Golmud was open steppe with nomad herders. After the railway reached town, immigrants from eastern China arrived in droves, leading to the present population of several hundred thousand and a sprawling town. Another major application of the railway reaching Tibet is strategic – with the line, it is easier to consolidate border defences.

The long-range blueprint for Tibet calls for four rail lines reaching Lhasa (the other three are from Lanzhou, Chengdu and Kunming).

POPULATION AND PEOPLE

The main groups are Tibetan and Han Chinese. The origins of the Tibetans as a race are sketchy: ethnologists place them in the Tibeto-Burman group. The earliest human habitation in Tibet can be traced back 4,700 years: it is believed that Tibetans migrated to the plateau in the late Neolithic Age. However, a recent find suggests that there was human presence in Tibet much earlier than that, as far back as the Ice Age. In 1995, researcher David Zhang Dian from Hong Kong University found remnants of a stove and 19 handprints and footprints pressed in rock on a mountain slope 85km from Lhasa. He brought back rock samples and had them dated. The tests revealed they were from the Ice Age. And in 2002, at a location 120km north of Golmud, Chinese archaeologist Xu Xinguo found artefacts dating to the microlithic period (10,000 to 30,000 years ago).

On the Tibetan Plateau there are a number of ethnic Tibetan subgroups, differentiated by cultural, dress and linguistic variations. These groups include the Topa (far-west Tibet), the Khampa (east Tibet), the Golok (from the northeast), and a number of minority groups closely related to Tibetans, such as the Qiang (from upper Sichuan) and the Monba and Lhoba tribespeople (far southern Tibet, near the Bhutan border). In the Barkor in Lhasa, it's possible to see groups from very different regions who have arrived on pilgrimage to the sacred city. The groups are often identifiable by their dress. From Amdo come nomad women, with their braided hair done in 108 strands (a sacred number). The waist-length tresses must be redone at least once a week and smeared with yak-butter. In former times, Tibetan women used to wear their wealth in the form of elaborate jewellery. This still holds true to some extent – you will see Amdo women with big chunks of turquoise or amber in their hair, or worn in bulky necklaces. From Golok come nomads who wear greasy sheepskin cloaks, yak-hide boots, and often sport felt bowler hats (a legacy of British invasion) or Stetson felt hats (made in eastern China). From eastern Tibet come the quick-tempered Khampas: the men have tassels of red or black yarn braided through their hair, and a dagger sheathed at the waist – not entirely decorative. Selling goods in the Barkor are also Nepali and Kashmiri traders, and Muslims from Xinjiang.

Any statistical data on Tibet – particularly on population – is dicey; facts and figures are fudged to suit whatever propaganda department is issuing them. Basically, the Chinese do not wish it to be known that they are flooding the region with Chinese settlers. In a 1996 figure, the Chinese claim the population of the

TAR is 2.45 million, of which 96% is Tibetan (around 2.35 million), and 4% is Chinese (around 100,000). This does not take into account the number of roving (non-resident) Chinese businesspeople in Tibet, nor Chinese military stationed in Tibet (estimated from 200,000 to 500,000 troops) – they would be registered in other provinces of China. It's possible, within the region of Ethnic Tibet, that the Chinese outnumber the Tibetans: in Lhasa, Chinese civilians and troops clearly outnumber Tibetans. The population of Ethnic Tibet could be 4.5 to 6 million, meaning more Tibetans live outside the TAR than in it. Within Tibet, nearly all Chinese live in urban areas, while 80% of Tibetans live in rural areas, some continuing their nomadic ways.

Last of the nomads

Traditional occupations for Tibetans are farmer, merchant, trader or monk. But the lifestyle that really manifests the rugged spirit of Tibet is that of the hardy nomad, dependent on yaks and livestock to survive. Tibetans are among the last nomads in Asia – other pastoral nomads include the Mongols (mostly in Outer Mongolia) and the Turkic tribes of China's far northwest, such as the Kazaks. Tibetan nomads face a great battle to retain their way of life as the Chinese are suspicious of those on the move, and attempt to make them settle: as a result the way of the nomad is fast disappearing.

Early travellers to Tibet remarked on how cheery Tibetan nomads were in the face of one of the harshest environments in Asia – a high, treeless, windswept plateau. Maybe it's their ribald sense of humour that sustains them in subzero temperatures and howling gales. Whatever the case, the nomads are part of the romance of Tibet, with their yaks, yak-hair tents, their elaborate costumes and jewellery, and their raucous folksongs.

It is thought that up to a quarter of Tibetans in the TAR – perhaps half a million people – are *drokpas* (pastoral nomads), moving households in search of pasture for their animals. Livestock – yaks, goats, sheep, donkeys and ponies – are central to the livelihood of the nomad, and the basis of their culture. Their movements are seasonal, linked to weather conditions and availability of pasture for their animals. Pure nomadic life is becoming rare: more often, nomadic groups move between designated areas with the change of the seasons. True nomads are found in the grasslands of northern Tibet, and at the peripheral zones of Kham and Amdo. Hastening the demise of the nomads are occasional bitterly cold winters. The winter of 1997–98 was particularly savage, with a long snowfall and temperatures of –30°C to –40°C, which wiped out large herds of yaks and sheep. The death toll for nomads was unspecified, but it is certain that a number died.

Playing a key role in the survival of the nomads is the yak – a comical creature best described as a cow with a skirt. The yak is the male animal: the female is called a *dri,* while a yak-cow hybrid is called a *dzo* (a very useful word to remember when you are playing Scrabble). Wild yaks can weigh up to 800kg – double the size of domestic yaks. Yaks are superbly adapted to high-altitude living and cold conditions, and are sure-footed on mountain slopes. Tibetans use all parts of the yak. With a harsh climate and a lack of vegetables, meat eating is a necessity in Tibet. Yak-meat is the principal meat eaten, preserved in dried or semi-dried form. The hair and hide of the yak are used for making thread, blankets, ropes, bags, clothing and boots. Yak milk, yoghurt, butter and cheese provide sustenance. Yak-dung is collected and stacked – it is the main fuel source on the treeless plateau. Yaks are also used for riding (though they hate the idea), as a pack animal, and in farm work (for ploughing). Yak-hide is even used to make ingenious small boats.

Nomads live in thick heavy tents woven from the hair of the yak. These tents can be dismantled piece by piece, rolled up, and loaded onto yaks or donkeys. Upon arrival at a new site, the tent is quickly reassembled. At the centre of the tent is usually a stove, fuelled by yak-dung; one corner of the tent always has a little altar. To beat the cold, Tibetan nomads cocoon themselves in long sheepskin jackets – the top and sleeves can be shuffled off when temperatures rise. Much warmer than sheep wool is fox fur, often used in hats. Cashmere goats provide a particularly fine wool, highly valued in the West. After several valiant efforts to obtain breeding stock for cashmere (wrong animals, two of same sex), the British finally procured some cashmere goats and took them to the far north of Scotland, leaving them out in the freezing cold. However, it clearly wasn't cold enough – or windy enough – for the goats, who refused to grow their cashmere undercoat.

Tibetans are among the few people in Asia who thrive on dairy products – mostly yak and goat derivatives (milk, butter, yoghurt and cheese). The Mongols and the Kazaks eat similar fare. You might have trouble recognising these dairy products: yak-butter floating in the tea, or tooth-breaking pieces of dried cheese, strung together like a necklace. Large amounts of tea are also consumed: three to five cups of tea are considered necessary for everyone in the morning, and some people might drink as many as 40 cups a day. Chinese brick tea was once considered so valuable it was a form of currency. Instead of milk, yak-butter is used, and since sugar is hard to come by in Tibet, nomads just use salt (there are copious salt deposits found near lakes). Tea is made in a wooden churn – a long cylindrical object.

Often mixed with tea and rolled into balls is the great staple of the nomads – *tsampa*. This flour is usually made by roasting barley, but can also be made from corn, wheat, millet or oats. Tsampa is a tasteless flour, but highly sustaining – it is obtained through bartering, and held in cloth bags. It stores very well. Often eaten raw from the bag, tsampa can be consumed in cakes or soup. Pardon the pun, but tsampa is so ingrained in Tibetan nomad life that it is virtually synonymous with Tibet. An American Tibetologist claims one of the key factors for determining if a person is Tibetan or not is whether he or she eats tsampa and actually enjoys it. Another barley derivative is *chang,* a milky fermented beer that is brewed on special occasions and is frequently offered to guests. Chang can also be made from rice, wheat, corn, oats or millet. Since chang is home-brewed, the alcohol strength varies wildly.

TIBETAN LANGUAGE

Mandarin Chinese is the official language enforced in Tibet. Tibetan is spoken and written, but given a very low profile in schools and very little media exposure. The literacy rate among Tibetans is very low – thought to be less than 25 percent. Many have no access to proper education facilities. The Chinese practice linguistic colonialism: if a Tibetan wants to get ahead and reach the echelons of higher education, he or she must speak and write Mandarin Chinese. Very few Chinese living in Tibet speak any Tibetan or attempt to learn it.

The Tibetan language is part of the Tibeto-Burman language group, although the written form is distantly related to Sanskrit. The existence of many dialects makes it hard for Tibetans to communicate with each other. Lhasa dialect is the standard, but Lhasa court dialect is dying out. The script is more uniform throughout the Tibetan world, and although different writing styles are employed, they're more easily understood from one end of the Himalaya to the other than the spoken word. There's one catch here: the very high illiteracy rate.

The elegant Tibetan script consists of 30 consonants plus four vowels, and is easily rendered on computer in Macintosh and PC formats, though not much of this is in evidence in Lhasa, where virtually all computer access is in the much more complex Chinese characters.

Tibetan is like the Latin of High Asia: it is hardly geared to the modern world. This ancient language lacks the vocabulary range for innovations like 'email', 'cell-phone' or 'barcode.' Tibetan is flexible enough that English or foreign words can be imported phonetically (which is the case for a lot of geographical terms) or Tibetans can try and make up new compound words. The Tibetan word for 'movie' is *log-nyen*, meaning 'electric picture', the word for 'airplane' is *namdru* ('ship of the sky') and in Amdo the word for 'bicycle' is *sherta* ('iron horse'). But new vocabulary requires consensus among the scattered groups of Tibetans to gain wide acceptance, and thus to be widely understood. There could be one term used within Tibet (taken from Chinese language) and a completely different one used in India (deriving from English or Hindi).

Scholars of Latin have achieved more success than Tibetans in agreeing on new vocabulary. They have used the internet to achieve this standardisation and to spread the word; societies in Europe regularly publish new Latin vocabulary. Nothing resembling this occurs in the Tibetan world, where computer access is rare or non-existent. Refer to the Tibetan language section (*Appendix 1*) at the back of the book for more about spoken Tibetan.

TIBETAN BUDDHISM

Tibetan Buddhism, practised by almost all Tibetans, is perhaps better described as 'showcase Buddhism' within the TAR, as it is rigidly controlled by the Chinese. Officially, the Chinese are atheistic, with the government and motherland as the reigning deities. The spiritual and political leader of the Tibetans is the Dalai Lama, who is vilified by the Chinese as a 'separatist' and even as 'a major hindrance to the development of Tibetan Buddhism'.

Tibetan Buddhism has all the trappings of a religion – temples, abbots, monks, monasteries, sermons, holy texts – but is actually not a religion. With no belief in a superior god, Buddhism does not qualify: in fact, it can be equated with agnosticism.

Buddhism is primarily a philosophical belief system based around respect for all living things, and the concept of compassion, providing a code of ethics to live by. Tibetans are an extremely devout people – Tibetan Buddhism forms a significant part of their lives and their identity. Material gain is not high on the list of priorities for Tibetans: spiritual fulfilment is.

At the core of Buddhism is the concern with suffering, and how to overcome that suffering and achieve a full life. The higher goal of Buddhism is to attain enlightenment, which means to be fully awake to the reality of life, to have an understanding of suffering and how it may be overcome. The Buddha is the 'enlightened one' or 'he who is fully awake'. Buddhism is fairly easy-going: it does not require (or expect) converts, or people to spread its message. Neither does it demand sole faith in Buddhism: you can be Jewish, or Christian, or atheist – or communist, for that matter. Except for monks, Buddhism does not require attendance at a fixed place of worship, nor does it have stringent rules or vows to follow.

There are a number of branches of Buddhism: the three major ones are Zen (mainly identified with Japan), Mahayana (identified with Tibet), and Theravada (identified with Thailand and Cambodia). Tibetan Buddhism is unique because it is a blend of Mahayana Buddhism (originally from India) and the ancient Tibetan shamanist cult of Bon, heavily associated with magic and sorcery.

In contrast to the stripped-down tenets of Zen, Tibetan Buddhism hosts a vast pantheon of animist spirits, protectors, tantric deities shown in blissful union with their consorts, and an array of bodhisattvas and Buddhas; other icons are real figures – founders of the various sects and past Dalai Lamas (see the *Jokhang Temple* section in the Lhasa chapter of this book for more on Tibetan iconography).

There are few female deities in the Tibetan Buddhist pantheon; women have a low profile in the leadership of Tibetan Buddhist sects. This is a contentious area of Tibetan Buddhism, and one difficult for Western women to accept. Compared with men, women are considered to be a lower form of incarnation.

Most Tibetan Buddhists believe in reincarnation – on a higher plane, a person is reincarnated as a human, on a lower plane as an animal or an insect. But there is, in addition, belief in the concept of different realms after death. Similar to Christian beliefs in Heaven and Hell (which may have derived from Buddhism), there is belief in an earthly realm, a heavenly realm, a hell realm, and limbo zones like the realm of hungry ghosts. For reincarnation, rebirth in the human world is far preferable to that of hell or hungry ghosts. Only high lamas are said to be able to direct a specific rebirth in their next incarnation.

A related concept is karma. Tibetans believe that they may have inherited some bad karma from previous lives, a situation that must be corrected by doing good deeds in the present life. Many Buddhist practices hinge on accruing merit by doing good deeds. Merit can be accrued by making donations to temples; by assisting in the building or repair of temples, Buddha images or shrines; or by going on pilgrimages to sacred Buddhist sites. In their lifetime, many Tibetans want to undertake a pilgrimage to Lhasa and to Mount Kailash, among other holy places. Karma is cause and effect: good deeds have good effects, bad deeds have bad effects. By following the right path in this life, a person can accrue merit, with karmic carry-over to the next life. A tree drops a seed that becomes a tree – but this tree is not the same as the original one.

One of the ultimate forms of merit-making is to become a monk or a nun. In old Tibet, it was an honour for a family to be able to send a son to a monastery – this was seen as an opportunity to gain a proper education, since monasteries in old Tibet were the only schools. Tibetan culture is closely linked to Tibetan Buddhist beliefs – in former times the majority of literature, music, dance and drama, painting, sculpture and architecture was inspired by those beliefs.

Since 1959, Tibetan Buddhism has been in a state of flux because traditions were severely disrupted by Chinese takeover, and lineage holders fled into exile. The Tibetans in exile say that real Tibetan Buddhism continues in freedom outside Tibet, but not inside Tibet. The Dalai Lama has attempted to draw the four main schools of Tibetan Buddhism together, the differences between them being more of a political nature than a religious one, but these attempts have seen little success.

The oldest school is the Nyingma sect, founded around the 7th century by Indian master Padmasambhava. The tradition is carried on through reincarnates of great teachers. The Sakya sect, founded in the 11th century, is not as prominent as the other three schools. At its head is the Sakya Trizin, who fled Tibet in 1959 and established his base in Dehra Dun, India. The Kagyu sect also emerged in the 11th century; the lineage holder is the Karmapa. The 16th Karmapa fled Tibet in 1959 and founded Rumtek monastery in Sikkim (a former kingdom in northeast India); on his death in 1981 a search was conducted for the 17th Karmapa. Eventually a boy from east Tibet, Ugyen Trinley Dorje, was installed at the traditional seat of Tsurphu Monastery near Lhasa in 1992. Ugyen Trinley Dorje escaped into exile in 2000, and now lives in India; a rival Karmapa candidate, Thaye Dorje, also lives in India. Finally, the Geluk sect, founded in the 14th century by Tsongkhapa, is closely associated with the Dalai Lama. The lineage holder is the Ganden Tripa, who is elected every seven years in Dharamsala.

A number of new schools, sub-sects and offshoots have been founded in exile by various masters. Some very strange permutations have taken place in the West. Exiled Tibetan Kagyu lama Chogyam Trungpa (1939-1987) established training centres and retreat communities where he promulgated his 'crazy wisdom' visionary approach. In 1970 he shocked his students in Scotland by marrying a young English woman and flying to North America, where he went on to establish a series of *dharma* centres under the banner of Shambhala International. Chogyam Trungpa was dubbed 'the cocktail lama' due to his scandalous predilection for women and wine, and his highly unconventional personality.

One thing that Tibetans in exile have attempted to do is cut down the amount of ritual involved in Tibetan Buddhist ceremonies, and to concentrate on the pure elements of Buddhism. In its 'purist form', Buddhism has gained wide appeal in the West. But how can the ancient faith of Tibetan Buddhism be in tune with the modern world? Buddhism appeals to the rational, scientific world because the Buddha did not insist that followers accept what he said: he told them to question everything, and test his words for their veracity. Attributed to the Buddha is this disclaimer: 'Like analyzing gold through scorching, cutting and rubbing it, monks and scholars are to adopt my word not for the sake of respecting me, but upon analyzing it well.'

That said, there remains a very un-scientific facet to Tibetan Buddhism, verging on high superstition. One of the reasons that Tibet fell to the Chinese was that the clergy failed to modernise. In pre-1950 Tibet, modern advances and technology were seen as threats to spiritual life and traditional values. The clergy were highly suspicious of new gadgets and new-fangled ideas: in 1943, the Regent banned the use of motorcycles and the playing of soccer (soccer fever, which had gripped Lhasa, was seen as a powerful force that would undermine social stability).

There was – and still is – great faith among Tibetans in auspicious days and bad omens, which are interpreted by astrologers. Tibetan astrology or astronomy could hardly be called scientific: like mediaeval Western models, the mapping of the earth and the planets was firmly rooted in religion beliefs rather than scientific observation with telescopes. The Tibetan cosmos places Mount Meru, the abode of the gods, at the centre of the universe (it is identified as Mount Kailash on this earth). On the summit of Mount Meru is the celestial city of Sudarsana; above Meru float 25 more heavens of the gods, while under the mountain lie the hell-realms. Mount Meru is surrounded by seven rings of golden mountains and seven oceans. At the outer edge of a flat circular disk, across the outer ocean from Meru, are a few spin-off worlds, like the one we're on. This is identified as the continent of Jambudvipa, trapezoidal in shape, where inhabitants live for a century, and where the dharma flourishes. East of Meru lies the continent of Videha, which is white and half-moon shaped, with inhabitants whose faces resemble half-moons – they are said to be twice as tall as humans and live up to 500 years. Two other continents lie to the north and west – Uttarakuru, a square continent populated by square-jawed giants, and Godaniya, a circular continent populated by round-faced giants. Beyond all this are the paths of planets, with the mandalic (see *Glossary*, page 271) model enclosed by massive rings of fire.

Tibetan Buddhists have had to seriously reconsider their traditional cosmology model in the light of modern discoveries. Some Tibetans cling to the literal truth; others claim that Meru is merely symbolic. There is obviously no huge mountain at the navel of the world, there is no city on the top of that mountain, and there is no continent of lanky giants with half-moon faces to the east, either.

Monlam and showcase Buddhism

On the surface, to the casual tourist in Tibet, it may appear that Tibetan Buddhist culture flourishes and that freedom of religion is permitted. Monks chant in deep tones in dark assembly halls, butter-lamps are lit in monastery courtyards by shiny-eyed pilgrims, and monastic festival days such as tanka-unfurling festivals are dutifully observed. But while monks and pilgrims appear to go through the ritual motions – turning prayer wheels, making offerings in temples, and prostrating – this may be all they are doing. These manifestations are largely cosmetic: the atheist Chinese tightly control what goes on through the Chinese Religious Affairs Bureau. This has led to a variety of 'showcase Buddhism' – purely ritualistic icing for tourists.

The crux of the problem for the Chinese is that monks and nuns are the ones who have spearheaded protests against Chinese presence in Tibet and demanded the right to freedom of worship, so a gathering of monks is something that the Chinese fear. Nowhere has this been more dramatically revealed than the case of Monlam, a major festival resumed in 1986. Monlam Chenmo, the great Tibetan prayer festival, coincides with lunar new year celebrations, and takes place around February or March. Or used to. There have been no full Monlam celebrations since 1988, after a series of explosive events.

In 1986, for the first time in over 20 years, Monlam was revived in Lhasa at the request of the Chinese. Whether this was to be a spectacle for tourists, or to show the world that religious freedoms were being resumed, is not clear. Whatever the case, photography of the 1986 Monlam pops up in all kinds of Chinese sources – in photo books, in brochures bolstering the Chinese claim that there is complete religious freedom in Tibet, and even in video format on the Beijing-produced CD-ROM *Wonders of Tibet*. But the actual festival is no longer held with all monasteries participating.

In the 1950s, with monks coming from all over Tibet, Monlam became a focus for anti-Chinese protests. On March 10, 1959, at the tail-end of Monlam, the Lhasa Uprising took place, with monks taking up guns against the Chinese, so the end of Monlam is a particularly volatile time. In 1986, over a thousand monks from the different monasteries around Lhasa gathered for rites. Huge butter sculptures were displayed outside the Jokhang Temple at the heart of Lhasa, attracting crowds of up to 10,000 people from Lhasa and the valleys beyond.

Versions vary as to exactly what happened at the third Monlam to be staged. March 5 1988 – the last day of Monlam – turned into a riot (close on the heels of the pro-independence riots of October 1987). Apparently, when a procession was in progress around Barkor Bazaar in Lhasa, some monks chanted independence slogans. Stones were thrown at them, and they were warned to keep quiet by the Chinese. When the monks repeated the slogans, a Chinese policeman advanced, drawing his pistol. A Khampa tribesman from east Tibet stepped in to defend the monks, and was shot in the head at point-blank range. Infuriated, the monks paraded the dead man's body around the Barkor. At first the Chinese did not interfere, but by the third circuit of the Barkor, they were using batons and tear-gas, then guns. Eighteen Tibetans died that day: hundreds of Chinese troops stormed the Jokhang Temple and beat a number of monks to death with iron bars; other monks were thrown off the rooftop. Some 800 Tibetans were arrested.

The following year, Monlam was boycotted by the monks. On March 5, 1989, the most severe rioting erupted – as many as 100 Tibetans were killed, Chinese shops were burned, a state of martial law was declared, and all foreigners were ordered out of Lhasa. Martial law was not lifted in Lhasa for 13 months. By late 1991, the situation was back to normal, according to the Chinese. The place was once again open to tourism and it was business as usual, albeit with lots of permits, restrictions, checkpoints, and frequent chopping and changing of regulations.

In 1996, Chinese work-teams occupied all of the monasteries and nunneries in Tibet as part of an extensive 're-education' campaign that involved signing of pledges by the monks and nuns to denounce the Dalai Lama and denounce those supporting Tibetan independence.

The Dalai Lama

He's funny, he's charismatic and he has a deep, booming voice. He's a thorn in the side of the Chinese, who vigorously protested the award of the Nobel Peace Prize to him in 1989. He cracks jokes on the Larry King show. He's been a guest editor at French *Vogue*, and has written introductions to scores of books about Tibet. He's been featured on the cover of numerous magazines, and in billboard ads by Apple Computers as one of the great thinkers of the 20th century – in the same league as Einstein and Picasso (the Dalai Lama's picture, however, did not appear in billboards in Hong Kong).

Who is he? The title is synonymous with Tibet: the Dalai Lama is Tibet's greatest campaigner. Revered as the living incarnation of the bodhisattva of Compassion, Tenzin Gyatso is the spiritual leader of all the Tibetan Buddhist sects. The Dalai Lama claims he is a simple monk ('a naughty Buddhist monk') but he's much more than that: his upper arm bears vaccination scars, revealing how well-travelled he is. He is a fighter for Tibetan rights, the foremost proponent of world peace, and a tireless promoter of what he calls his real religion: kindness and compassion.

The Dalai Lama is an international icon, an inspiration to millions of Buddhists, and to millions of advocates of non-violence and right-living. On a global basis, he has no equal (the Pope comes to mind, but the Pope is a proselytiser, seeking converts, while the Dalai Lama doesn't). He cuts across barriers of race, religion and creed. All this is even more remarkable when you consider that the Dalai Lama's first language is not English, and that no government is willing to recognise him as a political leader – they accept him as a Nobel laureate or as leader of Tibetan Buddhism. The Dalai Lama has significantly raised awareness about Tibet, and the countries of Costa Rica, Poland and Norway have voiced support for Tibet in international forums.

The Dalai Lama's life has undergone fantastic twists and turns: the stuff that legends – and Hollywood movies – are made of. The Tibetan system of finding reincarnates, based on oracles and visions, dates back to the 15th century. Since lamas in the Geluk sect were celibate, a method of selecting the leader had to be arrived at. The resulting system of choosing a reincarnate worked beautifully, with no king's sons fighting each other for the throne, and no dispute over who would reign. It was, in addition, egalitarian, since the reincarnate could come from an impoverished nomad family. The 14th Dalai Lama was born in a cowshed in Amdo Province, of a very poor family. At the age of two, he was identified by disguised lamas as the reincarnation of the 13th Dalai Lama, and hence the spiritual leader of four million Tibetans. His family were informed they would be moving to Lhasa. The boy was installed at the age of four upon the Lion Throne in Lhasa, and embarked upon a formidable course of monastic studies – training in Tibetan Buddhist metaphysics that would continue for the next 18 years. His new home was the dark, thousand-room Potala Palace.

In 1950, the Chinese invaded Tibet; a month after the attack, the Dalai Lama was rushed through an enthronement ceremony to give him his majority, and thus assume the leadership of Tibet in the face of Chinese aggression. He was just

15 at the time. At age 18, he was negotiating face-to-face with Mao Zedong and Zhou Enlai over the fate of Tibet. In 1959, at the age of 23, the Dalai Lama escaped from Lhasa – ironically disguised as a soldier – and fled into exile in India, losing his country and his people. He issued a statement condemning the Chinese. He was just a Tibetan refugee, and a humble monk – no passport, no country and no status.

The Dalai Lama still travels on a refugee's yellow identity certificate. If anyone had told the Dalai Lama back in 1959 that he would still be in exile over 40 years later, he would not have believed it. Other Dalai Lamas had fled Tibet during political crises – to Mongolia and to India – but only for a period of a few years. Tibetans going into exile in 1959 all believed they would soon return, and have not tried to take out Indian citizenship because it would mean a loss of their Tibetan identity.

The Dalai Lama's idol is Mahatma Gandhi, from whom he learned the path of nonviolence. But this path has produced no concrete results: the Dalai Lama is in a dilemma because nothing has come of his peaceful approaches in the last 40 years. The Chinese pre-condition for discussion about Tibet is that the Dalai Lama abandon any thought of independence. For a period, the Dalai Lama abandoned his position of asking for full independence and asked for autonomy within the PRC, a situation similar to what existed in Tibet from 1950 to 1959, and similar to the system guaranteed for 50 years in Hong Kong SAR (Special Administrative Region), whereby Hong Kong continues its free ways but cedes military power to the PRC. But even this did not bring the Chinese to the negotiating table, because the Chinese claim that Tibet already is autonomous and that what the Dalai Lama is really after is independence. What keeps the Dalai Lama going? 'A belief in the rights that we have,' he says. It is the Tibetan struggle in a nutshell.

After his dramatic escape in 1959, the Dalai Lama kept a low profile throughout the 1960s, engaging in personal retreats. In 1974, he took his first trip to the West. Since then he has globe-trotted at an astounding rate, spreading the message about Tibet and his ideas on world peace. The Dalai Lama's most endearing quality is what he calls a 'radical informality' – his uncanny skill at cutting to the heart of the matter, and being on the same wavelength as ordinary people. He is one of Tibet's most accomplished philosophers, trained in a traditional Tibetan system, and yet he comes across as a kind of jovial uncle.

Reincarnates

Tibetan Buddhism places great faith in master teachers, or *rinpoches* (high lamas), and in the concept of reincarnation. With most of these rinpoches living in exile, that means the survival of Tibetan Buddhism lies outside Tibet. There are a number of obstacles to continuing the tradition of the masters: a major obstacle is how and where to find incarnates.

In Tibetan Buddhism, only a high lama is said to be able to redirect his soul into the body of another. The young reincarnate is known as a *tulku*, or Living Buddha, and is usually found in a one- to three-year-old boy (if the search takes longer, the boy could be up to six or older). Most tulkus are officially instated at four or five years old. Finding the incarnation of a high lama upon his death is a complicated matter for the Tibetans – it involves the assessing of omens and portents, consulting the state oracle, performing divinations for clues, and perhaps visiting Tibet's sacred oracle lake, Lhamo Latso. Potential candidates are screened through extensive interviews; the final confirmation of a reincarnate is made by the Dalai Lama himself.

After the Dalai Lama's flight to India in 1959, the process of finding and verifying reincarnate lamas has become even more complicated because it must be determined if the incarnate has been born inside or outside Tibet. Most are now found outside Tibet: tulkus have been found among the Tibetan exile community in India and in Switzerland. If a tulku is discovered inside Tibet, it is difficult for the Dalai Lama's emissaries to carry out the selection process. This puzzles the Tibetan community-in-exile: where are the reincarnates to be found? And if one is discovered inside Tibet, what should be done about it? Can a reincarnate be a Westerner?

Asked about his own incarnation, the Dalai Lama has said that logically if he is in exile, his reincarnate can only be found in exile. But he has wavered on the question of whether the method of finding the Dalai Lama should be altered, and whether the Dalai Lama should be chosen democratically, like the Pope. In the case of the Geluk Sect throneholder, the process *has* been altered: the leader is elected in Dharamsala every seven years. The Dalai Lama has also taken the unusual step of saying in an interview that in future the Dalai Lama could be a woman (all 14 Dalai Lamas thus far have been men). Of course, that's only an idea, and one that would never stand a chance of getting off the ground with the Tibetan community in exile. The stories behind three controversial tulkus are briefly described here.

The Spanish lama

Dharamsala, March 1987: a two-year-old boy, Osel Torres, is enthroned with much pomp and ceremony as the reincarnation of renowned teacher Lama Thubten Yeshe. Lama Yeshe was the founder of the Foundation for the Preservation of the Mahayana Tradition (FPMT), an international organisation with over 80 dharma centres worldwide. Osel ('Clear Light') was discovered through oracles and dreams by Lama Zopa Rinpoche, who took over directing the FPMT after the death of Lama Yeshe. Subjected to traditional tests, Osel passed with flying colours, and at the age of two was recognised by the Dalai Lama. The one major difference is that Osel is Western. Since globe-trotting Lama Yeshe was one of the biggest transmitters of Tibetan Buddhism in the West, it was reasoned his reincarnate was Western also. Lama Osel is the son of Paco and Maria Torres, who were devoted followers of Lama Yeshe in Spain; the couple have five other children. Lama Osel went on to receive a formal Tibetan education at Sera Monastery in South India. Reincarnate lamas undergo severe training: without special qualities, most would collapse under the strain. The strain is greater on Osel because he is Western, thus making him a celebrity lama, and one often scrutinised by the Western media.

The politics of the Karmapa

Officially, the Chinese are atheist, and have ignored the selection of reincarnate lamas as 'feudal superstition'. This attitude, however, changed because the Chinese realised that these incarnates are very powerful, so it's become more a question of politics than religion. In 1992, the Chinese recognised an incarnate in the 17th Karmapa of the Kagyu sect, enthroned at Tsurphu Monastery and assisted by the Chinese Religious Affairs Bureau. This marked the first time since 1959 that the Chinese recognised an incarnate, although it appeared in this case they wanted to direct the choice of the incarnate. The choice of the 17th Karmapa, a boy from eastern Tibet, caused a rift among Kagyu sect followers at Rumtek Monastery in Sikkim, where the 16th Karmapa lived in exile until his death. However, it appeared from the choice of the 17th Karmapa that it was possible for an incarnate to be found within Tibet and approved by both the Dalai Lama and the Chinese. This concurrence was short-lived: in early 1995, the Chinese and the Dalai Lama had a severe falling-out over the choice of the 11th Panchen Lama (read following entry). See the *Tsurphu Monastery* section (Central Tibet chapter) to read more about the dramatic escape of the 17th Karmapa to India.

The case of the missing lama

In January 1989, when the 10th Panchen Lama died of a heart attack at Tashilhunpo Monastery in Shigatse, the Dalai Lama's government-in-exile started collecting names of potential candidates. In 1991, a divination was performed that determined the reincarnate had been born inside Tibet. Approaches to Beijing to co-operate in a search for the incarnate were rejected, but in 1993, a message was sent to India by Chatral Rinpoche, the head abbot of Tashilhunpo Monastery, explaining that the proper rituals were being carried out. The search by a committee from the monastery (sanctioned by the Chinese) had whittled down the number of candidates. A six-year-old boy from Nagqu (northern Tibet), named Gedhun Choekyi Nyima, looked the most promising.

Several divinations were performed in Dharamsala, India, in early 1995 to determine if the boy was the right candidate, and these proved positive. On this basis, in May 1995, the Dalai Lama declared the child the official 11th Panchen Lama. At this point, all the Chinese had to do was go along with the Dalai Lama's choice – the boy was, after all, one of their own sanctioned candidates. But Chinese officials were apparently infuriated that the choice of candidates had been 'leaked' to the Dalai Lama's government-in-exile.

This time, for the first time since taking over Tibet, the Chinese stepped in – in a big way. They condemned the Dalai Lama's choice, detained Chatral Rinpoche (the abbot responsible for the search), and took the six-year-old in question into custody – making him the world's youngest political prisoner. Neither the boy nor his parents have been seen in public since, leading to fears for their safety.

In the meantime, Tashilhunpo Monastery split into pro-Dalai Lama and pro-Chinese factions – an estimated 50 Tibetans were detained following the fallout. In July 1995 the leading lamas at Tashilhunpo were sacked, and replaced with pro-Chinese head lamas. In November that year, 75 Tibetan Buddhist leaders were rushed to Beijing, lectured by President Jiang Zemin, told to reject the Dalai Lama's choice, and asked to prepare another list of candidates. The new candidate would be selected by drawing a ball from the Golden Urn – a lottery system from the 18th century, from an outdated Mongolian treaty.

In November 1995, another six-year-old boy from Nagqu, named Gyaltsen Norbu, was virtually hand-picked by the Chinese as the new Panchen Lama. Ten days later, a highly publicised enthronement ceremony took place. Security was tight, with hundreds of PLA troops deployed at Tashilhunpo Monastery. In January 1996, Gyaltsen Norbu was in Beijing, shown being greeted by President Jiang Zemin. The Chinese choice for Panchen Lama does not seem to spend much time in Shigatse – the reason given is safety concerns (ie that he will be threatened by Tibetans).

The interference of atheist China in Tibetan Buddhist ritual is hard to fathom. Did it really matter to the Chinese which six-year-old boy from Nagqu was chosen? To the Tibetans it does – no Tibetan will accept a Panchen Lama who is not verified and sanctioned by the Dalai Lama. The only way the Tibetans will accept such a choice is under duress, and this is apparently the next step, as Chinese force monks in major monasteries to swear that the Chinese choice is the only legitimate one, and to renounce the Dalai Lama. A deluge of Panchen Lama posters, pictures, books and videos spreads the word of the Chinese choice. As for the Dalai Lama's choice, blackmarket pictures of the missing lama are sold in Lhasa, despite the risk of a jail sentence if found in possession of such a picture.

In the aftermath of these events, the abbot of Tashilhunpo Monastery, Chatral Rinpoche, was sentenced to six years in jail for 'leaking state secrets'. The head of the Tantric University at Tashilhunpo, Kachen Lobsang Choedrak, was detained; and the secretary of Tashilhunpo, Gyatrul Rinpoche, was fined and expelled for refusing to endorse the Chinese-chosen candidate. Chinese work-teams moved into Tashilhunpo Monastery to force monks to pledge their loyalty to the communist party – those refusing to do so were expelled or imprisoned.

Conflicting reports have been given by the Chinese concerning the whereabouts of Gedhun Choekyi Nyima, the Dalai Lama's choice. Chinese officials have variously said the boy is living in Beijing, or in a town in the north of Tibet. In February 1996, in the aftermath of the Panchen Lama run-in, an intense anti-Dalai Lama campaign was launched, with the removal of all Dalai Lama pictures, including those from the Potala. Monks were told to sign pledges denouncing the Dalai Lama and approving the Chinese choice of Panchen Lama.

MYTHOLOGY AND THE ARTS

Tibetan culture, isolated for thousands of years, developed along very different lines from that of neighbouring India or China. There are two streams to Tibetan culture: religious arts and folk arts – the sacred and the profane.

The folk arts of Tibet (the profane side) derive largely from the nomad herder culture, with hard drinking and partying at festival time, like the annual horse-racing festivals held all over the ethnic Tibetan region. Rather like Wild West cowboy rodeos, these events are a mixture of horse races and other competitions, plus song-and-dance events. They are also a prime venue for match making among the widely scattered nomad clans, so nomad women show up dressed in their finest clothing and jewellery. In exuberant foot-stomping dances, Tibetan boots become musical instruments all of their own, and with a simple horse-hair fiddle nomad musicians can create strident music. High-pitched Tibetan 'yodelling', performed by women, is especially haunting and evocative of the vast grasslands. Often performed in a welcome ceremony is the Yak Dance. Two performers don a single yak-skin costume, with one performer up front, shaking the head and horns, and the other performer at the back, wagging the tail. The feisty yak may perform back-rolls, or it may charge – with horns forward – causing members of the audience to scatter in all directions.

The sacred arts

Tibetan culture is closely linked to Tibetan Buddhist beliefs – in former times the majority of literature, music, dance and drama, painting, sculpture and architecture was inspired by those beliefs. The bulk of Tibetan literature is based on its religion, as texts were printed with inked woodblocks at certain monasteries.

Two massive works of religious literature are the *Kanjur* (Canon of Buddhist Law, 108 volumes) and the *Tenjur* (commentaries on the *Kanjur*, in 228 volumes). These are mostly translated from Sanskrit. An exception to religious literature is the epic of Gesar of Ling, the legendary king – this was a staple of Tibet's former wandering story-tellers, who committed the long tale to memory. This thousand-year-old tale runs to millions of words, and is Asia's equivalent to Homer's *Odyssey*.

Unlike Theravadan Buddhist traditions, monks at Tibetan Buddhist monasteries are actively involved in the creation of artwork, using formulaic methods. Inspiration is the goal of the artwork – assisting the viewer with meditation and in attaining spiritual realisation – and thus the creation becomes far more important than the creator: as a result, most Tibetan art is anonymous. However, there are instances where great lamas and teachers also happen to be creators, like the lama-teacher-sculptor Zanabazar in Mongolia. Sculpture at monasteries is generally of bronze or copper with highlights in gold or gilt. Fine silver statuary is also found. Murals covering the entrance and interior walls of monasteries depict Buddhas and *bodhisattvas*, protector deities, and other themes. Tankas (wall-hangings, either painted scrolls or appliquéd on cloth or silk) originated as objects of meditation and were formerly used for teaching purposes by travelling lamas (no longer seen within Tibet).

Assisting with meditation are mandala murals and mandala tankas – the mandala is a mystic circle design or cosmogram. A unique Tibetan monastic art-form is the creation of sand mandalas – circular sand paintings made by monks from coloured sand over a period of several weeks. Elaborate ceremonies take place at the monastery during and after completion of the sand mandala: it is then destroyed, to indicate the impermanence of all things.

Monasteries in Tibet used to stage an annual ceremony called Cham, with masked dances and accompanying long-horn music performed by the monks. In these rituals, the monks wore masks representing demons, spirits and mythical animals. Cham dance is still occasionally seen within Tibet, but authorities are highly suspicious of any large gathering of Tibetans, so the chances of seeing a Cham dance in Tibet are rare (in fact, the chances of witnessing one are higher in other parts of the Tibetan world).

Because of their close link with Tibetan Buddhism, many of the Tibetan arts are proscribed or no longer practiced in Tibet itself. That means you have to go to the exile community for the real culture. Tibet's cerebral sacred music is showcased in albums like *Freedom Chants,* recorded in India by the exiled Gyuto Monks, who are also featured on the soundtracks for the movies *Kundun* and *Seven Years in Tibet*. These monks have mastered the Tibetan meditation technique of chanting with a deep three-note chord, which places such a strain on the vocal chords that the singer is in danger of becoming mute if he overdoes it. Oddly enough, Tibetan sacred music has found a place in New Age offerings. Firmly established with New Age musicians is a former monk, Nawang Kechog. Kechog has mastered a number of instruments including the bamboo flute, the Tibetan longhorn and the aboriginal didgeridoo: his albums include *Quiet Mind, Sounds of Peace* and *In a Distant Place* (see *Further Information,* page 277).

SAVING TIBETAN CULTURE

The ancient Tibetan culture has developed along very different lines from others in high Asia. Saving this unique culture essentially comes down to the issue of religious freedom, because Tibet's cultural identity is tied in with its religion, and the Chinese do not respect that religion. Ultimately, it's a question of human rights.

December 10, 1998 marks the 50th anniversary of the United Nations' adoption of the Universal Declaration of Human Rights (UDHR). This document was principally crafted by Canadian law professor John Humphrey as the UN response to atrocities committed during World War II – ostensibly to ensure that horrors like the Jewish Holocaust would never happen again. In Tibet, they did happen again, within a scant ten years of that declaration. 1998 also marks the 48th year in a row that the UN has turned a blind eye to the devastation China has wreaked in Tibet, violating the majority of the 30 articles of the UDHR. The UN has no moral authority left. True, in 1959, 1961 and 1965, resolutions were passed at the UN demanding that China respect the UDHR in Tibet, but there was no punch

BLOWING IN THE WIND

Tibetan culture – ethnic stock, beliefs, customs, language, food – has little in common with Chinese culture. But possibly the best way to gauge a culture is not through its food or its customs, but through its mythology. Here, Tibetan culture truly comes into its own. On the roofs of Tibetan houses, atop nomad tents, on high passes, on sacred peaks, at holy lakes and on the upper ramparts of monasteries, you will always find prayer flags fluttering. There are a number of varieties of prayer flags, but the commonest are the five-coloured prayer flags, which are printed with Buddhist mantras. Depicted in the corners of each flag are the clawed supernatural animals of the four directions: garuda (wisdom), dragon (gentle power), tiger (confidence) and snow lion (fearless joy). A fifth mythical animal, appearing usually in the middle of the prayer flag, is the wind horse. Some of these mythical animals are found in other Asian cultures, but not the wind horse or the snow lion, which are uniquely Tibetan.

The Windhorse The beautiful steed that brings good fortune, symbolised by the jewel on its back. It is known as *lungta* in Tibetan. When prayer flags snap and flutter in the breeze, the wind horse printed on them is set in motion, carrying good fortune in all directions and galloping across the sky, spreading the teachings of Buddhism. The wind horse represents uplifting energy. Prayer flags are usually printed on cloth, using woodblocks. Some pilgrims cannot afford them, and resort to a modified inexpensive version – small squares of paper, embossed with wind horses. Pilgrims throw these in the air at sacred sites and shout *Lha Gyalo!* (Victory to the gods!).

The Snow Lion When the lion made the leap over the Himalaya from India, it became the residing deity of Tibet's snowy ranges, able to bound from snowpeak to snowpeak. This friendly dog-like animal (*sengye* in Tibetan) is shown in temple frescos with a white body and turquoise mane, or a blue body with vermilion mane and green eyes. The snow lion is a symbol of fearless joy – a mind free of doubt, clear and precise. The snow lion dance is performed at special events. Snow lions are part of the throne of Buddha, and are shown upholding the three precious jewels of Buddhism on the forbidden Tibetan flag. Snow lions appear on the crest and seal of the Dalai Lama; they also appear on Tibetan government seals of office, and on old banknotes and stamps.

There's a curious ideological battle involving snow lions, possibly because of their close association with the Dalai Lama and Tibetan nationalism. Snow lion statues stand guard at the gates of Norbulingka, the Dalai Lama's summer palace in Lhasa, but outside the front gates of the Potala stand statues of Chinese imperial lions, the same symbols of Chinese emperors found at the Forbidden City in Beijing. Chinese officials have even objected to a logo at a conference in Europe – the image in question was not the Tibetan flag, nor an image of the Dalai Lama, but simply a pair of snow lions.

behind the resolutions. They were promulgated before 1970, the year that the PRC became one of the five permanent members of the UN Security Council, with full veto power. The UN Human Rights Commission today includes voting members from such bastions of liberty as China, Cuba, Libya, Syria, Saudi Arabia, Sudan and Zambia, who do nothing but thwart its human-rights mandate.

Why Are We Silent? This is the title of a 60-second cinema ad about Tibet, marking the 50th anniversary of the UDHR. The clip features six movie and rock stars reading extracts from the UDHR against a background of Tibetan imagery. In early 1998, members of the Tibetan Youth Congress staged a hunger strike in Delhi. Six hunger strikers, representing the six million people of Tibet, demanded that the UN resume its debate on the question of Tibet; that it appoint a Special Rapporteur to investigate the situation of human rights in Tibet; and that it appoint a Special Envoy to promote a peaceful settlement of the question of Tibet and initiate a UN-supervised plebiscite to ascertain the wishes of the Tibetan people. The lengthy strike was broken up by the Indian police.

China has one of the worst human-rights violation records in the world. The US Department of State's 1997 report on Tibet slams China for 'serious human rights abuses in Tibet' and for imposing 'intensified controls on fundamental freedoms'. Evidence for reports like this is drawn from interviews with credible Tibetan refugees, who tell of forced sterilisations and abortions, as well as arbitrary arrest, torture in prisons, and cases of summary execution. Despite mounting evidence, China vigorously denies any transgressions, says that torture has been completely abolished, and claims that Tibetan people have gained real democracy and equality after 1959's 'democratic reforms'. Beijing blithely churns out glossy brochures in English that quote the UDHR to back up the Chinese claim that rights are better now than they were under the Dalai Lamas. This won't explain why Tibetan monks have been given long prison sentences for translating the UDHR into the Tibetan language. Meanwhile, Clinton, who in 1992 delighted in mocking George Bush for consorting with Chinese communists 'despite their undisguised contempt for democracy and human rights' did an about-face. The Clinton administration delinked human-rights issues from trade, and continued to affirm China's Most Favoured Nation trading status.

What human rights do the Tibetans want? The basic ones: the right to freedom of speech, freedom of thought, and freedom to follow Tibetan Buddhist beliefs. The right to a proper education, the right to use the Tibetan language. The rights of the child. Even the most fundamental of human rights are denied to Tibetans. These include the rights to clean water, sufficient food, a home, health care, proper education, employment, protection from violence, equality of opportunity, and a say in their future. In Tibet, Chinese violations of the UDHR are so blatant that they have led scholar Robert Thurman to say that 'Tibetans are the baby seals of the human rights movement'. The Dalai Lama puts it this way: 'The Chinese are entitled to their happiness, but not at the expense of another nation or people'. He accuses the Chinese of pursuing a deliberate policy of cultural genocide in Tibet. By the government-in-exile count, over a million Tibetans have perished – either directly or indirectly – at the hands of the Chinese since the 1950s.

Population transfer

Before 1950, there were no Chinese settlers in the TAR. Accurate figures on current Chinese population in Tibet are hard to come by: Chinese figures do not include the sizeable military contingent. However, it is certain that China is providing incentives to bring settlers into Tibet – higher salaries, more benefits and tax breaks. In the provinces at the edge of the TAR, Han Chinese settlers outnumber the Tibetans. The Chinese do not integrate with the Tibetans, nor bother to learn the language. Not only are they starting to outnumber the Tibetans, they are reducing them to second-class citizens in their own land. For doing the same job, Chinese workers are usually paid a higher salary than Tibetans.

In Inner Mongolia, after 1949, when the communists took control, millions of Han Chinese flooded onto the steppes, thanks to government encouragement and incentives. The Mongols are now a minority in their own land – there are now 20 million Han versus four million Mongolians. Mongol nomad livelihood has been severely disrupted by Han Chinese turning pasture into irrigated farmland. All this is in contravention of the Geneva Convention. A similar situation appears to be developing in Tibet.

Political prisoners

The number of political prisoners held in prisons in Tibet ranges from over a thousand (government-in-exile figure) to 50 (Chinese figure). The Chinese figure is skewed because Chinese officials maintain that prisoners in Tibet are common criminals, not political prisoners. If a prisoner is convicted for holding up a Tibetan flag, this is noted as 'prisoner trying to incite public disorder' so somehow it becomes a criminal offense, not a political one. Conditions in prison are poor, with beatings and torture routine. Across China, it is estimated that over 6,000 prisoners a year are executed (the exact number is not known, since figures are kept secret). In June 2001, Amnesty International reported that in the previous three months, an estimated 1,780 prisoners were executed across China, a figure which was more than those executed in the rest of the world combined *for the previous three years* (although large numbers were executed in Iraq – figures are unknown). In addition to those executed, Amnesty International reported that for the same period, 2,960 prisoners were sentenced to death in China. Prisoners are usually executed with a bullet to the back of the head: the bill for the bullet is often sent to the family of the executed as further humiliation. There is some evidence that body parts of executed prisoners are sold on the international market. Chinese spokespeople blithely deny that any of this ever takes place.

Believed to be the world's youngest political prisoner is Gedhun Choekyi Nyima, the Dalai Lama's choice for 11th Panchen Lama. His whereabouts are unknown: he has not been seen in public since May 1995.

In August 1995, Ngawang Choephel disappeared in Tibet. Choephel, a Fulbright scholar, was researching traditional music in Tibet and videotaping dance and song performances. It was not for another 14 months that his mother discovered that he was still alive, and in prison. He was charged with spying for the Tibetan government-in-exile and a sentence of 18 years was handed down. After a vigorous high-profile campaign by Western supporters, and after serving six years of his sentence, Ngawang Choephel was released on medical parole in January 2002, and flown back to the US, where he applied for political asylum.

Ngawang Sangdrol is a nun who was 13 years old when she was first jailed for demonstrating for a free Tibet. After her release, she was forbidden to rejoin her monastery. In 1992, she was arrested again for demonstrating and sentenced to three years in jail. In 1993, while in prison, Ngawang and 13 other nuns recorded Tibetan protest songs – the tape was smuggled out by a sympathiser and taken to the West. When they learned of this, the Chinese increased the nuns' sentences by a further six years. In 1996, Ngawang's sentence was increased by a further nine years: she is not due for release until the year 2010. In a rare protest from the UN, in 1995 the UN Working Group on Arbitrary Detentions ruled the nun had been punished for exercising her rights to freedom of opinion. The group called on China to release her, in line with the principles of the UDHR – a call that was ignored by the Chinese. In 1998, as part of a campaign commemorating the 50th anniversary of the Universal Declaration, Ngawang Sangdrol was featured in a joint campaign by the Body Shop and Amnesty International, putting added pressure on the Chinese.

Religious freedom

It is estimated that up to 70% of political prisoners in Tibet are monks and nuns. The reason they are imprisoned is a combination of their political attitudes and their fight for religious freedom. In the past, monks and nuns have spear-headed the Tibetan independence movement: their vows may empower them to act politically. Celibacy puts them in a better position to sacrifice their lives as opposed to those with families, and dying for Tibetan independence is a selfless act guaranteeing a human rebirth in the next life.

Since early 1996, Chinese officials have conducted a 'Strike Hard' campaign deliberately directed at monks and nuns. Chinese work-teams have been dispatched to all monasteries and nunneries in Tibet for 'patriotic re-education' (an on-going process). Dalai Lama pictures have been banned in all temples and public places, and Tibetan monks and nuns are required to sign a five-point agreement, pledging to oppose the idea of an independent Tibet, to denounce the Dalai Lama, to recognise the Chinese-appointed Panchen Lama, to oppose those advocating independence for Tibet, and to work for the unity of 'the Motherland'. According to China's own statements, the majority of Tibet's 46,000 monks and nuns in 1,700 monasteries and nunneries have come under the programme. As a result, in the first two years of the programme, it is estimated that 14 monks and nuns died, upwards of 300 were arrested, and over 3,000 were expelled from their monasteries or nunneries. In addition, seven monasteries and nunneries were completely closed down.

In June 2002, a tent encampment established in a remote valley near Serthar in Amdo (Sichuan province) was broken up by Chinese officials with pick-axes, and thousands of residents were ordered to leave. The encampment at one point attracted up to 8,000 monks and nuns, of whom nearly 1,000 were Chinese. They were drawn by the teachings of charismatic leader Khenpo Jigme Phuntsok, who started off Larung Gar encampment with a handful of students in the 1980s. At special teaching times, the numbers at Larung Gar swelled to over 15,000 participants – hence the Chinese nervousness that led to the break-up.

When Hollywood locks horns with Beijing

Gyantse, November, 1987: a young British tourist, Kris Tait, is accosted by a Chinese soldier on a bicycle, who tries to tear off her T-shirt. She at first assumes he's trying to assault her, but when a Tibetan crowd gathers chanting 'Dalai Lama!' it occurs to her that the soldier is after the T-shirt, which appears to bear an image of the Dalai Lama printed on it. Actually the T-shirt is embossed with the face of the late Phil Silvers, a cult figure from late night BBC re-runs of the 1950s American TV series, *Sergeant Bilko*. The woman manages to wrench free from the soldier, and flees to her guesthouse to change clothes. Kris Tait, an avid Bilko fan, later says there is a resemblance between Silvers and the Dalai Lama – the same quizzical eyebrows, the same thick glasses. Hollywood's dust-up with the Chinese over the Dalai Lama has just begun.

Dissolve to 1997, when the sleeves are rolled up, and the big brawls begin, as Hollywood takes on China in earnest, with full-length movies about the Dalai Lama in the works. Disney's Touchstone Pictures is faced with the most momentous decision of its corporate career – sell Mickey Mouse in China, or humour director Martin Scorsese? Which goes? Whose wrath will be greater to face – that of surly Chinese officials, or of Scorsese without his morning coffee? Scorsese is filming a movie about the early life of the Dalai Lama, one which has raised the hackles of the Chinese, who threatened to halt work on the creation of a Disneyland near Shanghai. The clash of the Titans has begun.

Flashback to 1937: Frank Capra's epic, *Lost Horizon*, is released by Columbia TriStar. The film, based on the book of the same name, is the first big budget movie to use a Tibetan setting: a Tibetan monastery high in the snowcapped mountains where the wisdom of the ages is preserved by wizened lamas. The film costs four times the amount of any Columbia TriStar film at the time, using a set considered the largest ever built in Hollywood. During WWII, Tibet remained neutral, a kind of Switzerland in High Asia (although the British Mission remained in Lhasa, without official diplomatic status). *Lost Horizon* was widely circulated among the armed forces during WWII – it bolstered the hope that there was a place during mankind's darkest days where the values of civilisation were preserved.

Sixty years later, Columbia TriStar released *Seven Years in Tibet*, quite a different version of Shangri-La – one man's vision of the last years before Tibet itself was engulfed in war and chaos.

Why the sudden Hollywood interest in Tibet after a 60-year silence on the subject? Why did the 1990s produce a rash of Tibet films? And why is Beijing upset about them? In part, Hollywood's interest in Tibet is attributable to the collapse of the USSR and the demise of the Cold War: China provides a new 'evil empire' to crusade against, in the vacuum left by the demise of Russia. China is the world's most populous nation, with expanding economic clout and a world-class nuclear arsenal. China is an up-and-coming superpower with a ruthless leadership: a change of Western attitude to China definitely occurred after the Tiananmen Massacre in 1989. Suddenly, what the Dalai Lama had been saying all along – that the Chinese were killing Tibetans – was blatantly demonstrated at Tiananmen when the Chinese opened fire on their own people. An indicator of this shift of evil empires was the plot of the 1997 James Bond film, *Tomorrow Never Dies*. No KGB here: the movie was originally slated to be about the handover of Hong Kong, but missed its timing so the script was changed to a stand-off between China and Britain, with the two teetering on the brink of war because of the ambitions of an out-of-control media megalomaniac (modelled on Rupert Murdoch!).

In part, Hollywood's interest in Tibet is related to new-found interest in Buddhism in the US, and to celebrity actors like Richard Gere, Harrison Ford and Uma Thurman supporting the Tibetan cause. Tibet has become chic following the popularity of the Dalai Lama after his 1989 Nobel Peace Prize award. The man has become Hollywood's favourite underdog – a nonviolent rebel with a cause. The Dalai Lama has mingled with Cindy Crawford and Sharon Stone at Los Angeles parties. Perhaps this is not so unusual: the Dalai Lama has been an avid fan of movies from an early age. In the late 1940s, he arranged for the building of a projection room in Lhasa to view films imported from India. In the early 1990s, he fine-tuned the script for *Kundun* (in readings with Melissa Mathison and Harrison Ford) and for *Seven Years in Tibet* (with Becky Johnston).

Another reason for Tibetmania is possibly that Tibet is the ultimate in exotic locations: there's renewed Hollywood interest in exotica following the phenomenal success of movies like *The English Patient*. More likely, however, is that Tibet is hot simply because controversy fuels box-office hits – and there's no shortage of controversy when it comes to Tibet.

In the case of *Kundun* and *Seven Years in Tibet*, the controversy started before shooting began. Both movies set out to portray an idyllic pre-1950 Tibet, with a smiling, soft-spoken Dalai Lama at the helm – a Dalai Lama sworn to nonviolence. The Chinese claim that pre-1950 Tibet was hell on earth – a medieval society where Tibetans had no freedom, and slaved away as serfs for the aristocracy. Both movies show the Chinese as brutal thugs. Sony, which owns Columbia TriStar, was threatened in China over *Seven Years in Tibet*, as was Disney, but no economic sanctions were applied. Both movie directors were blocked from filming in India, which was their first choice of location. One thing's for sure: films like *Kundun, Seven Years in Tibet* and *Red Corner* will never be shown in China. However, there's no reason why they can't be shown in Hong Kong, where technically the laws only empower authorities to check films for violence and sex. In fact, *Seven Years in Tibet* has been screened in Hong Kong despite stern criticism from Beijing. The movie brought Ngapoi Ngawang Jigme out on the attack in Hong Kong. He complained about the movie's portrayal of himself as a turn-coat who betrayed the Tibetan army and signed the 17-point agreement with China for its annexation of Tibet. It was poetic justice of a kind. Ngawang Jigme, now in his eighties, has rarely spoken to the press; he has lived in Beijing since 1967, where he and his clan hold high positions.

Seven Years in Tibet was also screened in Moscow, again despite Chinese embassy objections. The Chinese vigorously protested a screening of the movie at a film festival in Japan (the film performed well in Japan, where Brad Pitt has a cult following – among teenage girls, anyway). Other Chinese objections were raised over *Kundun,* a movie which glorifies the Dalai Lama (and in one scene portrays China's great leader, Mao Zedong, as a crass, evil, chain-smoking buffoon). In May 1998, the Chinese Embassy demanded that the film *Windhorse* be removed from the Washington International Film Festival because it was meant to 'obviously smear China's policy toward Tibet'. The festival director invited Chinese Embassy officials to come to the screening of the movie and participate in an open dialogue about the film – they did not show up. The film went on to become the festival-goers' top choice.

Words are the only weapon that Tibetans have in the fight against Chinese repression of Tibetan culture and occupation of their land, and Tibetans have found words can have great impact when they are spoken on the big screen. In the US and elsewhere, Tibetans have distributed leaflets and Tibet Action Kits outside screenings of the movies. China's problem with all of this is an issue of freedom of speech. Chinese embassies around the globe have tried to muzzle Hollywood, which thus far has only succeeded in drawing more attention to the Tibetan cause.

In a world where the international community has been spectacularly silent on the topic of Tibet, the films have pricked the Western conscience, and incurred the wrath of Chinese embassy officials. China's greatest fear is that one of these Hollywood films will become a cult hit, with TV reruns for the next 20 years – just like *Sergeant Bilko*.

Trans Himalaya

Trans Himalaya, under the direction of Dr Gyurme Dorje, a Tibetologist and Tibet travel writer, organise travel throughout the Tibetan plateau, as well as in Mongolia, China and the Himalayas (Bhutan, Sikkim, Nepal, and Ladakh).

Whether you are a first-time visitor to Central Tibet looking for a simple itinerary, or an experienced Tibet traveller planning an overland journey, trek or expedition in Ngari, Kham or Amdo, Trans Himalaya are the specialists, with a strong client base in the Americas, Europe, SE Asia, Australia and South Africa.

Accompanied by knowledgeable guides, you will be exposed to the diverse cultural heritage of Tibet, its distinctive Buddhist and Bon monasteries, and the life-styles of its people. Trans Himalaya's eco-tourism programme also enables you to participate directly in rural development or art restoration, working as a guest alongside Tibetan monks, villagers or nomads.

Circumambulate sacred Mts Kailash, Kawa Karpo & Amnye Machen!
Ride through the rolling grasslands of Amdo!
Witness the horse festivals and pageantry of sacred dances in Kham!
Explore the wilderness and wildlife of the Jangtang & Kunluns!
Appreciate the rich diversity of Tibetan art & architecture!
Tibet's exhilarating mountain panoramas, forested gorges, and pristine lakes invite you to breathe rare air!

For details and booking contact:

Trans Himalaya
4 Foxcote Gardens, Frome, Somerset, BA11 2DS, UK
Tel: +44-1373-455518 Fax: +44-1373-455594
Email: gd@trans-himalaya.demon.co.uk
Website: www.trans-himalaya.ndirect.co.uk

Trans Himalaya Chengdu Office:
1 North Shuangqing Road, Bldg 2, Suite. 2A,
Chengdu, Sichuan, 610072, China
Tel: 13688338152

Practical Information

The Chinese are very big on 'the rules'. Everything has stern rules: hotels have rules posted, temples have rules, restaurants may be told not to serve foreigners. Bus stations have rules posted about who can buy tickets and who can't. There are even rules restraining foreigners from riding bicycles. Trouble is, most of the time, the rules are written in Chinese – a deliberate strategy to keep foreigners in the dark. This section attempts to come to grips with rules and protocol and how to get around things like this. Some advice may appear cryptic, or won't quite make sense until you get there. Faced with so many rules, regulations and restrictions, you have to maintain your sense of humour. You can amuse yourself by making up your own road rules. Here are a few unofficial laws of the land, and maxims for touring Tibet (from the author): All roads lead to Lhasa. Lhasa is not Tibet – it's too heavily Chinese-influenced for that. If you get a chance to go to a countryside festival, go! And finally, one last cryptic piece of advice: when in doubt, split!

PLATEAU HIGHLIGHTS

Highlights are subjective – they really depend on your interests. Some travellers see two or three monasteries and get 'templed-out', while others seem to have an unlimited capacity for looking at monasteries. The key to visiting is to vary the sights – take in a temple or fort, go on a day-hike, or visit a hotspring. Sometimes you luck out and find these all in the same locale. The following is a shortlist of personal favourites, which is bound to be biased, of course. The main highlight of any visit to Tibet will be meeting the people. There are two guaranteed places you will see and meet lots of Tibetans: at festivals and at key pilgrimage sites. Tibetans have their own version of top sites, and these are sacred pilgrimage destinations like Mount Kailash – the trip of a lifetime.

Festivals These follow the lunar calendar, but timing is unpredictable as they're often not announced. If you get a chance, go – festivals offer great people encounters. Summer sees horse-racing fairs in Gyantse, Nagqu and Litang and other locations. Monasteries occasionally stage annual Cham dances – a majestic spectacle.

Top pilgrimage sites Potala, Jokhang, Barkor (Lhasa); Kailash (west Tibet); Tashilhunpo (Shigatse); and Kumbum (Amdo). Again, pigrimage sites are great for seeing – and meeting – people from all parts of Tibet.

Tibetan town architecture Distinctive Tibetan style can be found in these places: the Tibetan Quarter, Potala, Norbulingka (Lhasa); Gyantse (Kumbum fort, plus Pala Manor); Samye; and Xiahe (Labrang). It's becoming harder to find areas of pure Tibetan architecture due to encroachment by bland Chinese concrete-and-karaoke architecture.

Best forts The majestic administrative centres of old Tibet. Most have been destroyed but these remain: Gyantse Dzong (used in the battle against British forces in 1904) and Yumbulagang (a rebuilt fortress-temple near Tsedang). The Potala in Lhasa is a prime example of fortress architecture.

Top active temples Chanting, rituals and monastic life can be experienced at the Jokhang (Lhasa – centre of the Tibetan world, with many pilgrims), Sera and Drepung (Lhasa), Ganden, Drigung (Lhasa Prefecture – Drigung is famed for its sky burial), Samye Monastery (the oldest in Tibet), Tashilhunpo (Shigatse – a magnificent statuary), Sakya (Mongolian fortress-style temple with grand chanting hall) and Labrang (entire monastic citadel in Xiahe, Gansu).

Top ruins Guge Kingdom, in Zanda, west Tibet – though mostly destroyed, excellent murals can still be seen. Set in entrancing desert terrain riddled with caves.

Best hot springs Tidrom Nunnery, Lhasa Prefecture – beautiful valley with Tibetan village and three enclosed hotsprings for bathing.

Best day hikes Back of Sera Monastery in Lhasa; hike to Hepo Ri viewpoint in Samye; hikes around Sakya; hike to top of Shining Crystal Dzong ruins in Shegar.

Mountains, top treks Kailash, sacred mountain – four-day pilgrim circuit in a stunning place. Everest, north face – a three-day trek into the base camp; from here the highest trek in the world (without crampons) leads to advanced base camp at over 6,400m.

Sacred lakes Turquoise classics include Yamdrok Tso (with backdrop of peaks in Bhutan); Manasarovar (Kailash in background); Lake Namtso, with 7,000-metre peaks backdrop; and Basong Tso, east Tibet. Pilgrims undertake *koras* (walking circuits) around these sacred lakes.

Great road trips Lhasa to Kathmandu route; Lhasa to Chengdu or Kunming; Lanzhou via Songpan to Chengdu (Amdo); Chengdu via Daocheng to Kunming (Kham) and the Karakoram Highway. These are among the greatest road trips in High Asia.

Give it a miss The worst road trip is Golmud to Lhasa. The worst town architecture prize goes to Tsedang, a complete Chinese town of the bathroom-tiling school of architecture. The most shocking experience is seeing Chinese high-rises in Lhasa. The worst Chinese mega-project under way is the building of a railway to Lhasa.

PLANNING YOUR TRIP
When to go
Climate
April to October is the best time. November is starting to get cold. December and January can be freezing, with heavy snow blocking high passes. Few individuals visit at this time, which means it's hard to find people to share Landcruiser rentals. February is Tibetan New Year and though cold, it can be lively if you can get in. April can be windy; there's a rainy season around July and August, when flooding can cut off roads and wash out bridges. Because Tibet is so large, climate conditions change from east to west and with the elevation.

Timing, festivals and sensitive periods
Rules and regulations concerning travel in Tibet chop and change as often as the weather does with El Niño, so the following sections may be out of date by the time you plan your visit. If so, make adjustments. There are several times of year

when it is difficult or impossible to get into Lhasa. Winter is an obvious one – there are no flights from Kathmandu and fewer from Chengdu. The Chinese may be nervous if some military bigwig or political leader is visiting, and they might just shut the whole country down for a few weeks. Nothing is guaranteed in Tibet, and no guidebook written in stone. Allow for changing information.

The Tibetan calendar is filled with unofficial anniversaries, and security is tight at these times, with Chinese troops on alert ten days before and after the sensitive period. You may have trouble getting into Tibet or travelling around at these times. The easiest travel months are April, June and August (however, June to August is the most heavily booked period for flights into Lhasa). Among the 'hot' times are:

Losar	Tibetan New Year, around February
March 5	commemorating major protests in 1988–89
March 10	anniversary of 1959 Lhasa uprising
May 23	marks the 1951 surrender to the Chinese with the 17-point agreement
July 6	Dalai Lama's birthday
September 27	start of 1987 riots
October 1	1987 protest in which Tibetans were shot dead
December 10	international human rights day, which sparked a protest in 1988

Tibetans sometimes gather at countryside locations to picnic and throw *tsampa* in the air to mark special occasions – in Lhasa, this practice has been banned by Chinese authorities.

Because the Chinese are nervous about large gatherings of Tibetans, traditional festivals are low-profile – indeed, for a number of years, festivals were banned outright. If you get a chance to see something more formal, like a festival in the countryside, go! If you're lucky there might be a horse-racing festival in progress at Damxung or Gyantse, or a *tanka*-unfurling ceremony at one of the monasteries within reach of Lhasa. There used to be festivals at every full moon in Tibet, but many were abolished by the Chinese authorities. The festivals that survive are based on the lunar calendar, which is complex and unpredictable (usually only announced in February, at Losar or Tibetan New Year). Ask around when you arrive in Tibet to confirm if there are likely to be any festivals in progress.

How long do I need?
Ten to 20 days would be good. Six weeks would be better. Two months would be ideal if you plan on going trekking. You need time to adjust to the altitude, and you should build in extra time for delays due to breakdowns, road closures, overbooked flights and so on. The Western ethic of rushing around doesn't work well here.

How much will it cost?
Transportation will be your greatest cost: getting there by air can be expensive. If you have anything to do with Landcruiser groups or organised tours, the costs will rise dramatically. On their own, travellers have travelled around by local bus and on foot, and survived quite well on about US$10 a day.

Will I have problems with the altitude?
Tibet is the highest region on earth, so expect some problems adjusting to the altitude. Altitude sickness is unpredictable – some travellers have no symptoms, others suffer mild cases and get over it, others become quite ill. You should be OK if you take it easy for the first few days and allow your body time to adjust to the new environment. If you get *really* sick, the best advice is to get right out of there by plane.

GETTING TO TIBET

Getting into Tibet is a two- or three-part operation. First you have to make it to a staging-point like Bangkok, Hong Kong, Kathmandu or Chengdu. Then you wrangle with paperwork and ticketing, run the gauntlet of Chinese officialdom into China, and strike for Lhasa. Once safely in Lhasa, you can fan out to visit other parts of Tibet, although you might be stuck with the TTB monopoly for Landcruiser travel (your initial paperwork in, say, Chengdu, may restrict you to the TTB as exclusive agent for Landcruisers in Lhasa). Think of this exercise as 'Hitting the Roof' – an oblique reference to the way you will feel when you deal with Chinese officials. It's also what will probably happen to you when you ride in a Landcruiser in Tibet.

Group touring

The majority of travellers to Tibet are on group tours. The ones that aren't often end up one way or another on impromptu tours involving Landcruisers or trucks. The Chinese would prefer that all foreigners travel this way. Why? Because tours are easy to monitor and because they get a sanitised version of Tibet. Participants are carefully insulated from the Tibetans, and chaperoned by Chinese guides with a totally warped sense of history (no sense of culture). Group tour operators take care of all the logistical problems – permits, transport, food and so on – but in the process you may lose out on other dimensions. Tours to Tibet are quite costly – even the ones organised out of Kathmandu rack up the bills.

On the plus side, group tour operators seem to magically transcend all the permit obstacles. They can mount trips and treks that individuals drool over – the vanguard of what's possible. Groups cross the border from Kailash into Nepal or India; they trek into the Karta Valley east of Everest; they engage Bactrian camels to trek into K2 base camp north of Ali; they cross the Nepalese border into Tibet with their own Western truck and driver (some European outfitters have been permitted to use their own truck and driver on the route from Kathmandu to Lhasa, on to Dunhuang and Kashgar, and down to Islamabad – a six-week trip). Expeditions liaising with Tibet Mountaineering Association (TMA) or Tibet International Sports Travel (TIST) have arranged a number of firsts – taking on trekking peaks, white-water rafting, mountain-biking, hot-air ballooning and paragliding in Tibet. Commercial rafting companies have made test-runs along some sections of the Yarlung Tsangpo Gorges and claim there is potential for guided trips. Because of the specialised nature of these trips, a group may be assembled from clients from different continents through outfitter liaison.

For business reasons, many operators play the game of not offending Chinese sensibilities. However, some tour operators have Buddhist links and provide a tour leader well versed in the history and culture of Tibet. Funding generated from these high-paying tours may not benefit the Tibetans – if considering an operator, inquire whether your driver and guide will be Tibetan. If you are embarking on a trekking or mountaineering type tour, inquire about equipment and safety conditions for porters, as the tour company is responsible for their well-being. Outfitters that combine innovative trips with small groups and an ethical approach would be the most desirable.

Regardless of whether you intend to take a tour or not, check out the websites for outfitters listed here to glean ideas for your own trip. The following list represents a sampling of what's offered by operators, which should encourage you to research more. To find more operators (mainly featuring those in Nepal) check out the Tibet Cultural Region Directory of the www.kotan.org website.

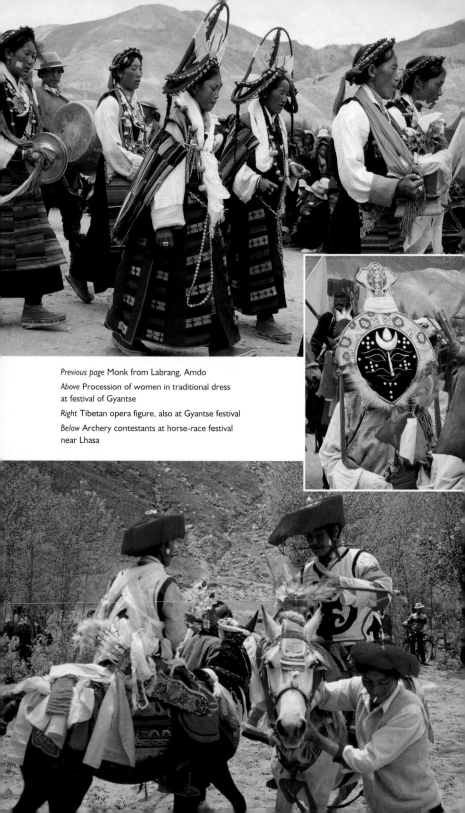

Previous page Monk from Labrang, Amdo

Above Procession of women in traditional dress at festival of Gyantse

Right Tibetan opera figure, also at Gyantse festival

Below Archery contestants at horse-race festival near Lhasa

Australia

Intrepid Travel 11 Spring St, Fitzroy, Victoria 3065; tel: 613 9473 2626; web: www.intrepidtravel.com.au. Small low-budget groups angled for younger travellers.
Peregrine Adventures 258 Lonsdale St, Melbourne, Victoria 3000; tel: 613 9662 2700; web: www.peregrine.net.au. Offers Hanoi-Lhasa-Kathmandu overland trip; allied with Exodus UK.
World Expeditions Level 5, 71 York St, Sydney 2000; tel: 612 9279 0188; web: www.worldexpeditions.com.au

Canada

Everest Trekking 2517 York Ave, Vancouver, BC V6K 1E3; tel: 604 731 7650; web: www.everesttrekking.com. Small-group trekking and touring to Tibet, Bhutan and other parts of the plateau.

France

Terres d'Aventure 6 rue Saint Victor, 75005 Paris; tel: 0153 737 773; web: www.terdav.com. Specialises in trekking.

UK

Alpine Mountaineering 62 Nettleham Rd, Sheffield S8 8SX; tel: 0114 258 8508; web: www.ottexpeditions.co.uk. For those seriously contemplating climbing an 8,000m peak.
Exodus 9 Weir Rd, London, SW12 0LT; tel: 020 8675 5550; web: www.exodus.co.uk. Mounts tours in central and east Tibet; runs overland trips using their own customised trucks.
Intrepid Travel UK PO Box 34429, London W6 0AF; tel: 020 8563 8244
Imaginative Traveller 14 Barley Mow Passage, Chiswick, London W4 4PH ; tel: 020 8742 3049; web: www.imaginative-traveller.com. Specialises in small-group touring.
Steppes East 51 Castle St, Cirencester GL7 1QD; tel: 01285 651010; web: www.steppeseast.co.uk
Trans Himalaya 4 Foxcote Gardens, Frome, Somerset BA11 2DS; tel: 01373 455518; web: www.trans-himalaya.ndirect.co.uk. Takes on all parts of the Tibetan plateau.
World Expeditions 3 Northfields Prospect, Putney Bridge Rd, London SW18 1PE; tel: 020 8870 2600; web: www.worldexpeditions.co.uk

USA

Adventure Center 1311 63rd St, Suite 200, Emeryville, CA 94608; tel: 800 228 8747; web: www.adventurecenter.com. Not much listed for Tibet, but acts as an agent for Intrepid Travel UK and other outfitters.
Boojum Expeditions 14543 Kelly Canyon Rd, Bozeman, MT 59715; web: www.boojum.com. Offers horseback and other innovative trips to Kham region.
Geographic Expeditions 2627 Lombard St, San Francisco, CA 94123; tel: 800 777 8183; web: www.geoex.com
High Asia Exploratory Mountain Travel PO Box 2438, Basalt, Colorado; tel: 800 809 0034; web: www.highasia.com. A goldmine for innovative ideas on trekking and mountaineering on the Tibetan plateau; this company even offers rafting and ski-touring trips in Kham.
Snow Lion Expeditions Oquirrh Place, 350 South 400 East, Suite G2, Salt Lake City, UT 84111; tel: 800 809 0034; web: www.snowlion.com. Offers overland, trekking and mountain-bike trips.
Wilderness Travels 801 Allston Way, Berkeley, CA 94710; tel: 800 368 2794. Focuses on trekking.

Non-group trips

Chinese officials secretly would like all travellers to be in coddled group tours that spend lots of money; on the other hand, they're reluctant to admit that Tibet is not open, or that Tibet is a special zone in China (which in fact it is). So a compromise is reached: if individuals get together and form a small group, it's acceptable. A group of four is fine. A group of two can work. And even a group of one might pan out (on a tour, with guide). If you come in from Chengdu by plane, the group may have to be ten people; from Kathmandu by plane, usually five people or more (the oldest person in the group is designated as the leader). You may be required to book a short tour (usually three days) as part of the charade. Once in Lhasa, you drop all pretence of being in a group and revert to your individual self.

However, once you reach Lhasa you will encounter several problems and won't be entirely free to roam around Tibet. The first is permits. Although some sites in central Tibet are open without permit, many other places require permits. The second is transport: there are few local buses and they're not in good shape. If there are not enough individual travellers in Lhasa to club together and rent Landcruisers, you may have trouble, since the TTB (Tibet Tourism Bureau) attempts to steer all individuals into their government-run, high-priced Landcruiser trips.

Red tape

On a group tour, getting into Tibet is no problem – the operator takes care of the red tape. As an individual, it's an elaborate game. The name of the game is: which door is open this week? The first target is Lhasa. There are three or four 'doors' to try – sometimes they're open, sometimes they're not. Flights into Lhasa arrive from Kathmandu, Beijing, Xian, Kunming, Chengdu and other parts of China, but you will be screened by China Southwest Airlines and will not be allowed to board unless you have the right paperwork. Land routes snake into Lhasa from Kathmandu (Nepal) and Golmud (Qinghai). The best chance is from within mainland China itself, with frequent departures from Chengdu (flight) or Golmud (sleeper bus). Here Chinese travel agents will put you into a group of say, ten aliens, for ticket purchase. The reason that Chengdu or Golmud are the best approaches is that you're already in China, and since Tibet is an integral part of China (in Chinese eyes), officials are less likely to stop you proceeding.

Visas

This may sound odd, but the best place to get a long Chinese visa is within China – in Hong Kong. Hong Kong, since the handover, operates as a Special Administrative Region (SAR), with the Chinese Embassy simply altering its name to PRC Visa Issuing Office. The office is located in the China Resources Building in Wanchai – you can approach this office yourself, but travellers usually go through agents for convenience. In short order, in Hong Kong, you can pick up a one-month visa (can be processed next day, HK$350/US$45), a three-month visa (HK$600/US$80), or a six-month visa, which takes two working days to obtain. Multiple-entry visas are possible.

There are certain things with which you should be careful when applying for a visa. Do not mention Tibet or Xinjiang as destinations. Travellers have had their visa application knocked back solely for doing this, and been told they need special permission to travel to those places. Safer destinations to mention are Beijing and Shanghai. Reason for visit: tourism. Your job: do not put down Reporter, Journalist, Writer, Photographer, Missionary, Diplomat or Politician, as your visa will not be processed. These people require special permission to travel in places like Tibet – this involves a complex procedure that may not succeed. Travel agents in Hong Kong will advise you how to fill in the application. For a short list of agents, see *Staging Point Hong Kong* in this chapter.

Visas have a coding on them: the L visa designates a regular tourist; the F visa is for a cultural exchange student (can create problems when flying from Chengdu to Lhasa, but seems to be okay through Kunming); the Z visa is issued to those working in China. A visa issued in Hong Kong may start running immediately (from the date of issue), which means you'll lose a week or so just getting to Tibet. Visas from other embassies usually start from the date of entry into China, and will give you a two- or three-month leeway to get there.

Embassies closer to China are the most liberal in issuing longer visas, it seems. Hong Kong is good (three-month visa or longer is possible); Hanoi is not bad (two months possible); Islamabad offers a two-month visa; the Delhi embassy may provide a two-month visa if prodded (but otherwise will only issue one month); the Bangkok embassy normally issues visas of only one month, but longer may be possible. You might try your home country to see if you can wangle a three-month visa. Explain that China is a big place and you need a long time to see it all. Visa extensions are difficult within Tibet, but easy in other parts of China.

According to the Chinese, Tibet is an integral part of China. When you apply for the visa, however, do not mention you want to go to Tibet. While a Chinese visa is good for Tibet, authorities there may not extend your initial visa in Lhasa without fulfilling demands like joining a tour. Therefore get the longest visa you can – two months, three months – at the point of origin. Not all Chinese embassies abroad are created equal. Some will grant you three months, others two months maximum, and still others only one month. As well as securing Chinese visas, group tour operators are issued with a separate permit on a quarto-sized (approximately A4) sheet of paper with all members of the tour and their passport numbers listed. This is in theory a 'Tibet permit' but it's not stamped in the passport.

Applying for a Chinese visa in Kathmandu is troublesome. The situation could change, but the Chinese Embassy in Kathmandu is in the habit of only issuing visas for the length of a tour to Tibet booked through an agent in Kathmandu. You cannot apply to the embassy as an individual: you can only approach them through a travel agent. Although there's no shortage of travel agents handling the Tibet trade in Kathmandu, prices can be steep – and then you have to work out how to jump the tour, since your visa may be short. Some agents are more amenable to the idea of booking you on a short tour while guaranteeing you a longer Chinese visa – ask around.

If you already have a Chinese visa issued elsewhere and apply for a short Tibet tour in Kathmandu, the embassy in Kathmandu may cancel it and reissue another visa valid for the length of the tour. So if you do not want this to happen, argue the case that you want to fly on from Lhasa to Beijing after their tour and need the extra visa time. See the following section about attempting the overland crossing to Lhasa from Kathmandu, using a Chinese visa not issued in Kathmandu.

Special entry permits
There is no such thing as a 'Tibet Permit'. This has been concocted by the airline, the TTB and crooked agents. What they're referring to is a piece of paper listing the group participants on a tour, which is needed before an airline ticket can be purchased. The list is sometimes issued *without* a visa by the Chinese Embassy in Kathmandu for those on a tour of Tibet round-trip from Kathmandu. You will most likely never see this piece of paper: ask for a copy of it, and the agent will probably say that's not possible. The 'Tibet Permit' is a farce.

Chinese embassies and consulates

Chinese embassies and consulates abroad are approachable for longer visas. Inquire whether the visa starts running immediately. Chinese embassies and consulates are found throughout Europe, Africa, the Middle East, Central Asia, Asia/Indian subcontinent, Australasia/Oceania and North America.

For a complete listing of Chinese embassies and consulates, with full address data including fax and email addresses, consult the website of the Ministry of Foreign Affairs of the PRC at: www.fmprc.gov.cn/eng. Click on 'Missions Overseas' for addresses, and 'Missions Overseas Online' for relevant embassy websites – which provide information on visa requirements and even downloadable visa application forms. A brief listing of relevant Chinese embassies follows: address and telephone data given may be the visa/consular section, which should be close to the embassy.

Western Europe

Austria Metternichgasse 4, A-1030 Vienna; tel: 431 710 3648.
Belgium Avenue de Tervuren 443-445, 1150 Brussels; tel: 322 771 3309.
Denmark Oregards Alle 25, 2900 Hellerup, Copenhagen; tel: 045 3961 9889.
Finland Vanha Kelkkamaki 9-11, 00570 Helsinki; tel: 2289 0130.
France 9 Ave Victor Cresson, 92130 Issy-les-Moulineaux, Paris; tel: 01 4736 0258; web: www.amb-chine.fr. Consulates located in Marseille and Strasbourg.
Germany Markischer Ufer 54, 10179 Berlin; tel: 030 275 880. Consulates located in Munich and Hamburg.
Ireland 40 Ailesbury Rd, Dublin 4; tel: 01 269 1707.
Italy Via Della Camilluccia 613, Roma 00135; tel: 06 3630 8534. Consulates located in Milan and Firenze.
Netherlands Adriaan Goekooplaan 7, The Hague; tel: 070 306 5061.
Spain No. 113 Arturo Soria, 28043 Madrid; tel: 341 519 242. Consulate located in Barcelona.
Sweden Lidovagen 8, 115 25 Stockholm; tel: 08 5793 6437. Consulate located in Gothenburg.
Switzerland Kalcheggweg 10, 3006 Berne; tel: 031 352 7333. Consulate located in Zurich.
United Kingdom 31 Portland Place, London W1B 1PD; tel: 0207 631 1430; web: www.chinese-embassy.org.uk. Consulates located in Manchester and Edinburgh.

North America

Canada 515 St Patrick St, Ottawa, Ontario K1N 5H3; tel: 613 789 3434; web: www.chinaembassycanada.org. Consulates also located in Toronto, Calgary and Vancouver.
USA 2201 Wisconsin Ave NW, Room 110, Washington DC 20007; tel: 202 338 6688; web: www.china-embassy.org. Consulates located in New York, Chicago, Houston, Los Angeles and San Francisco.

Australasia

Australia 15 Coronation Dr, Yarralumla, ACT 2600; tel: 02 6273 47890; web: www.chinaembassy.org.au. Consulates located in Sydney, Melbourne and Perth.
New Zealand 2-6 Glenmore St, Wellington; tel: 644 472 1382; web: www.chinaembassy.org.nz. Consulate located in Auckland.

Asia/India

Visa validity for the following embassies and consulates varies considerably. You can get two- (or even three-) month visas in Hanoi, but only one month might be given in Bangkok. Islamabad may hand out two months, but New Delhi only one month. Some visas allow up to three months to get there; others may start running immediately.

Cambodia Issarak Blvd at Street 163, Phnom Penh; tel: 426 271.

Hong Kong SAR Ministry of Foreign Affairs of the PRC, 5th floor, Low Block, China Resources Building, 26 Harbour Rd, Wanchai; tel: 2827 1881. Classed as a 'visa-issuing office'. Travellers often use agents.

India 50D, Shantipath, Chanakyapuri, New Delhi; tel: 011 611 6682. Consulate located in Mumbai.

Indonesia Jl. Mega Kuningan No 2, Jakarta Selatan; tel: 221 5724 3336.

Japan 4-33, Moto-Azabu 3-chome, Minato-ku, Tokyo; tel: 03 3403 3380; web: www.china-embassy.or.jp. Consulates located in Osaka, Fukuoka, Sapporo and Nagasaki.

Laos Wat Nak St, Sisattahanak area, Vientiane; tel: 315 103.

Malaysia 229 Jalan Ampang, 40450 Kuala Lumpur; tel: 603 242 8495. Consulate located in Kuching (Sabah).

Mongolia CPO Box 672, Zaluuchuudyn Urgun Chuluu 5, Ulaanbaatar; tel: 976 11 323940

Myanmar (Burma) No.1 Pyidaungsu Yeiktha Rd, Yangon; tel: 01 221 280. There's a consulate in Mandalay.

Nepal PO Box 4234, Baluwatar, Kathmandu; tel: 9771 413 916.

Pakistan Diplomatic Enclave, Ramna 4, Islamabad; tel: 9251 282 4786. Consulate located in Karachi.

Singapore 70-76 Dalvey Rd; tel: 65 734 3200.

Thailand 57 Ratchadapisek Rd, Dindaeng, Bangkok; tel: 02 245 7032; web: www.chinaembassy.or.th. Consulates located in Chiang Mai and Songkhla.

Vietnam 46 Hoang Dieu, Hanoi; tel: 825 3737. Consulate located in Saigon.

Customs and searches

Customs and checkpoint searches in Tibet are of the hit-and-miss variety. Some are waved through, others get the third degree. If a suspicious item is found in a Landcruiser, all the baggage may be searched. Your baggage may be searched on entry to Tibet, while in Tibet, and on exit. One passenger had a souvenir prayer wheel dismantled at Lhasa Airport upon exiting, to see if any messages were being carried in it. Even if you are on a domestic flight from Chengdu to Gongkar, you may have your bags searched. Body searches are rare. Military checkpoints on the Kathmandu to Lhasa route are on the lookout for material readily purchased in Kathmandu, like Dalai Lama pictures or tapes. Some foreigners have been hauled off at a military checkpoint and questioned about books in their possession – one of these was an autobiography by the Dalai Lama. On exit, Chinese customs may be looking for 'antiques,' which means anything Tibetan that is older than 1959.

Alien Health Declaration

You are required to fill in a Passenger Health Declaration when flying into China or Tibet. It starts out: 'Any Alien suffering from AIDS, venereal disease, leprosy, psychiatric disorder or open pulmonary tuberculosis is not allowed to enter the territory...' and goes on to solemnly ask you to declare if you are carrying any Biological Products, Blood Products, or Old Clothes. Your health certificate may be asked for, but probably won't be.

Access routes into Tibet
Route strategies

Direction of travel becomes very important in Tibet. Getting in from Kathmandu to Lhasa is a killer (problems with permits and altitude), but exiting from Lhasa to Kathmandu is a piece of cake. Because Nepal to Tibet is an international arrival, it leads to many more visa and red-tape complications, although some travellers have

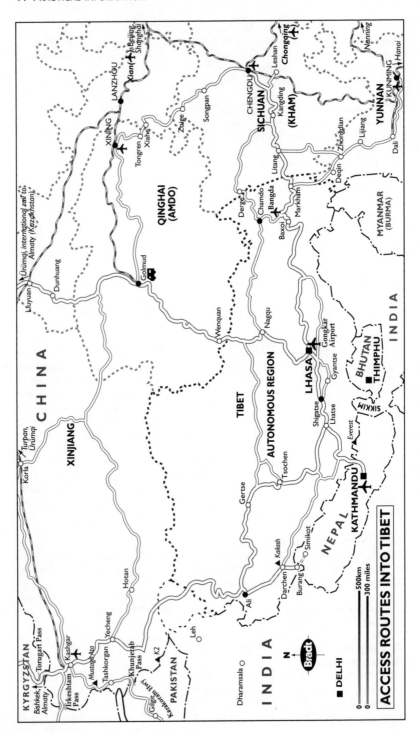

ACCESS ROUTES INTO TIBET

ROUTES INTO TIBET

The map opposite shows major access points into Tibet, as follows (clockwise from Chengdu):

From Chengdu, Sichuan Main air gateway to Lhasa, with daily flights. Rough overland route to Lhasa. Frequent flights to Beijing/Shanghai, Hong Kong/Shenzhen/Guangzhou, and Bangkok/Singapore.

From Chongqing, Sichuan Infrequent direct flight to Lhasa. Direct flights to Hong Kong and Macao.

From Zhongdian, Yunnan Weekly flight to Lhasa, Kunming and Chengdu. Rough overland route to Lhasa.

From Kunming, Yunnan Weekly flight or rough overland route to Lhasa. Rail route direct to Hanoi, Vietnam. Frequent flights to Bangkok, Chiang Mai, Hong Kong. Less frequent to Hanoi, Singapore, Vientiane, Phnom Penh and Rangoon.

From Kathmandu, Nepal Direct flight or spectacular overland route to Lhasa. Frequent flights to Hong Kong, Bangkok, India and Europe.

From Kashgar, Xinjiang Rough overland route via Ali to Lhasa. Rail, road and frequent flights to Urumqi. Spectacular Karakoram Highway route to Islamabad in Pakistan.

From Golmud, Qinghai Main overland route to Lhasa, using sleeper buses.

From Xian, Shaanxi Infrequent direct flight from Beijing via Xiang to Lhasa. Rail connection via Xining to Golmud.

Many travellers choose to enter Tibet from one point, such as Chengdu, and exit from another, such as Kathmandu, giving the opportunity to travel more widely in the region.

beaten the system by booking on a three-day tour to Lhasa from Kathmandu, and then jumping ship. Travellers obsessed with getting to Tibet go to great lengths: having found their route stymied in Kathmandu, some travellers have flown all the way back to Hong Kong and *back* to Chengdu, and then *back* to Lhasa! If you look at the map, you can see why that route costs a small fortune as opposed to a direct Kathmandu-Lhasa flight. Occasionally Chengdu is blocked too – possibly because of some Chinese official visiting Tibet – and travellers have proceeded all the way up to Golmud by land, and then overland to Lhasa.

More than most places, you need to think about your route to and from Tibet because of visa complications. There's only one consulate in Lhasa – the Nepalese Consulate (you actually don't need a Nepalese visa as you can pick it up on arrival). That's fine, but what about going overland to Kashgar, and then exiting on the Karakoram Highway into Pakistan? The nearest place for a Pakistan visa is Beijing, and that's a long, long way to go. A similar conundrum crops up in Chengdu if you want to go overland to Hanoi – there may be a Vietnamese consulate in Kunming, otherwise the closest one is in Guangzhou. There are Lao and Burmese consulates in Kunming. Visa acupuncture points for Asia include Kathmandu, Hong Kong, Bangkok, Hanoi, Singapore, Beijing, Islamabad and Delhi. Some visas are readily available upon arrival by land or air: these include the Nepalese visa, Thai visa, and Hong Kong entry visa.

TTB monopoly

Since 2000, the Chinese-government-operated TTB (Tibet Tourism Bureau) has created a monopoly for Landcruiser travel in Lhasa. They try to channel all individuals coming through by plane into TTB-affiliated travel agents in Lhasa. The paperwork for the airticket and three-day tour of Lhasa probably also stipulates that you are TTB property, and can only book a tour with Snowland FIT or Banakshol FIT (the same company). This is already decided on your initial permit, and other travel agents in Lhasa will not deal with you for fear of losing their licence (however, they will still accept you for travel to non-permit areas, like destinations in Lhasa Prefecture). The main agent dealing with the 'Tibet permit' in places like Chengdu, Kunming, Shanghai and other points is likely to be the TTB-affiliated office (so TTBS is Tibet Tourism Bureau of Shanghai). There are also TTB offices in Hong Kong and Kathmandu.

If you wish to get around the TTB monopoly, and you have a small group assembled, you could try and deal direct with a **Lhasa tour agent** to make customised arrangements. This is what the Western outfitters do, but it must be done from outside Tibet (and outside China). A short listing of Lhasa agents can be found in the *Lhasa* chapter, but there are very few which are not Chinese-managed in some way.

Staging points

The first stepping stone for many is to get to Hong Kong SAR, or Bangkok, or Kathmandu. More information on Kathmandu can be found in this book in the sections following.

Hong Kong SAR

No visa is required of most Westerners for stays of a month or longer in Hong Kong SAR. Supposedly, the economic, social and legal status quo will stay in place for 50 years from the handover to China on July 1, 1997. However, there are indications that this promise is falling apart after just five years. In 2002, dissident Harry Wu was arrested at Hong Kong Airport, held for half a day and deported. Falun Gong members have been refused entry at the airport also. There is pressure from Chinese authorities on the media and certain taboos are in place, amounting to self-censorship of sorts. Taboo topics include the Falun Gong, insulting senior Communist Party leaders, advocating independence for Taiwan or Tibet (or Hong Kong), and being off the mark about the Tiananmen Massacre. By 2002, the *South China Morning Post*, once one of the most opinionated newspapers in Asia, had laid off most of its foreign staff and replaced them with mainland stooges as reporters and editors.

All that said, there's a wide range of books available in stores, with material on Tibet freely available, but for how much longer is not known. The best bookstore is Pageone, with several branches, including Level 3 of Harbour City in Kowloon, and in the Times Square building at Causeway Bay. Hong Kong is a good place to stock up on US cash dollars, medicines, or whatever else you are short of.

Chinese visas are easy to get in Hong Kong SAR, and can usually be obtained within a few days. There is a direct charter flight from Hong Kong via Chengdu to Lhasa once a week, but this is only for groups and is quite expensive. You can achieve a similar routing, but at far reduced prices, by pre-booking an air ticket from either Shenzhen or Guangzhou to Chengdu. You proceed overland from Hong Kong to Shenzhen or Guangzhou and transfer to the airport the same day. The more scenic option is the ferry to Shenzhen, which connects with an airport shuttle bus.

Hong Kong travel agents include:

Phoenix Services Agency, Room A, 7F Milton Mansion, 96 Nathan Road, Kowloon, tel: 852 2722 7378; fax 852 2369 8884; email: Phoenix1@netvigator.com; this is a highly recommended agent.
Friendship Travel, Room 604, 6F, Mohan's Bldg, 14-16 Hankow Rd, Kowloon; tel: 852 2312 1888; fax 852 2366 1623.
Star Tours & Travel, 8F Wah Ying Cheong Kin Bldg, 236 Nathan Rd, Jordan, Kowloon; tel: 852 2367 6663; fax 852 2369 6173.

Bangkok, Thailand

No visa is normally required for most Westerners arriving in Thailand for a stay of one month. Bangkok is the major hub of Southeast Asia, and an excellent place to go shopping – or visa shopping. ATM machines abound, and it's easy to turn US travel cheques into US cash dollars at banks. To get around town, you would be wise to keep to the Skytrain or the Chao Praya express boats – everything else crawls. There are fine bookstores in Bangkok, including many branches of Asia Books; in the Emporium Building (Skytrain stop is Emporium on the Sukhumvit line) is a major bookstore called Kinokuniya.

Agents can arrange visas and ticketing onward from Bangkok, with direct flights to Chengdu or Kunming. However, you might not be able to get a longer visa for China from the embassy in Bangkok. Khao San Road has a large cluster of travel agents – make sure the phone is plugged into the wall. Two reliable agents in the Silom area are:

STA Travel Wall Street Tower, 14th floor, Room 1406, 33 Surawong Road; tel: 236 0262, fax: 237 6005; email: help@statravel.co.th
I&E Trading 190 Charoenkrung Soi 44, Bangrak; tel: 238 1525; fax 237 3236; email: inetour@cscoms.com. A smaller office near the back of the Shangri-La Hotel.

Hanoi, Vietnam

You need a visa in advance to get entry to Vietnam. Two-month Chinese visas are readily obtained in Hanoi within a few days, which makes Hanoi more attractive than Bangkok as a staging point. Also, getting from Hanoi overland to China is cheaper than flying. Hanoi is a very pleasant city, with lakes, cafes, bicycle rentals and streetside beer stalls (the beer is cheaper than bottled water). You can obtain cash US dollars from the Vietcombank for a small commission charge (changing from US dollar travel cheques). From Hanoi you can take a train to the Chinese border, then transfer for a stunning train-ride on the Chinese side to Kunming, twisting through mountainous terrain. From Kunming, you could board a plane direct to Lhasa, or continue by rail to Chengdu and arrange a package to Lhasa from there. An alternative is to fly from Hanoi direct to Kunming. A reliable agent in Hanoi is:

New Indochina Travel, 4 Dang Thai Than St, tel. 933 0599; fax 933 0499; email: new-indochina@fpt.vn; this agent is the STA representative for Vietnam.

Direct air routes

All flights into Lhasa are on Boeing 757s or Airbus A340s operated by the regional carrier China Southwest Airlines (CSWA), an arm of the national carrier CAAC. The hub for CSWA is Chengdu, so this has the best connections and options. Approximate flight durations are: Lhasa to Kathmandu, 1 hour 10 minutes; Lhasa to Chengdu, 1 hour 50 minutes; Lhasa to Xian, 2 hours 30 minutes. There's no sign

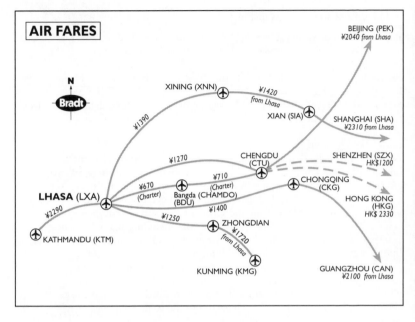

of any Tibetan pilots yet – call back in another 25 years or so – but there are some Tibetan stewardesses on the planes. They wear striped Tibetan trim on their aprons. This is progress. Inflight videos introduce you to the wonderful world of Tibet, but you would do a lot better looking out the window; the remote and savage snowy ranges between Chengdu and Lhasa are the stuff that dreams are made of.

You will not be allowed to purchase an air ticket to Lhasa on CSWA from any destination unless you have the right paperwork, meaning you have to go through an agent in those places, who will fix you up with a 'Tibet permit' (a useless piece of paper that says you can fly on CSWA) and a three-day tour of Lhasa. CAAC (affectionately known as China Airlines Almost Crashes) has a poor safety record: there have been several major crashes due to hijackers attempting to get to Taiwan, and others due to poor maintenance, but it does boast an impeccable record in Tibet.

Gongkar Airport
Pilots landing at Gongkar must be trained in aerial manoeuvres at 3,700m. Due to air currents, most flights in or out of Tibet are scheduled as early as possible in the morning (wind can pick up significantly in the afternoon). On arrival at Gongkar your baggage may be searched (even if you are on a domestic flight). Gongkar Airport is 96km from Lhasa. If you don't have a ride arranged from Gongkar, find out if there's a CAAC bus running into Lhasa, or else get together with others and hire a taxi. There is lodging and food in the town of Gongkar, an easy walk from the airport. For information on departing Tibet by air, see the *Lhasa* chapter.

Other plateau airports
While there are a number of military airfields in Tibet, there are only a couple of civilian airfields. Tested out in late 1999 by Boeing pilots is Bangda Airport, which is located about 100km south of Chamdo. Bangda is the highest airport in the world, with a runway at 4,334m. For the present, charter flights operate on this route (group tours only – Bangda is a closed town). It takes an hour to fly from Lhasa to Bangda.

There is another flight from Bangda to Chengdu. Confusingly, Bangda is also called Bamda, Pomda, and Changdu (so there's a Changdu-Chengdu flight).

A large airport at Zhongdian (3,275m) in Diqing Tibetan Autonomous Prefecture (upper Yunnan) started operation in early 2000. The airport is officially named Diqing Shangri-La Airport: this lies in Yunnan, outside the TAR, so no permits are required to fly into this place from Lhasa. You can also fly from Zhongdian to Lhasa on a package deal similar to those offered in Kunming (from where the flight originates).

Chengdu gateway

Chengdu is the main air gateway to Lhasa, with year-round flights and sometimes up to five flights a day. The flight into Lhasa crosses the snowcaps of eastern Tibet, with great 757 wingtip vistas. Flight time is 1 hour 50 minutes. You need to book a flight at least two days in advance to allow time for paperwork. It is the most reliable way to go for individual travellers. It is also the main hub for the airline CSWA, with frequent onward connections to destinations like Beijing, Shenzhen, Guangzhou and Hong Kong SAR.

You'll be hit for another Y50 for airport construction tax at the airport. Because it mounts the most regular flights into Tibet, Chengdu is a magnet for individual travellers, who are packaged into impromptu groups of 10-15 by local agents. The coding on the air ticket is CTU-LXA (Chengdu-Lhasa). Peak months, with heavy bookings, are July and August. You can fly into Chengdu from Hong Kong, Guangzhou, Bangkok or Singapore; you can also get to Chengdu overland from Hanoi via Kunming.

You cannot buy the ticket yourself. The best thing here is to stay at the Traffic (Jiaotong) Hotel in Chengdu and go through one of the lobby travel agents resident there – the agent will supply the air ticket by putting you in an impromptu group. From Chengdu, a one-way ticket with permit and three-day tour in Lhasa retails for Y2,700, which includes air-ticket (Y1,270), airport transfers (ours was by regular CAAC bus), 'insurance', 'Tibet permit', low-end dormitory accommodation in Lhasa, and a tour bus and tour-guide for three days. Not included are airport construction tax, and entry-fees for Lhasa sights (which are quite high). The Chengdu Mafia all stick to the same price for the three-day package, backed by TTB thugs. This 'tour' is marketed for backpackers. The TTB has other more expensive customised packages for those who would not stand for dormitory accommodation in Lhasa. Packages can be customised for groups of four or even two persons.

Agents may demand that you buy a round-trip ticket to Lhasa – or a ticket out of the TAR. To get out of this one, purchase (in advance) a bus-ticket from Lhasa to Golmud for Y300 (actual price is Y210 at the bus station in Lhasa). One more thing to consider: agents in Chengdu will most likely sign you up with your sole agent in Lhasa as Snowland FIT or Banakshol FIT (these are the same monopoly, run by the TTB). Inquire who the agent responsible for you is in Lhasa because you will be stuck with that agent for any Landcruiser tours starting from Lhasa. The Traffic (Jiaotong) Hotel happens – by more than coincidence – to be where backpackers stay, sharing rooms. The hotel is sited near the Jinjiang River at 77 Linjiang Road (tel: 028 555 1017). Right opposite, but across the river, is a travellers' hangout called Paul's Oasis – a good place to swap tales and dredge up the latest road news.

Chengdu agents

Permits all go through TTB Chengdu, located in Room 1418, 14th floor of Tibet Hotel, Chengdu. You cannot get a permit directly through them – you must go through an agent.

Chengdu New Pearl Star Travel Service, located on the ground floor of the Tibet Hotel (10 Renmin Bei Lu; tel: 028 318 3388; fax 028 318 7048; email: newpearl@mail.e-tibet.com) is the agent with the most clout, but it's not the cheapest. For cheaper rates, there are at least seven small agents in and around the Traffic Hotel that deal with backpackers. They're most likely branches of the same company – a load of monkey business. It's a jungle out there! Or so says George of the Jungle, chairman of one of these companies (his slogan: Life is a Jungle – Let George do it). Agents in and around the Traffic Hotel include the following:

Traffic Travel Service Outside the lobby of Traffic Hotel, tel: 028 545 4988; fax 028 667 8855; email: georgeofjungle@sina.com
Holy Land Tibet Budget Tour In the Traffic Hotel compound; tel: 028 544 0553
Chengdu Traffic Travel Service On the street near Traffic Hotel; tel/fax 028 545 8111

Kunming/Zhongdian gateway

The flight from Kunming to Lhasa via Zhongdian goes several times a week. Tibet packages go for Y2650 one-way, including insurance and three-day Lhasa tour. These are TTB-controlled. The best plan is to stay at the Camellia Hotel (Chahua Binguan), 96 East Dongfeng Rd; tel: 0871 316 3000 (dorms Y30, Y100-170 double). The Chamabar, located in the Camellia Hotel compound, is a great place to chat with travellers (and on the internet too). Kunming is connected by rail from Hanoi in Vietnam (pick up a Chinese visa in Hanoi), and you can go overland from Luang Namtha in Laos to Kunming (pick up a Chinese visa in Vientiane).

Kunming agent The main agent for Tibet tickets (overland or by air) is Mr Chen, Room 3116, No.3 Building, Camellia Hotel; tel/fax: 0871 318 8114.
Zhongdian agent The primary agent is the TTB-affiliated office at Room 306, Kangba Hotel; tel: 0887 822 7892; fax 0887 822 9028.They can book air-packages from Zhongdian to Lhasa, and possibly can arrange overland trips for a hefty tariff.

Other Chinese gateways

The flight from Beijing stops in Chengdu, then continues to Lhasa. Frequency may vary from once a week to daily; in any case, the Chengdu-to-Lhasa leg is daily. Less frequent flights go to Lhasa from Guangzhou via Chongqing (rumoured to be once or twice weekly), or to Lhasa from Shanghai via Xian and Xining (two or three times a week). There are several snags involved with these flights. The first is that they are pretty expensive – Beijing to Lhasa is Y2,040 one-way, and that's without tour-and-permit costs factored in. With the full package (one-way airfare, three-day Lhasa tour and transfers), TTB Shanghai (www.tibet-tour.com) quotes Y4,020 one-way from Beijing (US$490) and Y4,265 (US$520) from Shanghai. You cannot purchase your own tickets over the counter like you would for other destinations in China – you have to go through a local travel agent. Listing of a flight on a timetable does not guarantee that the plane will actually depart. Chinese planes only fly when seat space is sufficiently filled: if not, the plane could be cancelled or delayed.

Kathmandu gateway

The only international flight into Lhasa is from Kathmandu. A group of five is mandatory for ticket reservations. Flights should be booked two to four weeks in advance through a travel agent. The flight costs Y2,290 one-way (fare applies if leaving Lhasa; to go from Kathmandu to Lhasa you need a full package price). No Nepalese aircraft fly the route – it's all on CSWA, so again the ticketing problems come up (you can't buy the ticket yourself). Ticketing problems are worse here because the agent will take your passport to the Chinese embassy, which may

NOT LIKE SHANGRI-LA

In December 1943, the first airplane reached Tibet – or rather, crashed in Tibet. During World War II, American pilots used to ferry strategic supplies from India to southwest China, flying over the Himalaya. Tibet did not allow overland passage of these goods through its territory: despite pressure from the British and the Chinese, the Tibetans wished to remain neutral. And so it was that five American airmen in a B-24 bomber got blown off course at night, started running out of fuel, and circled Lhasa, believing it to be an Indian town. With no radio response from the town – and no obvious airstrip – they decided to parachute out of the plane. The startled villagers of Tsedang clothed and fed them; eventually the wide-eyed airmen were escorted to Lhasa, by now wearing fur-lined boots and fur coats.

Here, at the British Mission, the reception was quite different, as they faced angry mobs of Tibetans. It transpired that the airmen had committed great sacrilege by flying over the Dalai Lama's palace. As further proof of this, Tibetan priests had long predicted that any aircraft flying over the Holy City and daring to look down on the Dalai Lama would be doomed. This is exactly what happened to the B-24: it had crashed into a mountainside near Tsedang and exploded (eventually, Tibetan villagers salvaged usable parts of the plane). The airmen never got a tour of Lhasa: they were quickly hustled out of the country for their own safety, and because Tibet wished to maintain its neutrality in the war-theatre. Ironically, the next planes to arrive were war planes, of a kind: Russian turboprops – the standard Chinese military aircraft in the 1960s. Most airfields in Tibet are military. Gongkar Airport doubles as a military and commercial airfield, as does Bangda Airfield, to the south of Chamdo.

cancel a Chinese visa issued elsewhere and replace it with a visa valid for the length of the tour you've booked. Impress upon the agent that the visa must remain unchanged because you will be travelling onward from Lhasa to Beijing and other parts of mainland China after the Tibet trip. Kathmandu to Lhasa flights operate two or three times weekly in season (the flight is closed down for winter months – late October to March). Peak months, with heavy bookings, are July and August. The flight lasts 1 hour 10 minutes, and goes straight over the Himalaya – the pilot uses Everest as a navigation landmark when turning.

Here's an example of a trip booked from Kathmandu. A Dutch couple picked up 30-day Chinese visas in Holland. In Kathmandu, they booked a tour through Explore Nepal Tours & Travel for US$273 one-way airfare (each) and US$207 (each) for three-day tour. That brought it to a total of US$480 each for air-fare, good hotel in Lhasa and three-days of touring with a guide in Lhasa. This tour was superior to the TTB offerings – it included three nights at the Flora Hotel, which has comfortable doubles with bath, and the price included all entry fees to sights in Lhasa. After staying three days in Lhasa, the Dutch stayed to do their own travelling, for the duration of the 30-day visa, and returned overland to Kathmandu.

Kathmandu agents

You can find information about Kathmandu agents (with address and email and website listings) at www.kotan.org (go to Tibetan Cultural Region Directory, then click on Nepal). Some recommended agents are:

Kathmandu-Lhasa Tours & Travel PO Box 9179/5208 Jyatha, Thamel, Kathmandu; tel: 9771 231060; email: kktt@ktm.mos.com.np
Explore Nepal Richa Tours & Travel email: explore@enrtt.mos.com.np

Road routes into Tibet

There are two semi-sanctioned road routes into Lhasa – one from Golmud and one from Kathmandu. The first is boring, the second poses considerable logistical problems. Exiting Tibet by either route is not a problem, but entering can be. China uses the metric system, and there are kilometre marker-stones along all major routes, so you can track your progress. You can also use these marker stones to figure out turn-offs. In Tibet, there are usually road maintenance stations every 10km, just like in imperial Rome.

Overland routes opening up

Group tours might be able to cross overland from Tibet into Nepal at Gyirong, leading into the Langtang area of Nepal, north of Kathmandu. Another possibility that may open up is for group tours to cross into or out of Tibet at Nathu La pass, on the Sikkim-Tibet border. However, due to friction between China and India around this border, it may remain sensitive. This was the main gateway for British access to Tibet by horse in the early 20th century, coming up from Kalimpong and Darjeeling. On the Tibetan side, the road passes viewpoints looking across at Kangchenjunga, the third-highest peak in the world.

Golmud route

The 1,130km journey from Golmud to Lhasa is a two-day epic that qualifies for the most boring bus-ride in Asia. The journey takes anywhere from 24 to 40 hours – longer if you break down. Golmud (3,200m) is the Black Hole of China – a town of 90,000. It is normally reached by railway (although bus is possible). Travellers may have to wait in Golmud until a group of up to 20 assembles, and along comes a CITS bus. The sleeper-bus fare is a whopping Y2,000 a person one-way, which includes the mythical 'Tibet permit' and a three-day tour in Lhasa. There are also direct Xining-Lhasa buses, but foreigners are not permitted to travel on them. There's a military checkpoint 30km south of Golmud, and another at Nagqu. Some enterprising travellers have sneaked out past the first checkpoint, then got rides in trucks, hiding under blankets at subsequent checkpoints. The paved road traverses stark high terrain, passing the world's highest inhabited place (Wenquan, at 5,100m, established by the Chinese in 1955), and shortly after crossing 5,180m Tangu La into the TAR.

Here's the rub: from Lhasa (where you have choices on where to go) the price of a bus seat one-way to Golmud is about Y210 (as opposed to the Y2,000 it costs by bus from Golmud to Lhasa). If you've left Lhasa and reached Golmud overland, you might want to look into continuing overland from Xining via Labrang to Chengdu – a great run through Tibetan areas. For more details, check the *Amdo, Kham and East Tibet* chapter.

Kathmandu route

By contrast, the Kathmandu to Lhasa route cuts through diverse altitude zones and draws you past an enthralling Himalayan landscape. However, this route is better tackled as an exit, for reasons of permits, choices and altitude. See the Lhasa to Kathmandu Route chapter for details. The first problem you will have is getting a Chinese visa. Unless you book a tour from Kathmandu, the Chinese Embassy may not issue a visa. Some travellers have obtained Chinese visas in other places, such as Delhi or Bangkok.

The majority of travellers entering Tibet overland from Kathmandu do so on a four-day tour, and then stay on to the end of their visa validity on their own. A good package would be US$350 for a four-day tour, which includes a bus to the border, a Landcruiser for three up to Lhasa with a guide, and a stay at a low-end hotel in Lhasa. Because you can see a lot of great sites along this route, travellers prefer to try and book a seven-day tour, taking four or five days to reach Lhasa before being given the Lhasa tour.

On your own, with a valid Chinese visa, you might be able to cross at the Zhangmu border, and pick up a CITS Landcruiser, usually charging US$100 to US$150 a person to get to Lhasa (the lower figure is a two-day run with no sightseeing stops; the higher figure could be a four-day tour, with stops). Although the Chinese Embassy in Kathmandu may cancel Chinese visas issued elsewhere (and substitute a new visa valid for the length of your tour), the border at Zhangmu is an entirely different authority, over which the Kathmandu embassy has no control. Zhangmu border officials may honour a Chinese visa issued elsewhere and may allow entry because there's money to be made from CITS Landcruiser rentals in Zhangmu. Take a bus from Kathmandu to Kodari for a couple of dollars, take a half-hour truck or jeep ride to Zhangmu, and then try and wrangle through to the CITS official next to the Chinese immigration post. You're not supposed to leave the trip until you get to Lhasa, but some have wandered off into the sunset in Shigatse.

Longer overland routes

There are various epic routes into Lhasa that traverse the plateau and you get to see half of Tibet along the way. As with the other routes mentioned, your success rate is probably higher leaving Tibet by these overland routes rather than entering.

If you can muster a group, you can arrange Landcruiser rental in Lhasa for a ten- to 14-day trip eastward to either Derge or Deqin, where you leave the TAR and stop worrying about permits. These trips cost about Y15,000 and up for the Landcruiser, or around Y4,000 a person. Some operators want Y6,600 a person for the ride.

Chengdu to Lhasa overland takes about ten to 15 days without stops, and crosses some 15 high passes. Past Kangding, the route diverges, a northern branch going through Derge and Chamdo, and a southern route passing through Litang and Markam. Both routes join up again near Bangda, and the road continues past Namche Barwa, the highest peak in eastern Tibet, at 7,756m. For a very long time, geographers speculated that there had to be a huge waterfall in the area close to Namche Barwa because the Yarlung Tsangpo dropped radically as it transformed into India's Brahmaputra River. There's no big waterfall, but the river stages a dramatic U-turn around Namche Barwa, cutting through one of the deepest gorges in the world.

Towns along the Chengdu to Lhasa route are mostly truck-stops. Officials and truck-stop inns don't see a lot of foreigners, but if they do, they're liable to cause problems. One group in a Landcruiser, stopping at Bayi, was fined heavily for staying overnight at a non-PSB-approved hotel (PSB wanted them to stay at a very expensive approved hotel). Chengdu to Lhasa is 2,400km via Chamdo (north route) and 2,080 km via Litang (south route). The route is not covered in this book, but there is some information on Kham in The Tibetan World chapter. In that chapter are also details on a beautiful route linking Lanzhou to Chengdu.

Coming up from Kunming is a stunning route that travels through the scenic towns of Dali, Lijiang and Zhongdian before joining the route to Lhasa near

Markam. Kunming to Markam is 1,200km, and it's another 1,100km from Markam to Lhasa. Kunming is a good staging-point. If you're into long overland trips, you can reach Kunming from either the Lao Cai border (connecting to Hanoi by road or rail) or the Ban Boten border (connecting through Laos to Thailand). You would have to straighten out the visa situation well in advance to cover the route. There's a Lao consulate in Kunming, but no Vietnamese one; for Thailand you get a visa on arrival at any land border.

The wildest route of all into Lhasa is the 3,100km journey from Kashgar in the far west of Xinjiang province, southward through Yecheng and Mazar to Ali, and then on to Lhasa. The route traverses passes over 5,000m. Travellers are frequently turned back at Yecheng on this route, and permits are a problem. The old silk-route trading town of Kashgar looks like it's a long way from anywhere, but actually it's only a few days down the Karakoram Highway from Kashgar to Islamabad in Pakistan. This is one of greatest mountain road trips in High Asia, crossing the 4,700m Khunjerab Pass. Another way of reaching Kashgar is from Bishkek (Kyrgyzstan) over the Torugart Pass.

The Jules Verne challenge

By stringing together some of these routes, you can develop a journey on a grand scale, clocking up over 10,000km by road. In 1992, the London-based adventure tour operator Voyages Jules Verne sponsored a car rally commemorating an historic 1907 race from Paris to Peking. The 1992 rally cars left London headed for Saigon, by way of Moscow, Tashkent, Kashgar, Yarkand, Shigatse, Lhasa, Xining, Chengdu, Nanning and Hanoi. Taking a cue from this, you can set up your own Jules Verne challenge. You can overland from Saigon up through Hanoi, continuing by rail or road to Kunming and Chengdu, then go by road or air to Lhasa, continue by road to Kathmandu, and carry on overland all the way to Istanbul. A silk route variation would be to take the same trail to Lhasa, and head north to Golmud and Dunhuang, perhaps fly from Urumqi to Kashgar, zip down the Karakoram Highway into Pakistan, and then travel overland to Istanbul. There's an international rail crossing from Urumqi to Almaty, eventually connecting all the way to Moscow.

GETTING AROUND

All roads lead to Lhasa. Lhasa is off-limits until you get there: then it's wide open. Within Tibet you are classed as an alien, and you require an Alien Travel Permit (ATP). Various annoying pieces of paper with fancy chops (Chinese signature markers) and seals dog your movements into and around Tibet – this is not like mainland China where you can virtually travel without restriction. The ATP is for cities or sites that are supposedly not open to foreigners, but the list of what is open is top secret, and it appears that what was open a few years ago is now closed. So it goes – the Public Security Bureau (PSB) knows the rules, but you're in the dark.

Apart from ATPs, in Lhasa other permits are issued: TTB, military, Foreign Affairs, Cultural Bureau permits – there's no end to the red tape. Foreigners are usually never shown these documents, nor allowed to keep them – they're classed as secret. In Lhasa, a guide will arrange your permits when you've booked a Landcruiser tour, and the guide will keep the permits (you could try and get a photocopy). On your own, you'll have trouble getting a permit in Lhasa: travellers have, however, obtained ATPs themselves from Shigatse PSB (for destinations within Shannan Prefecture). Many areas of Tibet remain closed or sensitive: they could be off-limits because they are military zones.

Above View from courtyard inside Potala Palace

Left Prayer flags for sale, Lhasa

Below Pilgrim in Lhasa

奇正集团 优质产品

Above Chinese advertisement for mineral
water in Lhasa, using a Tibetan model

Below left Mural of Atisha

Below right Mural of snow lion, the mythical
animal that bounds from snow peak to
snow peak

THE BRIGHT FUTURE OF TOURISM

When not busy imprisoning monks or forcing them to renounce the Dalai Lama, Chinese authorities are preoccupied with building Tibet's bright socialist future. On the horizon are more plans for bigger cities, more cities, improved roads, and an expansion of tourist facilities. Among Chinese tourists, Tibet is seen as an exotic corner of the Chinese realm. Miss Tibet contests have been staged in Lhasa, and fashion magazine crews from Beijing have arrived to shoot models on location (we're talking about cameras here). So you see a picture of a Beijing model posing in semi-ethnic gear outside the Potala, or posing next to pilgrims outside the Jokhang.

What's next? Well, the Chinese haven't really yet begun to tap Tibet's tourist potential. There's a lot of scope for mountaineering, trekking, mountain-biking and other sport-touring. Eastern Tibet (Kham) has hosted activities like cliff-jumping (paragliding) and white-water rafting. Less well-advertised are hunting trips organised to parts of Qinghai province whereby Western hunters are allowed (for large sums of money) to shoot rare wildlife such as Argali bighorn sheep as trophies. Car rallies and motorcycle rallies across the rooftop of the world have been staged. Also on the board are plans for the creation of tourist theme locations, such as a therapeutic hot-spring centre for health care, or a fisherman's island where tourists can learn about yak-hide boats (and cruise around in them).

If you are hiring a Landcruiser and guide, the best thing to do is to make it very clear to the guide that you want all the necessary permits and that if permits required are not obtained, it will be his responsibility. Hiring a Landcruiser lends legitimacy to your travels: if you're in a Landcruiser and you're not sleeping at a place overnight, who's going to know if you have a permit or not? It's more likely that PSB will catch up with you if you overnight at the hotel in a place.

Getting around the towns in Tibet presents little problem: they are mostly small enough to walk around. Larger cities like Lhasa, Shigatse and Tsedang have public buses plying the streets, and fleets of VW taxis roving around (you can also hire these by the day or half-day). Another taxi-like option is using the motorised three-wheelers and foot-powered trishaws as transport. Renting a bicycle is another excellent way of getting around, if you can find one (easy in Lhasa). In Shigatse, you can take a walking-tractor – a tractor with handlebars controlling the engine up front, and a carriage at the back – across town for a small tariff.

Permits and prefectures

To get an overview of the complicated situation for permits, consult the map in this book showing Prefectures of the TAR with area codes. The TAR is divided into seven prefectures, each with its prefectural capital or seat, and each with its own telephone area code. Permits are normally only issued in the prefectural capital, although permits for any destination in the TAR can be issued in Lhasa through agents. Rules about permits chop and change – they can change overnight, in fact – so keep asking other travellers about the current situation.

Lhasa Prefecture Individuals have been able to travel in Lhasa Prefecture freely, including visits to many monasteries (Tsurphu, Drigung, Ganden) without permits or guides. Namtso Lake is also open to travellers without permits as it falls in Lhasa Prefecture.

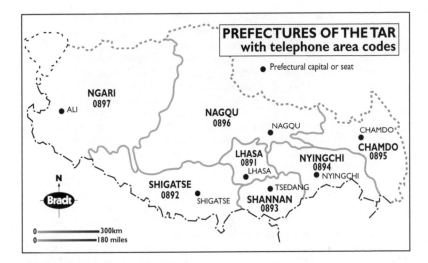

Shigatse Prefecture The prefectural capital of Shigatse is open without permit. Once you get there, you can ask Shigatse PSB for an ATP listing a number of destinations in Shigatse Prefecture; these permits cost Y50 and may only be valid for five to seven days. Gyantse and Everest base camp both fall in Shigatse Prefecture.

Shannan Prefecture Gongkar Airport is open without permit: you can stay in the vicinity without problems. Otherwise, most of Shannan Prefecture is closed unless you have the right documents. The Shannan prefectural capital of Tsedang may or may not require a permit to visit – the rules keep changing. Shannan Prefecture is troublesome: permits may be demanded by police for Samye, Yambulagang and Samding Monastery.

Ngari Prefecture Prior to 2002, it was possible to arrive permit-less in Ali (west Tibet), pay a fine to legitimise your arrival, and then ask for permits for an ATP with destinations in Ngari Prefecture (including Kailash). However, this situation may well have changed – it really depends on who is in charge of Ali PSB.

Other Prefectures The prefectural capital of Nagqu, on the Lhasa-to-Golmud road route, seems to be open without permit. The prefectures to the east are mostly closed to individuals unless they have the right paperwork. However, if you have a Landcruiser booked to go more or less straight through (on a route from, say, Lhasa via Nyingchi and Chamdo Prefectures on to Sichuan or Yunnan), these rules can bend.

Visa extensions
In Lhasa, these are linked to tours – that is, only if you book a tour will you be given an extension (which will be for the length of that tour). You might be able to cut a deal elsewhere, like Shigatse. Also try under-the-table payments through an agent in Lhasa – it will cost, but you'll get the paperwork done. Lhasa is tight for extensions, sometimes only granting five days.

Landcruiser and guide
The Chinese insist that the only way you (as a foreigner) can get around Tibet is with a hired Landcruiser with a driver and guide. This works out to about

US$110–170 a day which, split between four or five paying passengers, is around US$25-45 per person per day. That's a fair bit of money, and most of the operators are connected to Chinese channels. Routes may be monopolised by TTB-connected Landcruisers.

Landcruisers are the greatest expense you'll incur in Tibet. Many Landcruisers operate on the Lhasa to Zhangmu run (to the Nepalese border). You can find Landcruisers for hire in Zhangmu, and possibly in Shigatse (but don't count on it). The majority of Landcruisers are hired in Lhasa – refer to the *Lhasa* chapter transport section for more details.

One peculiar phenomenon you will have to deal with in Tibet is called 'hitting the roof'. This is when the Landcruiser (which has no seatbelts) hits a rut and launches those in the back seat straight into the roof. It hurts! To soften the impact, think about wearing a wool hat or something similar. The idea of padded interiors has not caught on yet.

By taxi

Taxis are intended to be a mode for getting around larger towns like Lhasa, Shigatse or Tsedang. However, they also commute from Gongkar Airport into Lhasa, a distance of around 100km, so think about this: they're much cheaper than Landcruisers, and they don't ask if you have a permit. Taxis are viable if the road is paved and in good condition, for longer trips from, say, Lhasa to Tsedang. You can also hire a taxi by the half-day or full day and use it as your touring vehicle, which makes sense if three or four travellers get together to share the rental.

On your own

You need considerable stamina, perseverance and devious ingenuity to mount your own trips in Tibet and break away from the Landcruiser Syndrome. While the regular bus service is sporadic – the crates wheeze over the passes, with frequent breakdowns – you may be able to get a ride to a trailhead, where you can start trekking. Hitchhiking in Tibet means you have to pay for lifts (negotiate with the driver), and it may mean heavy fines for the driver if caught transporting a foreigner. Crazy dreamers have found ingenious ways of getting around inside Tibet. Back in the early days of independent travel in Tibet, in the 1980s, two Americans transported their kayaks up to Lake Manasarovar and started paddling the Yarlung Tsangpo – they made it part of the way. A young Englishman managed to bluff his way through the Zhangmu border with a motorcycle, and he was out by the Great Wall by the time the authorities caught up with him. Others have rented (or bought) yaks or donkeys to carry their gear, and headed off on long hikes.

If you have money coming out your ears, of course, you can arrange to realise any dream you want through official channels. All the paperwork and aggravation might take some of the joy out of it, though. I've met several trios of motorcyclists from Europe who've been all over Tibet and Xinjiang on their imported bikes. They would not, however, divulge the cost of the entourage of vehicles accompanying them (with national guide, local guide, translators, medic etc). High-paying group tours walk to the Kojinath border crossing in western Tibet, trekking in for five days from Simikot (Nepal), and are then picked up by Landcruisers which take them on to Burang, and up to Kailash. In Nepal, that border crossing lies in a Maoist-controlled region, so it may not be operational. A similar trek up the Indian side, crossing at Lipu Lek Pass, is sanctioned for high-paying group tours. Another crossing at Nathu La, Sikkim, may be possible for high-paying groups.

Tour de Tibet

Mountain-biking is the only way to bring your own 'vehicle' into Tibet (apart from the odd kayaker or motorcyclist). Mountain-bikes are ideal for the dry terrain in Tibet. You can remain independent and still cover great distances, and it's a great way to meet people and savour the land at a slower pace. However, you need a road of some sort, or a trail. Technically, you're not supposed to be cycling around Tibet at all because you've got too much freedom and authorities have no way of tracking your movements, and that's something that the PSB doesn't like. In practice, the PSB often turn a blind eye. However, try and get permits in advance for sites where you know you'll stop the night. Organised tours to Tibet by mountain-bike have been conducted by a few operators (a few possibilities are listed with *Group touring*, pages 38–9), notably one based in Kathmandu. In this case, a sag-wagon usually accompanies the group, and picks up the stragglers if they're slow on the winding passes.

Independent travellers have been able to bring their own bikes in by plane from Chengdu or Kathmandu, or by train and then bus from Golmud. The Chinese don't bat an eyelid if you try to put a bike on a train or a plane, or bring it into your hotel room: they're used to seeing bicycles in strange places. Some travellers have reported wheeling a bike to the airport check-in. You can also buy American mountain-bikes made in Shenzhen (Cannondales and Diamondbacks) and sold in Chengdu, Kunming, Beijing, Shanghai, Guangzhou and Hong Kong. These may take a bit of work to track down as they're primarily for export. They cost about US$250–350 apiece, which is low compared to what you'd pay in the US. Taiwanese-made mountain-bikes like Giant are good quality, but hard to find (you can buy one in Beijing). Chinese-brand mountain-bikes like Forever are junk – they fall apart within a few weeks, and parts like pedals may suddenly break off. You can buy them for US$40 and up in a Lhasa department store – they are fine for running around Lhasa, but not reliable for crossing the plateau. Nevertheless, some *have* bought these bikes, reinforced them, and used them to make a run to Kathmandu. In Lhasa you can buy a 'Today' brand mountain bike for US$70 with front and back suspension. Some Westerners have bought these, customised them, and ridden them off down the road to Kathmandu. However, reported problems include: plastic pedals that are easy to break; there are no panniers for sale; and excess gear would have to be sent ahead somehow. The short seat-post on Chinese-made models is a problem – you might have to get it removed and a longer one substituted. If intending to cycle, bring all the (compact) supplies you need with you – Chinese pumps, for example, are monstrous steel things. It's difficult to find items like bicycle water-bottles in Lhasa. Cyclists revel in wearing a wristwatch that tells not only the time but the altitude.

If you fly a bicycle into Lhasa, you should conduct acclimatisation trips around the Lhasa Valley to get used to the altitude. This particularly applies to climbing hills. There are many fine rides within a day or two of Lhasa. Some travellers indulge in hybrid travel modes – biking a bit, then putting the bike on the top of a bus. You could make it out to Tibet's wild west (Kailash region) by this method.

Although cyclists have tackled all the major routes in Tibet (including the run to Kashgar), the most popular is the Lhasa to Kathmandu route. This run has it all – high passes, Himalayan camping sites, ancient towns and temples, high winds and surly PSB officials. An interesting facet of mountain-biking is being able to race the locals on horses – they win over a short distance, but the horse quickly tires, and then you start to gain, much to the surprise of the horseman. I once raced a Tibetan on a Chinese one-speed bicycle: he was leading by a good margin until we hit a hill, and then the 18 gears left him behind, flabbergasted. Gravity is something you have to consider on the Lhasa to Kathmandu route. If you start in Lhasa, you end up with a fantastic 4,500m drop off the plateau from Tong La. If you go the other way, you'll need to take a few energy bars along.

Cyclists are a peculiar breed; their talk centres around headwinds, gradients, water quality, and, in Tibet, animals. There are two animals to watch out for: yaks and dogs. Yaks are not a problem – they will bolt at the approach of a bike (mistaking it for a rival species?) but may upset the handler when they thunder off. Dogs, on the other hand, will come straight at you, fangs bared. Dogs are especially a problem when trying to sneak around checkpoints at night (which is what some cyclists attempt to do). Squirting a water-bottle at a dog may repel it; some cyclists carry fireworks, or have a pump at the ready to defend themselves.

Logistically, cycling in Tibet poses major problems. The route from Lhasa to Kathmandu is about 1,000km, crossing six high passes. It requires a minimum of two weeks, and preferably three weeks, to complete the trip. Carrying enough food for the three-week journey would mean your bike would be too heavy, so you have to back off on the weight (carry freeze-dried food, with all its moisture removed – available in camping stores) and find other ways of maintaining your food supply to stoke your energy levels. Water alone adds considerable weight (you need four litres a day). Camping gear is essential for the run.

Some cyclists have ridden all the way up to Everest base camp. This is not a road – in fact, it's a pain in the butt, made of pebbles and glacial moraine debris. Only parts of the route are rideable. Intrepid travellers have even mounted a combination of trek and bike: Victor Chan (author of *Tibet Handbook*, see *Appendix 3*, page 276) and his companion arranged to have porters carry their mountain bikes over a high pass into Tibet and then proceeded to cycle along the highway. There's always the option of strapping a bike to the side of a yak for transport over difficult terrain – this has probably not been attempted because yaks don't like anything unusual (and the yak might decide to roll over on the load). Some trekking terrain is suited to biking: the jeepable road out to Lake Namtso is quite passable, and grassland areas in parts of Tibet are eminently rideable – you don't even need a road here. Bicycling in Kham and Amdo – peripheral Tibet – offers some excellent terrain with grasslands and mountain trails. A great destination is the Kunming-to-Lijiang route.

WHAT TO TAKE

> Good heavy ammunition boots are the best for men, and stout ankle boots
> for women, and both may, if desired, be hobnailed. A pair of comfortable
> slippers is a great relief after the day's march is done, and should not be
> forgotten. Woollen socks and stockings are the best, and should be thick.
> To avoid chafing, boric powder should be dusted inside them before
> putting them on, and the toes and heels rubbed on the outside with soap.
> In the event of blisters developing, they should be pricked with a sterilised
> needle, Germolene applied, and a lint and cottonwood pad placed over
> them to protect them from further chafing while marching...

This paragraph comes from *Touring in Sikkim in Tibet*, a slim guidebook written in 1930 by David Macdonald, former British Trade Agent in Gyantse. He makes travel sound painful; in the 1930s, travellers rode or marched into Tibet with pack animals and an entourage of porters, carrying 30kg tents, a portable bath, hurricane lanterns, stove and so on. One porter was assigned to carrying the tiffin basket, which contained crockery, cutlery and provisions for lunch. Times have changed – those 1930s travellers would have been amazed at the strong, lightweight camping gear and clothing on the market now, with the wonders of Gore-Tex and Velcro.

Even so, on a trip to Tibet, you may end up with a lot of gear. What to take? Pepper spray for the dogs? A shovel for the propaganda? A shortwave radio to get your news fix? All kinds of equipment springs to mind, but can you carry it? A good idea, before you set out, is to assemble all your gear, shoulder it, and walk a dozen blocks – or better yet, hike up the nearest mountain. Carrying luggage at altitude is much harder work than at sea level: the emphasis in your gear should be on strong, lightweight stuff that performs multiple functions. And you should remember that the gear you take is not the final weight: you may purchase souvenirs or books en route, not to mention food and drink, all of which will add to the burden, so you have to figure out where the weight lies, and how to reduce it without compromising on essentials like medical supplies.

High on my list would be a good pair of hiking shoes with ankle support – lightweight, strong and well broken-in. You rely on your feet a lot in Tibet. The next priority would be a strong flashlight that has a long battery life (and a supply of spare batteries). Due to erratic or non-existent electrical supply in Tibet, you constantly need a flashlight – for illuminating dark frescos in monasteries, for finding your way around at night, for visiting the outhouse at night etc. Clothing for dealing with extremes of heat, cold and wind is essential. Rain and dampness are not so much of a problem – Tibet is high and extremely dry. Dust is a big problem. Silk items favoured by skiers are ideal for insulating – they're lightweight and durable. A thick pile sweater and a windproof jacket (Gore-Tex is good) should provide protection against biting wind and cold. For more on clothing, sunglasses and protection from the elements, read the *Health and Safety* section, which has a rundown of essential medical supplies.

If you plan to get off the track in Tibet, you need a good sleeping bag. These are bulky, but you'll find a Chinese quilt is much more bulky – though these are supplied in most guesthouses, off the track they may not be, and you can't afford to freeze or lose sleep. If a guesthouse is already warm enough, you can use a sleeping bag to cushion the bed. A sleeping bag with a down fill is recommended because it's compact, lightweight and insulates well – get one rated to sub-zero temperatures. A compact Therm-a-Rest (ultra-light air mattress) is also a good idea in case you end up sleeping on the floor of a teahouse. In the gadget line, an altimeter may be helpful – make sure it goes to 6,000m. Some wristwatches have in-built altimeters, so the question is not what time, but how high.

What you bring really depends on what kind of trip you're planning. If travelling in a Landcruiser, consider that luggage space in the back is minimal if sharing with three other passengers. Obviously if you want to go trekking, you will need to be fairly self-sufficient gear-wise. While supplies and food can be bought in Lhasa, these items will be heavy and clumsy. Discarded expedition gear is readily available in Kathmandu, and of high quality, but the same is not true of Lhasa. If high quality gear can be found at all in Lhasa, it will be very expensive. If you are planning to go cycling or do a lot of trekking, you might want to think about importing your own freeze-dried food and other supplies. Concentrate on food that can be 'cooked' by adding hot water to the package and letting it sit for a few minutes. This way you can use the thermoses of hot water supplied in most hotels. While you can buy a stove in Lhasa, it will be an unwieldy kerosene stove that weighs a ton. If you want a light, compact stove that operates off any fuel source, bring it with you. The rot-gut Chinese liquor sold in various parts of Tibet can power a stove.

If you're travelling by Landcruiser or truck, you may find that your backpack or main duffle bag is out of reach, buried under other baggage. Thus you need to keep a day-pack with essential items such as camera and so on with you; some day-packs have an external mesh holder for a water bottle. Within easy reach also should be food supplies if you stop for lunch: some travellers purchase a cheap vinyl bag in Lhasa to hold food supplies and things like candles, separating this from the main baggage. If staying longer in Tibet, you can use Lhasa as a base, so you could leave a duffle bag in guesthouse storage while off gallivanting around. Cargo duffles have lockable zippers on them to deflect prying fingers.

Bring all your **film** with you. To rephrase that: bring a lot more than you think you'll need. Certain slide films (high speed) and black-and-white film can be hard to find in Lhasa. If you're passing through, Hong Kong and Bangkok are good places to buy and process film. See the section on *Photography*, page 67, for more details on filming in Tibet.

A couple of other notes on gear: if you don't have it, maybe your fellow travellers do. Message boards at the budget hotels in Lhasa carry ads from travellers selling sleeping bags, film, camping gear, medicines, freeze-dried food – or even left-over oxygen. Travellers can become fixated with their stuff and spend hours in needless aggravation over what to take. Get that part over quickly and shift your attention to more important matters like plotting your route, reading up on the areas you plan to visit, reading up on Tibetan culture and learning some Tibetan language (buy a phrasebook). Knowledge is the most important thing to carry with you.

Electronic gear Electrical supply in Tibet is 220 volts, 50 hertz, with a variety of plugs: supply in Tibet is either intermittent or unreliable, with frequent blackouts. It's best to bring good battery back-up for any electronic devices, and use the power supply to recharge those batteries.

Maps

Research all map material before you go to Tibet, and bring it with you. Within Tibet, the only maps available are Chinese-produced. The best place to find maps of Tibet is in Kathmandu, where you can even find pirated editions of maps that are long out of print in Europe, like Stanfords' *South-Central Tibet: Lhasa to Kathmandu Route Map*.

Handy map collections can be found in several books. The best is the ambitious book *Mapping the Tibetan World* (see *Further Information*, page 276), which collates over 280 maps, with fine detail seen nowhere else. Victor Chan's *Tibet Handbook* (see *Further Information*, page 276), though somewhat unwieldy (it has been christened 'Vic the Brick'), contains a collated set of *US Department of Defense Aerial Survey Maps*. These provide selected coverage of Tibet's topography – very useful for trekkers – but they are old, and while the geographical features are fine, the size and location of towns may have changed.

Surely the strangest map-guide ever produced is *On This Spot-Lhasa*, issued by ICT Washington, 2001. This unconventional map is backed up by a wealth of detail on Lhasa's rapidly changing face and its tragic human rights situation; it tells you what happens behind the scenes in the capital and includes some subversive photos. The map was released as part of an International Campaign for Tibet (ICT) initiative to educate travellers about China's occupation of Tibet, and to redress the balance in guidebooks on Tibet, which often omit information on the human rights situation. The map can be ordered through ICT's website www.savetibet.org. Also available from ICT is a double-sided map titled *The*

Eastern Regions of Tibet, which gives details on Kham and Amdo, with a lot of historical annotations. For sheet maps, accurate German cartography of Tibet includes the RV Verlag/GeoCenter map, *Tibet, Nepal and Bhutan*; Berndtson & Berndtson's *Tibet*; and Himalayan maps in the Nelles series.

Tibetans themselves never really needed maps, nor bothered to create them, except in artistic renditions. So Tibetan-created maps of Tibet are a recent phenomenon. Published in Dharamsala in 1994 is a *Road Map of Tibet*, with place names in English and Tibetan: this map encompasses Kham and Amdo. From the Amnye Machen Institute in Dharamsala comes the finest map of Lhasa yet produced: *Lhasa City* (issued 1995) with a separate gazetteer. The map details 590 locations, including sites like educational institutions, prisons and PLA bases,which are of no interest to the casual tourist. This aside, the map provides an excellent overview of Lhasa, with contour lines useful for hiking sorties. For more information, consult their website www.amnyemachen.org.

Within China

The only maps available within Tibet and the PRC are the Chinese-produced ones. This is probably because of 'cartographic correctness' – Chinese maps show all of Arunachal Pradesh lying in Chinese territory, much to the chagrin of India.

On sale in Lhasa is the *China Tibet Tour Map,* a foldout map of Tibet (published by the Mapping Bureau of the TAR, 1993), and the *Lhasa Tourist Map* (published by Chengdu Cartographic Publishing House, 2001). The last map is also issued in a Chinese language version, with more information on it. Significantly, there are few Tibetan-language maps for sale. The best map of China is a joint-venture effort between the Cartographic Publishing House of China and Liber Kartor AB, Sweden (1995): it's a large wall map, but you could slice off the Tibet part to make it easy to carry.

Maps are very cheap in China, but the maps published in English are weak in detail, while the maps published in Chinese are more complete (a kind of reverse censorship – the Chinese need to find their way around their own colony but they don't want foreigners to access the material). For the traveller, maps with Chinese and English on them are best, so you can point to the characters for your destination when talking to Chinese drivers.

The basic problem with maps of Tibet is that the Chinese have all the data, but treat it as a military secret – it's only partially revealed in Chinese-produced maps. On Western maps, there are conflicting names for destinations depending on whether the Tibetan name, the Chinese name or the old English name is referred to, and which transliteration system is used. Everest, for example (English name), is known as 'Chomolungma' in Tibetan, and transliterated as 'Qomolangma' in pinyin Chinese. Maps of Tibet are an ideological battleground. Tibetan-exile maps show Tibet covering the entire Tibetan Plateau, while Chinese maps show the much-reduced area of the Tibet Autonomous Region, created in 1965 (Xizang Province). Street names in Lhasa may be referred to by a Tibetan name (such as Dekyi Shar Lam) or a Chinese name (Beijing Road). There are ongoing battles between cartography departments in China and neighbouring countries. Chinese maps continue to show Tibet extending into Arunachal Pradesh. Indian customs officials scrutinise books for any maps with these inflated borders, and handstamp over them this message: 'Borders neither authentic nor correct'.

MONEY AND PRICING

Two forms of readily-exchangeable money are travellers' cheques and US cash. It's wise to carry some of both. Credit cards are of limited use in China and Tibet, and are only usable at major hotels in Lhasa (Lhasa Hotel takes them). Cash advances on a credit card are possible in Lhasa at the Bank of China. Changing travellers' cheques or US cash is not a problem within Tibet or China. The whole idea is that you spend lots of money, otherwise Tibet wouldn't be open, so you can find Bank of China branches in Lhasa, Shigatse, Tsedang, Ali and other large Chinese towns. If not, major hotels can change travellers' cheques. The two most widely recognised travellers' cheques are American Express and Thomas Cook. Although cash and travellers' cheques in different currencies are accepted by the Bank of China, in places like hotels or on the street, US dollars are more easily negotiated. There's a very small blackmarket in US dollars, so if banks are closed, you can always change in a shop or maybe at a hotel reception desk.

Chinese currency is renminbi yuan (Y or RMB, people's money): it comes in denominations of 1, 2, 5, 10, 20, 50 and 100 yuan, and small change in the form of 100 fen to the yuan. The 10-yuan bill shows Tibet – well, the north face of Everest – and the newer 50-yuan bill shows the Potala. Exchange rates hover at around Y8.25 (renminbi) to the US dollar (with travellers' cheques, a small commission is deducted by the Bank of China; rates should be uniform across the country). The rate is slightly lower for cash – Y8.1 for US$1 – with no commission charged (the blackmarket rate may be Y8.2 for US$1). Other relevant exchange rates are: Nepal, about 78 rupees for US$1 (there's a blackmarket in US cash, with higher rates for bigger bills); and Hong Kong SAR, HK$7.78 for US$1.

Within Asia, you can use ATM machines to access your home bank account using your usual bank card with a 4-digit PIN number. ATM machines are common in Hong Kong, Bangkok and Singapore, and can also be found in Kathmandu and a number of Chinese cities (look for Bank of China ATM machines). ATM machines have even appeared in Lhasa, but are directed toward Chinese patrons.

Paying through the nose

Pricing in this book is quoted in either US dollars (US$10 for example) or Chinese yuan (Y20 for example), and sometimes in Hong Kong dollars (HK$40 for instance). Because pricing fluctuates and is often negotiable, variations may occur. Pricing is not a problem for restaurants and hotels in Tibet – you get used to the expected prices fairly quickly. Prices are negotiable because of the Chinese dual-pricing system (one country, two systems). The highest expenses in Tibet are for long-distance transportation – ie flights to and from Lhasa – and the cost of hiring Landcruisers.

Dual-pricing system

If you are from Europe, Australia or North America and have a beak-like nose, you are known as *da bizi* (big-nose) by the Chinese, or *waiguoren* (outland person) or *yangguizi* (foreign devil – derogatory). This is a kind of separate ethnic group – in the Chinese system, Tibetans are barbarians, and foreigners are aliens. The bigger the nose, the more you pay through it. Although in theory there is no dual-pricing system in China, in practice you can pay twice, three, ten, or a hundred times more for certain services. When you buy a US$9 ticket to go and see the Potala, you are paying at least ten times the going price that a Chinese or Tibetan person pays. Negotiating prices depends on what you look like, how desperate you look, and how long you're willing to argue. You can bargain for student price for some items (such as the Potala entry ticket, and even bus tickets), but this argument may only be accepted if you're a student in China, with valid ID. Chinese who live overseas (called Overseas Chinese) are often charged a rate that is above Chinese price, but lower than Western price. Usually, the seller deduces they are Overseas Chinese (or from Hong Kong) from their clothing or cameras. Westerners of Asian ethnic background who speak good Chinese can confuse Chinese sellers as they can't rank them in the pricing system.

Costs within Tibet
Restaurants and hotels are arranged in this guide from low end to high end.

Hotels
These can be easily sized up – they fall into budget, mid-range or group-tour (high-end) categories. Low-end guesthouses charge US$3–8 per bed in two-bed, three-bed or larger rooms. Mid-range hotels charge US$15–45 for the room (whether occupied by one person, two or three). High-end (group tour) hotels charge US$50 and up per room – the tariff can go to US$200 and up for suites in Lhasa.

Restaurants
The cost of food is not really a big issue in Tibet as food, if it is available, will be in cheaper teahouses or restaurants, costing around US$2–4 a head for a shared meal. Restaurants in deluxe Lhasa hotels could charge US$5–12 per dish. Occasionally, Chinese-run places might try to gorge Western customers by serving up something that looks like a banquet. Be wary of places that pile on extra dishes – ones that you never ordered – or lay on extras like face-towels and bowls of peanuts, as these will appear on the bill.

Permits and entry fees
Entry fees for monasteries and tourist attractions (forts, palaces etc) are usually US$2–6 a person, with the asking price for major monasteries hovering around US$5 (the Potala Palace charges US$9). Students can negotiate half price entry. Posted photo and video permission fees are high: at the Ramoche Temple in Lhasa, a US$6 fee for photography permission is levied, and double that for a video-camera (fees for video can go much higher). At the village of Chay an entry fee of US$8 per person is charged to access the Everest area to those arriving by Landcruiser. Permit fees to visit certain parts of Tibet can be high – usually one piece of paper is issued, so all names of passport holders can go on it to minimise costs. ATPs cost only a dollar (for the group) but a military permit can be US$10 a person. Cultural Bureau permits for Zanda and Tsaparang can run to US$50 or so. The 'permission' to buy a plane ticket or bus ticket into Tibet can run to US$50-60 a person. Fines if caught in the wrong place can run up to US$70, but are negotiable.

Transportation
Bicycle hire is about US$3–5 a day in Lhasa. Taxis are a few dollars to get across town. Local long-distance buses are cheap, even if you pay double as a foreigner. A run from Lhasa to Shigatse is US$8 for foreigners. Landcruisers cost about US$110–170 per day for the vehicle, which can take three to four passengers (or five passengers without a guide). This rate includes the driver, the guide, the vehicle and the gasoline, but nothing else. The formula is based largely on kilometres covered on the trip (gasoline consumption), terrain (wear and tear on vehicle), rest days, and so on. The guide fee is generally around US$15–20 a day, so if no guide is involved, the Landcruiser rate will be lower.

LODGING AND FOOD

Except in larger towns like Lhasa and Shigatse, be prepared for very low standards for food and lodging. It's best to bring your own supplies as back-ups: bring a Therm-A-Rest (ultra-light air mattress) and a good sleeping bag to soften the beds and to stay warm, and bring packets of soup, or whatever, to compensate for the lack of restaurants.

Hotels and guesthouses

Low-end guesthouses, teahouse inns and truck-stop places generally offer a bed and not much else. These usually work out to US$2–5 a bed, in dormitory-type accommodation with perhaps four beds to a room. If there's a dirt floor, a lumpy bed and a tap in the yard, you've hit rock bottom. Bedbugs can be a problem in low-end hotels. A notch up are Chinese concrete-blockhouse hotels, usually with several storeys, and possibly some internal plumbing. These places charge about US$10–25 for the room, no matter if your party is single, double, or triple, so you can reduce costs by sharing. The more creature comforts you get, the higher the tariff. If you get your very own bathroom, with your own plumbing, rates are even higher. Because of shoddy workmanship, it often turns out that half of these gadgets fail to function, and yet you are paying for them being in the room. Some foreigners have successfully bargained down the price of a room due to absence of electricity to power devices like the TV. In this range are hotels designed for visiting Chinese, some of which may be off-limits to Westerners.

At the high end are group-tour hotels, with rooms from US$30–60 and up (if you have three people sharing a room, which may still only be US$10 a bed). These definitely have plumbing – and even hot water – and rooms with real lightbulbs, and possibly even satellite TV reception. Even so, the prices for the rooms are often inflated, and discounts are frequently offered to tour operators. The hotel lobby often features a dining hall, souvenir shop, bar and so on. It may even have a foreign exchange counter and a small business section able to handle faxes and IDD calls. Even if you don't stay in a high-end hotel, you can wander in and shop or use the services there: naturally, the tariff will be higher than normal. There are half-a-dozen hotels of this standard in Lhasa, and one hotel in this class in Shigatse, Gyantse, Tsedang and Zhangmu. Another is found near Shegar. These high-end hotels may have cheap dormitories tucked away, so it's worth enquiring.

Plumbing notes Hot showers are a rarity in low- and mid-range hotels in Tibet, though they are easier to find in Lhasa and Shigatse. You are therefore often dependent on hot water from the large Chinese thermoses at hotels, which is boiled up by solar cookers on the rooftop or with a furnace. Hotels do not automatically provide thermoses. You may have to ask – or wheedle or cajole – to get one. By using a bucket or wash-basin, you can manage basic ablutions. The hot water thermoses can also be used for making soup or tea, and if you let it cool overnight, the water can be carried in your own bottle as drinking water. Tibetan and Chinese toilets are of the bomb-bay door design (squat and hope). They're usually filthy. In high-end hotels, there are Western sit-down models. When Shigatse Hotel started operation, fancy imported plumbing was brought in. An overweight woman on a group tour sat on one of these brand-new pieces of porcelain and the sit-down unit broke away from its mooring. The woman was not injured, but she was furious – she threatened to sue the manager over the poorly installed equipment. The hotel manager promptly confiscated the passports for the group and said that they would not be returned unless he was compensated for the full value of the imported plumbing that had been destroyed. Confronted with this, the group-tour leader decided to pay up.

Dining out

Tibet is not noted for its culinary arts. China, however, is – ergo, find a Chinese-run restaurant if you want more variety. There's lots of variety in Lhasa – you can find Tibetan, Chinese, Indian and Nepalese cuisine. On the streets you can find fresh fruit and vegetables in abundance, and fresh bread and tangy yoghurt. You can even find good fresh cheese imported from Nepal. Yak cheese is excellent, but only when made with Swiss technology (as it is in Bhutan, Nepal and in parts of northern India). Tibet has yet to catch up with the technology – mostly what you'll find on sale are small pieces of rock-hard yak-cheese, strung together like a necklace. These are almost impossible to eat, and are treated like sweets by the nomads, who suck on the pieces all day.

Tibetans are more inclined to run teahouses with low carpeted tables, which serve tea and momos (meat dumplings) and perhaps the odd potato. They offer lots of atmosphere, but not a whole lot of food. Lhasa is fine for food, but once out in the countryside, it's pretty much noodles all the way. In the wilder areas, it's *tsampa* – or roasted barley-flour – all the way. Tsampa is boring but quite sustaining, and you can mix it with soup or noodles (some connoisseurs add powdered milk or other substances to this Tibetan goulash). Not many travellers take to tsampa – the backpacker staple tends to be 761 army-ration biscuits.

Chinese packaged goods are not much more appetising. Olive-green army cans with stewed mandarins or pork or something equally disgusting are resold on the blackmarket. When travelling in Tibet, you should always bring along some food as a back-up, for the times when you're stuck. You can load up in Lhasa on packaged soup and so on. Some bring in freeze-dried food from the West. Bottled mineral water is available in Lhasa, Shigatse and larger towns in Tibet, where brands include Wahaha, and Potala Palace Mineral Water. Cheaper than bottled water is Chinese beer. Since beer goes through a fermenting process, it's safe to drink, but this is not advisable at altitude until you've acclimatised (beer should not be drunk if you have the runs, either). Available Chinese brands include Huanghe (Yellow River), Lhasa Beer and Pabst Blue Ribbon.

FACILITIES
Shopping

Facilities inside Tibet are poor compared to those in neighbouring regions. Most infrastructure and buying and selling are concentrated in Lhasa, so you can glean more about shopping from the Lhasa chapter and the section for Shigatse. You can ship purchases (even very heavy ones) out of Lhasa without problem through China Post, the main post office. Carpet companies in Lhasa will arrange the shipping for you direct from their showroom.

Entertainment

Unless you like karaoke bars, or parlours showing ear-splitting kung-fu videos, nightlife is mostly limited to restaurants. There are some restaurant venues where Tibetan dance is staged (see *Lhasa* chapter, page 113). For the performing arts, the best bet is to time your trip for a festival, like the Yoghurt Festival in Lhasa or the Horse-Racing Fair in Namtso.

Photography and film

Tibet is highly inspirational for photography and you will find yourself running through roll after roll of film. So it's a good idea to bring in *lots* of film, or digital camera supplies. Film is sold in Lhasa, but you're better off stocking up in places like Bangkok, Hong Kong or Chengdu (which also have good labs for processing film). Certain film types (ISO200, ISO400 slide-film, black-and-white film) are next-to-impossible to find in Lhasa. Print film can be processed in Lhasa and the results would make great gifts.

The light in outdoor situations in Tibet is so intense that you can make wonderful use of fine-grained, low speed slide film like Kodachrome 25, Fuji Velvia 50 or Fuji Provia 100. You will probably want a polarising filter to reduce glare. Another situation commonly encountered is exactly the opposite: a dim interior where you need a high speed film (ISO400 and up), as flash may be forbidden. Special hazards include yak butter, fine dust and frozen batteries (remove and keep in a shirt pocket, worn on your body – near your body is not close enough – overnight).

You can bring in as many rolls of film as you want. To bring in professional video or motion-picture equipment, special clearance is required, meaning you probably won't get it without a ton of paperwork and grovelling. There is no restriction, however, on bringing hand-held camcorders and amateur video equipment – plenty of Chinese and Asians on tour in Tibet bring such gadgets. The equipment is not the problem, it's how and when you use it. A policeman might overlook it if you are in a closed or sensitive region, but making a record that can later be aired in public is a very different case. Taboo subjects include the Chinese military (especially on manoeuvres and at checkpoints) and strategic locations like bridges or the airport. Tibetans do not appreciate camera flashes in temples, nor photography of sky burial rituals (which is particularly sensitive). Some foreigners have had their film confiscated, and even their camera equipment. At a checkpoint on the Kathmandu-Lhasa road, a bored passenger stood aside and photographed a luggage search in progress. An army officer promptly seized his camera, and it was only after considerable argument that the camera was returned, minus the offending film.

Media and communications

China's one-party state controls all forms of media, making independent reporting impossible. All local news media is closely monitored. In Tibet, foreign news media are not permitted entry unless reporters are considered pro-China and will toe the party line. The TTB produces a glossy magazine on Tibet called Tibet Tour (printed in Shenzhen), but this is mostly in Chinese language. Slick colour brochures on human rights and other 'hot topics' are distributed to major hotels in Chengdu and Lhasa.

The great electronic leap forward

What the fax machine was to the dissidents of the 1980s ('seek truth from fax'), the anarchic internet is to those of the new era. Surfers in Beijing can be fined if caught using the wrong websites – the crime is 'splitting the motherland'. Cybercafés are located in most of the popular tourist sites and cities of China, and in other parts of Asia (Kathmandu, Hong Kong, Bangkok, Kuala Lumpur etc). These offer email services – access is easier through web-based addresses. Small cybercafés are found in Lhasa and Shigatse, but access is limited or nonexistent in other parts of Tibet.

Printed matter

Anything printed outside China can be screened. However, non-political books like Gary McCue's *Trekking in Tibet* (see *Further Information*, page 276) have been spotted for sale at the Lhasa Hotel, along with *Tintin in Tibet* (which has been translated into 27 languages, including the Tibetan language itself). 'Printed matter' extends to messages on T-shirts: these have caused Westerners some trouble, although Tintin T-shirts are acceptable, and sold in Lhasa.

Photocopying A corollary to the above is that you may have to photocopy the relevant pages of books from other travellers. That's easy to do, as there are a number of places with good-quality photocopy machines in Lhasa, though they're tough to find outside of Lhasa. You might try high-end hotels for photocopy machines outside of Lhasa, as they often have a business centre for guests with photocopy, fax and internet facilities.

Radio

Tibet Radio is the official Chinese station in Lhasa, which is about all you'd want to say about it. If you bring a shortwave radio, you can pick up the BBC World Service (the Dalai Lama's favourite programme – he's addicted) which broadcasts in English. Voice of America (VOA) and Radio Free Asia (RFA) are operated by the US: both broadcast in Tibetan. RFA started in late 1996 and reaches Thailand, Indochina, Indonesia and China – it espouses a free press to authoritarian governments. Apart from a Mandarin segment, there's an RFA Tibetan Service. The Chinese don't seem to like either broadcast: in mid-1998, three RFA journalists who were due to accompany Clinton on his visit to China had their visas revoked. The head of the Tibet section in Washington is Ngapo Jigme, who is one of twelve sons and daughters of Tibet's greatest turncoat, Ngapo Ngawang Jigme. Ngapo Jigme defected in 1985 and works for the Free Tibet Campaign in Washington. Because Tibet is at such high altitude, there's excellent reception. However, around Lhasa, authorities jam signals by broadcasting on the same frequencies. Broadcasting in Tibetan is Voice of Tibet (VOT), a programme produced by Tibetan journalists stationed in India, Nepal and other countries (the target area is Tibet and neighbouring countries: VOT cannot be heard outside this range, but can be picked up in RealAudio on the website www.vot.org).

Television

Lhasa has two TV broadcasting stations: Xizang TV, which is parked near the Potala, and Lhasa TV, to the eastern fringe of town. Other stations or transmitters are located in Shigatse, Tsedang and Gyantse. A couple of channels broadcast in Tibetan, others in Chinese (these programs run the boring socialist gamut from pig farming in central China to ear-splitting Sichuan opera performances and revolutionary ballet performed by PLA soldiers). Beijing's CCTV broadcasts on four or five channels, with CCTV-9 broadcasting mostly in English or with English sub-titling on the programmes.

Because of the elevation, satellite TV reception is excellent on the Tibetan plateau, but dishes must be licensed and are carefully monitored. In Lhasa, the mid-range and high-end hotels pick up VTV, a kind of Indian MTV. On larger satellite dishes – notably the one at Lhasa Hotel – is CNN. Of course, the average Tibetan gets nowhere near a satellite receiver, but occasionally things work for the better. In 1996, stunned Tibetan staff at a Lhasa hotel gathered to watch a broadcast of the Larry King show where one of the guests was the Dalai Lama.

Hong Kong-based StarTV programming may also be available on satellite, including the Star Movie Channel (English movies), Star Sports, and a Chinese movie channel, but not BBC news. In 1994, Rupert Murdoch, chairman of the

News Corporation (which owns StarTV), removed the BBC news from his satellite services to China to calm tense relations with Chinese officials who complained about a BBC profile of Mao Zedong and objected to coverage of Chinese dissidents. Although Murdoch has styled himself as a foe of totalitarianism and a champion of individual liberty and free speech, in the PRC's case he decided to brush all that under the carpet because he has extensive holdings in China and ambitious plans to expand them. In 1997, the BBC came under further fire from the PRC because it aired a program on the disappearance of the 11th Panchen Lama.

More missing news: in October 2001, AOL Time Warner signed a deal with the Chinese government to expand its Mandarin-language cable channel China Entertainment Television (CETV) into Guangdong Province, southern China. AOL Time Warner acquired CETV from a Singapore entrepreneur who said his successful formula for reaching the Chinese market was 'no sex, no violence – and no news'. CETV shows dramas, game shows, and situation comedies from Taiwan and Hong Kong. The no-news part sounds quite bizarre for a company best known for CNN. Meanwhile, Time Warner Cable has agreed to distribute Beijing's CCTV-9 in the US, and that station carries Chinese news.

Staying in touch

May your mail be opened, may your phone-calls be monitored, may your faxes be scanned, may your email be scrambled. This is not an ancient curse – it's a reality in today's Tibet, policed by the paranoid Chinese. The mailing system in Tibet is quite efficient – letters can get from Lhasa to Europe or North America within a few weeks. Poste Restante exists at the main post office in Lhasa, or you can have letters mailed care-of specific hotels (a better option). Sending faxes is expensive, but still cheaper than repeating complex details over the phone (when you will still be charged even if you get an answering machine at the other end).

Once out of Lhasa or Shigatse, communication becomes more difficult. If planning to send postcards, buy all the stamps in Lhasa, because you may only find small-value stamps in other places, and they will cover the entire postcard. Bring your own posting materials if out of Lhasa. Although places are remote, if there's an army base around, there are probably communication towers and satellite dishes to serve the military. That means IDD phones, sometimes even in remote corners of Tibet.

Fax and phone

You can use IDD phones to call direct from Lhasa through major hotels or at the main post office. Most China-wide and international destinations can be reached direct. Pre-paid cards are much cheaper than hotel calls – around Y4 a minute for international calls (global reach) versus Y12-15 a minute for calls placed through a hotel system. There are two kinds of card: the IC yellow phonecard, and the IP hotel phonecard. The IC yellow phonecard can be purchased with a Y50 or Y100 value. You will see yellow phones on the street; they can also be found in some hotel lobbies. Special elongated yellow machines lurk in the lobby of Lhasa Hotel and at the China Telecom Office – these not only handle international calls, they can also process email. There is one drawback, however – no keyboard. You have to input using an upright touch-screen.

Phone area codes are designated by prefecture, which is very useful for figuring out whose jurisdiction you are in for permits. The area codes are: Lhasa Prefecture 0891, Shigatse 0892, Shannan 0893, Nyingchi 0894, Chamdo 0895, Nagqu 0896, and Ali Prefecture 0897. If dialling from outside the country, drop the 0 in this

THE TWILIGHT ZONE

Feeling out of synch? Having trouble figuring out what time of day it is in Lhasa? You wouldn't be the only one. All China runs on Beijing time, due to the communist craze for centralised planning, although it should strictly have five or six time zones from east to west. Even though Lhasa is thousands of kilometres to the southwest of Beijing and should be on the same time zone as Nepal (which is two and a quarter hours behind Beijing time), it runs on Beijing's clock. If you fly from Lhasa to Kathmandu, that means you actually arrive before you left! So everything is out of synch in Lhasa. Sunday is the non-working day; Saturday might be a half-day. From Monday to Saturday, Chinese business hours for banks and other offices like CAAC are (in summer) 09.00 to 12.30 mornings, then *xiuxi* (siesta – some offices have beds in the back rooms), and then 15.00 to 18.30. When they say 09.00, it's actually more like 07.00 in real time. Tibetans run on Tibetan time, which is like stepping back a few centuries. It's timeless: get up when the sun comes up, and go home when the sun goes down. Beijing time is Greenwich Mean Time +8 hours, or Pacific Standard Time +16 hours.

prefix. Let's say the local seven-digit number in Lhasa is 633 3446. If you are in Lhasa, you would dial the number as is. If you are in Shigatse trying to reach Lhasa, you would dial 0891 633 3446. If you are in Canada, trying to reach Lhasa, you would dial 011 86 891 633 3446. The 011 sequence gets you out of Canada, 86 is country code for China, 891 is area code for Lhasa (you drop the 0 prefix from 0891 for this dial-up), followed by the local number. Lhasa phone numbers are seven digit, but mobile phones are usually 11-digit (with 1390 often being the first four digits). That means if you are trying to reach a mobile phone in Lhasa from outside the country, you would have to dial around 20 digits.

Other areas of Tibet may have erratic five-digit numbers – or no phones at all. Some other area codes for Chinese cities are: Xining 0971, Zhongdian 0887, Kunming 0871 and Chengdu 028.

Email and internet

The rules of engagement for use of the net in China are that many sites are 'sensitive.' However, you are not told which ones. It's possible that the laws that apply to locals do not apply to foreigners. If foreigners are used to looking at their favourite newspaper and suddenly find it blocked, they might get upset.

The net is your lifeline for news and information: consult the appendix at the back of this book for useful sites. Email is apparently monitored, though with the sheer volume of web-based mail, it is hard to fathom how this could possibly work. There is good email access in Lhasa, limited access in Shigatse, and extremely limited access elsewhere in Tibet. Email in Lhasa is useful for finding other travellers and for arranging Landcruiser rides.

ETHICAL GUIDELINES
Customs and conduct

Tibetans are a spontaneous lot – they have no trouble breaking the ice. They'll probably examine your camera, fondle your luggage or shake you down for Dalai Lama pictures. Or give you a big grin. Tibetans have a great sense of humour, they're self-reliant, amazingly hardy, and have none of the shyness or coolness that the Chinese bring to bear on foreigners. They are usually direct, open and honest in their dealings. Tibetan women have a fairly high status, although they still do heavier work than the men. Outside of Lhasa, few Tibetans speak English: those that do are likely to have been educated in India. Put a Tibetan phrasebook to good use: any attempt at speaking the language is greatly appreciated. There are other ways to communicate: gestures like thumbs up and thumbs down go over well, as does singing in any language. If you're patient enough, it's only a matter of time before you are invited in for tea – or something stronger. Any kind of pictures you have are a great way of communicating. That extends to picture books on Tibet – these are engrossing to your host.

Interactions with Tibetans are not always so pleasant. Unfortunately, for a lengthy period Tibet was only open to group tours, who were in the habit of handing out pens, candy and Polaroid pictures to Tibetan kids: these same urchins may expect the similar gifts from you, and will get antsy if nothing is forthcoming. On a more serious note, when interacting with Tibetans, you have a responsibility. When it comes to an overheard political discussion, not a lot will happen to you, a foreigner – at worst, you'll be booted out of Tibet. For the Tibetan, however, it could mean interrogation and jail. An Italian tourist interviewed a monk on video about Tibetan independence, and then took the videotape to a Chinese Embassy back in Italy to protest the treatment of Tibetans. The monk in the video was traced and received a 14-year jail sentence. Avoid putting Tibetans at risk – if a Tibetan talks to you about something politically sensitive, make sure to keep your interaction private and guard their identity. There are Tibetan informants as well as Chinese ones. Common sense will serve you well in most situations, but keep in mind just how serious Chinese authorities are toward punishing Tibetans who speak their mind, or express their support for any notion of independence.

The following section has been adapted from a set of ethical guidelines published by the International Campaign for Tibet. For further up-to-date information and advice, contact The International Campaign for Tibet, 1825 K St, NW, Suite 520, Washington, DC, 20006 (website: www.savetibet.org).

Respecting customs

Tibetans are extremely religious people and appreciate foreigners respecting a few simple customs; always walk clockwise around Buddhist religious sites and within monasteries or nunneries. Take hats off, do not smoke and do not touch figures or use flash photography inside monasteries or nunneries unless it has been cleared with the monks or nuns. Do not jump queues of pilgrims within monasteries nor interrupt ceremonies. Try to be an unobtrusive visitor but feel free to show interest and ask questions. It is also important not to touch the heads or point your feet towards monks or nuns, and be careful with physical contact with them. Dress appropriately when going to any religious site – remember, it is a holy place.

Sky burial

Do not encroach on Tibetan burial rituals (known as sky or celestial burials). This unique system of disposing of the remains of the dead is a sacred and private affair – it is not proper for visitors to Tibet to intrude into a family's last rites. Some Tibetans believe photos can steal their soul. At any rate, taking pictures of people can be rude and intrusive. Put yourself in their place before you take each and every photograph.

Support religious freedom

Entry fees at large monasteries will go to a committee controlled by the Chinese Communist Party, and not necessarily used for religious purposes. Donations left on

DALAI LAMA PICTURES

As of 1996, the trade in Dalai Lama pictures is banned, and there have been several incidents of tourists being detained, interrogated and searched after they were seen giving pictures to Tibetans. Of course, the gifts most appreciated by Tibetans are photos and postcards of the Dalai Lama and books by or about him. However, if a Chinese guide or the police see you giving them to a Tibetan, both you and the Tibetan could get into serious trouble. There's nothing to stop you talking about the Dalai Lama, however – if you have seen the Dalai Lama on television, or have read a newspaper story about him, tell the Tibetans about it and assure them of his good health. Tibetans like to have a Dalai Lama picture to place on their home altar (if they can, under current conditions). However, that's not the only picture they put there. They'd be quite happy to place a picture of the Potala Palace or the Jokhang Temple or sacred Mount Kailash there as well. Pilgrims would be very happy to receive these pictures, and they're all street legal.

altars may benefit monks and nuns, or donations can be made directly to individual monks and nuns, or given in kind. Clothing, food, film or books are much appreciated, but don't give your dirty castoffs. Donations to smaller, out-of-the-way monasteries will be used properly, according to traditional Tibetan custom, since they are not as tightly regulated by Chinese authorities. Items such as candles, prayer flags, a bag of tsampa or some tea are always appreciated at remote monasteries. A wonderful way to spend some time with monastic people is to share your food. Walk the Barkor at sunrise with the Tibetans! It's a peaceful experience and allows you to be with the Tibetan people in a way that shows your support for their religious freedom.

Buy from Tibetans

If you want to support the Tibetan people, culture and economy, buy from Tibetan shops and stalls. A large influx of Chinese immigrants in Lhasa and other Tibetan cities is now taking over the economy and putting Tibetans out of work. The Dalai Lama has called this influx possibly the greatest threat to the survival of Tibetan culture. This general rule also applies to Tibetan restaurants and tea stalls. Eat Tibetan food rather than Chinese imported foodstuffs. Inflation is also a very real problem in Tibet. You contribute to this by paying exorbitant prices to vendors, which can increase prices Tibetans must pay for goods. Don't be cheap, on the other hand. If you find a piece of finely woven cloth or a carving you like, pay a fair price for the amount of work entailed. Bargaining is a part of Tibetan life – unfortunately, being ripped off by tourists is also becoming a part of their life.

Do not buy antiques Most of Tibet's artistic treasures have already been destroyed or plundered by Chinese troops. Please leave antiques in Tibet. This goes for all family heirlooms as well as religious items. Since it is difficult to tell what is antique and what is not, a good rule of thumb to follow is that if someone tries to sell you something secretly, don't buy it. Stick to public stores and stalls. Families are often forced to sell their treasured items to put food on the table. Be creative and find other ways of helping Tibetans without taking away their culture.

Eco-tourism

Help protect Tibet's wildlife – do not buy products made from wild animals, especially from endangered species (ie: skins of the snow leopard and tiger, horns of Tibetan antelopes, paws of the Himalayan brown bear, or any medicinal products made from animals). If you see these items, take photographs and notify the Worldwide Fund for Nature (WWF) or the International Campaign for Tibet. This holds true for cities in Tibet, as well as Nepal, China, Hong Kong or anywhere else you come across them.

Leave only footprints The Himalayan ecosystem is a fragile one. If you go trekking use kerosene, even where wood is available. Trash should be buried 30m (100ft) from a water source, paper burned, and cans and bottles packed up and taken to a hotel or large town. Do not leave this up to your guide as environmental awareness is often low, especially among the Chinese. Plan ahead and bring food that has little packaging. Travel light and don't demand five-course meals. Bring your own food as villages rarely have surplus. If you want to bring presents for locals along the way, think carefully. Don't bring plastic baubles or contribute to begging by handing out a lot of freebies. It is much more appropriate to share time and a cup of tea with people, or play a game of jacks with the children. Tibet is becoming littered with human waste and toilet paper – bury excrement and burn toilet paper! Be careful where you hike as erosion and damage to fragile plants are increasingly becoming a threat to the environmental health of the plateau and mountains.

Interacting
Try and use knowledgeable Tibetan guides. All travel companies must work through a travel operator in Lhasa. It is important to select a company which works with a Lhasa-based operator, run and staffed by Tibetans as opposed to Chinese. To quote one experienced guide, 'When you go to France, you don't want a German tour guide; when you go to Tibet you don't want a Chinese one.' Moreover, using Tibetan-staffed companies promotes Tibetan culture and employs Tibetans. Check and see if one of the Tibetan-run agencies is operating at the time of your visit to Tibet.

If you are on a tour with an official Chinese government guide, do not expect accurate answers to historical, religious, or political questions. Educate yourself before you leave! Read books about the history of Tibet and its people. John Avedon's *In Exile from the Land of Snows* is a classic and the Dalai Lama's autobiography *Freedom In Exile* is very informative (see *Further Information*, page 276). Reading some Chinese propaganda before you leave may help you to recognise false statements when encountered in Tibet.

Breaking away
Almost everyone who visits Tibet says that the best part was their interaction with Tibetans. In small groups, wander the streets, follow the hillside paths or get outside of the town and visit a village. Revisit a monastery without the group or spend time at a tea stall in the market. Photos of your family and neighbourhood or Tibetan communities and celebrations abroad are great conversation pieces – don't worry about the language barrier. Tibetans would much rather have you attempt their own language rather than speak Chinese. Be mindful of approaching Tibetans in front of Chinese, particularly soldiers. Depending on current Chinese restrictions, Tibetans can be openly criticised or interrogated for associations with foreigners. Always be careful around dogs; they are numerous in most parts of Tibet and trained to protect their territory.

Being critical
Don't be frightened by dire warnings that the Chinese will lock you in jail and throw away the key for your support of the Tibetans. You should, however, be

careful, and never endanger the Tibetans, but let the Chinese know when you disapprove of actions such as the use of monasteries for grain storage, the malevolence shown by police in and around religious sites, and unfair hiring and school enrolment practices. You can do a lot for the Tibetans and their cause, and will most probably want to after you come to know these wonderful people.

DEALING WITH OFFICIALDOM

The following PSB notice appeared on the walls of budget hotels around Lhasa. The first five items of the notice are quoted (out of seven). Curiously, there is no mention of 'Tibet' or 'Tibetans' – the latter are referred to either as 'Chinese citizens' or 'minority nationality.'

NOTICE: Ladies and Gentlemen: Welcome to Lhasa. So you may have safe and enjoyable travels, we would like you to be aware of the following government regulations.

1 Foreigners travelling to China must abide by Chinese law and must not endanger the national security of China, harm its public interests, disturb the public order, or engage in any other activities incompatible with tourist status.

2 If Chinese citizens are holding a rally or demonstration, it is strictly forbidden for foreigners to participate, follow along with, take pictures, or video film any of these activities. Foreigners are not permitted to interfere in Chinese internal affairs.

3 Foreigners are forbidden to distribute any propaganda material and join in any religious activity.

4 In accordance with regulations, foreign tourists must go through all registration formality and stay only at a designated hotel. Without prior permission, it is forbidden to travel in unopened areas, to operate individual business or privately take up an occupation.

5 It is forbidden to visit or photo the sky burial site according to the local government's regulations for the minority nationality's habits and customs. the tourist who breaks this regulation will be punished strictly.

Being watched

Without being too paranoid about things, you should be aware that if you appear to be any kind of activist or have any connections to the Tibetan government-in-exile, your actions may be watched. You may be followed, your interaction with Tibetans noted, and your room may even be bugged. Sounds unreal? It has happened. In one case, in Beijing, a person speaking on the phone in French was asked by a Chinese wire-tapper to switch to English because he couldn't follow the conversation! In Lhasa, in 1996, a traveller wrote a political comment about Tibet in a book (for complaints) at the counter of the Bank of China: the PSB promptly tracked him down, exacted a confession, cancelled his visa, and gave him an exit visa – meaning he had three days to fly out of Lhasa, back to Kathmandu. The Chinese are not good sports when it comes to criticism.

Encounters with the PSB

There's no particular reason to be worried when dealing with police, army or other officials. If you are formally arrested, your embassy must usually be notified within four days. You have the right to speak to a consular officer and can demand that a call be placed to your embassy. Incidents involving foreigners in Tibet have ranged from warnings to hotel interrogations, to confinement to a hotel for four days (Dalai Lama tapes found in baggage in Shigatse after police were tipped off), to deportation. Three tourists watching demonstrations in Lhasa in 1994 had their passports confiscated. There have also been reports of Westerners being given a mild dusting-up – kicked or punched – when dealing with security officials.

In the Chinese system, if you are arrested, you are automatically guilty of something. Do not assume that innocence in a Western situation would mean you're in the clear in China. Chinese logic is different. Cast aside any notions of justice, put aside ideas of politeness and gentility, and respect. There is no innocent here: you're either guilty and you admit it – and you'll get off lightly – or you're guilty and you deny it, in which case you'll be heavily fined, deported at your expense, or otherwise punished. The arresting person would lose face if you were entirely innocent. You must leave a way out for the arresting officer – the usual method is making a written confession. There is nothing binding about these confessions – they're not legal documents. You can promise to the hilt on a confession, and then go out and break those promises the next day.

Under no circumstances should you let someone else write that confession for you (especially in Chinese!) to be signed. Insist that you write it yourself. Irksome though confessions may sound, they are really meaningless pieces of paper. Phrases that please are: 'my ancestors would be ashamed of me', or 'I will never even think of doing this again'. In the early days of Tibet travel, a British backpacker was busy writing his confession about being in a closed area when the arresting officer noticed that he'd extended his own visa – the highest level of naughtiness conceivable. Unperturbed, the traveller continued writing his confession: 'In addition to the above, I must humbly confess that I have extended my own visa, for which....'

Close encounters are usually of the PSB kind – ie: over travel permits. As long as your papers are in order, there's nothing to worry about: if you get off the track, the legality of your travels is sometimes at the whim of the particular PSB official you are dealing with, at which point a small 'fine' may be levied, going directly into his pocket. These fines are negotiable: if he asks for US$100, wait until it drops to US$20 or US$10. Packets of foreign-brand cigarettes go down well with the Beijing Boys. Sometimes the crime is just too 'serious' and the PSB won't back off. Two Germans who were caught collecting high-altitude bug specimens were fined over US$300 by PSB for their illicit activities. PSB officers have amusing English-language phrasebooks for dealing with foreigners in situations like this ('Please sign your interrogation' – things like that). The military – mostly teenaged recruits – do not seem particularly concerned about foreigners, except at checkpoints.

GIVING SOMETHING BACK
Brian Harris

There are estimated to be 45 million blind people worldwide: 90% of these people live in non-affluent countries. Remarkably, 80% of this blindness is avoidable – either preventable or curable.

In the Tibet Autonomous Region alone, there are probably over 30,000 blind people. In the Tibetan-populated regions of neighbouring provinces, there could be a further 30,000 blind people. That makes a total of perhaps 60,000 blind Tibetans. With cataract surgery, over half of these people could see again. The main cause of cataract blindness is simply the aging process; however, in Tibet the incidence is believed to be increased due to poor nutrition and to a greater exposure to ultraviolet light. At 4,500 metres there is less atmosphere to filter out the harmful effects of UV light.

The Seva Foundation in the US and its sister organisation Seva Canada are among the few NGOs working in Tibet to address the problem of reversible blindness. Seva has worked with the Tibet Development Fund, centred in Lhasa, for over seven years to help Tibetans develop eye-care services in each of the main hospitals in Tibet, by building a regional eye-care program to reduce this immense backlog of cataract surgeries.

Although more than 40 doctors work in various eye clinics in Tibet, few have medical degrees and none are fully qualified ophthalmologists. Eye-care services in the region are very limited; the eye doctors are poorly trained, equipment is inadequate and outdated, and complication rates have been very high. Seva's Tibetan Sight Program attempts to address these urgent needs. Seva has developed training programs for surgical teams from each of the 12 principal hospitals in Tibet, to teach staff safe cataract surgery techniques and other eye-care skills. Seva has also supported eye camps in Tibet, providing up to 500 cataract surgeries each to supplement the limited eye-care services available. Now, the Tibetan doctors Seva has trained are conducting their own eye camps each year.

When Seva first started working in Tibet seven years ago, one of its first major goals was to find and train local medical doctors in modern cataract surgery. Among the early trainees was a team of doctors from Menzikhang, the hospital of traditional Tibetan medicine in Lhasa. Actually, Seva did not plan to work within the traditional medical model, but the Menzikhang had the space to conduct eye camps and its traditional doctors were very keen to learn modern ophthalmology. Tibetan medicine is a complex system of medical practice, inseparable from its spiritual foundation in Tibetan Buddhism. The Tibetan medical tradition has historically included a form of surgical treatment for cataract. Thus Seva was not challenging any major conceptual assumptions of Tibetan medicine. Several years later Seva also learned that Tibetan Medicine includes the recognition of different eye diseases and several treatments for these conditions.

Now, after years of training and participating in many cooperative eye camps, there is an effective local cataract surgery team. However, despite having excellent surgical techniques, these doctors don't understand many of the basic tenets of Western medical ophthalmology. There are inherent dilemmas and very practical risks that arise when modern ophthalmology is incorporated into traditional medical practices without this new way of medical thinking to act as a bridge. Providing this theoretical 'bridge' without undermining the very important traditional medical system is one of the many challenges Seva encounters in Tibet.

Another instructive example of the conundrums created by modern ophthalmology's meeting with traditional belief is when an elderly Tibetan refuses to have this free, 15-minute, sight-restoring cataract surgery because this person's blindness is understood to be his or her Karma or spiritual destiny. It is very important to respect such deeply held religious belief.

Seva continues to work with Menzikhang because they are clearly committed to serving the poorest people in Tibet and this hospital is the most trusted by the local people. In order to develop a comprehensive blindness prevention program, Seva is still exploring the best way to add preventative care and medical treatments for other diseases to its existing program of cataract surgery.

Seva does seek skilled volunteers for Tibet. Ophthalmologists, optometrists and ophthalmic assistants who can make a long-term commitment are especially welcome. Non-clinical volunteers including computer and health education specialists are also sought.

The rewards? Here's what ophthalmic surgeon Dr Pratt-Johnson says of his volunteer work in Nepal, India and Bangladesh: 'You soon get the feeling that you are doing so little and yet it means so incredibly much to our partners and particularly to the patients, who express their overwhelming gratitude in a mixture of gestures, tears and happy smiles. You try and wish you could do more. You return with an afterglow that warms your heart and soul. This psychologically resets the equilibrium of one's life, fulfillment and joy. We ophthalmic surgeons need to be conscious of having skills that place us in a privileged position, coming close to performing miracles – restoring sight to the blind. Share it with as many as you can. Giving through volunteering is such an adventure and a lot of fun.'

For more information about Seva's work in Tibet and other parts of the world you can contact the following offices in the US and Canada: Seva Foundation, 1786 Fifth Street, Berkeley, CA 94710; tel: 510 845 7382; fax: 510 845 7410; email: admin@seva.org; web: www.seva.org; and Seva Canada, Suite 100-2000 West 12th Avenue, Vancouver, BC, V6J 2G2, Canada; tel: 604 713 6622; fax: 604 733 4292; email: service@seva.ca; web: www.seva.ca.

Toenpa Shenrab, a Bon version of Sakyamuni Buddha

Health and Safety

HEALTH
In consultation with Dr Felicity Nicholson
An alternate title for this section might be 'Staying Alive'.

This material is not intended to scare you away from visiting Tibet. Rather, it is intended to make you aware of the dangers involved if you happen to get really sick, to encourage you to travel with at least one friend as a back-up in case things go wrong, and to encourage you to obtain comprehensive evacuation insurance before visiting Tibet.

Informing yourself
The following medical matters may venture into uncharted territory, especially concerning altitude sickness. This section is a broad outline – it does not cover matters in great detail. Draw your own conclusions – and then consult other sources and experts for more thorough answers. Information on altitude sickness is hard to come by because it's not a common problem in the West. There are some books out on the subject, but these tend to get out of date as knowledge evolves. For general health concerns, The Centers for Disease Control and Prevention, based in Atlanta, Georgia, maintains a website at www.cdc.gov/travel with the latest information on prevention guidelines and strategies. See the short listing of other websites at the back of this book.

Before you go
Some important facts to know before you go: Tibetan and Chinese hygiene standards are atrocious, and Chinese medical facilities within Tibet are appalling. Some conclusions to draw: you have to be your own doctor in Tibet, you have to be willing to help fellow travellers in dire situations, and you have to be prepared to evacuate if the need arises, so you need good medical insurance.

Prior to departure, go and visit your local health unit or travel clinic (see below) and get an armful of relevant shots. You would be wise to be up to date with **tetanus**, **polio** and **diphtheria** (all ten yearly), **typhoid** and **hepatitis A** (Havrix Monodose or Avaxim). For longer trips (four weeks or longer) consider **meningitis**, **hepatitis B** and **rabies**. The last two require three injections given over a four-week period, so go in plenty of time. Talk to your doctor and arm yourself with drugs – ciprofloxacin (for dysentery), tinidazole (for giardia or amoebic dysentery) and Diamox (to deal with altitude). Assemble a good medical kit (see below). Check out where your embassies lie in China and in the neighbouring region – note down the addresses and contact numbers. Bring a health certificate to China (it may be checked). Find out your blood group and record it on that document. If you haven't had time to get all or any of your vaccinations/medicines before you leave home then the **Ciwek Clinic** in

Kathmandu is an excellent place to go. It is run by Western doctors and is located just off Durbar Marg (the main street coming out of the Royal Palace).

Travel clinics and health information

A full list of current travel clinic websites worldwide is available on www.istm.org/. For other journey preparation information, consult ftp://ftp.shoreland.com/pub/shorecg.rtf or www.tripprep.com.

UK

British Airways Travel Clinic and Immunisation Service There are now only three BA clinics, all in London: 156 Regent St, W1B 5LB (no appointments); 101 Cheapside, EC1V6DT (tel: 020 7606 2977); 115 Buckingham Palace Rd, SW1W 9SJ (Victoria Station; tel: 020 7233 6661); see also www.britishairways.com/travelclinics. Also sell a variety of health-related goods.
Fleet Street Travel Clinic 29 Fleet St, London EC4Y 1AA; tel: 020 7353 5678
Hospital for Tropical Diseases Travel Clinic Capper St (off Tottenham Ct Rd), London WC1; tel: 020 7388 9600; web: www.thhtd.org. Offers consultations and advice, and is able to provide all necessary drugs and vaccines for travellers. Runs a healthline (09061 337733) for country-specific information and health hazards. Also stocks nets, water purification equipment and personal protection measures.
MASTA (Medical Advisory Service for Travellers Abroad) Keppel St, London WC1 7HT; tel: 09068 224100. This is a premium-line number, charged at 50p per minute.
NHS travel website, www.fitfortravel.scot.nhs.uk, provides country-by-country advice on immunisation and malaria, plus details of recent developments, and a list of relevant health organisations.
Nomad Travel Pharmacy and Vaccination Centre 3–4 Wellington Terrace, Turnpike Lane, London N8 0PX; tel: 020 8889 7014; email: sales@nomadtravel.co.uk; website: www.nomadtravel.co.uk. As well as dispensing health advice, Nomad stocks mosquito nets and other anti-bug devices, and an excellent range of adventure travel gear.
Thames Medical 157 Waterloo Rd, London SE1 8US; tel: 020 7902 9000. Competitively priced, one-stop travel health service. All profits go to their affiliated company, InterHealth, which provides health care for overseas workers on Christian projects.
Trailfinders Immunisation Centre 194 Kensington High St, London W8 7RG; tel: 020 7938 3999. Also at 254–284 Sauchiehall St, Glasgow G2 3EH; tel: 0141 353 0066.
Travelpharm The Travelpharm website, www.travelpharm.com, offers up-to-date guidance on travel-related health and has a range of medications available through their online mini-pharmacy.

Irish Republic

Tropical Medical Bureau Grafton Street Medical Centre, Grafton Buildings, 34 Grafton St, Dublin 2; tel: 1 671 9200. Has a useful website specific to tropical destinations: www.tmb.ie

USA

Centers for Disease Control 1600 Clifton Rd, Atlanta, GA 30333; tel: 877 FYI TRIP; 800 311 3435; web: www.cdc.gov/travel. The central source of travel information in the USA. Each summer they publish the invaluable *Health Information for International Travel*, available from the Division of Quarantine at the above address.
Connaught Laboratories PO Box 187, Swiftwater, PA 18370; tel: 800 822 2463. They will send a free list of specialist tropical-medicine physicians in your state.
IAMAT (International Association for Medical Assistance to Travelers) 736 Center St, Lewiston, NY 14092; tel: 716 754 4883. A non-profit organisation that provides lists of English-speaking doctors abroad.

Canada
IAMAT (International Association for Medical Assistance to Travellers) Suite 1, 1287 St Clair Av W, Toronto, Ontario M6E 1B8; tel: 416 652 0137; web: www.sentex.net/~iamat
TMVC (Travel Doctors Group) Sulphur Springs Rd, Ancaster, Ontario; tel: 905 648 1112; web: www.tmvc.com.au

Australia, New Zealand, Thailand
TMVC Tel: 1300 65 88 44; web: www.tmvc.com.au. 20 clinics in Australia, New Zealand and Thailand, including:

Auckland Canterbury Arcade, 170 Queen Street, Auckland City; tel: 373 3531
Brisbane Dr Deborah Mills, Qantas Domestic Building, 6th floor, 247 Adelaide St, Brisbane, QLD 4000; tel: 7 3221 9066; fax: 7 3321 7076
Melbourne Dr Sonny Lau, 393 Little Bourke St, 2nd floor, Melbourne, VIC 3000; tel: 3 9602 5788; fax: 3 9670 8394
Sydney Dr Mandy Hu, Dymocks Building, 7th Floor, 428 George St, Sydney, NSW2000; tel: 2 221 7133; fax: 2 221 8401

South Africa
SAA-Netcare Travel Clinics PO Box 786692, Sandton 2146; fax: 011 883 6152; web: www.travelclinic.co.za or www.malaria.co.za. Clinics throughout South Africa.
TMVC (Travel Doctor Group) 113 DF Malan Drive, Roosevelt Park, Johannesburg; tel: 011 888 7488; web: www.tmvc.com.au. Consult the website for details of clinics in South Africa.

Switzerland
IAMAT (International Association for Medical Assistance to Travellers) 57 Voirets, 1212 Grand Lancy, Geneva; web: www.sentex.net/~iamat

Evacuation insurance
You are strongly advised to carry comprehensive air evacuation insurance for a trip to Tibet. Hopefully, you will never have to use it. Your best strategy if you fall really sick in Tibet is to get right out of Tibet – and China – as fast as you can, and make a beeline for somewhere with hospitals that have real doctors, like Singapore. Use regular scheduled flights to get out of Tibet if possible. If the plane looks full, insist that a regular passenger gets bumped off the flight for the emergency patient.

Evacuation by chartered flight can cost a fortune. Check your travel insurance to ensure that it covers emergency evacuation costs, and more specifically, if it will cover evacuation by crews like SOS/AEA, which has clinics in Beijing with expat doctors and imported medicines. Better yet, take out direct insurance with SOS/AEA (check their www.internationalsos.com website for addresses and contact numbers, and see the section on evacuation that follows, page 90).

Himalayan medical kit
Failing adequate health care in Tibet, you really need to be your own doctor. There are Chinese pharmacies in Lhasa, but medication may bear Chinese instructions and may not be familiar to Western eyes. Kathmandu and Hong Kong are quite well-stocked with Western drugs and will issue medication without prescription. You can easily find drugs like Diamox in Kathmandu (check expiry dates). While you can't be a travelling drugstore, you'll need a larger-than-usual medical kit in Tibet. If travelling with a friend or a small group, divide up a medical kit to share the weight. Camping and outdoor stores in the West sell pre-packaged medical kits that you can customise to your needs (you can even find 'Himalaya kits'). Items

like antiseptic cream and bandaids (plasters) are hard to find in Lhasa. Take along a Swiss Army knife with scissors and tweezers. You'll need your own water bottle and purifying tablets (or filter).

A medical kit may contain a ready-made package – sealed and labelled – with sterile needles and syringes. It is highly recommended you carry these in case blood samples or injections are required. Take along any prescription drugs you need, as well as back-ups of things you are dependent upon – such as glasses. Your chances of finding contact lens solution in Shigatse are zero: dust can be a major problem for contact lenses in Tibet (take along regular glasses as a back-up). Glasses or no glasses, dust can cause eye irritation – you might want to take along soothing eyedrops.

Read the following sections for ideas on arming yourself for the rigours of Tibet – you will need medications like cough lozenges, codeine and decongestants (for colds); moisturisers, lip balm, sunglasses, sunscreen and other balms will help combat the effects of sun, wind and altitude. Recommended drugs for Tibet include: Diamox to help acclimatise, Ciprofloxacin for diarrhoea associated with blood or mucus and/or a fever, tinidazole for giardia and amoebic dysentery and a phial of iodine tablets for purifying water.

Travellers buy a medical kit but overlook the importance of the medical knowledge required to go with it. A pocket-sized booklet would be worth bringing along – there are several on the market, such as *The Pocket Doctor* or *Holiday Health*. There are also specialised booklets like *Altitude Illness: Prevention and Treatment*. If you're leaving Tibet and returning directly home, you should consider selling or donating your precious cache of medicines and other supplies to incoming travellers. Drugs like Diamox have an expiry period and will be of little use to you in the West anyway.

The buddy system

When you go diving, you use the buddy system. You watch out for your friend underwater, which is an alien environment and a potentially dangerous one. You could draw close parallels in Tibet: high altitude is an alien environment. If someone gets altitude sickness, he or she becomes confused and disorientated, and cannot make the right decisions. Someone else has to take those decisions. Back yourself up in Tibet with at least one buddy. And be prepared to watch out for others in a Landcruiser group if someone falls sick.

Common health problems in Tibet
Running on empty

To keep your system ticking properly, you need proper nutrition and high fluid intake. And that's hard to achieve outside Lhasa. So carry vitamin pills and carry freeze-dried soups, and carry extra food supplies – dried fruit, whatever, to supplement the meagre local offerings. You should think in terms of what can be 'cooked' with the hot water supplied in thermoses in hotels and truck-stops: check the cooking times on soup packets (ideally, only a few minutes in hot water). Packets of soup are the best item here – soup is easily prepared and gives the illusion of a hot meal. *Tsampa*, the Tibetan food staple, is sustaining but tasteless – it can be mixed in with soup to make it more palatable. You can get run-down without proper nutrition intake: this makes you more susceptible to coming down with other ailments.

Fluid intake

Two essentials concerning water: making sure the water is safe to drink, and drinking enough of it. Even though Tibet is high and the water looks crystal clear, it could be contaminated by herders and livestock on higher ground. It's best to always filter water or boil it. Staying hydrated is essential in Tibet to combat dryness and the effects of altitude. Even if you have to overload your system, keep drinking your quota of water – about four litres a day. If you get a case of the runs, you'll lose a lot of body fluids, so you need to keeping drinking water to stay hydrated. You can buy bottled water in Lhasa and larger towns in Tibet – make sure the seal is intact. The water supplied in Chinese thermoses in hotels is usually reliable since it has been boiled at high temperature. You have to wait for this to cool down, or else drink it in tea. You should take along your own water purifying devices – the simplest is an iodine cup filter. Iodine tablets can be purchased cheaply in the West. Iodine-treated water tastes horrible – but you can buy another tablet that removes that taste. Or take along Gatorade flavouring crystals to neutralise the taste. These and other electrolyte powders (such as Electrolade) are sodium and potassium, which will help restore body fluid balance (one of the main ingredients in sweat is sodium).

Hygiene hazards

Washing and cleaning activities are a low priority with Tibetans: explanations range from lack of hot water to layering themselves with dirt to protect the skin from sun. Both Tibetan and Chinese hygiene standards are shocking; toilets are disgusting. You have to be careful about the handling of food and water – do not accept the cold face-towels offered in restaurants. In restaurants, stick to well-cooked hot food (noodles are fine). Boil it, peel it – or forget it. Some travellers prefer to use their own eating utensils, bringing an aluminium mug and spoon (soup can be served in the mug).

Although hot showers are readily available in Lhasa, in the rest of Tibet you won't be so lucky. There are the occasional hot springs to soak in, but that's about it: the rivers and lakes are pretty cold. Out of Lhasa, you have to rely on the thermos of hot water supplied to your room (or ask for it). The thermos is a source of hot water for tea, or for making soup – and can also be used for bathing. A metal basin is often supplied in the room (sometimes with a special wooden stand to hold it), so you can pour water in and wash yourself in stages (hair one day, and so on). Another technique is to soak a thin towel (preferably your own) and apply it Japanese-style, as in a sushi restaurant. Thin, spongy Western sport-towels are ideal for this as you can wring them out to dry quickly.

Diarrhoea

Because of low hygiene standards, it is eminently possible that you will get a case of the runs. Usually, this is not a problem – just stick to a simple diet with liquid back-up: water, clear soups, and unsweetened juices. Do not drink beer or milk, and avoid spicy or fatty foods as they can aggravate your condition. The problem should pass within a day or two. In Kathmandu you can buy packets of rehydration crystals – a mixture of glucose and salt. If these are unavailable, you can make your own by adding two or three teaspoons of salt – and a similar amount of sugar – to a litre-bottle of purified water. Packets with electrolyte rehydration powders (sodium/potassium crystals) are efficacious. If problems persist, it may be a case of bacterial diarrhoea – refer to the section on *Intestinal bugs* (page 85).

The elements

Sunburn, windburn, chapped lips, lobster-face and red-eye are definite hazards in Tibet due to the (at times) ferocious effects of the sun, wind and cold. Once you get cracked lips or chapped hands, you'll find these take a long time to heal and can be very bothersome. Moisturisers are the answer: bring along hand- and face-cream moisturisers (these can also be purchased in Lhasa). You need a good sunblock cream (preferably containing Paba) and Chapstick (also with Paba). A hat of some kind – preferably covering the ears and neck – is essential, as are high-quality sunglasses or glacier glasses that block UV rays (ideal are *dark* polarising lenses). The use of certain drugs such as the antibiotic Tetracycline can render a person more sun-sensitised, and result in bad sunburn. One of the greatest hazards in Tibet is dust. It can get into your eyes, so contact lenses are not a great idea – dust can be very irritating if it gets under them. A silk scarf or bandanna, wrapped around your nose, throat and mouth (bandito-style) will generally filter the dust out of your breathing apparatus in extreme conditions, and the same scarf can be used round your neck to keep you warm in a sudden change of temperature.

Coughs, colds and sore throats

Respiratory ailments are quite common in Tibet, and can turn very nasty when combined with the effects of extreme dryness and altitude. Take care. These are not your normal colds – they can be persistent and debilitating. New (mutating) strains of flu, originating in China, can be knock-outs. The best way to avoid this syndrome is to make sure you don't undergo drastic changes of body temperature. Make sure that you have clothing that you can layer on or off, to cope with the extremes of heat and cold – sometimes occurring on the same day in Tibet. This also applies to sleeping arrangements – there's not much heating in hotels in Tibet. Bring your own medicines for coughs, colds and sore throats. Some stronger drugs (codeine compounds) can be multipurpose – for headache, pain, coughs or colds. Tuberculosis exists in Tibet: the airborne bacteria are transmitted through coughing, sneezing or spitting by people in an infectious stage of TB. Conditions can be very smoky in Tibetan teahouses – with a fire burning away in the middle, and no ventilation.

Danger zone
Accidents

It's unknown how many foreigners have perished in Tibet due to driving accidents, but there have certainly been cases of trucks and Landcruisers being totalled, and foreigners killed. There are no safety devices along precipitous mountain roads in Tibet and few warning signs. Your fate rests with your driver's road skills. Drivers range from excellent to downright dangerous. Assess the state of your driver and his judgement calls – if he's going too fast or taking unnecessary risks, tell him to slow down and get his act together. If he looks sleepy, keep him awake – or rearrange the itinerary so you stay in the nearest hotel, where he can rest up. Avoid driving at night.

You are bound to experience some pretty close calls in Tibet. One Landcruiser hit a flock of sheep – resulting in a smashed front windshield (the passengers were all right – the incensed shepherd had to be compensated, and the group continued, albeit a bit frozen with the windshield missing). Another tour group in a Landcruiser rounded a corner near a high pass and clipped an oncoming truck in a Chinese military convoy. The drivers got out to argue. Meanwhile, another truck in the same convoy came round the corner and hit the Landcruiser again. More arguments broke out. And then a third truck hit the Landcruiser – this time moving it closer to the edge of a precipice, at which point the passengers scattered. In another situation, our driver played chicken with a military convoy, doing daredevil overtakes on mountain roads with sheer drop-offs. After overtaking all the trucks, the driver called for a pit-stop – at which time all the army trucks overtook us again.

You most likely don't want to even think about this, but you have to consider what would happen if there was an accident. The biggest problem could be loss of blood. It's not known to what degree hospitals in China or Tibet screen their blood – tainted blood carries all kinds of viruses, including those for hepatitis and HIV. Then there's the question of whether your blood type will even be stocked. Blood Type O is rare. The Chinese neither have nor store Rh-negative blood for transfusions: you'd have to be evacuated to the nearest Rh-negative country.

Dogs, curs, mongrels, hounds

Tibetans are fond of dogs: these hounds perform guard duties in many villages around Tibet. Dogs are believed to be reincarnates of renegade monks who didn't quite make the grade, and hence are accepted as guard dogs at monasteries. Some are in good shape; others are mangy and fleabitten. Sometimes dogs operate in packs around monasteries, in which case they can be benign (lazing around, or curled up in corners) or they can be extremely dangerous. Travellers have been attacked and dragged to the ground in some places, and then rescued by monks. This can lead to lacerations requiring stitches – not a pleasant thought.

If a bite from a dog punctures the skin, it can lead to a far greater problem: rabies. If bitten, scratched or licked over an open wound by a dog, clean the wound thoroughly with soap and water. The incubation period for rabies is variable, depending on where the victim is bitten. If the victim is not given rabies shots within a certain time, then the result is fatal. Dogs are known to carry rabies in Tibet and rabies is endemic in most parts of Nepal, where rabid street dogs are a cause for concern. To be on the safe side, if a dog draws blood, you have to get a course of rabies shots as soon as possible. You can get rabies vaccine at the People's Hospital in Lhasa, and also at clinics in Kathmandu (though there may be a shortage of the vaccine). If you are sensible you will obtain pre-exposure vaccinations before you go. Three injections are ideally given over a four-week period, but if time is short then even one injection is better than nothing. Each will cost around £40/$US60, but do shop around – prices vary. Having at least two pre-exposure vaccinations will reduce the number of post-exposure shots required should you be bitten, and, more importantly, will obviate the need for rabies immunoglobulin (RIG). This product is scarce and very expensive (about US$800 a shot).

The best strategy here is not to get bitten in the first place. Treat all dogs with extreme caution: carry a stick, or an umbrella, or pick up a stone if a dog approaches. If a dog attacks, try and clobber it on the sensitive snout area. You might also consider squirting a water bottle at a dog or using pepper spray.

Intestinal bugs

If diarrhoea is persistent, with blood or mucus in the stool, this indicates a more serious illness such as amoebic or bacillary dysentery. In this case, you need a stool test to identify the culprit – merely guessing and indulging in 'drug cocktails' may be detrimental. Facilities to identify bugs like this are not available in Lhasa; the nearest place is a Western-run clinic in Kathmandu (Ciwek clinic, see page 79). From Chengdu, the closest reliable medical testing facilities are found in Bangkok, Singapore and Hong Kong. For bacillary dysentery (recognised by blood or mucus in the stools, which may be accompanied by a fever), the best treatment is to take Ciprofloxacin (500mg tablet repeated 6–12 hours later) or Norfloxacin. More of a problem is giardia, caused by a microscopic parasite that can elude some water filters (iodine kills it). Giardia-like symptoms include stomach cramps, sulphurous burps or gas, and persistent diarrhoea: it's like something is bubbling away down there. You can treat it with tinidazole (another drug is metronidazole, also known as Flagyl, though this is not as good and has more side effects). Hepatitis is a viral infection of the liver, primarily spread through contaminated food and water (hepatitis A), or dirty needles (hepatitis B). Since both types are prevalent in Nepal and Tibet and prevention is better than cure, obtain vaccinations prior to travel. At the very least have one shot of either Havrix Monodose or Avaxim (for hepatitis A). This will last for a year when a booster dose can be given to extend coverage for ten years. Protection for hepatitis B (Engerix B) consists of three shots over a four-week period. You can now do both at once (again three shots over four weeks) by using Twinrix.

Various types of intestinal worms are also prevalent in Nepal – the larvae are often present in unwashed vegetables or undercooked meat. Intestinal worms are awful to contemplate, but not of great concern since drugs like mebendazole are highly effective in killing them. Stool tests can detect the culprits.

Acute exposure

It can get *very* cold overnight in Tibet – and if you happen to be in the back of a truck, you may get frozen solid. Silk articles, favoured by Western skiers, are especially useful for countering the cold – they're light and pack easily (balaclavas, long-johns, T-shirts, scarves, gloves). Wool and polypropylene clothing also insulates well. A woollen tuke or similar headgear will go a long way toward countering the cold. A dangerous condition, caused by rapid heat loss, is hypothermia: this is brought about by physical exhaustion when cold and wet. Symptoms include uncontrolled shivering. Shelter is the most important thing here: strip off wet clothing and replace with dry. In severe cases, the person should be stripped and placed in a sleeping bag with another person to share body heat. Do not rub affected limbs.

Frostbite is the most extreme result of rapid body-heat loss. It affects the tips of the extremities first – toes, fingers and nose. In these areas the blood freezes, preventing circulation as ice crystals expand in the cells. Again it is essential to find shelter, and immerse the affected part in lukewarm water if available. Surface frostbite can be thawed with another person's body heat – do not rub the affected part. Snow blindness results when bright sun reflected off snow (or ice or water surfaces) burns the cornea of the eye. The eyes feel like there is grit in them, appear bloodshot, and eyelids may puff up and swell shut. The condition is alarming but temporary – rest and soothe the eyes with cold compresses or eyedrops, and the condition should clear up in a few days. Wearing glacier glasses with total UV block is the way to prevent this condition.

Altitude sickness

When Sherpas say climbing is in their blood, they may mean it literally. Sherpas have a physiology adapted to the high-altitude environment – their blood has a higher red-cell count, and their lung capacity is larger. Ability to adapt to altitude is thought to be in your genes. That may mean you either have the high-altitude genes or you don't. If you do, you can adapt quickly; if you don't, it will take longer – or so the theory goes. At higher altitudes, air pressure is lower, and the air is thinner. Although it contains the same percentage of oxygen as it does at sea level, there's less oxygen delivered in each lungful of air. So you have to breathe harder, and your body has to convert to more red blood cells to carry the oxygen through the system.

Altitude sickness is something of a mystery. It does not appear to depend on being in shape: athletes have come down with it, and it may occur in subjects who have not experienced it before. Altitude sickness can occur at elevations above 2,000m, and about 50% of people will experience some symptoms at 3,500m. The higher you go the more pronounced the symptoms could become. So adjustment is required at each 400m of elevation gain after that.

Terrain above 5,000m (common enough in Tibet) is a harsh, alien environment – above 6,000m is a zone where humans were never meant to go. Like diving at depth, going to high altitudes requires special adjustments. To adapt, you have to be in tune with your body. You need to travel with someone who can monitor your condition – and back you up (get you out) if something should go wrong. Consider this: if you were to be transported in a hot-air balloon and dropped on the summit of Everest, without oxygen you would collapse within 10 minutes, and die within an hour. However, a handful of climbers have summited Everest without oxygen: by attaining a degree of acclimatisation, they have been able to achieve this. A similar analogy could be drawn with flying in from Chengdu, which is barely above sea level, to Lhasa, at 3,650m. That's a 3,500m gain in an hour or so. You need to rest and recover. Coming by land from Kathmandu, you rise from 1,300m up over a 5,200m pass at Tong La – a gain of 4,000m over a few days (to soften the blow, it would be worth staying a few days at Nyalam, which is 3,750m).

The study of altitude sickness is still evolving. Recent studies suggest that altitude sickness may be due to leaky membranes – which are more permeable as you go up in elevation. It was unknown if a person could survive above 7,500m without oxygen until 1978, when Messner and Habeler summited Everest. Actually, a hundred years earlier, in 1875, French balloonist Tissandier reached 8,000m after a three-hour ascent and lost consciousness: the balloon descended and Tissandier survived but his two companions died. Messner was told he would come back from Everest a raving madman, or, at the very least, a brain-damaged automaton if he attempted the peak without oxygen. Messner got his timing right, got to the top, and went on to bag all the 8,000m peaks without oxygen. Climbers like Messner, however, will admit to impaired functions at higher elevations – and to strange encounters. Messner recalls talking to his ice axe, talking to his feet, talking to an imaginary companion and having hallucinations.

Altitude strategy

It is essential to take it easy for the first three or four days after arriving at altitude; most acclimatisation takes place within the first ten days (it can take two or three months to fully acclimatise). When reaching altitude, most travellers experience discomfort – headaches, fatigue, nausea, vomiting, lack of appetite, swelling of the hands or feet, difficulty sleeping. This condition is usually mild and short-lived. Headaches can be treated with aspirin: if a headache persists, or intensifies – or if the person wakes up with a headache – this is a sign of real altitude sickness. The critical question is how to distinguish between mild altitude sickness and more serious cases – read on. You don't acclimatise by sitting around doing nothing – get some simple exercise like walking, and drink lots of water. Do not drink alcohol, as it contributes to dehydration. Smoking, of course, will be a major problem at altitude.

Never underestimate altitude – it can be a killer. Go slow, be careful, experiment before you go higher. The climber's maxim is 'walk high, sleep low' – climbers may trek higher during the day, but retire to lower levels to sleep. The maximum rate of ascent when trekking should be about 400m a day. If you're acclimatised to Lhasa (3,650m) you really need to undergo a second acclimatisation phase to handle a visit to Lake Namtso (at 4,650m). On a brighter note, once you've acclimatised to a particular altitude, the altered blood-chemistry should stay with you for about ten days. So if you acclimatise to the 5,000m level and then go down to 3,500m, you should be able to go back up to 5,000m again without ill effects, provided you do so within ten days.

HIGH-ALTITUDE DRUGS

This text comes with a few caveats. Mainly, that there are a lot of unknowns when it comes to altitude sickness. What works for one person may not work for another. The only guaranteed cure for altitude sickness is immediate descent to lower elevations and administration of oxygen to the patient. Drugs can reduce symptoms of altitude sickness, but may also mask symptoms: the taking of these drugs should never be used to avoid descent or to enable further ascent.

Herbal drugs

Dr Stephen Bezruchka, in his book *Altitude Illness: Prevention and Treatment* (Mountaineers Books, 2001), says: 'The herb, Ginkgo biloba, 80mg to 120mg twice a day, beginning five days before ascent and continued a day at altitude, appears to prevent AMS. It interferes with platelet activity in the blood, so its safety for those taking other drugs that have such effects is unknown. It also improves blood circulation to the hands in the cold. Its role at altitude remains to be clarified, but it has few side effects and should be considered.'

Chinese visitors to Tibet use a variety of traditional herbal medicines to counter the effect of altitude. These include small vials of liquid concocted from the Tibetan *Radix rhodiolae* plant, which grows on the plateau at elevations of 3,500 to 5,000m. It is called 'plateau ginseng' and according to Chinese sources, research has shown it efficacious for high blood pressure, high blood fat, diabetes, senility, and 'internet addiction'. In any case, it

Acute mountain sickness

Acute mountain sickness (AMS) is a general term for a whole raft of altitude-related maladies. Symptoms of AMS include gastrointestinal turmoil (loss of appetite, nausea, vomiting), extreme fatigue or weakness, dizziness or light-headedness, and difficulty breathing or sleeping.

A case of severe AMS may result in high-altitude pulmonary edema (HAPE), when a small amount of fluid that appears in the lungs at altitude is not absorbed normally. Instead, it accumulates, obstructing the flow of oxygen and drowning the victim in his or her own fluids. Symptoms include rapid respiratory rate and rapid pulse, cough, crackles or wheezing in one or both lungs, frothy or bloodstained sputum, and severe shortness of breath. Another serious complication is high-altitude cerebral edema (HACE), where the fluid problem is in the brain. A person with HACE is disoriented, has an unsteady gait and trouble using the hands, is irritable, suffers from drowsiness and nightmares, and may suffer hallucinations. Memory, judgement and perception are impaired.

To counter HAPE and HACE, mountaineering expeditions sometimes tote a Gamow bag, which weighs about 8 kilograms. It is a body-enclosing bag that can be hand-pumped to replicate atmospheric pressure at much lower levels. Recent studies suggest that a one-hour treatment corresponds to a descent of 1,500 metres: this leads to short-term improvements, but nothing lasting. Some group tour operators carry a tank of oxygen to deal with cases – but that tank may only hold 30 minutes of oxygen (Landcruiser drivers sometimes carry oxygen). Drugs like Diamox are also used to counter the effects of altitude. The best solution, however, in all cases, is simply to transport the patient to a lower elevation – as fast as possible (if this means moving in the middle of the night, do so). Unfortunately, on the appears to improve blood flow, which is good at altitude.

Available in Lhasa is a kind of high-altitude tea. Similar to *maté de coca* (the Andean remedy, from coca leaves), this tea is said to relieve headaches, insomnia, nausea and dizziness brought about by altitude. The tea is called Gaoyuanan, and is made in Tibet. You can buy a box of sachets in Lhasa at several of the hotels, or at Dunya Restaurant.

Diamox

Diamox (acetazolamide) is a diuretic that can help alleviate the symptoms of altitude sickness. It does not prevent you getting altitude sickness, nor does it solve the problem, but it may ease your passage when, say, arriving in Lhasa by air, or when going up and over and down a pass within the same day. It may also improve the quality of sleep at altitude. Since it's a diuretic, it leads to increased urination and to dehydration, so you need to keep drinking more if you use it. Other side effects include a tingling sensation in the lips and fingertips, and the medication may give a strange taste to carbonated drinks. You don't have to follow the dosage – the normal dosage is 250mg every 12 hours, but you could take half the recommended dosage (cut the tablets in half). If a person comes down with AMS, the dosage can be increased slightly to 250mg every six hours. With no alternative drugs for altitude sickness, it might be worth carrying Diamox along. However, its use is controversial, and it's a sulphur drug, which some have allergies to. Check with your doctor.

Tibetan plateau, descent to lower elevation is not always feasible. In serious cases, the focus is often evacuation by road to Kathmandu, or by air to either Kathmandu or Chengdu.

Chinese medical facilities

Chinese hospitals are appalling in China generally, and completely primitive in Tibet. Avoid hospitals like the plague: you would do a lot better by taking a good hotel room instead. I have personally seen, in Tibetan clinics, rusting antiquated equipment, and filthy wards and operating theatres (and filthy doctors – I sighted one doctor greeting patients wearing a blood-spattered apron and smoking a cigarette). There's a shortage of sterile equipment and supplies; the most basic facilities for diagnosis and treatment are generally absent; doctors and nurses are poorly trained. Surgical gloves may be washed and re-used – and the same with syringes. A disturbing trend in some hospitals in Tibet is to subject the patient to a cardiogram, an X-ray and a glucose drip – regardless of what illness is presented – and then charge for these services. A person suffering from altitude sickness doesn't need an X-ray.

In Lhasa, the best facilities are at the Military Hospital, but this place is not usually accessible to tourists. The People's Hospital has an emergency centre, but no mechanism for dealing with seriously injured people. An Italian NGO has been supplying equipment and training at the People's Hospital. Costs for foreigners staying at the People's Hospital in Lhasa can be very high, and payment may be expected in Chinese cash (travellers' cheques will probably not be accepted, and nor will credit cards).

The nearest places in China for good medical attention are Chengdu (a hospital can run to US$120 a day for foreigners), Hong Kong (even more expensive), and in major cities like Beijing and Shanghai. Elsewhere in Asia, any place that has a lot of foreign embassies is good for clinics and hospitals with Western standards, often staffed by Western doctors. The best are found in Singapore, Nepal (the Ciwek clinic – see page 79) and Bangkok. See also *Medical services* in Lhasa, page 114.

Medevac crews

International SOS is a Singapore-based medevac organisation which comes under the umbrella of parent company Asia Emergency Assistance (AEA). International SOS will evacuate to Hong Kong or Singapore if possible; there are branch offices in Beijing, Shanghai, Guangzhou and other locations in the PRC. Check their www.internationalsos.com website for contact numbers. Their head office is at International SOS, 331 North Bridge Rd, #17-00 Odeon Towers, Singapore; tel: 65 6338 2311; alarm centre tel: 65 6338 7800; fax 65 6338 7611; email: corpcomm@internationalsos.com. The Hong Kong office is International SOS, 16F World Trade Centre, 280 Gloucester Rd, Causeway Bay; tel: 852 2528 9998; alarm tel: 852 2528 9900; alarm fax: 852 2528 9933. Another emergency medical assistance firm is MEDEX, whose packages are more economical for long-term travellers. See their www.medexassist.com website for details: there are regional offices located in Beijing, Hong Kong, Singapore, Thailand, the Philippines and Japan. AEA has been able to fly a Lear Jet from Hong Kong into Lhasa for an evacuation, but the procedure is extremely complicated and costly.

Risky situations and evacuation

The best advice that can be offered in risky medical situations in Tibet is this: when in doubt, evacuate. Get on a regular scheduled flight to Kathmandu or Chengdu (an alternative is to take a Landcruiser down to Nepal, but this could take three days or more). If the patient can be brought to Gongkar Airport without too much trauma, then you can organise the evacuation yourself. When sufficiently pressured, airline authorities will bump passengers off a regular flight to Chengdu or Kathmandu to create space for an emergency case, so the idea is to get to Gongkar Airport as fast as possible.

Although helicopter evacuation is employed for injured trekkers in Nepal, it is simply not an option in Tibet. Although the Chinese military have Sikorsky and Boeing CH-47 high-altitude choppers, these are strictly for military applications and under no circumstances will be diverted for civilian use. The elevation limit for conventional helicopters is 6,000m, so only the high-altitude choppers would work in a situation like this. If the condition of the patient is not so critical, and there is leeway of a few days to transport, then another option is use of a Landcruiser as an ambulance – getting the patient down to Kathmandu as fast as possible.

If it's a case of altitude sickness, it's essential to get oxygen for the patient as fast as possible. Lhasa Hotel has oxygen 'pillows' (pillows with nasal tubes attached); you can also buy oxygen in a sort of aerosol can (or larger tank) in Lhasa itself at a commercial outlet just west of the Potala.

The above evacuation advice is offered because (a) medical facilities in Tibet are completely primitive; (b) there is no system of helicopter rescue in Tibet; and (c) the Chinese don't give a fig about sick or dying tourists anyway.

If you think that last statement is unfair, then allow me to present the following macabre case, the details of which have been verified by the Western tour operator. In 1987, an elderly tourist on a group tour to Tibet died of a massive heart attack in his sleep. It was just a few days into the tour; his wife (back in North America) was phoned to inform her, and was asked what should be done. She requested that her husband be cremated, and that the ashes be brought back with the tour. The cremation was promptly carried out – and the ashes were transported around in the group leader's carry bag, in a small jar-like urn with a sealed top. Some time later, the dead man's wife requested a refund for the trip from the tour operator, who duly contacted CITS in China. CITS informed the operator that the wife did not qualify for a refund, because her husband had indeed completed the tour – posthumously, in the urn. Logical Chinese thinking at its best.

Worst-case scenarios

Several foreigners who have died in Tibet could have been saved by evacuation. In 1991 a British tourist died from altitude sickness after being admitted to the People's Hospital. Repeated requests by a Western doctor to evacuate him were overruled by the senior medical staff at the hospital, who claimed the patient would recover. An American tourist who visited the patient said that when she checked his oxygen tank, it was empty and he was gasping for air. There seemed to be no sense of emergency on the part of the nurses. The following year, a Swiss woman with a similar altitude problem was evacuated from Lhasa by a team sent to collect the patient at the insistence of the Swiss Embassy. Again, Chinese medical opinion held that her case was not serious. Due to evacuation, she survived. Moral of the story: don't trust the opinion of unconcerned Chinese medical staff.

In another case, a young backpacker in the rear of a truck was sleeping with his arms and elbows resting on the edge, where the tarpaulin meets the metal compartment. Somehow the truck was sideswiped by an oncoming truck – the impact smashed one arm and ripped the other right out of its socket. Quick action by fellow travellers saved his life. The missing arm was found on the highway, and the truck raced back to Lhasa – fortunately, a fellow traveller with some medical knowledge managed to stem the flow of blood on key arteries for the 12-hour ride. The backpacker was then airlifted to Chengdu and on to Europe. He lost the arm. He was very lucky – he could easily have died through blood loss. Good medical insurance covered the air and hospitalisation bills.

SAFETY AND SECURITY

As with any Third World travel situation, you need to keep your wits about you in Tibet. Theft of luggage is uncommon on the plateau, but it does happen. Ditto with rented bicycles -- lock yours in a secure, highly visible site. Luggage has even gone missing from some budget hotel storage rooms in Lhasa: to reduce the risk of this happening, identify your baggage with your passport number prominently displayed on an attached label. Keep an eye on your bags when on the move. Pilfering of personal items is known to be risky when trekking in some areas, particularly the Everest region.

Because of the heavy Chinese military presence in Tibet, armed robbery or crimes like this are extremely rare, though in old Tibet banditry certainly existed in remoter areas. A greater threat to life and limb is on Landcruiser sorties and through resulting confrontations that may develop on these trips. Apart from the major health hazard it presents, high altitude is known to befuddle the brain, making you irritable and unable to focus when making decisions or when judgement is required. And there are important decisions that need to be made: for example, to size up quickly those on whom your life depends. That means that, if a Landcruiser or taxi driver refuses to slow down and keeps overtaking recklessly, you may have to bail out.

Confrontations between Landcruiser drivers, guides and passengers over changes of itinerary or other problems can turn ugly. Incidents have involved both

Tibetan and Chinese driving crews. In the Everest region, when a Landcruiser driver and his guide (both Tibetan) refused to drive beyond Rongbuk Gompa for the extra dozen kilometres to Everest base camp, a passenger swore at the guide. The guide picked up a rock and hurled it at the passenger. The rock missed, but the passenger was in a state of shock that he would even attempt such a thing. Disagreements between passengers themselves can also turn nasty. Other arguments may erupt over permits and permission with Chinese authorities, who are not noted for their politeness. In all of these situations, mediation skills are called for: stay cool, be patient, be polite yet insistent, and keep your temper to yourself.

Women travellers

Although Tibetan Buddhism promotes a code of respect, there have been cases of harassment of Western women by Tibetan men, especially on crowded buses and when hitching rides in trucks. Tibetan women dress modestly, with little flesh exposed, and that may be the key here: a Western woman wearing shorts and a revealing top may send out the wrong message, and is bound to attract the wrong kind of attention. For these reasons, travelling solo in Tibet is not advisable for a woman. However, a woman who speaks enough Tibetan – and who dresses modestly – should not have a problem. Chinese men and Chinese military appear to have little interest in sexual advances to Western women, perhaps due to the phenomenon of numerous Chinese prostitutes plying their trade at karaoke bars in the larger towns of Tibet.

Part Two

The Guide

Tsongkhapa

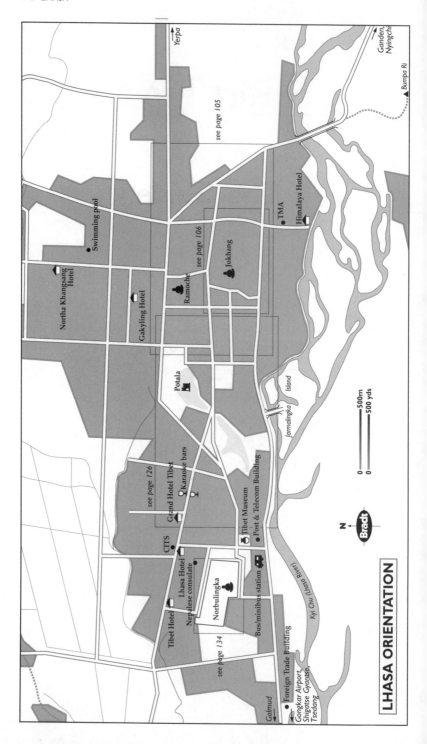

LHASA ORIENTATION

Lhasa

SECRETS OF THE CITY

The name Lhasa is thought to derive from the Tibetan words *Lha* (Sacred) and *Sa* (Earth). In the late 19th and early 20th centuries, Lhasa was the most reclusive city on the face of the planet – a sacred place that was as difficult a goal as Mecca to reach. Even the greatest Western explorers of the era – Nikolai Prejavalsky, Sven Hedin – failed to make it.

Now this shroud of secrecy has been ripped away ... to reveal ... a humdrum Chinese town. Lhasa is one large Chinatown now, with rows and rows of faceless Chinese apartment blocks and government buildings. 'It's just another Chinese city with a few Tibetans thrown in for colour,' says a Tibetan-born American visitor. The most disturbing aspect of Lhasa is not only the overwhelming Chinese presence: it is the Tibetan absence. The Tibetans are a minority in their own capital, with perhaps 60,000 Tibetans out of a population estimated at 180,000 (the real figure could be much higher – possibly 400,000). A sizeable contingent of the Chinese population is an occupation force: military, para-military, police and bureaucrats.

If you are disappointed with Lhasa, or feel cheated of the mystique you had expected, you won't be the first. The eccentric English traveller Thomas Manning tried to forge a route through to Peking, and by chance reached Lhasa in 1812, disguised as a Chinese physician. He found the Potala extraordinary, and the rest of the place a dump. Here's his description of Old Lhasa, one of the first 'snapshots' of the Potala ever recorded by a Westerner:

> The road here, as it winds past the palace, is royally broad; it is level and free from stones, and combined with the view of the lofty towering palace, which forms a majestic mountain of a building, has a magnificent effect. The roads about the palace swarmed with monks; its nooks and angles with beggars lounging and basking in the sun.... As a whole [the Potala] seemed perfect enough; but I could not comprehend its plan in detail.... If the palace exceeded my expectations, the town as far fell short of them. There is nothing striking, nothing pleasing in its appearance. The habitations are begrimed with smut and dirt; the avenues are full of dogs...

Manning not only managed to get to Lhasa, he also garnered an unprecedented audience with the seven-year-old Dalai Lama (IX), which he recorded as a moving experience. Almost a century later, in 1904, the invading English under Younghusband found their triumphal march into Lhasa impeded by piles of refuse, stagnant pools of water, open sewers, and various rabid animals foraging for putrid scraps of food. They did, however, note that the gleaming gold roofs of the Jokhang and other temples restored the balance in favour of the majestic.

Lhasa was never a big city. There was no census taken in the Lhasa of 1949 or earlier, but the population was estimated at 30,000. There were an additional 7,000 monks at Sera Monastery, and 9,000 monks at Drepung. This brought the figure to around 45,000, and probably double that number would be in Lhasa during festivals. Lhasa's design was based not so much on practical as sacred aspects. In the 7th century, King Songtsen Gampo moved his capital from the Yarlung Valley to the site of Lhasa. Later, as the residence of the Dalai Lamas, Lhasa became the religious centre of Tibet, and the seat of government. Lhasa was (and is) dominated by the Potala Palace, the winter residence of the Dalai Lama, with his summer palace, the Norbulingka, below. Within the front, walled section of the Potala was the entire Tibetan government administration, where the nobles lived – these buildings have now largely disappeared. Across town, separated by meadows, was the Jokhang Temple with a market and artisan section. A third edifice was the Palace of the Regent – the man who ruled in times when the Dalai Lama was not of age.

Old Lhasa disappeared with the Chinese invasion of Tibet in 1950 and with the flight of the Dalai Lama to India in 1959. Transformation was swift: few of those Tibetans who fled in 1959 would have recognised Lhasa in 1964, when pro-Chinese writer Israel Epstein said:

> Lhasa is becoming a beautiful modern city. Not long ago, the Potala, the temples and a few mansions stood amid hovels and cesspools of medieval squalor. Now there are miles of well lit, asphalted streets and underground drains... Electricity is supplied to 90 per cent of all homes for illumination and often for cooking (ex-serfs and slaves get it free). A working people's Cultural Palace and a hall seating twelve hundred is used for meetings, plays and films; there are also two other film theatres. A State Emporium built this year, the biggest of many new shops and stores, sells everything from needles and thread to sewing machines, bicycles and transistor radios...

Picture this process accelerated over the next 40-odd years, and you get an idea of what's occurred in Lhasa. A Tibetan resident commented that Lhasa had changed more in the 1990s than it had over the last few hundred years. The urban area of Lhasa has rapidly expanded, with many new Chinese-built apartment buildings and offices. An industrial fringe has also cropped up, with a concrete factory and a brewery in northern Lhasa.

While technological change is a positive thing, the fact is that in Lhasa these changes have not been in the interest of the Tibetans – they're for the Chinese. The Tibetans 'still preferred independence to electricity, and freedom to sewers', as French explorer and writer, Michel Peissel, put it. The Chinese settlers demand electricity and street lighting, Chinese soldiers need roads, and Chinese officials need cultural palaces, and girlie bars and karaoke salons with their glitter and neon. Rows of barbershops near the Potala do a brisk business late at night. Why? Because they are fronts for prostitution – one of Lhasa's dirty secrets. Holy city or whorehouse? For Tibetan pilgrims, Lhasa remains the Holy City, but to even the casual visitor, the Chinese layering of scores of bars and karaoke salons is glaring. And that's not to mention the heavy Chinese military and para-military presence, with army bases ringing the city, and a network of prisons. The end result is that Lhasa has become increasingly sinicized. You see it in small details, like the statuary around the city – pairs of Chinese lions outside the entrance to the Potala, a Chinese dragon sculpture in the fountain in Potala Square, a concrete statue of Chinese mountaineers atop Everest, Chinese flags flying at strategic points, and – at night – glowing Chinese neon signs.

LHASA GOES HIGH-RISE

When you picture Lhasa, you may not conjure up a metropolis of high-rises and soaring telecom towers, but this is the way Lhasa is going: upward. Previously, the only building that approached a skyscraper was the Potala (which gets most of its height from the hill it sits on). It is still the tallest place in town, but only because of the hill. Back in 1990, the tallest structure in the Lhasa Valley was a wing of the Holiday Inn, reaching a height of seven floors. It has an elevator – the only one in Tibet at the time and an object of great curiosity among Tibetans. But now there are lots of elevators in Lhasa, and they ride much higher. The Tibet Foreign Trade and Economic Cooperation Building, to the west side of Lhasa near the Kyi Chu river, takes the skyscraper prize with 17 floors, shimmering with a green-tinted glass facade. The China Telecom building rises ten floors, and the Post and Telecom Trade Building reaches eleven floors. And builders have completed a 13-storey eyesore on the Sera Road—it's a police office tower. Tibetan-style buildings were rarely built higher than four floors, so it is startling to see modern interpretations that exceed that height. Daji Hotel, built in neo-Tibetan style, is five floors high, and there's an eight-storey Tibetan-style building opposite the Xiong Bala Hotel.

To make Lhasa more attractive to coastal entrepreneurs (who, according to the Chinese 'go to Tibet to offer their expertise to help develop the local economy') some anomalies have popped up. Chinese office blocks are going up around the town; for the first time in its long history, Lhasa is seeing traffic jams, caused by the importation of taxis. Chinese taxi-drivers can earn up to five times as much in Lhasa as they can in other cities; other incentives for Chinese immigrants include preferential tax and loan policies. Keeping track of investments is the Tibet Stocks Business Centre, which has a satellite feed listing prices on China's stock exchanges in Shenzhen and Shanghai. Keeping Chinese residents comfortable requires improved communications – satellite reception is provided by Lhasa's Xizang TV station, constructed in the early 1990s.

TRANSPORTATION AND PERMITS
Getting there and away

Getting to Lhasa is practically synonymous with getting to Tibet, since Lhasa is the main transport hub: all flights and overland travel are routed through the capital. Consult the route descriptions in the *Practical Information* chapter for details on the intricacies of long-distance travel to Tibet (Lhasa) by road or by air.

Getting out of Lhasa is considerably easier than entering because permits are less of a problem. Possibilities by road include the deathly-boring bus to Golmud, and the riveting Landcruiser journey to Zhangmu (and on to Kathmandu). Direct Landcruiser runs to Zhangmu (pure getting there, no sightseeing stops) are cheaper. See the *Lhasa to Kathmandu Route* chapter for road-trip strategies.

While you can't buy a China Southwest Airlines (CSWA) ticket yourself when flying into Tibet, you most certainly can buy one in person when flying out. Tickets to Chengdu, Zhongdian, Kunming, Beijing or Kathmandu, though they can be booked ahead, are generally not handed out until two days before the actual flight (sometimes you can get them a week in advance). Due to computer glitches, some flights get overbooked – be prepared for delays. You can make bookings and pick up tickets at the Civil Aviation Administration of China (CAAC) office downtown; tel: 633 3446. There's a smaller office in the basement of Tibet Hotel (out past Lhasa Hotel) called TibetAir Travel Service; tel: 632 2567. CAAC arranges its own bus to the airport for Y25 a person. Inquire about departure times, and buy the ticket the day before. Otherwise club together and arrange a Landcruiser or a taxi to pick you up at your hotel for the one-hour run to Gongkar. Another option is to take a bus out to Gongkar the afternoon before your flight and overnight in Gongkar.

Getting around Lhasa

Lhasa is a small town. It's easy to navigate by prominent landmarks like the Potala or the TV tower atop Chakpori Hill. Key roundabouts are conveniently identified by statuary – Golden Yak statue, Golden Archer statue, Mountaineers-on-Everest statue. You could call them the 'Golden Yak roundabout' or the 'Mountaineers-on-Everest roundabout.' Although a local minibus system exists, most travellers don't bother with it unless heading out to, say, Drepung Monastery or Sera Monastery. Inquire at your hotel about which bus to take for a longer journey. You can mostly walk or bicycle around town.

Foot-powered bicycle-taxis rove the streets – they seat two up front. Regular VW cabs (imported from east China) cruise the streets and are easy to flag down. They don't have meters – you usually pay a flat rate of Y10 for any distance, but if your destination is a long way out, it may be Y15. You can also hire taxis by the hour, or by the half-day or full-day for touring, which makes sense if you have three or four people.

Bicycling is an excellent way of getting around Lhasa – since the town is mostly flat, you can go a long way on a gearless Chinese roadster. Chinese bicycles can be hired from the Banakshol, Snowland or Pentoc hotels (the Pentoc also has a few mountain-bikes). There are some bicycle rental operators on the street along Tengyeling Road. Hotels generally prefer bikes to be reserved for use by their own guests, and usually require a hefty deposit. Snowland Hotel, for example, charges Y30 a day for rental plus Y400 deposit. Rental bicycles are often in poor condition – before renting, check that at least one of the brakes works, and that both wheels actually go round. Bike theft can be a problem – make sure you lock yours when you stop, or better yet, leave it in the care of a shopkeeper at your destination. If staying longer in Lhasa, consider buying a Chinese-made mountain-bike from a department store – you can buy one for only Y340 with gears, fat tyres, the works. However, they have plastic pedals and some weak components. A problem for Westerners is that the seatpost is usually too short, so if you're tall, customise it by changing to a longer seatpost. For Y550 you can buy a mountain bike with front and back suspension. A good accessory is a battery-powered bicycle bell with six different warning tones that you can set.

Getting around Tibet
Buses and minibuses
At the crack of dawn (around 06.30) minibuses patrol the streets near the Yak Hotel looking for passengers for Shigatse, Samye or Nagqu. Sometimes they're parked in the alley toward the Ramoche Temple. Also at the crack of dawn are pilgrim bus departures from the west side of Barkor Square, heading for Ganden (and less frequently to Tsurphu or Drigung). For Gongkar Airport, there are departures by CAAC's own bus, leaving early in the morning from the CAAC office downtown (other buses may depart later – inquire).

Minibuses also congregate in the vicinity just south of the Norbulingka. Around the corner from this is Lhasa's main bus and minibus station, with a large board listing places all over the map, but you may have trouble buying tickets to many towns. Destinations they will sell tickets for include Tsedang, Shigatse and Damxung. Foreigners have been able to buy tickets to Golmud without problems. Others have got around refusal to sell tickets by ambushing the bus on its way out of town (the fare goes in the driver's pocket). One foreigner managed to hop on a bus to Chengdu – a trip of about two weeks. This Lhasa-Chengdu direct epic trip is not exactly legal for foreigners, but if you don't mind a bit of round-about routing, there is another epic sleeper-bus ride that apparently goes from Lhasa to Xining, and then from Xining down to Chengdu. This routing would be legal for a foreigner as long as the visa is valid long enough to complete the bus-ride.

Landcruiser travel and agencies

There are a number of agencies – large and small – that operate Landcruiser trips out of Lhasa, hired by the half-day, by the day, for several days, by the week, and even by the month. However, since late 2000, most travellers have been channelled into the Foreign Independent Traveller (FIT) travel agents at the Snowland and Banakshol hotels. These rip-off merchants are both run by the Tibet Tourism Bureau (Chinese government) and constitute a monopoly. If you get a plane ticket from Chengdu to Lhasa with a package, that package designates which travel agent you must deal with in Lhasa. It is invariably Snowland FIT or Banakshol FIT. The FIT agents are out to make money – their pricing is well above other Lhasa agents, and the quality of service is not good.

Here are some examples: Snowland FIT wants an outrageous Y3000 (US$370) for a two-day Landcruiser trip from Lhasa to Samye. If you did the same thing yourself by taxi, it would cost Y400 (return), because once you get to the ferry crossing at Samye, the Landcruiser driver sits on the south bank waiting for you to return. And Snowland FIT is asking Y1,200 for a one-day Landcruiser trip just to Ganden monastery (take the bus for a few yuan and you can do the same trip). When asked about the Ganden to Samye trek (normally five days on foot), Snowland FIT quoted Y5,800 (US$710) for a group of five people, which was then bargained down to Y4,800, and it was then revealed that this staggering amount of money did not include food or cook, nor porter, nor yaks. What did it include? It included a driver to staging-points, and guide and permits. In a place where Y1,000 is the average monthly salary, and Y3,000 a month is considered a high-end managerial salary, that's quite a wad of money to pay someone who's on foot, though presumably most of the money goes into other deep pockets somewhere. Snowland FIT tells you that their rates are set by the government, but if you're not happy, go and talk to Banakshol FIT (which is the same TTB-controlled company!).

Your options here are not great, because other agencies in Lhasa won't touch the FIT-agent clients for fear of having their licences revoked. When other agents apply for permits, the paperwork could be rejected because PSB would notice that you are meant to be with FIT. However, there are ways of getting past the insidious TTB/FIT monopoly. First, for the Lhasa Prefecture area, no guide or permits are required. That means you can go with another operator for this region (encompassing Lake Namtso, Drigung, Reting, Ganden). Another by-pass method is to go with a Landcruiser operator to Shigatse PSB, pick up all the permits for the Lhasa-Kathmandu route, and carry on regardless. You can find some driver-guides around Lhasa who might set off on a sortie like this.

The TTB (Tibet Tourism Bureau, aka China Tibet Tour, or Tibet Tour, or Tibet Autonomous Region Tourism Bureau) is the all-powerful force behind the FIT scam. The TTB controls the running of the tourist business in Tibet, particularly the registering of guides. Hotels that deal with foreigners invariably carry a TTB seal of approval, as do restaurants catering to big-noses, and Landcruiser drivers must carry the TTB logo (a black yak, white mountain, and 'China Tibet Tour' inscription) on the windscreen. This TTB seal of approval indicates that the agency has the licence to deal with foreigners; other Lhasa agents may deal exclusively with Chinese tourists (who far outnumber foreign visitors).

If you go with a Landcruiser group, insist on a Tibetan driver and guide, even if the outfit is Chinese-backed (which it invariably is). Your experience on the trip will be very different if your driver and guide are Tibetan – they will steer you to Tibetan restaurants and teahouses, and Tibetan-style hotels.

A number of Lhasa travel agents have offices in the hotels. At Yak Hotel, upstairs near Dunya Restaurant is Shigatse Travels, which is efficient. Higher-priced and CITS-linked are the agencies operating out of the ground floor of Lhasa Hotel; across the street is the head office of China International Travel Service (CITS), with TTC (Tibet Tourist Corporation), Tibet Adventure Travel, and Tibet/China Travel Service all coming under the CITS wing. Handling sports aficionados is TIST (Tibet International Sports Travel), operating from the grounds of the Himalaya Hotel. Close by is the TMA (Tibet Mountaineering Association) which deals with mountaineers. Golden Bridge Travel Service is run by the PLA, and Asian Dragon Travel is run by the dreaded PAP. The Catch 22 is that agencies linked to the military or CITS can arrange permits more easily than others. It is difficult to recommend a travel agent in Lhasa because (a) the trade is heavily controlled by the TTB and Chinese official management, and (b) independent operators may refuse to deal with you for fear of having their licences revoked. Here is a shortlist:

Shigatse Travels In Yak Hotel compound, 100 Beijing Donglu, Lhasa; tel: 633 0489; fax 633 0482; email: amdo@public.ls.xz.cn. Has Tibetan staff in management and can arrange a Tibetan driver and guide.

Wind Horse Adventure 1 North Minzu Lu, Lhasa; tel: 683 3009; fax: 683 6793; email: wha@public.ls.xz.cn. Specialises in higher-end, customised tours and innovative trekking, bicycling and camping trips. Has Tibetan staff in management and can arrange a Tibetan driver and guide.

Tibet FIT Travel Snowland Hotel, Lhasa; tel: 634 9239; fax: 634 3854, email: ttccits@public.ls.xz.cn is a front for the TTB, as is the FIT office at Banakshol (same company). Although they control most of the tourist trade, you cannot deal directly with TTB Lhasa. Their office has no English sign out front: it is located to the south of the Golden Yak Statues at 18 Yuanlinlu, Lhasa; tel: 683 4315; fax: 683 4632.

Chamdo International Travel Service Room 403, Gao Zheng Hotel, 77 Beijing Middle Rd; tel: 681 3564; fax 681 3584. This TTB-affiliated office may be able to assist with overland travel to east Tibet and further into Yunnan.

Tibet Nagqu International Travels In Kirey Hotel, 105 Beijing Donglu; tel: 632 8851; fax: 632 8822; email: tints@public.ls.xz.cn

Landcruiser logistics

Four-wheel-drive vehicles are the best way to go anywhere in Tibet. Toyota Landcruisers are the most common rental vehicles available in Lhasa. A superior version is the Toyota Landcruiser 4500, which has double-capacity gasoline tanks, giving it a range of perhaps 700km without refuelling. It comes with an array of fog lights and other extras, and is higher off the ground. Other 4WD vehicles sighted include the Mitsubishi Pajero and the Beijing Jeep Cherokee. In a Toyota Landcruiser you can squeeze in four passengers plus a guide and driver – that makes three in the front, three in the back. However, because of the gearstick, the front seat won't be comfortable. If you can afford it, go with only three paying passengers. In some situations you may *have* to go with only three passengers: if you all have a lot of gear the baggage weight alone will limit the vehicle to three passengers. It is sometimes possible to go with five passengers (with light luggage) – if you're going to a place like Lake Namtso, for example, you don't need a guide, since Namtso is open without permit, so that frees up the extra seat.

Landcruisers cost about Y500–1,200 (US$70–140) and upwards a day, depending on the route, the distance, the itinerary and so on. Pricing may be based on kilometres covered: calculate on Y3.5–4 per kilometre in a Landcruiser. If you go to Lake Namtso, no permits or guides are required, so the price drops, and if you stop for a day there, the vehicle is not using gasoline, which reduces costs. If you go into Everest, there's a lot of wear and tear on the vehicle, which operators don't like, so the price will rise for that itinerary. If you're making a one-way run to the Nepal border, the agency expects a return subsidy to cover cost of gasoline (even though the driver will probably pick up new passengers).

Always arrange to check the condition of the vehicle (and crew) before you put any money down. Don't pay everything up front: perhaps put half down, and pay the rest in stages as an incentive for the driver and guide to complete the trip as outlined. Make out a basic contract to confirm conditions you have agreed to verbally: include the itinerary, timing, amounts to be paid and so on. It's extremely important to be flexible with Landcruiser arrangements: you can't push your driver if a bridge is down, and you won't get much out of a driver if you back him into a corner. On a contract, put down a rate for extra days. If a delay is caused by the driver or vehicle breakdown, then the agency covers the cost; if the delay is due to illness of a passenger, the group covers the cost; if the delay is due to bad weather or road conditions, you can divide the cost between the agency and the group.

Allow extra time on the itinerary for delays. Travellers have a litany of horror stories to tell: vehicles that break down (or *disintegrate*) in transit, drivers who refuse to follow the itinerary, stroppy guides – the nightmare goes on. Others have had absolutely no problem – just a few loose kidneys at the end of the ride. A last thought on Landcruisers: make sure you get along with the others in your group – you'll be seeing a lot of them. If you spend 25 days on the road to Kailash, you'll want congenial company. Compatibility is a very important consideration for long road-trips like this.

Permits and paperwork

Getting travel permits or visa extensions is tricky in Lhasa – both depend on joining a group with a firm itinerary. You might be better off having an agency approach the relevant offices. Tibet PSB, to the east side of town, handles ATPs and travel permits. These are normally obtained through the guide on a trip, and list all passport holders on a single document (usually one sheet of paper). There are several kinds of permit – ATPs (to visit towns on route), military permits (for restricted areas and getting past military checkposts), and Cultural Bureau permits (for visiting sites of special architectural or cultural interest). While Tibet PSB will not normally issue permits to individuals who apply directly, Shigatse PSB probably will.

The TTB (Tibet Tourism Bureau), near the Golden Yak roundabout, appears to be involved with permit-issuing, but is not approachable directly. It seems that guides need to get TTB permits before they can get ATPs from the PSB for a trip (but in Shigatse, no TTB permits are required from the PSB office). Most Landcruisers in Lhasa carry a TTB sticker on the front window that says 'China Tibet Tour.'

> ## TIBET CHIC: CHINESE TOURISTS
> It's late afternoon on the rooftop of the Jokhang, and a Chinese woman with her hair braided Tibetan-style (with small chunks of turquoise in it) is on her cell-phone, chatting with relatives in Shanghai. The monks are doing a roaring trade selling drinks and lucky charms to a cluster of Chinese tourists, all happily snapping pictures of each other. Among them are some 'military tourists' – in uniform, off-duty, and carrying cameras with big lenses.
>
> These are well-heeled Chinese tourists: a trip to Tibet is not cheap. Some wear their wealth: one tourist I met came armed not only with a video camera but with two digital still cameras – he downloaded the images to his laptop and then sent them off to friends from a cybercafé in Lhasa. Tibet is a 'cool' place to go among the well-heeled. In 1997, statistics say 260,000 Chinese visitors came to Tibet; in the year 2001, there were 560,000 Chinese tourists – though it is unclear whether 'military tourists' are included in this count.
>
> The Chinese tourist phenomenon in Tibet means that you will inevitably mix with sometimes-unwieldy numbers of them at key sites, like the Jokhang. Interactions are interesting here – not a single Chinese tourist I came across would venture an opinion on the Dalai Lama or Buddhism in Tibet. Of course, to broach such topics with Chinese settlers, hard-nosed administrators or the military living in Tibet is impossible, but you'd think that a Chinese tourist might be willing to talk.
>
> An obligatory stop for Chinese visitors is Potala Square, where they dress up

Tibet PSB handles visa extensions, but usually only if you have a tour booked. If your tour itinerary is for 6 days, then the extension is for 9 days or so (to enable you to complete the tour and leave Tibet). If you have booked a Kailash tour itinerary, you might be able to get a month's extension. Under special circumstances, travellers have been able to negotiate a visa extension through Tibet PSB, but the maximum time they give appears to be five to seven days, which is not very useful.

Nepalese Consulate
The only consulate in Lhasa is the Royal Nepal Consulate-General (tel: 683 6890), located to the north side of the Norbulingka; open 10.00 to 12.30 Monday to Friday. You can pick up a 30-day or 60-day Nepalese visa within a day for US$30 or Y255. Double-entry or multiple-entry visas can also be obtained (price will double or triple), and there may be a half-price visa valid for 15 days. It's not really necessary to obtain a Nepalese visa as you can get the same visa for the same price on arrival in Nepal by air or by road. However, some like the cachet of the exotic visa issued in Lhasa.

WHERE TO STAY
The following hotels and guesthouses are arranged by location and pricing. Location means a lot in Lhasa – the closer you are to the Barkor, the better, because that's where all the Tibetan action is and where you can stroll around at will. There are other factors to consider. How is the plumbing? What time does the front door close at night? Is there secure storage if you leave bags behind for a week or more? Apart from location and price, there's one very important factor to consider: who runs the place? More kudos to you if you stick with Tibetan management.

As for Chinese management: well, they may not want you in their hotel at all. Apartheid is a standard Chinese practice: segregating Chinese tourists from foreign tourists. A number of hotels are restricted to Chinese only, and PSB in Tibetan cloaks and foxfur hats to have their photos taken with the Potala in the background. Despite communist leadership vilification of the Dalai Lama, trendy Chinese can shop for Tibetan jewellery at boutiques in Shanghai, or buy an astonishing variety of Tibetan products (made by state-run companies) like ginseng-berry juice or Tibetan barley wine (Shangelila label). And stranger still, you will find, at some pilgrimage sites around Tibet, Chinese (who are officially atheist) participating in rituals like tying on prayer flags, burning juniper, and chanting *Om Mani Padme Hum* (see the entry '*mantra*' in the glossary, page 271).

That's exactly what Chinese chanteuse Dadawa did on a track of her 1995 album, *Sister Drum*. Dadawa achieved the remarkable feat of infuriating both Tibetans and Chinese simultaneously with this album. On the album she croons songs like *Sky Burial* and *The Sixth Dalai Lama's Love Song*. On the cover art, she appears dressed in monastic robes, but her hair is not shaven (it is hidden under a monastic hood) and she is wearing jewellery, which neither monks nor nuns do in Tibet. In London, Tibetans gathered outside the office of her record label to protest exploitation of Tibetan culture. But in Tibet itself, reticence turned to jubilation when Tibetans discovered that in the background track of her top hit was the voice of a woman praising the Dalai Lama in Tibetan! Dadawa had to recall her album and have it re-edited, and her videos are still banned in Tibet. She claims she's had it with Tibet Chic and will not produce any more albums like *Sister Drum*.

would rather keep foreigners isolated in a select number of hotels where they can keep an eye on them. To the southeast side of the Barkor, the Khada Hotel appears to be for Tibetan truck drivers. Out near the Mountaineers-on-Everest roundabout, the Plateau Hotel seems to cater exclusively to a Chinese clientele. The same appears to be true of Gold Grain Hotel (tel: 633 0357), which is a bland 50-room block on Mi Mang Lam – prices are in the mid-range. Catering to well-heeled Chinese clientele is the modern Tibet Royal Hotel, with a big disco-karaoke complex, on the southern section of the Lingkor. Out on 'Karaoke Row' (west of the Golden Yak roundabout) are some glitzy Chinese places with names like Hotel Dream Paris.

Pricing notes: many hotels in Lhasa charge the same for single, twin (two beds) or double rooms (one large bed); others offer discounted rates for singles. Some hotels include all service charges in the price; others include breakfast as well – and even, in high-end hotels, free oxygen! In mid-range and high-end hotels, a service charge of 10% may well be added to bills. These hotels claim to accept a wide range of credit cards: American Express, Visa, Diners, Mastercard, Dragon, JCB, Great Wall, and Peony. The high season for travel to Tibet is April to October: prices may fluctuate seasonally, dipping lower in the shoulder (between high and low seasons) and low seasons.

Addresses are confusing in Lhasa because three different names may surface: Tibetan, Chinese and Western. For instance, Dekyi Shar Lam, Beijing Donglu, and Beijing East Road are one and the same road. Beijing Zhonglu and Beijing Middle Road are the same. And Tengyeling Road is the same as Danjelin Road. Check Lhasa maps for precise locations.

Low to mid-range hotels

A number of hotels in Lhasa offer accommodation from dormitory up to deluxe double-rooms. The tariff in this group is Y15–50 for a dorm bed, Y80–120 for a double room, and Y120–380 for a double with bath. The hotels listed in the Barkor and Sera Road areas are mostly Tibetan-managed, which is why they are placed up front here. Those in the Lingkor area are likely to be Chinese-run.

A British traveller who stayed at a mid-range hotel (included with an arrival tour by mistake), says that his Y500 room at the Shangbala Hotel was equivalent to a Y50 room at the Yak Hotel (but with no bathroom included at the Yak for this price). For a double with bath, much better value is to stay at the Yak or Snowland for around Y260, or at the Flora Hotel for Y180. Very popular with travellers are the Tibetan-run Yak, Kirey, Snowland and Banakshol hotels, which operate on a similar formula – they offer a range of accommodation, and have on-site shop, internet access, restaurant, and travel agent. These hotels have hot showers, laundry facilities, will rent bicycles, and will store baggage while you're off on a trip.

Barkor area

Snowland Located just off Barkor Square; tel: 632 3687. This Tibetan-managed courtyard-style hotel is popular with backpackers and those on group tours. Good central location, but toilets are sloppy if staying in dorms or a room without bath. Hot shower stalls are grubby. Has email centre, bike rentals, and FIT Travel Centre (official monopoly, high prices). Rooms are Y25 dorm (4-bed to 8-bed), Y30 common triple (per bed), Y80 double. In the newer wing: Y260 double with bath, Y360 deluxe.

Tashi Targyal Near Snowland; tel: 632 5804. Chinese-run hotel with 74 rooms, some very dim and run-down. Charges Y15-25 dorm, Y100 double with bath.

Pentoc On Tengyeling Rd; tel/fax: 633 0700; email: pentoc@public.east.cn.net; web: www.pentoc.com. Although it claims on the website that 'pentoc' is Tibetan for 'helpful', Pentoc is also short for Pentecostal: this hotel is operated by a group of evangelical Europeans. Their connections with the authorities are not clear, given that a foreign-run operation is rare in China, and very rare in Tibet (and given the fact that evangelists would never be tolerated anywhere else in China). The Pentoc Hotel is very small, very clean, and has good facilities – even the plumbing works. Here's a refreshing twist: the Pentoc looks Chinese on the outside, but decor is all Tibetan on the inside. Pentoc runs video-nights (movies), and has email hook-ups. The management can arrange camping and biking tours in the Lhasa Valley and beyond; the Pentoc also rents camping gear, but prices are steep. Runs about 25 comfortable rooms for Y30 dorm (3-bed room), Y50 single, Y80 double/twin, Y90 triple, Y120 for 4 beds.

Yak 100 Beijing Donglu (Beijing East Road); tel: 632 3496; fax: 633 6906; email: lhasayak_hotel@hotmail.com. A large, efficient operation with central courtyard. The quiet main section is removed from road. Excellent rooftop dormitory and rooftop viewing area. The Yak courtyard tent is a favourite meeting place for travellers staying here. The Yak is much cleaner than Snowland. About 75 rooms for Y20 dorm, Y50-60 double no bath, Y100 triple no bath, and Y260 double deluxe with bath.

Kirey 105 Beijing Donglu; tel: 632 3987. Large internet café. Free baggage storage. Mad Yak restaurant at centre of courtyard stages dinner-dance soirées. Has over 100 rooms, for Y25 dorm (in 3 to 9-bed rooms), Y50-60 double, Y120 double with bath.

Gang Gyen Hotel Further east is the nondescript Gang Gyen Guesthouse, which is lacking in atmosphere but has functional rooms. Resort to this hotel only if desperate.

Banakshol On Beijing Donglu; tel: 632 3829. Has bike rental; FIT travel centre (the same rip-off one as in Snowland Hotel). Offers about 100 rooms, ranging from budget upward – the better ones are those on the upper floors, where there's more sunlight. Walls are thin at the Banakshol – a definite minus. Tibetan management is very friendly – a plus. Charges are Y25 dorm (in 30 rooms of 4 to 5-beds), Y30 single (10 rooms), Y60 double (45 rooms), Y150 with bath (20 rooms with deluxe Tibetan-style decor).

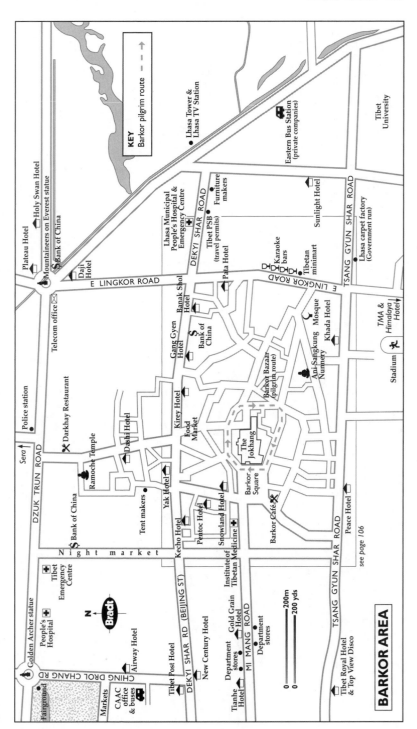

BARKOR AREA

KEY
--- Barkor pilgrim route

Plateau Hotel
Holy Swan Hotel
Mountaineers on Everest statue
Bank of China
Daji Hotel
Telecom office
E LINGKOR ROAD
Lhasa Municipal People's Hospital & Emergency Centre
DEKYI SHAR ROAD
Tibet PSB (travel permits)
Pata Hotel
Furniture makers
Lhasa Tower & Lhasa TV Station
Eastern Bus Station (private companies)
Tibet University
Sunlight Hotel
Karaoke bars
Tibetan minimart
Lhasa carpet factory (Government run)
TSANG GYUN SHAR ROAD
E LINGKOR ROAD
Mosque
Khada Hotel
Ani Sangkung Nunnery
TMA & Himalaya Hotel
Stadium
Banak Shol Hotel
Gang Gyen Hotel
Bank of China
Barkor Bazaar (pilgrim route)
Police station
Sera
Darkhay Restaurant
DZUK TRUN ROAD
Ramoche Temple
Dashi Hotel
Tent makers
Kirey Hotel
Food Market
The Jokhang
Barkor Square
Peace Hotel
see page 106
Yak Hotel
Kecho Hotel
Pentoc Hotel
Snowland Hotel
Institute of Tibetan Medicine
Barkor Café
Bank of China
Night market
Golden Archer statue
People's Hospital
Tibet Emergency Centre
N
Brod
CAAC office & buses
Fairground
Markets
CHING DROL CHANG RD
Tibet Post Hotel
Airway Hotel
New Century Hotel
DEKYI SHAR RD (BEIJING ST)
Tianhe Hotel
Gold Grain Hotel
Department stores
MI MANG ROAD
Department stores
Tibet Royal Hotel & Top View Disco
TSANG GYUN SHAR ROAD
0 200m
0 200 yds

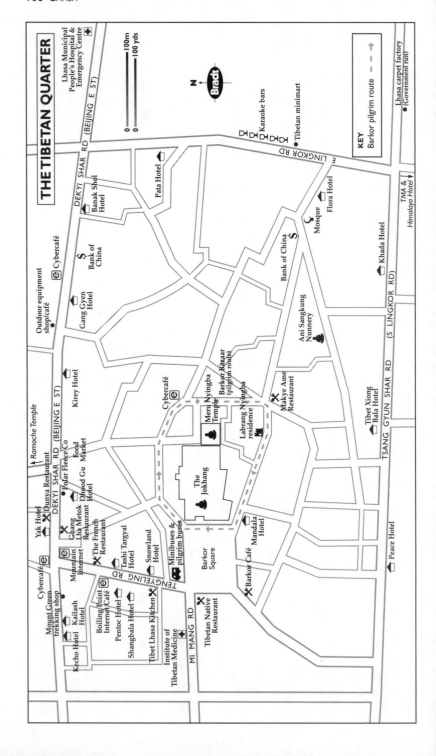

THE TIBETAN QUARTER

KEY
Barkor pilgrim route - - -

Flora Off east Barkor on Hobaling Road, near the mosque; tel: 632 4491, fax: 632 4901. The main building has 20 rooms for Y180 double, including bath – excellent value. Another building offers Y35 dorm beds in 4-bed rooms upstairs, or Y20 in 6-bed rooms downstairs.
Kecho (aka Kechu or Kyichu) 149 Beijing Donglu; tel: 633 8824; fax: 632 0234; email: jqfd@public.ls.xz.cn. Small, five-storey place with good facilities; very clean and highly recommended. Small restaurant and giftshop. About 40 rooms for Y260 double; there are also a few single rooms for Y180.
Kailash 143 Beijing Donglu; tel: 632 2220. Group-tour hotel with some Tibetan-style standard rooms and some attempt at Tibetan décor, with Tibetan staff, although it's Chinese-run. Prices are similar to Kecho Hotel, with rooms for Y160 single or Y380 double.
Dashi Near Ramoche Temple; tel: 634 4888; fax: 683 6999; email: tdi@public.ls.xz.cn. Although this looks like a large 4-storey building, the ground and 2nd floor are taken up with reception and bars, leaving only the 3rd and 4th floors for accommodation. Good views from the rooftop. Ten rooms with bath for Y140, and eight rooms without bath for Y120.
Mandala South side of Jokhang Temple at 31 South Barkor St; tel: 633 8940. Hotel is centrally located and has Tibetan staff. On the ground floor is a great dining area and bar; you can access the rooftop for views over Lhasa. Group-tour hotel, with 35 rooms for Y180 single, Y260 double, or Y300 triple.

Sera Road area
Gakyiling Off Sera Road on sidestreet; tel. 632 6685. Favoured by NGO groups. Has 48 rooms for Y75–150 double, and Y350 suite.
Tashi Mandala Near Gakyiling. Arrayed around a Tibetan-style courtyard, this hotel is also a favourite of NGO groups.
Northa Khangsang 35 Sera Road; tel: 634 1734; fax: 634 1735; email: nothps@public.ls.xz.cn. The hotel is constructed around a large Tibetan-style foyer with teahouse; the room interiors are Western-style. Has 30 rooms for Y380 standard, Y488 suite, and Y688 deluxe suite.

Lingkor area
Pata On East Lingkor. A Tibetan-style hotel with three floors; great balconies with potted plants. Some NGOs lodge here. The hotel is Tibetan-run. There are 18 double rooms for Y120 each.
Peace On South Lingkor at 10 Jiangsu Road; tel: 632 4253; fax 634 8612. A concrete block with Tibetan trimmings, and Chinese-run. In an isolated spot – not much atmosphere. The hotel offers 38 rooms for Y288 single, Y380 standard, Y260 triple, and Y680 suite.
Tibet Royal Hotel On South Lingkor; tel: 675 7849. This hotel sports a mock-Tibetan facade, but is Chinese to the core. Charges Y268 standard (24 rooms) or Y388 suite (6 of these). The hotel has a large entertainment-disco-karaoke complex at the back called Top View Disco, with an advanced light and sound system, and a rabbit-warren of karaoke rooms leading off it. This is favoured by the military brass.
Sunlight Located to the southeast side of Lhasa; tel: 633 1124; fax: 633 5675. Has 90 rooms (some with attached bath) and a range of services. A little way out of the action: both the Sunlight and the Himalaya (following) are bland, lacking in atmosphere, but are favoured by group tours and adventure tours.
Himalaya Hotel 6 East Lingkor Rd; tel: 633 4082; fax: 633 4855; email: sdhh@public.ls.xz.cn. Operates over 140 rooms with bath, arrayed in several wings, one of them a nine-storey building. Sports-related groups often lodge out this way because TIST (Tibet International Sports Travel) and the TMA (Tibet Mountaineering Association) have offices in the vicinity.

Mid-range hotels

Tariff is Y400–800 (US$50–100) for a double in these hotels, rated 3-star by whoever rates them thus. You can easily tell classier hotels by elevators in the lobby, oxygen piped into rooms (or supplied through a machine), and saunas. Although they may have some token Tibetan interior design, the following mid-range hotels are Chinese-run (except for the Dhood Gu). Most offer rooms with hot water, colour TV, IDD phone, air conditioning and other comforts. Lobby facilities include business centre, fitness centre, travel agent, gift shops and so on. A peculiar item on the tariffs is the 'o'clock room': this is a room that is rented by the hour for Y100–200, probably for short-time flings. Even the high-end Tibet Hotel has them.

Shangbala In Barkor area, near Snowland Hotel at 1 Tangyeling Rd (Danjelin Rd); tel: 632 3888; fax: 632 3577. Used by tour groups. Over 70 rooms – pricey at Y400–480 single or double, Y1,200 deluxe suite.

Dhood Gu In the Barkor area, near the market at 19 Sharsarsu Rd; tel: 632 2555; fax 632 3555; email: dhoodgu@public.ls.xz.cn. Five-storey Tibetan-style hotel (also interior decoration) with 67 rooms. All rooms include bathroom and breakfast; rates are posted in dollars: US$40 single, US$60 double or twin, US$80 Potala view room, US$45 for triple, US$125 suite. Has a few cheaper options: eg US$15 per bed in a 3-bed room (includes bath).

Holy Swan In East Lingkor area at 3 Lajin Rd; tel: 632 6999; fax: 632 6696. Constructed in 1998, this is a soul-less place with white bathroom tiles, tinted blue glass and mock-Tibetan trimmings. It has 82 rooms for Y460 single, Y488 double, Y580 triple, and Y880–1,088 suite.

Daji (aka Tarjye) 34 East Lingkor Rd; tel: 633 7777; fax: 6328999. This curious piece of architecture was built in 1998, at a cost of US$4.4 million by Sichuan-based Tibetan entrepreneur Mr Tarjye, according to the hotel brochure. The architecture is an odd mix of Tibetan and Chinese styles, with a choice of Tibetan-style or Han-style luxury suites within. Attendants also dress in exotic silky garb – both Tibetan and Chinese styles. The expansive lobby is Tibetan-style, and there are two elevators. Oxygen can be obtained through a card system – feed in a card for Y50 (four hours). There are six restaurants and teahouses in the hotel. On the 2nd floor is a Han restaurant; on the 4th floor, a Tibetan restaurant-teahouse, with staff in silky robes. The Sacred Capital Nightclub boasts karaoke rooms of different décor. The 5th floor contains a greenhouse-like area with views toward Potala; there is also a rooftop perch with umbrellas. The hotel's sauna health centre on the 4th floor features equipment imported from the US. The 45 rooms at the Daji go for Y400 single, Y1,200–1,600 for suites.

Tibet Xiong Bala Hotel In South Lingkor area at 28 Jiangsu Rd; tel: 633 8888; fax: 633 1777; email: xiongbl@public.ls.xz.cn. This Chinese-run hotel opened in 2000. On the ground floor is a large, Tibetan-style restaurant with private booths. There are 83 rooms for Y370 honeymoon room, Y518 deluxe standard room and Y1,188–2,388 suite.

Lhasa Department Store Hotel Next to Lhasa Department Store, of course; tel: 632 1018. Has 35 rooms for Y380–420 standard, and Y880–980 suite.

New Century Hotel On Beijing Middle Rd; tel: 633 4895. Has two elevators. There are 80 rooms: prices are Y500 standard and Y1,000 suite.

Tibet Post Hotel 33 Beijing Middle Rd; tel: 682 1999; fax: 681 3999; email: xzyzjd@163.net. Affiliated with China Post and located on the same block. 80 rooms for Y568 double, and 6 suites for Y1,680 (includes free oxygen).

Grand Hotel Tibet West of the Potala at 195 Beijing Zhonglu; tel: 682 6096; fax: 683 2195. The Grand Hotel Tibet is a bit of an anomaly because rooms are not necessarily mid-range prices. However, it has some exclusivity to it – it is patronised by visiting delegations and is close to Lhasa's high-end hotels. Dining Hall Number One has a capacity for 1,000 guests at a conference; there are six other (smaller) restaurants in the hotel. The 'Oxygen

THE FORMER HOLIDAY INN

In late 1997 it was announced that the Holiday Inn management group would not renew its contract for running the branch in Lhasa – the only luxury hotel in Tibet. No reason was given – and the international giant continues to run its numerous other branches around China. Victory was claimed by various campaign groups in the West, particularly the Free Tibet Campaign in England, which launched a boycott of Holiday Inn operations and those of its British parent company, Bass PLC (makers of Bass beer), in 1993. In 1997, Students for a Free Tibet and fifty other Tibet support groups joined the campaign.

In its heyday, the Holiday Inn Lhasa was run in partnership with the Chinese government and was the largest foreign currency earner in Lhasa – catering to well-heeled group tours. The original hotel was completed by the Chinese in 1986: the Holiday Inn corporation modernised the building and renamed it. A trusted brand name like Holiday Inn brought a certain amount of prestige, a veneer of respectability, and a seal of approval for Chinese operations in Tibet. There were even Miss Tibet contests conducted in 1992 to attract tourism during the slack winter months. You had to wonder how long it would take McDonalds, Pizza Hut and the rest of the multi-national gang to get there in the wake of Holiday Inn.

Although Tibetans work at the hotel, there is no Tibetan presence in the management – profits only benefit the Chinese. Top-ranking Chinese military like to stay there, and it appears that the staff are in cahoots with security forces. After the Holiday Inn management left, the building reverted to its original name, Lhasa Hotel, but the sign out front and the hotel brochures still bear the legend: 'The Former Holiday Inn Lhasa.' A hilarious account of life at the former Holiday Inn is given in Alec Le Sueur's book, *Running a Hotel on the Roof of the World.*

Another joint-venture enterprise sparking protests from foreigners is the beer company Pabst. Pabst Blue Ribbon operates a Sino-American joint-venture: in 2001, their Chinese partner strung up a large banner in Lhasa congratulating the Chinese on the 50th anniversary of the take-over of Tibet. The oil giant BP has come under fire too, for assisting PetroChina in laying an oil pipeline into Tibet. BP is a shareholder in PetroChina, which is China's biggest oil producer.

Bar' turns out to be part of the hotel clinic, with a few armchairs where you can siphon from a 10-minute oxygen bag for a Y10 fee. There are a whopping 540 rooms at the Grand, arrayed in four wings. The tariff is Y160 economy double (about 100 rooms), Y280 standard (185 rooms), Y460 deluxe (180 rooms) and Y2,000 suite.

High-end hotels

Lhasa's top hotels lie west of the Potala and charge Y800 a room and up. Both of the following are Chinese-run.

Tibet Hotel 64 Beijing Middle Rd; tel: 683 4966; fax: 683 6787. A mock-Tibetan abomination of a building that is favoured by Asian group tours and Chinese clientele. Unfriendly and surly staff. The giftshop is worth checking out. There are over 200 rooms and suites for Y880 single or standard, Y980 triple and Y2,800 suite.

Lhasa Hotel 1 Minzu Lu; tel: 683 2221; fax: 683 5796; email: sales@public.ls.xz.cn. The top hotel in Lhasa, rated as 4-star, and the only one with a swimming pool (nobody seems to use it, however, because it's poorly maintained). Even if it is a luxury hotel, Lhasa Hotel has its problems – built in 1985, it is falling apart in places, with water-damaged walls. Lhasa Hotel still has a sign up, 'Former Holiday Inn Lhasa', but does not explain the background (see box, page 109). The hotel boasts three tower wings, each with an elevator (the first to arrive in Tibet). The hotel has the full gamut of services, including telecom and business centre, currency exchange counter, and several giftshops. There's a fitness centre with sauna and jacuzzi. Restaurants include the Tibetan-style Himalaya (styled like a Tibetan teahouse), Chinese-style Kailash restaurant and the Western-style Hard Yak Café. The banquet hall can seat 600. For the price of a drink you can drop in and watch CNN and other programs on satellite TV by going to tiny Chang's Bar, located on the ground floor. The 468 rooms and suites at Lhasa Hotel go for Y778 economy, Y1,010 superior, Y1,180–2,220 suite, and Y8,888 presidential suite (over US$1,000 a night).

FOOD AND NIGHTLIFE

Lhasa is well-supplied for food: you can even buy fresh bananas (from central America), and peaches and mangoes from street vendors. You can throw together your own food in Lhasa: there are places where you can find fresh-baked flatbreads, delicious yak curd (yoghurt) and bananas – start putting these things together and you'll have a great breakfast. It's fun to wander the streets around the Barkor to get your daily yoghurt.

A number of restaurants listed here double as suppliers of food for trekkers and those on Landcruiser trips. In the self-catering line, Lhasa Department Store mini-mart is good, with plenty of fruit juices, dried fruit, almonds, nuts, and Dove chocolate. A Tibetan-run mini-mart can be found on East Lingkor Road, in the Flora Hotel vicinity: it stocks supplies like trekkers' muesli from Nepal, mango frooti drink, peanut butter from India, sunblock and so on. Chinese-made Ziploc plastic bags can be purchased at Outdoor Equipment, east of Yak Hotel.

Watch out for dirty restaurant kitchens – diarrhoea and food poisoning are the threats here. Many travellers in Lhasa have stomach problems or coughs, colds, and flu. Stomach problems are probably traceable to water that's not properly boiled, or to uncooked vegetables. Having said that, the tented street stalls at the night market to the west of Yak Hotel are worth a visit – even if you don't eat there. It's a lively place packed with Muslim traders and kebabs on braziers.

Near Tashi I are several Muslim noodlehouses with hearty fare at low prices: these bear green banners with the Muslim crescent moon on them. Opposite Sheng Shia hotel, west of the Potala, is a string of hot-pot places – food is cooked at the table. Watch out for 'heavy' Chinese food, or greasy food. Peking duck, for instance, is very rich – and hard on your system. You need to be acclimatised. What? Food too?! Yes, that's right: in Beijing there's a phenomenon known as Jetlag Duck Attack, whereby an unsuspecting tourist arriving with a jetlag hangover is taken straight to a Beijing duck dinery, and promptly keels over after eating the rich food. I guess the Lhasa equivalent would be to step off the plane, go and eat at a Peking duck restaurant, and then climb the central staircase of the Potala. Anyway, Beijing duck is delicious – it comes with duck soup, duck crêpes and other duck dishes.

If you are feeling really acclimatised, you can wash all this down with some wine. Avoid the cheap Chinese champagne on the shelves – this is only good for bathing in. The bottle to purchase is Dynasty White Wine, which is bottled in Tianjin as part of a French joint-venture enterprise. Another good brand is Great Wall Red.

OVER THE FIREWALL

The Dalai Lama's image has been banned in Tibet since a major fallout over the choice of Panchen Lama in 1996. Even more incriminating are tapes or books by him or about him, or movies about him. Even the Potala Palace is bereft of his portrait – the last big portrait was taken down around 1997. The image you might see in monasteries (possibly) is of a younger Dalai Lama with Mao Zedong in Beijing in the 1950s, as this seems to be politically correct. Otherwise, the Dalai Lama is commonly denounced as a 'revolutionary splittist' or 'a wolf in monk's garb'.

But the irrepressible Dalai Lama is easy to find on the internet. You can bring him up at any time – he's on so many sites, they can't be blocked. He pops up on the cover of all his books, for starters. In a cybercafé in Lhasa, I was hunting for information on the Karmapa (who is not yet blacklisted by the Chinese), when a magazine cover popped up. It was an issue of *Time Asia*, with a cover story on political repression in Tibet. And featured on the cover were two monks in burgundy robes – the Karmapa and the Dalai Lama. *Time Asia* itself is firewalled in China, but somehow this cover arrived by a different route, past the firewall. Amazed Tibetans crowded round the screen to witness this, probably the first time they'd seen a photograph of the two high lamas together. But the cybercafé operator, fearful of having his licence revoked – or fearful of starting a riot – asked me to switch sites.

Makye Ame Located at the back of the Barkor, this second-floor restaurant has a laid-back atmosphere and big bay windows overlooking the Barkor, where you can watch the Tibetan pilgrim world turn – and turn. The restaurant is Tibetan-run and serves an eclectic menu from *thukpa* (noodle soup) to pizza. You can also visit for drinks alone – go up to the tented rooftop section for even better views of the Barkor. Makye Ame also rents books if you leave a deposit.

Dunya Next door to Yak Hotel, Dunya has cornered the market in safe eating. The place is run by Europeans and is very clean and spacious, with wooden tables, candles at night, and a great ambience. It features a mixed menu, including Tibetan, Italian and Indonesian. On the menu is 'yak sizzler', which is yak-steak, French fries and vegetables served in a hot skillet – so hot that it sizzles. Chicken sizzler is similar. Take a look at their site at www.dunyarestaurant.com.

The French Restaurant (Tcheu Tang) The name brings wine and cheese to mind, right? Well, yes, you're in luck. Espresso coffee, sweet and savoury crêpes, croissants, chocolate mousse, quiche and homemade bread are on the menu. Great Wall Red is Y58 a bottle, or Y14 a glass. Great Wall White is Y45 a bottle or Y12 a glass. It also has bulk cheese for sale, which is good for trips.

Snowland A few notches up in décor and price is Snowland Restaurant, which is attached to Snowland Hotel but is a separate operation, with Nepali cooks. This place is very comfortable, with a larger section at the back for group tours. On the menu is a selection of Western, Chinese, Tibetan and Nepali food. The Tibetan dishes are curious: yak tongue salad, yak noodle soup, yak fried chilli. The breakfast menu may sound more familiar, serving muesli with fruit and curd (tangy yoghurt), banana milk porridge, or scrambled eggs and coffee. Snowland Restaurant also sells supplies for those off on excursions – you can buy excellent brown bread, canned goods, Swiss chocolate and other delicacies, imported from Nepal.

HAVING A BLAST

Need an blast of oxygen? A high-altitude cocktail? Lhasa Hotel was reputed to have rooms where oxygen was piped in, but this system no longer seems to function because guests kept going out and leaving the oxygen on. If guests have trouble with the altitude, they are usually given an oxygen pillow to make sleeping smoother. There is nothing more scary than sleeping at altitude and waking up in the middle of the night completely out of breath, heart pounding, gulping for air, with a throat like the Sahara. This is where the oxygen pillow comes to the fore – it is a pillow of oxygen with nasal tubes attached. The pillows are also taken along on Landcruiser or minibus trips from Lhasa Hotel in case a guest is feeling under the weather. Landcruiser drivers may also keep a tank of oxygen in the vehicle, rather like a fire extinguisher unit. Oxygen does not solve the acclimatisation problem, but it does provide temporary respite.

Several outfits in Lhasa sell oxygen devices, manufactured as far afield as Xiamen. These range from small scuba-like tanks to aerosol spray-cans for those who need a blast of fresh air. You can rent the scuba tanks for a dollar or so a day (with a large deposit) – the capacity is 30 minutes of oxygen. At top-end hotels guests can use a card system to hook up to a larger oxygen-dispensing device.

Kailash This Nepali-run restaurant inside Banakshol Hotel serves great vegetarian food, rents out books (including guidebooks), and sells trekking food supplies.

Tashi 1, Tashi 2 Family-run and with fair prices, but food is a bland. Tashi I is upstairs on the corner of Tengyeling Road and Beijing Road. Tashi II is inside the Kirey Hotel. On the menu are yak-burgers, spaghetti, French fries, vegetable dishes and apple momos.

Yeti Café At 206 Beijing Xilu (Beijing West Rd), close to Lhasa Hotel, it has a big menu of Sichuan, Western and Tibetan food. The café features Tibetan-style teahouse décor, with carpeted seats. It can handle groups. In this area are trendy cafés, catering largely to a Chinese clientèle.

Lhasa Hotel Has several over-priced restaurants, including the Hard Yak Café (serving yak-burgers) and an ice-cream café (with good gelato). The Himalaya Restaurant at Lhasa Hotel serves a range of food from Indian to German, plus Tibetan dishes like Yak Tartare, or Minced Yak with Tibetan Spices. Traditional Tibetan music groups sometimes perform at the restaurant.

Teahouses and rooftop cafés

There are pleasant teahouses in Lhasa where you can soak up the views as well as the drinks. One of these is Lukhang teahouse, in the northeast corner of Lukhang Park – it offers a great view of the back of the Potala and is a peaceful place. The teahouse serves 'eight treasures tea' and there are often fresh flowers on the tables from the adjacent nursery. Another viewpoint on the Potala is from the front, at a Chinese pavilion with restaurant and teahouse, overlooking a lake to the Potala's south side. There's a Tibetan-style teahouse inside the Red Palace of the Potala itself.

On the rooftop of the Jokhang is a tented teahouse, run by the monks, although only in the summer months, and only for tourists. Offering a view across Barkor Square is the upper deck of Barkor Café. In the same vicinity is a fourth-floor tented rooftop patio at the Native Tibetan Restaurant. Most ignore the menu of over 200 items and just settle for a beer or a fruit juice – and the view, of course.

Around the back of the Barkor, Makye Ame restaurant's rooftop on the third floor has great views over the parade of pilgrims. From various hotel rooftops, you can also get good views of Lhasa, and see paper kites launched from other rooftops. Some hotels like the Kecho may have rooftop cafés.

Entertainment and nightlife

Lhasa's handful of hotels and restaurants are nightlife and entertainment venues by default: they are gathering points for information exchange. Source and sauce: other travellers provide the latest information, and you digest it over a steaming bowl of noodles. Snowland, Tashi I, Dunya, and Kailash restaurants function as traveller cafés. This is how travellers mostly pass their nights. Chinese nightlife consists of crooning, carousing and chasing Sichuan women around in karaoke bars or places like Top View Disco (some Westerners venture in here too). Other night-time Chinese endeavours include dwarf-tossing contests. Tibetan nightlife consists of crowding into tiny video salons where sound distortion and flasks of chang are the big things.

Dinner-dance venues

The Mad Yak restaurant, inside the Kirey Hotel, and the Crazy Yak restaurant, located next to the Kirey (off the road a bit) may stage dinner-dance events. The cost is Y50 including dinner, or you can probably get by on a beer for Y10 only. These places cater mostly to foreign group tours, but they don't mind if individuals show up. Dinner starts at 19.00 and the show takes place from 19.30 to 21.30. The show is a mix of traditional dance and music, with the highlight being the exuberant yak dance, performed by two Tibetans hidden inside a yak skin. It is traditionally performed as a welcome dance. The dancers roll on the floor, flick the tail around, and charge into the audience. There may be other Lhasa restaurants with dinner-dance shows. Check the Tibet Lhasa Kitchen restaurant.

Bars

Popular with foreigners is the upstairs bar at Dunya restaurant, next to the Yak Hotel. You can't miss the Heineken sign out the front – the bar was set up by a Dutchman.

Opposite the Yak Hotel is Ganghla Metok, a trendy Chinese-run restaurant and bar, with Chinese artwork on the walls masquerading as Tibetan. The food is bland, but the place is fine for drinks, and stays open late.

INFORMATION
Traveller network

Your best information source is other travellers, encountered at cafés or guesthouses. Make other contacts through the message boards at Snowland, Yak, Banakshol, Pentoc or Flora hotels – you can buy or sell medicines, sleeping bags, tents and freeze-dried foods. Assembling small groups for Landcruiser trips is often achieved through the boards.

Books and maps

You might dredge up the odd map, poster or Tibetan music cassette from the Xinhua Bookstore at the west end of Mi Mang Lam; otherwise, pickings are slim. Prices for maps and books can be absurdly low if produced by the Chinese government. There's a Xinhua bookstore branch out near Lhasa Hotel. Look for a sheet map called *Lhasa Tourist Map*, produced by Chengdu Cartographic

Publishing House, dated 2001 and sold for Y16. This large, double-sided map carries an impressive wealth of detail and a selection of mini-guide material.

The souvenir shops at Lhasa Hotel and Tibet Hotel are good for books, though more expensive. Also selling books and postcards are souvenir kiosks near the Potala ticket entrance and inside the Norbulingka. Rule of thumb: when you see something you really want, bargain and buy it – you might not see it again. Other Chinese bookstores are scattered around; there's one at the east side of Barkor Bazaar.

SERVICES
Banking
The main branch of the Bank of China is located just northeast of the Golden Yak roundabout. It provides full services, including credit card advances (although commissions can be high). The BOC is open 10.30 to 13.30, and 15.30 to 18.00 Monday to Friday; from 11.00 to 15.00 Saturdays; and it may be open on Sundays. There are sub-branches in a few other locations – notably one near the Banakshol hotel. Major hotels like Lhasa Hotel have their own exchange counter, but the rate is not as good. ATMs exist in Lhasa, but with instructions in Chinese you should not count on this option.

Medical
You're best off moving to a comfortable hotel in the event of a medical problem. High-end hotels usually supply oxygen pillows and may have a doctor on call. Hospitals in Lhasa cost a fortune for foreigners to stay in, and the medical attention is dubious anyway. Lhasa's finest is the Military Hospital at the north end of town, but that's not for foreigners. The People's Hospital is basic, although one unit is supported by an Italian NGO project for equipment and training and there's an X-ray unit there. The Emergency Centre (tel: 632 2200) at this hospital has a small ambulance.

Communications and media
The Potala post office awaits you: the main branch for telecommunications lies near the Potala, on Beijing Road. The sending of regular mail and parcels takes place here; bring along your own packing materials as few are supplied (for larger items, you might have to open your package for customs inspection). Some hotels handle mail too – they deliver to the post office. Part of the China Post complex on this block is a large store devoted to Chinese magazines – everything from car magazines to fashion periodicals – to keep the settlers happy. The news is all from China, and thus all screened. There is a media blackout in Tibet – you cannot find any foreign magazines at all. And despite the great advances the Chinese say they have made in Tibet, there is not a single Tibetan newspaper to be found for sale on the streets of Lhasa.

Fax and phone
There's a long-distance calling office next door to the main post office (calls are most likely routed through Beijing); the same office will allow you to send faxes. A second telecom office is located at the Mountaineers-on-Everest roundabout. Faxes can also be sent at Lhasa Hotel's business centre, but they're more expensive. International phone calls can be placed through hotels, even at the budget hotels. It's cheaper to use a pre-paid card with a yellow phone (these phones are sometimes found in hotel lobbies, and sometimes on the street). The country code (China) is 86; the Lhasa area code is 0891 (for calls within China) or 891 (for incoming international calls).

KHAMPA MONA LISA

Mona Lisa's enigmatic smile undergoes a twist in Lhasa. You will see her painted with Khampa-style dress and turquoise jewellery studded in her hair. This is definitely not traditional. In fact, it is not even Tibetan. The painting was done by a Chinese who describes himself as a 'local artist'. The art studio below the (Chinese-owned) Barkor Café says it is for 'Tibetan artists to express their Tibetan heritage.' Not quite – the studio also sells imitation, Van Gogh-style wares which are all done by Chinese artists. All of this is blatantly misleading and begs the question: who makes the high-kitsch art hanging on restaurant and café walls and in shops and hotel lobbies around Lhasa? A lot of it seems to derive from Chinese artists, not Tibetan ones. Can Chinese tanka painters be far away? A number of the trendy Tibetan-style cafés and shops that tourists frequent are actually Chinese-owned and managed, including the huge tanka shops on the Barkor.

The neo-Tibetan phenomenon, with Chinese masquerading as Tibetans, extends to actual dress-up. At some tourist sites, the ticket-sellers dressed in Tibetan costume are in fact Chinese and cannot speak a word of Tibetan. At Lhasa Department Store, some of the counter servers are Chinese dressed as Tibetans, and similar charades occur at the reception desk of some of Lhasa's high-end hotels.

Email and internet

Net access is available through a growing number of cybercafés, and through hotels and guesthouses. Connection speeds vary – connection is sometimes good, sometimes slow and sometimes non-existent (come back later). Internet use is cheap – mostly under Y5 an hour. There are two Tibetan-run cybercafés at the north end of Tengyeling Road, another round the corner near the Yak Hotel, and one at the northeast side of the Barkor circuit. The main post office has an email and internet section, and most hotels have at least one or two computers available for guest use. It is rumoured that emails are monitored through Beijing, though it's difficult to see how such a large volume of messages could be scrutinised. However, it's possible that monitoring is done by flagging keywords ('independence' for example). Chinese authorities are extremely sensitive about what you can access on the net (see the back of this book for a listing of websites). Taboo sites are those concerned with human rights, Tibetan exile groups, Taiwan; the list goes on. That means sites could be blocked or firewalled, but it's surprising what you can still pick up in Lhasa. If you do get through to sensitive sites, it could mean trouble for the cybercafé owner. However, there is no official list of what is forbidden and what is allowed. In theory, though, there is filtering software in place at cybercafés that will block certain sites: if material is not filtered, the café could be closed down. It is dubious whether foreigners are subject to these regulations. It's a CNN situation: foreigners at Lhasa Hotel can watch CNN, but locals can't.

Satellite TV

High-end hotels may have satellite TV reception, picking up VTV (India), StarTV (Hong Kong) and CNN. Access to these stations is strictly controlled: even if the hotel has a satellite dish, this does not guarantee it has permission to receive certain channels (for which a decoder is needed). Lhasa Hotel seems to have the best contacts for permission: there's a place within the hotel (Chang's Bar) where non-guests can watch the tube. The larger the dish, the greater the reception: satellite receivers require special permission to operate within China, and the foreign programs are not intended for local eyes. Xizang TV and Lhasa TV are the local stations; CCTV from Beijing broadcasts a nightly news service in English, and on Sunday in French. CCTV channels 3, 5, 6 and 8 are from Beijing. CCTV-9 broadcasts all in English or else Chinese with English sub-titles – this is the Chinese, pan-Asian voice.

Photography and film

There are Kodak and Fuji labs in Lhasa. You can get print film developed at shops south of the main post office or near Potala Square. The quality is reasonable, and prints of Tibetans will make fine gifts. The quality of film purchased in Lhasa varies – there are some rotten rolls, some good – so check expiry dates for freshness. High-speed film and black-and-white film is very difficult to purchase. Slides cannot be developed in Lhasa.

Shopping

If you can't find it in Lhasa, you probably won't find it anywhere in Tibet – except possibly Shigatse. Whether outfitting for a trip or shopping for Tibetan artefacts, Lhasa has the biggest selection, though it has nothing on Kathmandu.

Trip gear

For camping gear, try making purchases from other travellers via message-boards. Pentoc Guesthouse rents some camping gear. You can buy (or rent) some gear from Mount Green Trekking Shop, near Kecho Hotel. Opposite Kirey Hotel is a place called Outdoor Equipment, stocking high-quality imported gear,and renting it too (tents, sleeping bags, stoves etc). And in Potala Square is North Col equipment store, with goods brought up from Nepal. Department stores sell formless but functional clothing, and there's PLA surplus gear for sale on the streets.

Fresh/packaged food

If going on a long trip – for instance, to Kailash – stock up on as much food as you can in Lhasa (the only other place to get supplies is Shigatse). For fresh food, the Tibetan market to the north of the Jokhang has the biggest selection (for items like potatoes, dried fruit and so on). Department stores downtown are a source of packaged goods, such as teabags, chocolate, and biscuits. Lhasa Department Store has a good stock in its minimart. For muesli, peanut butter and other items imported from Nepal try Snowland Restaurant or Kailash Restaurant (Banakshol Hotel). There is a Tibetan-run mini-mart on East Lingkor road with a good stock of Nepalese-imported items – it is in the general vicinity of Flora Hotel.

Tibetan artefacts

The main array of souvenir shops lines Barkor Bazaar, but watch out for Chinese clones. Some souvenirs are obviously not Tibetan at all: a few brass Buddha statues are from Thailand; others come from Kathmandu. Much the same stock is sold at giftshops in major hotels at more inflated prices, at souvenir kiosks at the Potala entrance, and at the Norbulingka. Watch out for fake turquoise and other stones if buying jewellery.

You might want to get to the source of items crafted in Lhasa – the factories are a sight themselves. There are several Tibetan tent-making workshops in the city – the easiest to find is in an alley near the Yak Hotel. Among other items, this place sells fine cotton door-hangings with Tibetan lucky symbols hand-embroidered on them. There are several carpet factories in town, including one to the southeast side of Lhasa and another out near Drepung. Potala Carpet Factory, 300m past the turn-off for Drepung, welcomes visitors – you can see women weaving and singing here as they work on complex patterns. There is an exhibition and retail room on the premises. Check out the various designs: a Tibetan dragon has four claws, the Chinese imperial dragon has five claws. A German joint-venture outfit displays yak-leather products at a showroom under the Pentoc Guesthouse – items include wallets and yak-wool sweaters (and some pretty heavy socks). Nearly opposite the Pentoc is Tibet Yekyl Tour Shop, a Tibetan-run place stocking a small but good-quality range of Tibetan handicrafts.

WHAT TO SEE
Orienting yourself

To get a better idea of the layout of Lhasa, there are a number of places that offer expansive views. The highest place is, of course, the Potala rooftop. The Jokhang rooftop has stunning views, too. Some hotels like the Yak, Mandala and Kecho offer rooftop views over the Barkor area.

Traditionally, Tibetan pilgrims approaching the holy city embarked on three sacred circuits: the inner circuit of the Jokhang Temple (called the Nangkor), the 20-minute outer circuit of the same temple (around the Barkor), and a 90-minute circuit around Lhasa itself, called the Lingkor. The first two are eminently possible, but the Lingkor is no longer easy to follow – it has been disrupted by modern Chinese building. The description of sights that follows is based on clockwise circuits of the Nangkor, Barkor and Lingkor – that is, starting at the Jokhang Temple, and spiralling outwards around Lhasa. On the outskirts of Lhasa lie the great monastic citadels of Sera and Drepung. You have to read between the lines in Lhasa when it comes to the sacred and the secret. There's been so much upheaval in the Holy City that half the time you don't know if what you're looking at is sacred or not – whether the statuary at the Jokhang is real or not, whether the West Gate is original or reconstructed.

Entry fees

It all starts to add up when you are charged Y70 to enter the Potala, Y30 for Tibet Museum, Y35 for the Jokhang, and other temples ranging from Y15 up. These tabs are not paid by some tour operators – notably the ones packaging three-day sorties from Chengdu.

Barkor area

There are two areas left in Lhasa where the Tibetan pulse can still be felt: at the Potala (a faint museum pulse) and Barkor Bazaar (throbbing pilgrim pulse). Other than that you're looking at Chinatown. It seems absurd to put it this way, but you really have to visit the 'Tibetan Quarter' – the quarter around the Jokhang Temple and the Barkor – to catch any Tibetans in action. Sadly, this quarter only comprises a small fraction of Lhasa's land area.

The Jokhang

The Jokhang or Tsug Lakhang (central cathedral) is Tibet's most sacred temple – the heart of Tibet – with streams of pilgrims coursing through. The temple was built in the 7th century by King Songtsen Gampo when he moved his capital to Lhasa. Apart from his three Tibetan wives, the powerful Songtsen Gampo had two wives offered by neighbouring nations – Nepalese Queen Tritsun and Chinese Queen Wencheng. The Jokhang was originally designed

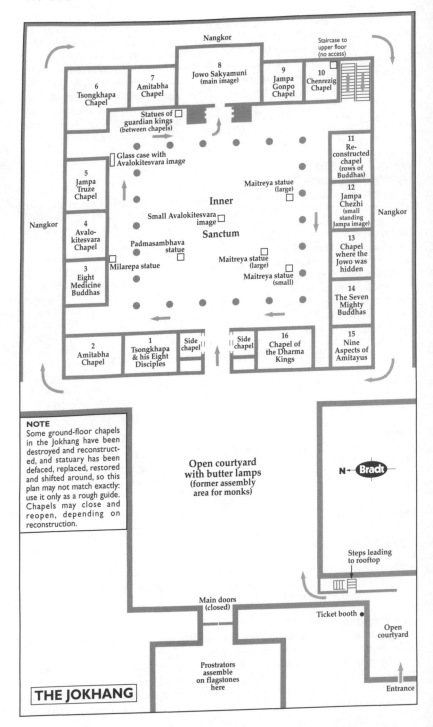

THE JOKHANG

by Nepalese craftsmen to house a Buddha image brought by the Nepalese queen. Upon Songtsen Gampo's death, Queen Wencheng switched the statue she had brought (the Jowo Sakyamuni) from the Ramoche Temple to the Jokhang, apparently to hide it from Chinese troops. That's why one part of the Jokhang (Chapel 13) is called the Chapel where the Jowo was Hidden. In time, the Jowo Sakyamuni statue became the chief object of veneration. The Jokhang was enlarged and embellished by subsequent rulers and Dalai Lamas. Although the building is as old as Lhasa, much of the statuary is quite new. During the Cultural Revolution, the temple was used as a military barracks and a slaughterhouse; later it was used as a hotel for Chinese officials. Much of the statuary was lost, destroyed or damaged, so it has been replaced with newer copies of the originals.

In 2000, the Jokhang was inscribed on the UNESCO World Heritage List as an addition to the Potala Palace, which is good news because it may bolster protection of the buildings in the immediate vicinity.

Outside the Jokhang

Fronting the Jokhang are flagstones where Tibetans gather to prostrate before the temple. A bit further back are two small walled enclosures with obelisks inside. One enclosure shelters two stone obelisks with an edict in Chinese about curing smallpox – the edict, from 1794, is largely illegible because Tibetans gouged pieces out of it, supposing that the stone itself had curative properties. The second enclosure, with a tall thin obelisk, bears a bilingual inscription about a peace treaty between Tibetan king Ralpachen and Chinese emperor Wangti, concluded in AD823, delineating the borders between the nations of China and Tibet. The brick enclosures around the obelisks were put up when Barkor Square was created in 1985.

Access

Exit and entry are by a side-door off the Barkor: an entry fee of Y35 is charged. However, if you go straight to the Jokhang rooftop, you can skip the entry fee. It's best to visit the Jokhang in the mornings, from 08.30 to noon. The Jokhang may be closed on Mondays. Entering the inner sanctum of the ground floor chapels may be difficult for Tibetan pilgrims. As a tourist, you are privileged to be allowed in. Photography is allowed in certain parts of the Jokhang – if in doubt, ask first. Second floor chapels may be closed off and only accessible to monks residing at the Jokhang – you should respect this limitation. It should be all right to access the rooftop, however, and you might be able to visit the rooftop at times when the ground-floor chapels are closed.

The rooftop

You can take a staircase near the ticket booth at the front straight up to the golden rooftop of the Jokhang, with excellent views over Lhasa rooftops and the Potala in the distance. In the summer months there is a tented teahouse up on the Jokhang rooftop, run by the monks. Visiting the rooftop seems to be a privilege reserved for tourists – both Western and Chinese – as you don't see Tibetan pilgrims up here. The monks at the teahouse do a roaring trade with Chinese tour-groups, selling Jokhang talismans and postcards, and T-shirts, books and souvenirs, plus drinks. Chinese tourists excitedly chatter on their mobile phones to callers across China (they even talk on cellphones when visiting the shrines in the Jokhang – including the Jowo shrine). Although it can, at times, turn into a Chinese photo-taking zoo, the rooftop is a bright, peaceful spot – a refreshing place after the dark, smoky chapels of the Jokhang interior. There are beautiful ornaments hanging from the eaves of the gilded sloping roofs, some in the shape of dragons, others in the shape of mythical birds.

Ground-floor icons

Walking through the dark corridors and chapels of the Jokhang, you enter another world – dim light is provided by a galaxy of butter lamps; the air is thick with the odour of yak-butter and incense; echoing through the halls is the sound of murmuring, from throngs of Tibetan pilgrims. If your timing is right, the inner sanctum may reverberate with the sound of deep, hypnotic chanting of monks at prayer. About 100 monks live at the Jokhang, residing on the upper levels.

Some of the chapels in the Jokhang have been destroyed and reconstructed, and statuary has been defaced, replaced, restored and shifted around, so the plan on page 118 may not match exactly with what is on the ground. Chapels may close and reopen, depending on reconstruction. With this jumble of old and new, it is also debatable which statuary is original and which is copied.

The world you enter seems quite complex and confusing, withno point of reference, no rhyme or reason. However, that may be a matter of familiarising yourself with the icons of Tibetan Buddhism – which, admittedly, are bewildering in their scope and number. If you want to explore Tibetan temple iconography, the Jokhang has the lot – a virtual Who's Who of the Tibetan Buddhist pantheon. Using the plan of the Jokhang in this section, you can identify which images are Avalokitesvara, Sakyamuni, King Songtsen Gampo and so on. The same icons pop up in many other temples in Tibet, and are referred to in other parts of this book. Only some of the ground-floor chapels are described here: the emphasis is on the icons.

Unlike most temples, the Jokhang is not identified with a particular sect. Leaders and teachers from the different sects are shown in statuary and murals. **Tsongkhapa** (Chapel 1) is the founder of the Geluk (Yellow Hat) sect. There's a finer image of him in Chapel 6, wearing monk's robes and a pointed yellow cap; he lived from 1357 to 1419. Between Chapel 3 and Chapel 4 is an image of the great poet-saint **Milarepa** (1040–1123), with his hand cocked to one ear so that he can better hear the music of the spheres and the voice of teachings. The sage appears with skin of a greenish hue – a case of nettle anaemia (he dined solely on nettle soup for a number of years). Milarepa was a founding member of the Kagyu sect. Another historical figure seen in chapels and in larger statues at the inner sanctum is **Padmasambhava**, the 8th-century tantric Indian master who is credited with establishing Buddhism in Tibet. He is the founder of the Nyingma sect, and is shown with a stern expression and a curled moustache, wearing a folded red hat.

In the Tibetan pantheon are many Buddhas and bodhisattvas. A bodhisattva is a being on the way to becoming a Buddha, but one who has decided to delay the pursuit of nirvana and devote himself or herself to the welfare of others. The Dalai Lama is thought to be an emanation of **Avalokitesvara**, the bodhisattva of Compassion (Chenrezig in Tibetan). Often shown in a standing statue, Avalokitesvara has 11 heads (one of which is wrathful) and multiple arms, and may be encircled by a thousand hands. The many heads are said to have burst from the original head as a result of contemplating the suffering of living beings.

The figure of Avalokitesvara is found in several parts of the ground floor – in Chapel 4, outside Chapel 5 in a glass case, in Chapel 10, and right at the centre of the inner sanctum. The image in Chapel 4 has a long story behind it: some parts of the statue are original, some are copies. The image was commissioned by

Songtsen Gampo in the 7th century. During the Cultural Revolution, this image and others were tossed into the streets. Tibetans managed to salvage a wrathful and a peaceful aspect of the faces of Avalokitesvara – the images were smuggled out via Nepal to India. The faces were eventually made into a new image of Avalokitesvara at the Tsug Lakhang in Dharamsala.

Tara (Drolma in Tibetan) is said to be the spiritual consort of Avalokitesvara, and possesses more than 20 forms. **White Tara** is identified with Queen Wencheng and the fertile aspect of compassion, while **Green Tara** is identified with Queen Tritsun and the motherly aspect of compassion. Green Tara is the patron female saint of Tibet; she sits with her right leg extended slightly, resting on a lotus blossom. White Tara sits cross-legged upon a lotus flower – she is easily recognised by the eyes depicted in the palms of her hands: she is believed to have sprung from a tear of compassion falling from the eye of Avalokitesvara. While there is little statuary of Tara in the ground-floor chapels, her image appears in a number of murals – a Tara fresco is shown on a wall recessed at the back of Chapel 16.

Tibetans believe that the historical Buddha (Sakyamuni) is the Buddha of the present era, but only one of the many Buddhas to appear – past, present and future. The Buddha is 'he who is fully awake' – an enlightened being. **Amitabha**, appearing in Chapel 2, is the Buddha of Infinite Light (*Opame* in Tibetan) – usually depicted in a red colour, with hands clasping an alms-bowl. The Panchen Lama is thought to be an incarnation of Amitabha. A row of eight **Medicine Buddhas** is shown in Chapel 3 – these are the Buddhas of healing, and caring for the sick. **Jampa** is the Buddha of the Future, also known as Champa or the Maitreya Buddha. This Buddha is not usually shown cross-legged, but seated conventionally on a throne. The Jampa statue shown in Chapel 5 is a copy of one brought to Tibet from Nepal by Queen Tritsun. In Chapel 9 is an image of Jampa (brought in from Drepung to replace a destroyed image); this statue was once paraded around the Barkor at Monlam. In the inner sanctum are two Jampa images.

The centrepiece of the Jokhang is a 1.5m-high gilded statue of **Jowo Sakyamuni**, the Buddha of the Present, born in 543BC in Nepal. The image was brought to Tibet by Queen Wencheng. It depicts the Sakyamuni Buddha at the age of 12: features such as long earlobes and a cranial bump are special marks of the Buddha. The highly revered statue bears an elaborate headdress and is encrusted with jewels; pilgrims crowd in to make offerings, and to walk around the statue.

Revered as deities are the early religious kings of Tibet, who converted to Buddhism. Easily identified in the ground-floor chapels is **King Songtsen Gampo** (circa 608–650), the first of the great religious kings, considered to be a manifestation of Avalokitesvara. He wears a high orange or gold turban; his Chinese wife, **Queen Wencheng**, is on the viewer's right; his Nepalese wife, **Queen Tritsun**, on the viewer's left. This is the arrangement for a group to the left of the Jowo Sakyamuni image. The three great religious kings of Tibet are found in the Chapel of the Dharma Kings (Chapel 16) – the central figure being Songtsen Gampo; to the viewer's right, **Trisong Detsen** (the second religious king, who ruled from 755–797); and to the viewer's left, **Tri Ralpachen** (who ruled from 815–838). On the way out of the area, take a closer look at the two **side chapels** by the entrance: these contain guardian deities, designed to ward off evil forces.

Entering or exiting the inner Jokhang sanctuary, you pass two side chapels. The side chapel to the left (on the north side) contains a statue of Palden Lhamo, the main protective deity of the Jokhang, as well as fierce guardian deities. To the right, on the south side, are three Naga deity statues, also with a protective role.

Barkor Bazaar

Barkor Bazaar is a lively combination of market-place, pilgrim circuit and ethnic melting-pot. The 20-minute hexagonal circuit, running clockwise around the Jokhang and other structures, is always busy, especially at dawn and dusk. Join the pilgrims for a few circuits – it's good for exercise and good for people watching.

At the front of the Jokhang, the flagstones are worn smooth – polished from many years of pilgrims performing prostrations. Two-metre-high conical incense-burners billow clouds of smoke, and the smell of juniper fills the air. Vendors – mostly Chinese making a buck off Buddhism – sell *kata* scarves (see *Glossary*, page 271), prayer flags and prayer-wheels to the pilgrims. Arriving on pilgrimage from far-flung regions – such as the Kham or Golok areas – pilgrims mutter mantras as they circumambulate. You might see nomad women from eastern Tibet, their long tresses smeared in yak-butter; or an old woman leading her favourite sheep around the circuit; or a proud Khampa from eastern Tibet with tassels of red yarn braided through his hair, and a dagger on his belt (not entirely decorative); or a hardy prostrator with rubber apron and padded gloves flinging himself forward on the ground, completing the circuit on his stomach.

The Barkor is a magnet for beggars seeking alms, and for pilgrims seeking funds for their return home (and to support themselves in Lhasa in the meantime). More sophisticated are sutra-chanters: for a small sum, they will recite from sacred texts. And finally, there is the bazaar itself – shops and businesses line the entire circuit. Competing with these are open-air stalls laden with souvenirs and household goods; and there are roving vendors with bags of Tibetan music cassettes or other items. Since 1987, Barkor Bazaar has assumed another role – as the focus of protesters who encircle the Barkor when demonstrating against the Chinese occupation of Tibet. This explains the presence of police and security personnel in the area, ready to intercept any demonstrators.

Barkor Square

Officially, Barkor Square was completed in 1985 to mark the 20th year of the creation of the TAR. Unofficially, it was built to provide full military access to the troublesome Tibetan quarter and the maze of alleyways in the Barkor beyond. In the process, the Jokhang – previously hidden from view – has been exposed by a large plaza. There used to be a small square in front of the Jokhang – used as a marketplace – but nothing on the scale of the present plaza. This architectural approach might suit a grand European cathedral, but it is a travesty when applied to an intimate corner like the Jokhang.

Barkor Square is lined with shops and eateries, but it is also an elaborate parking lot for army trucks should trouble arise. A lot of older housing was ripped up and then replaced with mock-Tibetan-style shops, but these do not quite look the same. For one thing, the outer walls of these newer buildings are vertical, not bevelled as in old Lhasa. Old Lhasan housing is conservative in style, with an 'extraordinary biblical severity … preserving for us living architectural forms of ancient civilisations', as one writer noted. Typical housing consisted of flat-roofed two- or three-storey structures made of stone or sun-baked brick. Some buildings in the Barkor area date back to the 17th century and have withstood the test of time. Like the great masons of ancient Egypt or the Inca empire, Tibetans used no nails or cement: they fitted large blocks of stone closely together and relied on gravity, which meant inward-sloping walls were constructed.

In the PRC, squares like this are used for mass shows of solidarity with the Party, but occasionally (as at Tiananmen Square in 1989) they can be used for mass demonstrations against the Party. In Barkor Square, if 20 or so Tibetans congregate, the police will break the gathering up, nervous of a repeat of the rioting that has taken place in the past.

Barkor back-alleys

The Barkor area was proposed as a UN World Heritage site, but ironically it did not qualify because of too much destruction. However, in 2000, the Jokhang Temple was inscribed on the World Heritage List, so hopefully that will slow down Chinese dismantling of the area. The Chinese are systematically tearing down as much of the old quarter as possible on the grounds that the buildings are unstable: these same buildings are then replaced with newer ones of a similar design. The area around the Barkor used to be prime real estate, with residences of high-ranking nobles or lamas in this vicinity. Some of the better-preserved residences are at the southeast side of the Barkor: here you can find Labrang Nyingba, the former residence of aristocratic families.

Despite destruction and re-construction, the Barkor area is a real delight for strays and alley-cats, with small markets and temples tucked away – and Tibetans playing billiards. You can explore on foot or by bicycle. Around here, you step into a timewarp, catching glimpses of what life must have been like centuries, or even a millennium, ago: Ramoche Temple, to the northern side of the Barkor, is thought to date back to the seventh century – it is older than the Jokhang. The Ramoche is Lhasa's second-largest temple and is best viewed during prayer sessions (early morning or late afternoon) for real atmosphere. An entry fee is charged; you might be allowed to access the rooftop, with good views of the area. The wide alley that leads to the Ramoche Temple is lined with curious shops, some merchants selling gold teeth, others gilded temple-top ornaments.

Waiting for you to discover them are a host of small temples and shrines tucked into the back-alleys. Easy to find are two temples directly at the back of the Jokhang (east side), off the Barkor circuit. The larger of these is Meru Nyingba, founded in the 17th century as the Lhasa residence of the State Oracle. On the edge of the Barkor area, on the southeast side, is Ani Sangkhung, one of the three nunneries in Lhasa. Upward of 80 nuns live at Ani Sangkhung, while a number of nuns from this place are serving time in Drapchi Prison for demonstrating. The nunnery is difficult to find – keep asking for Ani Gompa. Also in this vicinity are several small mosques, combining Muslim and Tibetan architectural features.

Institute of Tibetan Medicine

Tibetan medicine is an amalgam of herbal cures, astrology and Tibetan Buddhism. No surgery is used – for this, the patient would have to go to other practitioners. Diagnosis in Tibetan medicine is done mainly by reading the pulse (urine samples are also checked). By reading the pulse, a traditional physician determines which humour-flow (bile, wind or phlegm) has been blocked, or is excessive, and which herbal remedies to prescribe to set the system in harmony. Apart from the three main 'humours' there are over 20,000 'channels' operating through the body. Though this may sound like medieval alchemy, in fact there is strong evidence to suggest the herbal cures, developed over a millenium, have considerable effect.

Since the medical college on Chakpori Hill was razed in 1959, the institute is the only traditional medicine facility left in Lhasa. In its present form – a bland concrete building located just west off Barkor Square – the institute opened in 1977. It has in-patient, out-patient and pharmaceutical production sections, as well as an astro/medical teaching institute.

Put together a small group and you can arrange a short tour of the Institute of Tibetan Medicine (Monday to Saturday, 09.00–12.30 mornings), which will

BEGGAR WITH A MOBILE PHONE

Lhasa has an air of mystery and intrigue still – but not quite the way you'd think. The big mysteries today are what all those Chinese buildings are, with the guards out front holding AK-47s or with pistols on their belts. The Chinese military have their own living quarters, exclusive markets, teahouses, restaurants, bars, discos and clubs tucked away, but you can walk into some of them. A lot of buildings are off-limits or Chinese-only or sensitive, and photography is frowned upon. Army bases are self-contained units with high walls – they usually have their own shops and facilities within, including their own video-cinema.

To assist the paranoid Chinese in their endeavours to snoop on Tibetans is a nefarious network of informants – human listening posts – and video surveillance cameras. The video cameras are mounted around the Potala and Barkor areas, and at major intersections of the city. The cameras were initially sold by Western countries to China for use in monitoring traffic flow. Since Lhasa doesn't have a traffic flow problem, obviously they are being put to other uses here. The Chinese network of Tibetan informants includes plainclothes police, monks in robes, and beggars. One Tibetan described these people as 'Tibetans who do Chinese work'. In the Barkor area, a man in rags was seen begging one moment, and the next using a mobile phone to inform police of what was going on.

The Chinese are convinced that demonstrations by the Tibetans could flare up at any moment. And then there is the threat of bombs. There have been sporadic reports of bomb blasts around Lhasa starting in the mid-1990s. The nature of the bombing is mysterious – Chinese authorities have largely remained silent on the subject. The bombs do not appear designed to cause loss of life – rather, to drive home a message of protest.

In June 1995, police defused an explosive device at the Qinghai-Tibet

include a visit to a second-floor museum, and the top floor medical tanka room. Here hundreds of rare medical tankas are stored – teaching devices showing which plants should be collected, anatomical charts with energy channels, and so on. You will be shown copies of the originals. In the same section are three statues of famous medical practitioners – in the middle is a white-bearded figure (Yutok Yonten Gonpo, 9th-century founder of Tibetan medical science), flanked on the left by the regent of the 5th Dalai Lama (Desi Sanggye Gyatso, 17th-century founder of Chakpori medical college) and on the right by the most renowned physician of the 20th century (Khyenrab Norbu, physician to the 13th Dalai Lama).

Potala area
The Lingkor

The Lingkor is the outer pilgrim circuit of Lhasa, taking about 90 minutes to complete on foot (or half that time by bicycle). Tibetans still follow the full Lingkor circuit, though it has lost much of its sacred appeal on the eastern and southern sides, where small bars and karaoke salons have mushroomed. These places are often fronts for prostitution. Nudes or noodles? Probably a bit of both, washed down with beer. Prostitutes are flown in from Sichuan province. Other fronts: barbershops west of the Potala, and certain restaurants with partitioned sections. How big is the trade? Very big. At Jarmalingka Island bridge, the news doesn't get any better. An old wooden bridge here used to lead to an undeveloped area where

Highway monument, an obelisk to the west side of the city, opposite the bus station. The monument commemorates the completion of roads linking the TAR to the provinces of Qinghai and Sichuan. Authorities were nervous because the explosive device was discovered a few months before the 30th anniversary of the founding of the TAR, scheduled for September 1995. With about 500 government officials and their families from all over China expected for the celebration, security was considerably tightened, and half a dozen checkpoints established on the Gongkar to Lhasa road. Two European tourists who took photographs of the obelisk a week later were detained and questioned for two hours, and had their film confiscated. In another 1995 incident, a tourist sent a fax from the Holiday Inn speculating about a bomb explosion: Chinese police intercepted the fax, arrested the tourist in the middle of the night, detained him for 48 hours, and then deported him.

In May 1996, Chinese authorities admitted to three bomb blasts in Lhasa, blaming them on separatists. In December 1996, a bomb damaged the gatehouse of the Metropolitan District Government Offices. The blast was confirmed on Tibet Radio, which described the incident as 'yet another counter-revolutionary bombing staged by the Dalai clique in Lhasa City' and calling it 'an appalling act of terrorism'. A substantial reward was posted for information leading to the capture of the person or persons responsible.

There are closed-circuit surveillance cameras mounted inside the Potala to eavesdrop on the caretaker monks there. Even though the Potala is Lhasa's major tourist attraction, and one of its most sacred sites, its last resident – the 14th Dalai Lama – is vilified by the Chinese. His picture is banned, along with that of the young 11th Panchen Lama (the one chosen by the Dalai Lama). So the whole trade in Dalai Lama and Panchen Lama pictures – once freely pursued in the Barkor – has simply gone underground.

Tibetans would congregate under the trees for picnics. The bridge was torn down and replaced by a wider concrete one – to develop Jarmalingka. The island-park was completely destroyed before it erupted with Chinese-style row-housing, brothels, karaoke bars, restaurants and cheap hotels. The area is today known as Kumalingka.

The Lingkor as a sacred circuit really gets underway at a cairn of stones with some prayer flags, just west of Jarmalingka Bridge. This marks the turn-off for a walking track that leads to the Blue Buddha. Apart from walking, you can bicycle the route, but there are steps near the Blue Buddha which require you to carry the bike. Otherwise, it's easy riding, with smooth, flat sections.

Blue Buddha

The way up past the south base of Chakpori Hill is a staircase lined with prayer flags. Further on is an entire cliff face depicting religious figures, which have been carved in bas-relief and painted in bright colours. Some carvings date back over a thousand years, with countless additions over the centuries. The largest carving is the Blue Buddha, shown seated in a meditation pose. In this area, pilgrims pay their respects, and off to the side, carvers chip text into mani stones. If you follow the pilgrims, you'll eventually arrive at Dekyi Nub Road. Right where you arrive at this major road, there's a section with some well-worn rocks. These are special rubbing stones that pilgrims apply their knees or backs to. From here, pilgrims continue past the Golden Yak statues to Lhasa's West Gate, although these were not part of the original Lingkor circuit.

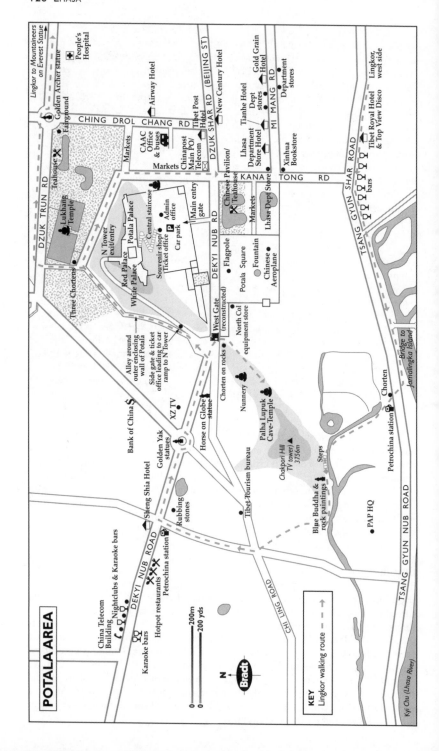

POTALA AREA

KEY

Lingkor walking route - - - →

0 ____ 200m
0 ____ 200 yds

N

Bradt

Kyi Chu (Lhasa River)

Golden Yak statues

Two golden yak statues were unveiled in May 1991 to celebrate the 40th anniversary of the 'peaceful liberation' of Tibet by Chinese troops. Tibetans have christened the incongruous statues 'Tenzin and Raidi,'a reference to the two Tibetan deputy secretaries of the Communist Party in Tibet who are trotted out when the Chinese need to present a Tibetan face to the media. In the background at this site sits the modern office building housing Xizang TV (XZ TV), the main radio and TV broadcasting unit in Lhasa. The operation is solar-powered. The Golden Yak statues are something of a navigation landmark, referred to in this section as the Golden Yak roundabout.

West Gate

As part of the 1995 'celebrations' of the 30th anniversary of the founding of the TAR, Lhasa's West Gate and two accompanying chortens were resurrected. Passing through the chorten-like West Gate was once the only way into the sacred city, and reaching it was the dream of many explorers. It was the gate that British troops marched through in 1904; the gate that Heinrich Harrer and Peter Aufschnaiter reached in rags in 1946, after two years of wandering. Now you see it, now you don't: the original West Gate was completely destroyed in the Cultural Revolution, and then completely rebuilt for the 1995 ceremonies. Tibetan pilgrims pose next to the 1995 version of the West Gate for photos, but Tibetans say that the structure was not properly consecrated by monks, and in any case, there are no hidden treasures within the chorten-like structure that required consecration. Nevertheless, there is some fine artwork lining the interior of the West Gate, especially a mandalic mural on the inside ceiling.

Detours

From the West Gate, there are several hiking options. Some pilgrims make a kora (complete loop) of the outer enclosing wall of the Potala and come back to the West Gate, and then visit Palhalupuk cave-temple. Others go from the West Gate to Palhalupuk first, then trace the wall of the Potala north to a site with three chortens, where they diverge past Lukhang Park to Dzuk Trun Road, and then continue eastward past the Golden Archer statue on the Lingkor circuit. Another hike to consider is a climb to the top of Chakpori. This hill was once crowned by the fortress-like medical college of Lhasa – the institute, founded in the 15th century, was razed by shelling in the 1959 uprising. The hill is now crowned with a TV tower – you can climb to the top for views of the Potala.

Palhalupuk Cave-temple

Palhalupuk is an extraordinary cave-temple set into the lower section of Chakpori Hill – you can reach it by a path leading from the West Gate. The brown and ochre-coloured Palhalupuk temple, with a dozen monks in residence, offers a superb viewpoint of the Potala, giving it a foreground of rocks and trees. Close by are two small caves – the larger one is lined with several rows of brightly painted bas-relief images, believed to date back as far as the 7th century (which qualifies them as the oldest in Lhasa). The central image here is Sakyamuni, while at the back is a small statue of Palden Lhamo, the protectress of Lhasa. The intimate scale of the temple and cave make Palhalupuk very special – it offers perspectives that you will find nowhere else in Lhasa. There's a second (minor) cave with an image of Avalokitesvara in the vicinity; above Palhalupuk to the right is a small active nunnery.

THE MYSTERIOUS SIXTH

The Sixth Dalai Lama was Tsangyang Gyatso, whose name means 'Ocean of Melodious Songs'. He is thought to have lived from 1683 to 1706. The Sixth took over as Dalai Lama under very unusual circumstances. The Fifth Dalai Lama had died during the construction of the Potala but his death was concealed by the Regent for some 15 years to ensure completion of the work (the Fifth was replaced by a double and was said to be engaged in long meditation retreats). The Sixth Dalai Lama took over as an adolescent, not an infant like his predecessors. He did not take any celibacy vows and was never fully ordained as a lama. He showed little interest in either his political or religious duties. His passions lay elsewhere. He was a prolific rake – no woman in Lhasa was said to be safe from his indulgences:

> I dwell apart in the Potala
> A God on earth am I
> But in the town the chief of rogues
> And boisterous revelry

Lukhang Temple has been variously described as the Sixth's personal retreat, and as his favourite trysting place. He was said to sneak out of a back gate of the Potala to meet his lovers. Apart from his love of wine and women, the Sixth was renowned as a melodious singer of love songs, and writer of romantic lyrics:

> Drops of rain wash away
> The love songs written in
> Black and white
> But love, though unwritten,
> Remains long after, in the heart

Despite his behaviour, the Sixth was revered by the people, who came to the conclusion that the living Buddha had two bodies – one which stayed in the Potala and meditated, and the other that got rotten drunk and chased Lhasa women. The Sixth disappeared under mysterious circumstances at the age of 23. One account claims that he had a son by a special lover, and that high lamas – fearing the office of the Dalai Lama would become hereditary – drove the Sixth into exile and imprisoned his lover and their son. Another account claims he was murdered at Litang.

Lukhang Park

The park at the back of the Potala was a site where Tibetan aristocracy used to picnic or drink tea. It has since lost its noble atmosphere – it's down at the proletariat level now, re-named Jiefang (Victory) Park. However, you can still take tea here, and contemplate the excellent views of the Potala. There are three entrances to the park – one at the north side, one at the east, and one at the southeast side. On the western side, the way in is blocked by walls and Lukhang Lake. At the entrances, you pay a token fee (extra for a bicycle). Lukhang Park attracts picnickers, strollers and people relaxing, and it's great for cycling around. In the far northeast corner is a fairground, with some mangy Bactrian camels serving as photo-props. Not far off is a teahouse with outdoor tables and umbrellas – it overlooks a small artificial lake, with the towers of the Potala looming above. A plant nursery is attached to the teahouse: potted plants and flowers make this a very pleasant place. You can park yourself over a cup of *ba bao cha* (eight treasures tea) – this is provided in a cup with a lid, and contains a big lump of rock sugar with dried berries and herbs, to which steaming hot water is added.

Lukhang Temple

On an island in the middle of the lake is Lukhang Temple, a tiny three-storey chapel constructed in the form of a mandala. The building of the temple is attributed to the Sixth Dalai Lama, and it was used as a quiet retreat for arcane meditation practices by successive Dalai Lamas.

Lukhang Temple is one of those corners that provides an illusion of old Lhasa: it is sequestered in greenery, with only the back of the Potala visible, so you can get a feeling for what Tibet once was. There are a few monks currently in residence at Lukhang Temple. You can visit, but not all parts of the building are accessible. There are murals on each of the three storeys: the most interesting are those on the third floor, believed to date to the 18th century. You will need a flashlight to see these gems – they are protected by a wire shield, which doesn't make the viewing any easier. The murals show subjects that are rare to find in Tibetan temples today. Among them are depictions of Indian ascetics in yogic poses, and others striking blissful tantric poses. One wall shows the stages of human life, with detailed anatomical pictures acting as a kind of Tibetan medicine primer (in which system an imbalance of humours leads to sickness and dysfunction). Attached to this is a set of murals based on *The Tibetan Book of the Dead*.

Potala Square

Potala Square was created in time to mark 'celebrations' for the 30th anniversary of the TAR. A large area of ramshackle Tibetan housing was razed to create the paving; the inhabitants were moved to concrete housing north of the Potala. The concept of a large square or plaza is alien to Tibetan town planning: this is a Chinese idea. The Tibetans would have no use for such a square because it allows the bitter winter wind to roar through. Potala Square has a lot in common with Beijing's Tiananmen Square, including the same chandelier-lamp fixtures with propaganda speakers attached. Tiananmen Square was Mao Zedong's creation, designed for military parades and mass solidarity parades, and meanwhile used for weekend amusement like photo-taking or kite flying.

This is exactly what Potala Square is used for: the military use it as one big parking lot; concerts for the military have been staged here; shows of force and parades by the PLA have taken place; and trade fairs with vendors promoting Chinese products have been conducted here. The emphasis at Potala Square is on entertainment, too, although it's mostly aimed at the Chinese. In the mid-1990s, Lhasa's biggest Chinese disco, called JJ's, was located in a large building on the west side of Potala Square, but it closed down within a year. Toward the back of the square are amusement rides for children, a fountain with a Chinese dragon sculpture, and an old aircraft which is used as a photo-prop. Potala Square is the premier Chinese photo opportunity site. There is a slew of photo-shops just to the west of the square, catering to Chinese tourism. A flagpole at the front of the square is a favourite place for Chinese tourists to have their photos taken. All Chinese dignitaries and military honchos arriving in Lhasa stop near the flagpole to have photos or video taken with the Potala in the background.

In 2002, a 37-metre-high concrete monolith was constructed near the fountain to commemorate the 50th anniversary of the liberation of Tibet. This monstrosity, said be an abstract rendition of Everest, is flanked by two concrete bunkers, intended as exhibition halls. The monument is reported to have cost US$1.7 million to build, prompting exiled Tibetans to call it a million-dollar insult.

Potala Palace

The Potala was inscribed on the UNESCO World Heritage List in 1994. The citation says: 'The Potala, winter palace of the Dalai Lama since the 7th century AD, symbolises Tibetan Buddhism and its central role in the traditional administration of Tibet'. Chinese authorities conducted a five-year multi-million-dollar restoration of the Potala, completing work in 1995. Why restore a palace that is former abode of Public Enemy Number One? Because it's a tourist attraction, of course. Unlike the Jokhang or the monasteries around Lhasa, the Potala is run by Chinese tourist authorities: the practice of Buddhism is essentially banned in the palace.

Once humming with activity, the Potala is now a lifeless museum, a haunted castle. A lot of the Chinese restoration was directed at the enclosing walls, which were damaged by Chinese shelling during the 1959 uprising. Adding considerably to the bill is the 'wiring' of the Potala. Electrical hook-ups have been enhanced and video surveillance cameras have been installed throughout. The cameras are to monitor the 60-odd caretakers at the Potala – mostly monks who are not permitted to wear robes (it appears that a number of them were replaced by ordinary cleaners in 1997). On a more practical note, fire extinguishers and other devices have been installed (following a disastrous fire that broke out in 1984 due to a short circuit).

Below the Potala, within the enclosing walls, used to lie the Tibetan administrative quarter of Shol. Some buildings in this zone have been destroyed. One building has been turned into a hotel; the others are used as art galleries, souvenir shops, or occupied as residences. In pre-1950 days, Shol quartered the offices of the Tibetan government, Tibetan Army officials, guard offices and a prison. Other sections of the Potala were used to house Namgyal Monastery, as well as a community of monks and a school for monk officials.

History and architecture

The Potala is a 13-storey castle – rising over 117m high – built of rammed earth, wood and stone. Crowning a mass of solid rock, the maze-like structure contains over a thousand rooms, and is thought to house 10,000 shrines and 200,000 statues. The architecture at first appears to be regular, but is not – storeys are not continuous, and access to halls may be hidden behind pillars or shrines. The walls – varying in thickness between two and five metres – were strengthened against earthquakes by pouring in molten copper. No steel frame was used, and no nails were used in the woodwork. The Potala is a layered structure: successive Dalai Lamas worked on the project. Although original construction dates back to the 7th century, the White Palace was not completed until 1653, and the Red Palace not until 1694: at this time, the wheel had not been introduced to Tibet, so stones were lugged in on donkey-back, or on the backs of humans. Simple equipment was used to fashion this skyscraper – an achievement on a par with the building of the pyramids.

The skyscraper itself created a transport problem. The Potala had no plumbing, electricity or heating, so there was – in previous times – a constant stream of porters with water for tea, yak-butter for the prayer-lamps, and firewood for the fireplaces. The Dalai Lama was portered in and out of the palace in a palanquin; high lamas were piggybacked up to the entrance of the Potala by porters.

Access

Hours of opening for the Potala seem to chop and change, and may vary with the season. You can follow the logic of the hours described here, but there could well be modifications. In theory, the Potala is open to tourists from 10.00–17.00 daily, including holidays. The best time to visit is mornings; the last ticket is sold at

15.30. Entry costs Y70 (charged at both the front gate and the west gate) for big noses and Y35 for foreign students (with proof of status). In the 'slack season' (November 1 to March 31) tickets drop to Y50. Once you enter the Potala, a further charge of Y10 is later levied to get on the rooftop, and another Y10 to get into the Cultural Relics Museum near the teahouse in the Red Palace. There may well be an additional charge for use of a video camera, and for still cameras at certain interior spots.

The Potala is open to Tibetan pilgrims, who pay a token entry fee and enter at the front gate. It appears that the pilgrims are allowed entry on Monday, Wednesday and Friday mornings, but this could change. When there are lots of pilgrims, key shrines may become very crowded, with long queues. Here's a paradox: things are much more lively with Tibetan pilgrims around (you can observe what they are doing – muttering mantras, flinging katas, and spooning yak-butter into lamps at shrines) but at the same time, it's more crowded and uncomfortable. Try and visit the Potala several times if you can: first to see the architecture and statuary, the second time to go and mingle with the Tibetan pilgrims.

If you consult the Potala Area access section of the Potala Area map, you can discern the main entry/exit routes. There are two ticket kiosks where you pay to enter the Potala; near the central staircase, or near the West Gate, at a large wooden door leading to a car ramp that brings you out to a parking area at the North Tower. You can enter and exit using a combination of these options. Group tours usually drive up in vans to the North Tower, and make their way through the Potala, exiting down the central staircase, where the vans pick them up again. This requires a minimum of physical exertion, which is what the tour operators want. Freelance travellers can walk up the same ramp to enter the Potala, but most opt for the traditional approach – the route the pilgrims take – which is via the central staircase. You walk slowly up the central staircase, reach the rooftop, spiral down through the Red Palace, and exit at the North Tower (the exit is difficult to locate – it's at the back of statuary, so just follow the pilgrims). You can then walk back down the car ramp to the West Gate area. A word of caution if you are tackling the central staircase – it's like Stairmaster at altitude. Ensure that you are reasonably acclimatised before tackling these steps, or they can knock the wind out of you.

The description in this book follows the entry up the central staircase and exit via the North Tower: if approaching from the reverse direction (as group tours often do), read the entries backwards. Only a fraction of the Potala's 1,000-odd rooms are accessible to the touring public: the contents of many are rumoured to have been destroyed or carted off. The rooms seem to open and close without rhyme or reason, so the following description may hit the mark – or it may not.

Inside the Potala
The Potala is divided into the White Palace and the Red Palace. The White Palace was secular in nature (used for offices, printing house, and so on), while the Red Palace fulfilled a religious function (comprising the tombs of the Dalai Lamas, scores of chapels and shrines, and libraries of sacred texts). Most of the White Palace is inaccessible; you can see a fair number of rooms in the Red Palace.

The 14th Dalai Lama's quarters
After huffing and puffing up the central staircase, you arrive near the roof of the Potala, reaching an open area. Green-maned snow-lions are the gargoyles here – pilgrims touch the mouths of the lions and ring attached bells. To the west side of the open area are the former living quarters of the 13th and 14th Dalai Lamas, attached to the White Palace. The only section accessible here takes you into the

former Reception Hall, dominated by a large throne. On the wall nearby hangs a portrait painting of 13th Dalai Lama, but a portrait of the 14th that used to hang alongside it has been removed. So ludicrous is the Chinese removal of 14th Dalai Lama images that in a lavishly illustrated Beijing hardcover about the Potala, he is only seen in one picture – shaking hands with Mao Zedong in 1954.

In the same Reception Hall, near the entrance, is a large mural of the legendary land of Shambhala. Beyond the hall lie the private quarters of the 14th Dalai Lama. You may or may not be allowed to see these, depending on the mood of caretakers. Try tagging along behind an official tour. At the 14th Dalai Lama's tearoom and meditation room, pilgrims leave katas and other offerings; beyond is His Holiness' bedroom, vacant since 1959.

Back out in the open courtyard, you can fork out another dollar or so to take rickety ladders that lead right onto the roof of the roof of the world. Here you can see what the Chinese have wrought in Lhasa, and the full extent of Potala Square. Chinese tourists hire historic Tibetan costumes here for photo-taking sessions.

The Red Palace

Entering the Red Palace from the rooftop area, you spiral downward through four levels, eventually exiting at the North Tower. The upper levels of the Red Palace enclose an open skylight space, with chapels arrayed in a gallery-like rectangle around that space. Interspersed through the many chapels and shrines of the Red Palace are the eight gold-plated stupas, each containing the salt-dried body of a past Dalai Lama – from the 5th to the 13th, with the exception of the 6th, who disappeared. Four of the reliquary stupas are on the upper level, and four are on the ground level.

Upper level The upper level provides access to chapels with the stupas of the 7th, 8th, 9th and 13th Dalai Lamas. You may have difficulty getting permission to see the stupa of the 13th Dalai Lama, which is 14 metres high, made of gold, and fronted by a three-dimensional mandala said to contain 200,000 pearls. The tomb ranges over several storeys and is well lit. One wall bears fine murals of the 13th Dalai Lama surrounded by his ministers and tutors, as well as scenes from his life. Another highlight of the upper level is the former throne room of the 7th Dalai Lama, which contains a beautiful silver image of eleven-faced Avalokitesvara, the bodhisattva of compassion – this statue was commissioned by the 13th Dalai Lama.

Revered by Tibetan pilgrims as the most sacred part of the entire Potala is the Avalokitesvara Chapel (Phakpa Lakhang), on the northwest side of the upper level. The tiny chapel gets very crowded when there are lots of pilgrims. It is reached by a small triple staircase. The centre of pilgrim attention is a tiny gilded standing statue of Avalokitesvara, thought to have come from Nepal. Legend has it that the image was found miraculously embedded in a Nepalese sandalwood tree when its trunk split open. Flanking it are two other images derived from the same source, one of Avalokitesvara again, the other of Tara. To the right of this chapel is the massive funerary chorten of the 7th Dalai Lama, rising to a height of nine metres, and studded with precious stones. Next to that is the tomb of the 9th Dalai Lama.

Mid-levels Downstairs, there is a Tibetan-style tearoom with a souvenir shop. On the same level is the Cultural Relics Museum, which charges Y10 entry and features a display of armour and instruments. There are two levels of galleries at the mid-levels, but rooms on the lower level are most likely to be closed (these contain murals depicting the construction of the Potala and major Tibetan monasteries). The highlight of the mid-levels is the Kalachakra Chapel (Dukhor Lakhang), which contains a stunning three-dimensional mandala of the palace of the Kalachakra deity. Made of copper and gold, it measures over six metres in diameter. To one side of the mandala is a life-sized statue of the multi-headed, multi-armed Kalachakra deity in union with his consort. On shelves nearby are the seven religious kings of Tibet and the 25 kings of the mythical realm of Shambhala.

Very popular with Tibetan pilgrims on this level is the oldest chamber in the Potala, the Chapel of the Dharma Kings, thought to have been the meditation chamber of King Songtsen Gampo. This cave-within-the-castle is approached by a ramp; the niches lining the cavern are filled with statuary of past kings, royal family members and ministers. The most highly-regarded statue is that of Songtsen Gampo himself. You can expect a pilgrim traffic-jam in this area and foreign group tours are likely to be ushered past the line-ups.

Ground level After negotiating several steep, dark flights of stairs, you come into a large assembly hall with columns – the Great Western Assembly Hall. This is the largest room in the Potala Palace, with dozens of pillars wrapped in raw silk. It contains the throne of the 7th Dalai Lama; the walls are coated in murals and appliqué tankas.

There are four chapels open on this level. The first you come to is Lamrin Lakhang, dedicated to the ancient lineage masters of the Geluk school, particularly Tsongkhapa. The next chapel, Rigdzin Lakhang, is dedicated to the great Nyingma lineage holder, Padmasambhava, showing eight manifestations of the master; in the same line-up of statues here are seven other great Indian masters.

The next chapel, Dzamling Gyenchik, contains the astounding tomb of the 5th Dalai Lama, which reaches a height of over 14 metres, and is said to contain 3,700kg of gold. It is studded with jewels and precious stones. In this line-up of tombs are eight more dedicated to Sakyamuni Buddha, commemorating the eight major events in his life. In the same chapel are the more modest stupas of the 10th and 12th Dalai Lamas, who both perished as minors, failing to attain their majority. The Dalai Lamas from the 6th through to the 12th all died young and under mysterious circumstances – possibly poisoned.

The last chapel on the ground level is Tungrab Lakhang, featuring a central double throne with two statues – a gold one of Sakyamuni and a silver one of the 5th Dalai Lama. This chapel contains the tomb of the 11th Dalai Lama; three statues of the Buddha (past, present and future); and statues of the eight Medicine Buddhas.

North Tower Exit

You can exit Tungrab Lakhang by a dark hidden corridor at the back of the statues – this leads out of the rear of the Potala at the North Tower. Heading down the hill you get a view of north Lhasa that is not revealed from the rooftop of the Potala: a sea of apartment blocks stretching toward Sera – the heavy Chinese concrete hand at work. You leave the Potala Palace grounds by the doorway near the West Gate.

Norbulingka area
The Norbulingka

In contrast to the lofty, monumental Potala, the Norbulingka is a small-scale, down-to-earth summer palace. In former times, an elaborate procession would wind out of the Potala, escorting the Dalai Lama to the Norbulingka, his home for up to six months of the year. In better days, the walled summer palace exuded an idyllic atmosphere, with picnic pavilions and well-tended gardens, peacocks roaming the grounds, and Brahminy ducks flocking to the lakes. Norbulingka in

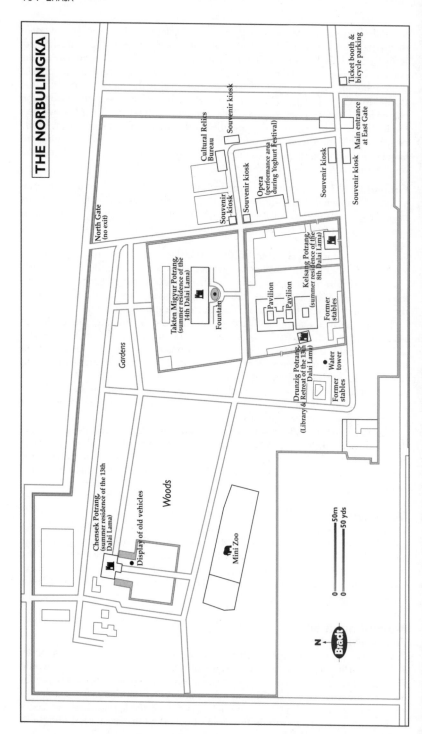

THE NORBULINGKA

Ticket booth &
bicycle parking

Main entrance
at East Gate

Souvenir kiosk

Souvenir kiosk

Opera
(performance area
during Yoghurt Festival)

Souvenir kiosk

Souvenir
kiosk

Cultural Relics
Bureau

Souvenir
kiosk

North Gate
(no exit)

Takten Migyur Potrang,
(summer residence of the
14th Dalai Lama)

Fountain

Gardens

Pavilion

Pavilion

Kelsang Potrang,
(summer residence of the
8th Dalai Lama)

Former
stables

Drunzig Potrang,
(Library & Retreat of the 13th
Dalai Lama)

Former
stables

Water
tower

Chensek Potrang,
(summer residence of the 13th
Dalai Lama)

Display of old vehicles

Woods

Mini Zoo

0   50m
0   50 yds

N

Bradt

fact means 'Jewelled Garden'. Visiting in the 1930s, members of a British delegation were astonished to find roses and petunias flourishing at 3,650 metres, as well as hollyhocks, marigolds, chrysanthemums, and rows of potted herbs or rare plants. As well, there were apple, peach and apricot trees – though the fruits did not ripen in Lhasa – and stands of poplar trees and bamboo.

The Norbulingka was shelled during the 1959 uprising, and a number of buildings were destroyed. Although there are roses and bamboo thickets around the 14th Dalai Lama's former residence, the gardens are mostly derelict, and the fountains and miniature lakes have dried up, so the flocks of birds have long gone too. The Norbulingka is mainly identified with the 13th and 14th Dalai Lamas, who commissioned most of the structures you see here. In 2001, the Norbulingka was added as an extension of the Potala for inscription on the UN World Heritage List, along with the Jokhang Temple. The citation quoted preservation of the last vestiges of traditional Tibetan architecture (what is meant here is saving the last traditional structures in the face of rampant Chinese development and reconstruction in Lhasa).

Access

The Norbulingka is open 09.30–12.30 and 15.30–18.00 (summer hours); closed Sundays. To get to the Norbulingka, you can walk, bicycle, take a taxi, or take a number 2 bus from the Barkor Square vicinity. Although there are several gateways at the Norbulingka, the only one open for entry/exit is the East Gate, with a ticket booth and bicycle-parking nearby. When Tibetan opera is held here during the Yoghurt (Shoton) Festival, around August/September, the grounds are crowded with picnickers. Flanking the massive east gates of the Norbulingka are two snow- lion statues, draped in katas. Tibetans like to get their photo taken next to the mythical snow-lion (the one to the left side shelters a lion cub). The snow-lion is the symbol of Tibet – it is reputed to be able to jump from one snowcapped peak to another. Only a few buildings inside the Norbulingka are open – others are locked up, or used as storage, or as residences or offices by those involved with the upkeep of the Norbulingka. Some more recent building additions or renovations are souvenir kiosks selling drinks, souvenir books and some Tibetan artefacts.

Residence of the 14th Dalai Lama

The main attraction at the Norbulingka is **Takten Migyur Potrang**, the summer residence of 14th Dalai Lama. It's a pilgrimage site for Tibetans, who leave katas and other offerings in the various rooms here. The building was constructed from 1954 to 1956, and was the place where the Dalai Lama meditated before he escaped to India. Access is only to rooms on the upper floor.

In the Assembly Hall, murals portray a detailed history of Tibet, from its mythical beginnings to its early kings to the discovery of the 14th Dalai Lama. Several other rooms can be seen here: the Dalai Lama's study chambers, with a beautiful tanka of Atisha; and his bedroom, with an art-deco bed and a 1956 Phillips radio (a gift from India). A sidedoor leads to a bathroom with state-of-the-art (for Tibet at the time) plumbing. You may be allowed to visit a small library and a meditation room.

In the Reception Hall is a carved golden throne which was used to carry the Dalai Lama when he went outside the Norbulingka for special occasions. One entire wall of the Reception Hall is covered with fine murals, painted in 1956 by artist Amdo Jampa. The murals show – with photo-like realism – the 14th Dalai Lama at the centre, flanked by his mother at the right, ministers and relatives at the left, secretary below him, his four tutors above him, various tribes of Tibet at lower right, and foreign dignitaries at lower left. Under all this is a row of mythical figures. Among the foreign dignitaries you can make out Hugh Richardson (hat and tie) who originally worked for the British and stayed on to represent the new Indian government. Also visible is an Indian dignitary, a Russian wearing medals and a Mongolian ambassador. Unfortunately, most of the mural – especially the section showing the Dalai Lama – is likely to be roped off, and light reflections make it difficult to view. An overhead surveillance camera ensures that pilgrims get no closer. This is one of the rare images of the Dalai Lama still left in Lhasa and thus the object of great veneration by pilgrims passing through, an activity the Chinese do not wish to encourage.

The opposite wall bears a large portrait of the Great Fifth Dalai Lama, surrounded by smaller portraits of the first through to the 13th Dalai Lamas. As you exit the doorway, there's a round Shambhala fresco with a Kalachakra mandala (see box, page 218). Harder to access are other sections of the building, including the dining room, and various meeting and reception rooms.

Retreats, vintage cars and a mini-zoo

Moving along through the grounds of the Norbulingka, of milder interest is **Kelsang Potrang**, the summer residence of the 8th Dalai Lama, completed in the 18th century. This section may be closed; if it's open, you can view some fine tankas depicting White Tara. On the eastern wall in this area is a viewing pavilion that looks over the opera grounds. The Dalai Lamas would sit here to take in performances, which are still held during the Yoghurt Festival (in August or September). To the west of this, in a separate compound (approached from the west wall), is **Drunzig Potrang**, constructed as the library and retreat of the 13th Dalai Lama. It has the atmosphere of a place of worship, with an assembly hall redolent of butter-lamps. It contains a newer wooden statue of Avalokitesvara, and thousands of sacred texts. Nearby is an area with outdoor pavilions, probably used for picnics or drinking tea. The mini-lakes they overlook have dried up.

There are several locations where horses were formerly stabled, though these are hard to pinpoint today. The back of each stable was decorated with bright frescos of equestrian subjects, ranging from horse anatomy to legends of flying horses, and nearby was the Dalai Lama's garage.

The Dalai Lama's cars, however, have been shifted over to a display of vehicles at Chensek Potrang. A fair walk away, in the northwest corner of the grounds, **Chensek Potrang** is the summer residence of the 13th Dalai Lama. It was built in 1922, and is preserved much as it was in 1933, when the 13th Dalai Lama died. Only the assembly hall here may be accessible.

In the courtyard of Chensek Potrang is a fascinating display of vehicles, ranging from palanquins (covered litters for one person, moved on foot by bearers) to landaus (elaborate horse-drawn carriages with sidelamps). There is even a bicycle and a tricycle (gifts from the British to the 13th and 14th Dalai Lamas). This is all the more fascinating when you consider that the wheel was not much used in pre-1950 Tibet, and the use of vehicles like motorcycles was banned by the monastic powers.

Among the vehicles in the courtyard you can see the rusted remains of several cars that originally belonged to the 13th Dalai Lama and were inherited by the 14th. The cars were gifts from British political officers, carried in pieces by yaks over the Himalayas from India and reassembled by an Indian chauffeur and mechanic. Two were 1920s Baby Austins (one with the numberplate Tibet 1); the third was a 1931 orange Dodge. They were used for special occasions, and were the only cars in Tibet at the time, apart from an American jeep. Their range was limited by a lack of roads and a lack of fuel, which had to be carried in from India. By the 1940s, they had fallen into disrepair, but the young 14th Dalai Lama managed to get them running again. He took a Baby Austin out for a spin at the Norbulingka – and promptly crashed into a tree. One of these cars was later adapted to power a generator for the 14th Dalai Lama's private cinema. Somewhere in the inner gardens of the Norbulingka there used to be a movie-theatre, constructed in 1949 for the Dalai Lama by Heinrich Harrer (there was another cine-projection room at the British Mission, run by radio operator Reginald Fox).

In the same vicinity, south of Chensek Potrang, is a derelict mini-zoo, with some cages lying empty. In residence is a motley collection of bears, spotted deer, rhesus monkeys, foxes, lynxes, Argali bighorn sheep, barheaded geese and bearded vultures, none of whom look especially thrilled about living on bare concrete.

Tibet Museum

Located in the same vicinity as Norbulingka Summer Palace is the largest structure built in Tibetan style in the last few decades, which is … a museum. Completed in 2000, the multi-million-dollar Tibet Museum encloses a vast exhibition space, spread over three floors. It is long on ethnography and short (or warped) on history, short on religion and very short on the Dalai Lamas (not a single picture of the 14th Dalai Lama is on display). The museum is liberally sprinkled with Chinese propaganda: the history section features such items as an original copy of the 17-point agreement signed in 1951, marking Tibet's take-over by the Chinese; and the Golden Urn, used by the Chinese to determine their choice of 11th Panchen Lama in 1995. Despite this slant, with its large collection of manuscripts, tankas, masks and costumes, the museum marks the passage of a great civilisation, with original, striking art and architecture. The ground floor focuses on pre-history and manuscripts and tankas; the middle floor is largely devoted to nomad culture; and the top floor concentrates on Tibet's flora and fauna. Given out with tickets are audio-tour devices programmed with different languages and available in English, Chinese, Japanese, and, yes, even in Tibetan. Entry tickets are Y30, or Y20 for students, but no audio device is included for that price. The museum is open daily, 09.00–13.00 and 14.00–18.00.

OUTSKIRTS OF LHASA

One of the saving graces of Lhasa is its clean air – far cleaner than in Kathmandu or other Asian cities. Traffic in Lhasa is light, and the place is ringed by mountains. The outskirts of Lhasa present great hiking opportunities. Offering novel perspectives on Lhasa Valley are ridge-top viewpoints – at Bumpa Ri to the southeast side, above Sera to the north side, and at Gephel Ri to the northwest side. The easiest one to tackle is Bumpa Ri. To get to the base of Bumpa Ri, you can bicycle out over Lhasa Bridge, the only bridge to span the Kyi Chu River. The bridge was built in 1965 – it is 530m long, and is guarded by sentries at both ends. Find a place to keep your bike and climb up toward prayer-flags planted on top of Bumpa Ri. If you want something less strenuous, you can take on smaller hills in this area, also planted with prayer-flags.

At the back of Sera Monastery are fine hiking trails linking shrines. You can take a bus or minivan service to either Sera or Drepung monasteries, bicycle out, share a taxi, hitch a ride, or walk. If you have a mountain-bike, day trips or overnight trips can be mounted – due east and northeast of Lhasa are the best directions to go, as there is less traffic.

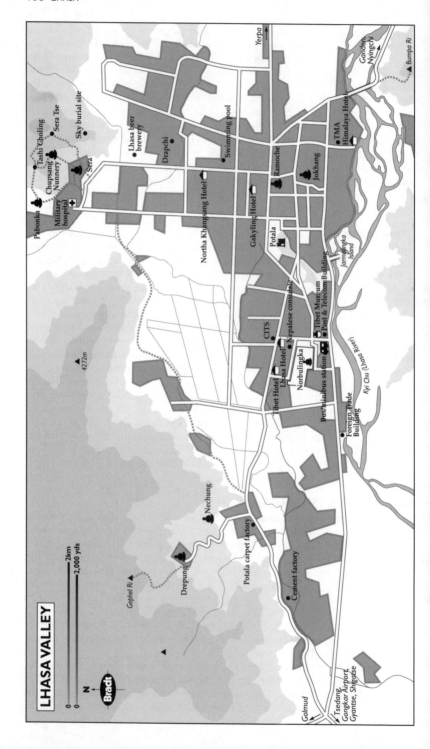

Sera

The three great Geluk monastic citadels close to Lhasa – Sera, Drepung and Ganden – developed a considerable rivalry in old Lhasa. They were all established in the early 15th century – Ganden in 1409, Drepung in 1416, and Sera in 1419. Sera's population hovered around 7,000 monks, eclipsed by the 9,000 at Drepung, while Ganden's quota was probably 5,000 monks.

Sera, 4km to the north of Lhasa, was at one time famous for its fighting monks, who spent years perfecting the martial arts. They were hired out as bodyguards to the wealthy, and even took on the Tibetan Army in 1947 during protests following the imprisonment of Reting Rinpoche. Once a year, the fighting monks of Sera used to race starkers along the Kyi Chu riverbank for several kilometres to toughen up. Sera means 'merciful hail' – the origin of the name is thought to derive from the fact that Sera was in constant competition with Drepung ('rice heap monastery') and that the 'hail' of Sera destroyed the 'rice' of Drepung. Today, only a few hundred monks remain at Sera, a shadow of its former self. You can wander around and view the interiors of the two main colleges – Sera Me and Sera Je – as well as the Main Assembly Hall.

Entry to Sera costs Y35. Near the entrance to Sera is a monastery restaurant that serves noodles, vegetables and bread at low prices. There's a pleasant outdoor section at the back, shaded by birch trees, where pilgrims gather.

Hiking behind Sera

A bigger draw than the temple interiors is the hiking out this way. Behind Sera to the northeast, on a mountainside, is the hermitage of Tsongkhapa – a simple shrine. In the vicinity are striking rock carvings, painted on boulders. A walking circuit around Sera takes about an hour to complete. If you are well acclimatised, there are more ambitious, longer, steeper hikes behind Sera that offer superb views. Dotted around the hill backing Sera are a number of caves, hermitages and sacred sites that are among the oldest in Lhasa. A circuit of sorts leads past Sera to Pabonka, a small temple with two dozen monks; from there you can carry on to Tashi Choling hermitage, and climb a ridge to Chupsang Nunnery, which has 80 nuns in residence. This makes for a worthwhile but fairly strenuous day.

Sera to Drepung

Instead of going back through downtown Lhasa to get from Sera to Drepung, you can take a more interesting shortcut by traversing a marshy area southwest of Sera. Some of the time there's a dirt road to follow, other times not. It's possible to bicycle most of the route, which leads past a rock quarry. Unless you have a mountain-bike with gears, it's better not to attempt the steep route up from the base of the hill leading to Drepung. Leave the bike with a shop-owner (with a token payment) and hitch a ride with whatever comes along (most likely a walking-tractor or number 3 bus).

Drepung

If Sera used to be famous for its fighting monks, Drepung was famed for its scholars. Spectacularly sited – enclosed on three sides by boulder-strewn peaks – Drepung is an entire monastic town that once housed a community of some 9,000 monks, qualifying it as the largest in the world. There are perhaps 500 monks living here today, although their numbers are uncertain following a major re-education campaign in the late 1990s, where monks were forced to denounce the Dalai Lama. Drepung has been singled out as a priority for re-education because of

SKY BURIAL

To the north of Lhasa is a kind of 'dead end', with Drapchi Prison, Lhasa Military Hospital, and – to the northeast – a large flat-topped boulder, on top of which sky burials take place. Upon death, the body is thought to return to one of the elements – earth, air, fire, water, or wood. Earth burial is rare in Tibet: the ground is hard to break up, and could be frozen in winter. Cremation (return to fire) is also rare because wood is a scarce commodity. A high lama might be cremated, and the ashes placed in a silver chorten in his monastery. Two other forms reserved for high lamas are wood burial (the body is placed in a hollow tree trunk), and embalming (the body is preserved in a seated pose by an ancient Tibetan embalming technique). Water burial – whereby the body is eaten by fish – is reserved for small children and paupers.

In Tibet, the most common form of dispatching the dead is not under the ground, but the opposite – releasing the body to the air. This is sky burial. The body is taken to a site on a rock on a mountainside and hacked into pieces with machetes. The bones are pounded together with tsampa, and when the work is complete, a signal is given to waiting flocks of vultures – which know the timing well – to feast on the rock. This way, the body is thought to be taken closer to the heavens. Sky burial takes place all over Tibet, but is more common in Lhasa because of the larger resident population.

In the mid-1980s, travellers were allowed to sit near the rock where sky burial takes place. As long as they were respectful of the customs and did not take photos, they were tolerated by the Tibetans. However, a number of ugly incidents involving photo-taking upset the Tibetans. In particular, one Westerner climbed up behind the rock, intending to sneak photos of the site with a long lens. In the process, he scared off the vultures who sit on the ridge above the sky burial site, so they did not come down at the completion of rites – a very bad omen. Since the early 1990s, the site has been off-limits to tourists. However, you can still see the sky burial ceremony at Drigung Monastery, to the northeast of Lhasa.

Tibetans are not the only people to dispatch the dead this way. The Parsees in India follow a similar custom. However, the ancient Parsee religious custom may soon disappear because the vultures that eat the bodies are headed for extinction in India. Populations of both the long-billed and white-backed vulture have crashed since 1996 due to a virus of some kind.

its larger contingent of monks and because of its previous involvement in Lhasa demonstrations.

Drepung is 8km west of downtown Lhasa. You can bicycle out this way, or take a number 3 bus, which runs past the Potala and goes all the way up to the gates of Drepung. On the way in or out of Drepung, you might want to visit the Potala Carpet Factory, which is about 300m west of the turn-off to Drepung. You can see women weaving and singing at the factory.

Like other large-scale monasteries, Drepung is divided into colleges with attached residences, rather like a campus where different disciplines are pursued. There are four major colleges – Ngakpa, Loseling, Gomang and Deyang. In previous times, all the monks at Drepung would gather on special occasions at the vast Main Assembly Hall. Now the hall is little-used. The hall is three storeys high: you can climb onto the flat rooftop for great views over Lhasa Valley (Drepung lies a few hundred metres above Lhasa). If you like climbing, there's a very strenuous hike behind Drepung to the top of Gephel Ri. The climb up and back would take a full day and you need to be very well acclimatised, as the top of Gephel Ri is 5,200 metres in altitude.

Nechung

On the lower slopes of the hill leading up to Drepung is Nechung Monastery, a small temple that fulfilled an important function in old Lhasa. It was the seat of the state oracle, who was consulted by the Lhasa government when making important decisions. The monks who lived at Nechung were trained in the secret rituals that accompanied the trances of the oracle. When in a trance, the oracle was said to be possessed by the spirit Dorje Drakden – the oracle shook, trembled, barked, rolled his eyes and stuck out his tongue. Monk-attendants quickly strapped on the oracle's impossibly heavy headpiece and he would dance around. Questions were asked, cryptic answers were given. The state oracle's last cryptic answers in Tibet concerned whether the Dalai Lama should leave or not – the answer was interpreted as yes. The state oracle himself escaped to India with the exodus of exiles in 1959: he died in 1985, but his successor was found, and the tradition has been kept alive in Dharamsala, India.

In keeping with its unusual function, Nechung Monastery has some strange, striking and imaginative murals lining the walls of the inner courtyard and main chapel – paintings of flayed humans held from the rafters by serpents, figures with dangling eyeballs, disembodied heads and legs, wrathful deities with garlands of skulls, and other ghoulish artwork. It also features an array of mythical animals, such as murals of snakes and dragons coiled around support beams in the main hall. There's a statue of Dorje Drakden in the main assembly hall, as well as a photograph showing the Nechung Oracle in a trance. Adjoining chapels were once used by the various Dalai Lamas when they visited or conducted retreats here. Some 20 monks currently reside at Nechung.

Yaks

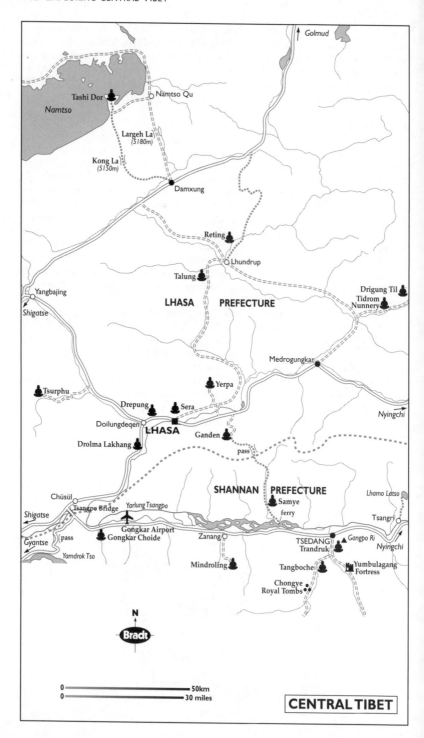

CENTRAL TIBET

Exploring Central Tibet

KEY PILGRIMAGE SITES OF THE REGION

Lhasa is not Tibet – it is too heavily Chinese-influenced for that. If you want to see a more genuine Tibet, you have to get out into the countryside, where 80% of Tibetans live. This chapter covers areas within easy reach of Lhasa by Landcruiser. You might also consider combination routes involving Gyantse and Shigatse when on a round-trip out of Lhasa. See the *Lhasa to Kathmandu Route* chapter for details on Gyantse, Shigatse and sites further westward.

While destinations when touring by Landcruiser are commonly monasteries, what's along the way is often more interesting. If you see an opportunity to stop or get off the track, take it. On one trip, we spotted some horse riders in costume. We pulled over and got the driver to ask where they were going. It turned out there was an impromptu horse-racing and archery event not far away. We spent several hours watching the races and drinking chang. Our Tibetan driver didn't mind – he was enjoying himself too.

If you string together a lot of temples on a Landcruiser trip, you run the risk of becoming 'templed out'. That is, after visiting the first two or three temples, they all start to look the same. The key to a well-designed trip is variety – visit a temple, a fortress, then take in some countryside, and make impromptu stops along the route. Samye is a good combination of natural sights (eg: crossing of the Yarlung Tsangpo River) and temples. A visit to Lake Namtso places more emphasis on natural beauty.

Logistics

Some of the sites mentioned here (Tsurphu, Damxung, Samye, Tsedang) can be reached by bus or minibus from Lhasa, but services are intermittent. For greater freedom, hire a Landcruiser with driver and guide for a period of two to seven days, depending on how much ground you want to cover, splitting the tariff between four or five passengers. The permit situation for Central Tibet seems to vary. At the time of writing, destinations falling in Lhasa Prefecture (such as Lake Namtso) did not require permits. However, those falling in Shannan Prefecture (such as Samye) definitely require permits. Both Samye and Tsedang have PSB offices that may check on you if you're staying overnight. If not overnighting, this is less of a problem. Gongkar Airport area, which falls in Shannan Prefecture, is open without a permit.

NORTH OF LHASA

Popular destinations north of Lhasa are Tsurphu Monastery and Lake Namtso, and the monasteries of Ganden, Drigung, Tidrom and Yerpa. Neither permits nor guide are needed to visit these places, which means the price should drop considerably on the Landcruiser tariff. There are several possibilities for touring this northern sector by Landcruiser, or by taxi: you could head straight for Lake Namtso on a two-day sortie; or you could easily spend five days going to Namtso and cutting across overland to Lhundrup, Reting and the monasteries of Drigung, Tidrom and Ganden. Some travellers just target the valley with Drigung, Tidrom, Ganden and Yerpa in two or three days. Apart from hiring a Landcruiser or taxi, another option for reaching Tsurphu, Ganden or Drigung is to take a pilgrim bus, leaving downtown Lhasa early in the morning from Barkor Square.

You can also indulge in trekking (which can be rough in Tibet) at various points. Resourceful travellers have forged round routes by various non-Landcruiser means. You could, for example, take a pilgrim bus to Ganden, and after seeing the *gompa*, trek off for four or five days toward Samye. From Samye, cross the river by ferry, make your way to the highway and pick up a bus coming from Tsedang – and going all the way back to Lhasa; or you could hitchhike back. Another possibility is to take a regular bus from Lhasa to Damxung, then trek out to Lake Namtso and back.

Sample itineraries
When working out itineraries, you should keep road conditions in mind: what looks like a short distance on the map might be over atrocious roads, which means it will take a long time to cover the ground. The run from Lhasa up to Damxung is along a sealed road and thus a very fast ride; however, the side-road to Tsurphu is abysmal and will chew up a lot of Landcruiser time. The sector from Ganden to Damxung cuts through a high rough road and will consume at least eight hours, and probably longer.

Three-day itinerary: Lhasa to Namtso/Tashi Dor
Day 1 Lhasa-Tsurphu-Damxung (overnight Damxung)
Day 2 Damxung over Largeh La to Tashi Dor (overnight Tashi Dor)
Day 3 hike at Namtso for a half-day, and drive back to Lhasa

Three-day itinerary: Lhasa to Ganden, Drigung, Tidrom and Yerpa
Day 1 visit Ganden for half a day and drive to Drigung (overnight at Drigung)
Day 2 sky burial at Drigung, drive to Tidrom hotsprings (overnight at Tidrom)
Day 3 more time in Tidrom, drive to Yerpa (extended hiking time needed), drive back to Lhasa

Five-day itinerary: Lhasa to Drigung, Tidrom and Namtso
Days 1 and 2 same as above (Lhasa-Ganden-Drigung-Tidrom)
Day 3 depart early from Tidrom and drive to Reting and Damxung (a long day over rough dirt roads, overnight in either Lhundrup or Damxung)
Day 4 drive to Lake Namtso (overnight at Tashi Dor)
Day 5 hike at Namtso half a day and drive back to Lhasa

Tsurphu Monastery
Lying 70km northwest of Lhasa, Tsurphu is the traditional seat of the Karmapa, head of the Karma Kagyu sect. At the beginning of 2000, the Chinese-sanctioned 17th Karmapa made a dramatic escape from Tsurphu, crossing into India just as his predecessor, the 16th Karmapa, had done 40 years earlier. Though the escape was a major embarrassment for the Karmapa's Chinese overseers, the 17th Karmapa has not yet been blacklisted: photos of him are still freely displayed at the monastery. However, the gompa does not attract the same volume of pilgrims as it

used to – previously, many travelled here to receive the young Karmapa's blessing. There is an air of dereliction at the monastery today; following a witch-hunt for collaborators in the escape, the monastery was turned upside-down and many older monks were replaced with novices. Several hundred monks currently live at the monastery.

The monastery was founded in the 12th century by the first Karmapa, Dusum Kyenpa. As the seat of the Karmapa, Tsurphu was headquarters for instruction of monks from far-flung monasteries of the order, some as distant as Kham. In the 1950s, Tsurphu was home to a thousand monks. In 1959, the 16th Karmapa left for exile in Sikkim, where he founded Rumtek Monastery. Tsurphu Monastery was razed during the Cultural Revolution, but a few parts have been rebuilt, including the impressive assembly hall. The monastery flies its own flag, a blue and yellow ensign. In May 1997, sacred Cham dances were performed at Tsurphu as part of festivities for Saka Dawa (Buddha's birthday) under the watchful eyes of Chinese officials – this dance had been banned for decades. The most curious part of the monastery is a back protector chapel where (dead) animals appear to be the offering: previously whole stuffed yaks, a kangaroo, and stuffed birds were suspended from the rafters, but on my last visit these had all been removed, and only stuffed tiger heads remained.

Getting there

Tsurphu lies 70km northwest of Lhasa, at the end of a dirt trail off the main road (the turn-off is at the KM3853 marker-stone). It takes about two hours to get there from Lhasa: there is an inclined rough road to get to Tsurphu, which sits at 4,420m. Should the need arise, there's a small monastery guesthouse and shops near the gates. Apart from a Landcruiser, the only other transport option is a daily pilgrim bus that departs early in the morning from the west side of Barkor Square, and returns the same day in the afternoon.

The case of the two Karmapas

And how exactly were two Karmapa candidates chosen? The selection actually ripped the Tibetan exile community apart. The lineage of the leaders of the Karma Kagyu sect of Tibetan Buddhism goes back to the 12th century. The 16th Karmapa was born in Tibet in 1924. After fleeing Tibet in 1959, he founded Rumtek Monastery in Sikkim as his principal seat in exile. He died in the US in 1981, but followers could find no letter or sign from him on how to locate the next incarnate. Four regents of the Kagyu sect in Sikkim were appointed to conduct the search for the 17th Karmapa: Situ Rinpoche, Gyaltsap Rinpoche, Jamgon Kongtrul Rinpoche and Shamar Rinpoche. In 1990, Situ Rinpoche said he found a letter left by the 16th Karmapa, giving clues about his reincarnate. The letter was not shown to the other regents until 1992: its authenticity was disputed. Nevertheless, in April 1992, with Chinese approval, a search party of lamas left Tsurphu Monastery to find the new incarnation.

A few weeks later, Jamgon Kongtrul Rinpoche was killed in a car accident – he had previously been designated as the person to find and check the incarnate. A boy from a nomad family in eastern Tibet – appearing to match details given in the letter – was brought to Tsurphu in July, 1992. The boy was officially recognised by the Chinese – the first time they recognised a Living Buddha since 1959. On evidence from the search party, the Dalai Lama then recognised the boy also. In September 1992, eight-year-old Ugyen Tinley was enthroned in an elaborate ceremony at Tsurphu by Situ Rinpoche and Gyaltsap Rinpoche, with Chinese media and government widely represented.

ESCAPE FROM TIBET

Times have changed dramatically since Heinrich Harrer's account of his amazing escape in *Seven Years in Tibet*, tracing his flight from a British internment camp in India to the safe haven of neutral Tibet in the early 1940s. Since 1959, the escape route has been in the opposite direction, away from Chinese oppression.

That's exactly what the Karmapa miraculously carried out at the dawn of the new millennium. The youth – then 15 years old – was growing increasingly restless about his monastic education. He had been denied access to his spiritual mentors: the Chinese had reneged on promises to allow these lamas to visit Tibet, and refused to allow the Karmapa to visit India. Worse still, he was clearly being groomed as a patriotic alternative to the Dalai Lama. It was simply a matter of time before he would be called upon to denounce the Dalai Lama publicly.

The stakes for the 17th Karmapa to attempt an escape from the Chinese were very high: any mistake would be costly for the highest-profile religious figure living in Tibet. Meticulous planning was essential. In late December 1999, the Karmapa informed his Chinese minders that he was going into solitary retreat in his private quarters for a week, and would not entertain any visitors. Nothing unusual about that, or greatly suspect. But parked outside the monastery was a Mitsubishi SUV, requisitioned by a senior Tsurphu monk for a fund-raising trip. And distracting the attention of everyone inside – including Chinese overseers – was a newly acquired television set.

Late on the night of December 28, with monks and minders engrossed in the new television, the Karmapa changed into civilian dress, slipped out a back window at Tsurphu, jumped into the waiting SUV and stole off into the night. At Tsurphu, meanwhile, his teacher and cook kept up the charade of attending to him while 'on retreat.'

The Karmapa's real retreat was from Tibet: he and his four trusted companions proceeded on a circuitous route across Tibet in the SUV, travelling day and night. They dodged military checkpoints along the way: fortunately, during winter there was little military presence, with several posts unmanned. Approaching a dangerous checkpoint by night, the Karmapa and two others got out of the SUV and skirted the area on foot, scraping their hands and legs on thorn scrub in the darkness. To their immense relief, the SUV driver eventually showed up: he had driven past the checkpoint in darkness.

Meanwhile, in Sikkim, violence flared at Rumtek Monastery as rival camps of monks brawled over the Karmapa issue. Indian troops were brought in to hold the peace. The 16th Karmapa's monks were evicted, and Situ Rinpoche's monks forcibly occupied the grounds in late 1993. In 1994, Shamar Rinpoche announced in Delhi that the true Karmapa had been found – a boy from Lhasa by the name of Thaye Dorje. The boy was able to procure travel papers to leave Lhasa by way of Chengdu and Hong Kong to India, where he now lives.

Namtso circuit

Namtso is Tibet's largest saltwater lake, and at 4,700m, also one of the highest. You would be unwise to visit Namtso shortly after arriving in Lhasa, as the altitude can be hard on your system. However, if you have been around Lhasa for a while and are contemplating taking trips at higher elevations, Namtso is a good testing

And then the SUV simply drove across the unmanned Nepalese border right into the kingdom of Mustang. Here, they abandoned the SUV and switched to travel on foot and by horseback. Hiring fine horses from the Mustang region, they rode hard from Lo Monthang for a few days to reach Kagbeni, and then forged on to a helicopter rendezvous site at Manang, on the Annapurna Circuit. From Nepal, they telephoned Tsurphu to find out what was happening: when a stranger answered, they hung up (the fates of the teacher and the cook at Tsurphu are unknown). Flying into the Pokhara vicinity, the Karmapa and his entourage took a taxi to the Indian border, bribing their way past Nepalese border guards.

From here, train and taxis took them through northwest India to Dharamsala. The Karmapa arrived, exhausted, on the morning of January 5th, 2000. An hour later, the Karmapa was greeted in an audience with the Dalai Lama. It was a moment of astonishment and delight – the meeting of two bodhisattvas, and the end of an amazing journey.

The Karmapa's escape echoed the flight of the Dalai Lama from Tibet 40 years earlier. The Dalai Lama is the one person in the world that the Chinese did not want the Karmapa to meet. The Chinese insisted the Karmapa left the Motherland on a shopping trip – to get his hands on a Black Hat, certain musical instruments, and other ceremonial items belonging to his predecessor, the 16th Karmapa, who was based at Rumtek Monastery in Sikkim. You can almost imagine the headlines in China: *Soul Boy Steps out of Motherland on Black Hat Shopping Expedition.*

The Black Hat they talk about is sacred. The rightful owner must keep one hand on the hat while wearing it, as it is reputed to have the ability to fly away by itself. That's because, according to legend, the Black Hat is woven from the hair of countless *dakinis* – celestial female deities, or 'sky walkers'. First mentions of the Flying Crown date to the 12th century; the present hat dates from a few centuries later and was smuggled out of Tibet to Rumtek. Controversy rages as to whose head the crown will grace, since there is a rival Karmapa candidate in India, but both young Karmapa appointees seem impervious to the conflict. There's a lot more than a hat at stake here: worldwide Kagyu sect assets are estimated to be worth over US$1.2 billion. Who is the real Karmapa? Will he ever take up residence at Rumtek? Will he wear the sacred Black Hat? Will it fly off his head? Whatever the case, Ugyen Trinley Dorje is not out on a religious-relic shopping spree: he has been granted refugee status by the Indian government.

ground: spending a few days here will help you to acclimatise to the 4,500-metre zone. Some arrange Landcruiser trips for two days up to Namtso; others hire a Landcruiser for five days or more to take in the much wider zone of Reting, Tidrom and Drigung monasteries.

Along the Lhasa to Namtso direct (paved) route, you pass by **Yangbajing** (elevation 4,200m), where a small settlement has developed around geothermal power units supplying Lhasa. Yangbajing hot springs, which are 4km off the main highway, are nothing to get excited about – the water is channelled into a large concrete swimming pool with a few deckchairs lying around. It's all a bit derelict and scummy. Next stop is **Damxung** (elevation 4,200m), a deadly boring Chinese-built town 170km from Lhasa. Think of this town as an elaborate truck-stop on the Golmud road. There are several basic guesthouse. Foreign traffic is channelled to the Tienfu Hotel, located at the crossroads on the west side of town.

There is no English sign, but the place has a TTB plaque and is a green-tiled building. Cost is Y50 a bed in two- or three-bed rooms. The hotel is clean and the restaurant is good. There are a number of roadside restaurants in Damxung where truck drivers congregate – you can negotiate rides with them to Lake Namtso.

A further 40km from Damxung brings you to **Lake Namtso**, reached by two rough routes – in a Landcruiser you can enter one way (motoring over Largeh La, 5,180m) and leave by another route (over Kong La, 5,150m). Annoying entry charges are levied for the Lake Namtso region: a Y35 entry charge on one road, and a Y5 additional charge near Tashi Dor. The road runs through a grassland valley, with the odd nomad encampment visible, and herds of yaks, sheep and goats roaming around. For the nomads, life is dependent on yaks: they live in yak-hair tents, and use yak-dung as their main fuel source. Some travellers hitch a ride in and walk back (about 12 hours), or trek both ways – a tough hike.

There are several possibilities for basic guesthouses. Apart from the guesthouses in Damxung, you can overnight at Namtso Qu, a tiny village at the eastern fringe of Lake Namtso. And at Tashi Dor there are two rudimentary longhouse buildings – the charge is Y35 for a dorm bed, or Y15 for a bed in a tent. Group tours bring their own tents and camp out here. Bring food, a flashlight, and a good sleeping bag. Beer can be purchased from the nuns.

Namtso is a sacred lake: there are cave-temples, hermitages and a nunnery for the contemplation at **Tashi Dor**. Hermits from the Kagyu and Nyingma sects occasionally occupy the caves. Two large rock towers near the nunnery are considered to be sentinels for the region. It's worth spending a day or more exploring the area, hiking in the hills around Tashi Dor, and poking around the cave-temples. The beautiful turquoise hues of the lake are a source of inspiration, and the vistas will redefine your sense of space. In the distance, to the south, the 7,088m snowcap of Mt. Nyanchen Tanglha looms up, along with the range of the same name. A walking circuit of Namtso is a tall order indeed. The lake is roughly 70km long and 30km wide, with a surface area of 1940 square kilometres: it takes nomad pilgrims up to 20 days to circle it. A short walk to the east of Tashi Dor is a site that operates as a bird sanctuary – between April and November there are good chances of sighting migratory flocks, including, if you're lucky, the black-necked crane.

Classic gompas, mountain settings

Northeast of Lhasa are a number of ruined or semi-active monasteries, amid spectacular settings. Getting to these places takes you right off the track into small villages. Roads are rough, and the going can be slow.

Ganden

Located 40km east of Lhasa, Ganden is a Geluk lamasery founded in the 15th century. Additions in later centuries increased its capacity to support upward of 5,000 monks. Ganden was dynamited to rubble during the Cultural Revolution. Remarkably, a number of its main halls have been rebuilt from scratch. In early 1996, following a ban on Dalai Lama pictures, the 400 monks at Ganden were involved in a riot. PLA troops arrived and fired on the monks – two were believed killed and a number were injured. It is thought 100 more monks were arrested; an equal number probably fled into the hills. Life has since returned to Ganden – there is a large population of monks (currently estimated at around 400), and reconstruction has continued at a brisk pace. A permanent PSB building up on the hill above the monastery guesthouse keeps a wary eye on everything.

There's an early morning pilgrim bus that leaves Barkor Square in Lhasa for Ganden. The monastery has a Y25 entry fee, and posts a Y20 still camera fee, plus a whopping Y1,500 video camera fee (Y750 for 'inland tourists', meaning Chinese). You can stay at the basic but pleasant monastery guesthouse, near the front gates. The tariff is Y15 a bed in six-bed dorms. Trekkers, Landcruiser arrivals, pilgrims and visiting monks or nuns all lodge here. Further on is a monastery-run shop, selling the usual dismal selection of packaged noodles, sweets and candles.

The main assembly hall of Ganden is located near a vast square: it is a white structure with gold-capped roofs. If your timing is right, you can hear monks chanting. There are many gilded images of Tsongkhapa in the main chapel. Pilgrims come to be tapped on the head with Tsongkhapa's hat or else the 13th Dalai Lama's shoes. Adjacent to the main assembly hall is maroon and ochre building which houses a Sakyamuni Buddha statue. A section of this chapel is devoted to the hand-printing of scriptures from woodblocks. In one corner is the *gonkhang* (protector chapel), which is only open to men and which showcases wrathful deities such as 32-armed Yamantaka and six-armed Mahakala, on a horse with a crown of skulls. You can access the rooftop of this building for views.

Ganden is set in a natural, hilly amphitheatre. You can hike around the monastery on a one-hour *kora* route, with stunning views over the surrounding valleys. Start from the monastery guesthouse and go up the hill to a white building with a red flag and a satellite dish (this is the PSB building); from there head for hilltop prayer flags and follow other prayer-flag markers along the route – and other pilgrims. At the far end of the clockwise kora is a rock that is said to be able to talk.

Ganden-to-Samye trek

For those with stamina and a good food supply, there's an arduous four to five-day trek from Ganden to Samye, over several 5,000m passes. Groups arrange a guide, yaks and yak-handlers to carry gear – all are self-sufficient with food and camping equipment. Even for just two trekkers, the entourage for a tour would include seven or so yaks loaded up with food and cooking gear, and tents. If you stay at the monastery guesthouse in Ganden, you can probably find a yak-handler who would be willing to make the trip and carry your gear. However, some are prone to turning back at the half-way point, so negotiate carefully. Yaks are apparently not permitted to walk right into Samye, so you would have to carry gear for the last stretch, or use a walking-tractor. The trek to Samye starts on the hill above Ganden guesthouse.

Drigung Monastery

Further to the northeast, about 130km from Lhasa, lies Drigung, a monastery impossibly grafted onto a sheer cliff-face. Drigung (elevation 4,150m) was originally the base of the Drigung sub-order of the Kagyu sect, dating from the 12th century. At one time it housed over 500 monks. Going up switchbacks in a Landcruiser, you may pass a donkey bearing a body under a blanket: Drigung is reputed to have the best sky burial ceremony of all. It is said that bodies dispatched here will not fall down in the 'three bad regions'. *Danchag*, or sky burial, is in fact the macabre main interest at Drigung, one of the rare places where you are permitted to see the ceremony.

Plan to spend the night at Drigung, as sky burial takes place in the early morning. Most arrive by Landcruiser (taking about four hours from Lhasa), but there is a pilgrim bus that makes the run from Lhasa several times a week. You can stay at Drigung's monastery guesthouse, which has two 12-bed dorms for Y20 a bed. There's no electricity, just candles. Although the dorms are basic, the atmosphere is special—you are staying inside the monastic grounds. Monks supply hot water in thermoses, and there's a small shop selling packaged noodles, candles and drinks. Some group tours camp out in the valley below.

The monastery offers stupendous views over the entire valley—you can clamber up to the gold-capped roofs for better vistas. The sky burial site is located about 600 metres from the gompa – a trail to get there starts just below the monastery and then turns uphill. You gain about 200m of elevation on this hike and it takes about 15 minutes to reach the site from the monastery. The site is a large fenced-off area surrounded by prayer flags. It's high on a ridge, with a large rock at centre-stage. The ceremony takes place on the rock, with monks present to bless the departed. Sky burial does not take place every day: sometimes there is no body. Other times, there could be four bodies. The timing is also a bit random, but about an hour after sunrise is the probable time. Vultures assemble on the upper slopes waiting for their cue to descend to the rock.

This spectacle is not for the faint of heart – it's a grisly ritual where bodies are chopped into pieces and fed to the vultures. Photography is absolutely forbidden – please do not rile the monks by trying to sneak shots with long lenses. You are privileged to be allowed to view the ceremony, but that privilege will only last as long as travellers comply with the no-photography stipulation.

Tidrom Nunnery

About 45 minutes by Landcruiser from Drigung is Tidrom Nunnery (another option is a half-day, or four-hour, hike from Drigung to Tidrom). Tidrom is set in a beautiful valley with numerous hermitages and caves in the surrounding hills. Miraculously, there's not a Chinese building in sight, although the nunnery has a huge satellite dish mounted on its traditional rooftop. The nunnery, though small, is home to over a hundred nuns. Pilgrims and visitors come to Tidrom for the sulphur hotsprings, also frequented by the nuns. The hotsprings are said to be good for the treatment of arthritis, gastritis and other ailments.

A charming aspect of Tidrom is that it is a walking zone: no vehicles can enter the village.

Landcruisers and other vehicles stop at a parking lot at the edge of Tidrom, a short walk from the hotsprings. The nunnery offers a few rooms, and close to the river is an older guesthouse with adobe flat roofs, and beds going for Y5 each. The best accommodation is in two blocks with corrugated roofs overlooking the hotsprings, with rooms for Y60 double or Y15–30 a person. There's a teahouse on top of one wing but offerings of food in Tidrom are meagre (there are some shops), so best to bring some back-up supplies.

Better rooms at the main guesthouse are supplied with slippers and bathrobes so you can pad down to the hotsprings in this garb. Tibetans bathe *au naturel*; others wear swimsuits. You should be aware that piping-hot water at this altitude (4,300m) can be a shock to the system, and can make foreign visitors feel dizzy. Best to take this in small doses until you get accustomed to it; take a dip for ten minutes, get out, rest, and go back in again. Those with high blood pressure or a heart condition (or if pregnant) should not partake. That said, these have to be the finest hotsprings in central Tibet: the springs are located right near a river, where the water bubbles under a great rock and disappears. There are three hotspring pools with attractive stone-laid enclosures surrounded by wooden fencing (no concrete!). One pool is for men, another for women, and the third pool is mixed: it is extra-hot and lies across a small footbridge. If you stay overnight, you can indulge in a moonlit soak with candles, and – if skies are clear – a magnificent canopy of stars overhead.

Previous page Crest of the pass overlooking Lake Yamdrok Tso

Above Yumbulagang Fortress, central Tibet, is reputed to have been the first structure built in Tibet. This copy of the original was constructed in 1982.

Right Three generations of a nomad family, near Namtso Lake

Below Monks assisting in construction of temple roof at Drigung Monastery, central Tibet

Yerpa, Talung and Reting

Three other monastic sites worth looking at lie north of Lhasa: Yerpa, Talung and Reting. **Yerpa**, 45km northeast of Lhasa (well off the main road), used to be a complex of monasteries, with more than 80 meditation caves tucked away in the hills. The area suffered extensive damage during the Cultural Revolution: restoration is on-going, but in 1998 a major set-back occurred when Chinese officials destroyed several temples and caves. There are, however, half a dozen restored temples to reach. Getting to Yerpa is not easy; a Landcruiser takes about half an hour from the turn-off to reach the foothills of Yerpa. The driver parks in a village, and then you embark on a strenuous hike. A steep trail ascends to about 4,400m, so you must be acclimatised.

Further north is a rough back-route leading to Lake Namtso (see map). In this direction, the once-great **Talung Gompa** lies in ruins, a victim of the Cultural Revolution. Several temples have been restored and over 100 monks have taken up residence. The monastery overlooks a village.

If you continue along this route past Lhundrup, you'll reach **Reting**, about 150km from Lhasa. Reting is the seat of the Reting Rinpoche: this lineage started in the 18th century when the 7th Dalai Lama appointed his tutor as abbot of Reting. Several of the Reting Rinpoches served as regents during the minorities of the Dalai Lamas. The 5th Reting Rinpoche ruled from 1933 to 1947 during the minority of the 14th Dalai Lama, and was actually responsible for his discovery. Involved in political intrigue and sexual scandal, the 5th Reting Rinpoche died in prison in 1947. There is considerable controversy over the authenticity of the current Reting Rinpoche, a boy essentially chosen by Chinese officials. He lives in the now-administrative compounds near the river at Reting. Tibetan pilgrims can make arrangements for an audience with the Reting Rinpoche, but police registration procedures make this rather difficult. Monks are guarded in talking about the situation.

Little is left of the splendour of Reting – it was all destroyed in the 1960s. A small assembly hall has been rebuilt, with a few dozen monks in residence. The area is unusual for its grove of juniper trees, which appear to be twisted and gnarled as an arboreal response to the problems of high altitude and high winds. It is possible to stay at Reting. You can also backtrack and find lodging in the village of Lhundrup, which has a few poky shops and a gas-refuelling station where Landcruisers can fill up (remind your driver as this is the only one in this region). Backing Lhundrup is the startling and seemingly unreal vision of a perfectly conical mountain.

YARLUNG VALLEY

Southeast of Lhasa lies the cradle of Tibetan culture – the Yarlung Valley. The Adam and Eve of Tibet – from a myth involving a monkey and a demoness – were supposed to have dwelt in Tsedang. The Yarlung dynasty kings had their base in the Yarlung Valley – in the 7th and 8th centuries, they unified the Tibetans and strengthened their identity as a nation. The burial mounds of all the Yarlung dynasty kings are at Chongye. However, these are rather dull to look at: the main attractions southeast of Lhasa are the Samye Temple Complex and Yumbulagang Fortress. By Landcruiser, you can visit half a dozen sites mentioned here in two or three days. If you're planning to do any hiking, allow more time. You can trek from Samye to Ganden by an arduous route over high passes. You need to be completely self-sufficient for a trip like this. Some group tours tackle the trek with guides, and donkeys or horses to carry gear.

From Lhasa up to the airport no permits are needed. Gongkar Airport technically falls in Shannan Prefecture, but the airport is open because that's where

THE CASE OF THE STOLEN BUDDHA

Among the statues at Drolma Lakhang is one that has been on a sort of world tour. This is a 1,200-year-old statue of the Buddha that was stolen from Drolma Lakhang in April 1993 by two men with a minivan. It was immediately sold to smugglers in Chengdu for an estimated US$300,000, according to a report in the *People's Daily*. Then it disappeared without trace, until Lhasa customs discovered that it had been shipped to the US, where a buyer was prepared to pay US$8 million for it, according to the news source. The FBI seized the Buddha statue on arrival, but demanded photographic evidence that it had come from Drolma Lakhang before they would return it. The Tibetans did not have such evidence. Finally, after two years of wrangling, Lhasa customs found a picture taken by a foreign tourist, and the FBI returned the statue to Drolma Lakhang in late 1997.

Interpol estimates that the black market in stolen art and antiquities worldwide results in upward of US$10-billion changing hands annually, making it the world's biggest illegal trade after arms and drugs. The motivation is vast profits with a short turnover time. Original Tibetan art is, of course, highly sought after, and there is little doubt that Chinese smugglers have been involved in the traffic, dismantling Tibet's heritage piece by piece.

travellers arrive in Tibet. However, from here on east, destinations in Shannan Prefecture require permits, probably including the prefectural capital at Tsedang. That means Samye requires a permit.

Lhasa to Samye
Drolma Lakhang
The exquisite Tara Temple (Drolma Lakhang) is one of the best-preserved in Central Tibet. This temple lies along the main road, 25km out of Lhasa. It is associated with the Bengali sage Atisha who arrived in Tibet to teach in the 11th century. He died in this area in 1054. The temple is dedicated to the goddess Tara, with whom Atisha had a strong connection. The temple was apparently spared damage in the 1960s because of a request from the government of Bengal, where Atisha is a highly revered figure. The temple is small and active, with 25 monks. The most striking feature is a sutra-chanting chapel where 21 life-sized bronze statues of Tara enclose the space. The main image is a Sakyamuni statue; to the left is a small statue of Atisha. On the upper floor is a library, plus some meditation rooms.

Gongkar
The name 'Gongkar' is today associated with Tibet's only commercial airport, but in the days before the first planes arrived in the 1960s, it was known to Tibetans as the location of Gongkar Dzong and Gongkar Choide. The dzong was mostly destroyed, but Gongkar Choide remains. The monastery is located 10km west of the airport (turn off at the KM84 marker and go 1km off the road). It was ransacked during the Cultural Revolution: the main hall was used as a barley silo, and murals were defaced with Mao Zedong slogans. Despite the destruction, the surviving mural work at Gongkar Choide makes it worth the visit.

Gongkar Airport (elevation 3,700m), lies further east (95km from Lhasa), just off the main road to Tsedang. It was constructed in the late 1970s, with elaborate terminal facilities and a second runway added in 1994. Not far from the airport gates is a crossroads with a cluster of small Chinese hotels and restaurants, and a mini-mart. Several guesthouses in this area charge Y30–50 a room; the best is a second-floor guesthouse, running along the top of a string of restaurants. There's also a ramshackle Tibetan guesthouse in the vicinity. Within the airport compound is Airport Hotel, tel: 618 2447, with 115 rooms ranging from Y140 to Y380. The airport has a post office and a bank with foreign exchange facilities (near the gates).

By Landcruiser or taxi, it's about 50 minutes from Gongkar to Lhasa. Gongkar falls in Shannan Prefecture but it is open without permit. That means you can use Gongkar Airport zone as a base to reach out into the Yarlung Valley (where places require permits) on daytrips. You've heard of airports with duty-free zones – this one is a PSB-free zone. Do not confuse Gongkar Airport with Gongkar County (the village 10km east of the airport) or Gongkar Choide (the monastery 10km west of the airport).

Map: GONGKAR AIRPORT

- Air terminal
- Airport Hotel
- Taxis for Lhasa & Tsedang
- CAAC bus
- Flying Horses statue
- N — Bradt
- 0 ———— 100m
- 0 ———— 100 yds
- Bank $
- Post office
- Restaurant ✗
- Minimart
- Lhasa (93km)
- Guesthouse (top floor)
- Restaurant ✗
- Restaurant ✗
- Tsedang (97km)
- Restaurant ✗ ✗ Restaurant

Mindroling Gompa

Mindroling is the largest Nyingma sect monastery in Central Tibet (a second large Nyingma lamasery is Dorje Drak, on the north bank of the Yarlung Tsangpo). Founded in the 17th century, Mindroling was razed by the Mongols in the 18th century, then rebuilt, and again razed during the Cultural Revolution (and rebuilt). Mindroling's imposing facade is constructed in monastic citadel style; the gompa impresses with its surprising size and austerity, and skilful construction in stone. The most important chapel lies at the back: it houses a huge Sakyamuni image. To get to Mindroling, turn off the main road near Zanang (aka Zhanang or Dranang) – the monastery is a further 8km away, on a dirt trail.

Samye

Samye, an attractive walled temple complex, sits at 3,650m on the north bank of the Yarlung Tsangpo. Samye is fascinating because you get a feel for old Tibet as the buildings are all Tibetan (with rare exceptions). Samye is also unusual because it is fully enclosed by a wall with gates at the compass points. Within the walls, most things are run by the monastery, it appears. There is a small cluster of shops and a restaurant just outside the east gate. There is some build-up, too, outside the west gate, but nothing at the south gate and very little at the north gate.

Getting there

You can get to Samye by regular bus (Y30 a head, takes about five hours), by hired taxi from Lhasa (about three hours, costs around Y180 for the whole taxi) or by taxi from Tsedang (taking about 40 minutes, Y80 for the taxi), or by Landcruiser.

Transport drops you on the south bank of the Yarlung Tsangpo River at a small compound (KM155 marker-stone) with a truckstop inn (Y15 a bed) and a few small shops. A Landcruiser driver waits with the car for a day or two while the guide takes you along on a ferry ride across the Yarlung Tsangpo. On the other side, a truck picks you up for the 20-minute run into Samye. The 'ferry' is a barge designed for the transport of goods back and forth from Samye. There have been a number of nasty arguments between foreigners and locals over the cost of the barge and the truck (foreigners are charged at least double the going rate). You will most likely be charged Y10 for the ferry and Y10 for the truck. The ferry will cost more if your small group are the sole passengers. Bargaining doesn't work well here as this is a monopoly situation and the operators know it. To avoid ill feelings, leave the matter in the hands of the guide (if you have one), and focus instead on the entrancing Yarlung Tsangpo vistas. Because the barge has to navigate around sand-bars, the trip across the Yarlung Tsangpo can take up to an hour. The route changes seasonally with the water levels.

Permits and PSB
You need a permit for Samye. If you don't have one, keep a low profile. The PSB will be checking the hotel registration book, but are unlikely to do so before or after their working hours. You could check in at, say, 19.00, and depart next morning at 06.00 (or leave your bags with reception and explore some more). It's also worth noting that the PSB does not work on Sundays. The PSB office is located about 120m from the east gate (the building is set back a bit – it's the only white-tiled building in the vicinity and has Chinese-style reddish roof-tiles fronting it). It's best to avoid this area if your paperwork is not in order.

Lodging and food
The best place to stay is the guesthouse attached to Samye monastery. It lies near the front entrance of the main temple. The three-storey guesthouse was built in the late 1990s and is arrayed around a courtyard. Rooms go for Y50–60 (doubles, triples, quadruples), or Y20–25 a bed. On the ground floor is a souvenir shop, and next door is a large restaurant venue (on the second floor) serving passable fare. Because of very little ambient light, there is a fantastic star-show at night— assuming clear skies—from the flat rooftop of the guesthouse. Adjacent to the guesthouse is another older place which is reserved for visiting monks. There's another small guesthouse just outside the walls at the east gate, and a place to eat called Friend Snowland Restaurant.

What to see
Samye Temple Complex
Samye is thought to be Tibet's first monastery and its first university. It has been deconstructed and reconstructed a number of times. The monastery is thought to have been founded in the 8th century by King Trisong Detsen, in consultation with Indian sage Padmasambhava. The temple was destroyed in civil war in the 11th century, by fire in the 11th and 17th centuries, by earthquake in the 18th century, and by Mao Zedong's fanatical hordes in the 20th century. Today, only a fraction of its original 108 buildings survive or have been reconstructed. Adaptations for visitors within the walls include the monastery guesthouse with restaurant and monastery shop. Most Samye villagers live outside the walls.

Samye's layout is based on Buddhist cosmology: it is a mandalic 3-D replica of the Tibetan Buddhist universe. The temple complex has been constructed

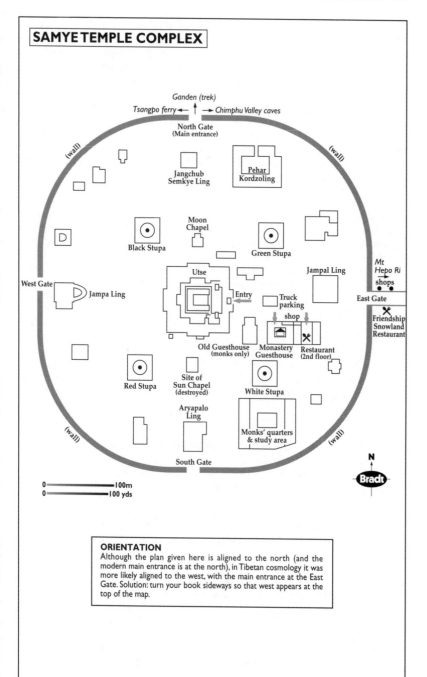

SAMYE TEMPLE COMPLEX

Ganden (trek)

Tsangpo ferry ← ↑ → Chimphu Valley caves

North Gate
(Main entrance)

(wall)

(wall)

Jangchub
Semkye Ling

Pehar
Kordzoling

Moon
Chapel

Black Stupa

Green Stupa

Jampal Ling

Mt
Hepo Ri
→
shops

Utse

West Gate

Jampa Ling

Entry

Truck
parking

East Gate

shop

Friendship
Snowland
Restaurant

Old Guesthouse
(monks only)

Monastery
Guesthouse

Restaurant
(2nd floor)

Red Stupa

Site of
Sun Chapel
(destroyed)

White Stupa

Aryapalo
Ling

Monks' quarters
& study area

(wall)

(wall)

South Gate

N

Bradt

0 ▬▬▬▬▬ 100m
0 ▬▬▬▬▬ 100 yds

ORIENTATION
Although the plan given here is aligned to the north (and the
modern main entrance is at the north), in Tibetan cosmology it was
more likely aligned to the west, with the main entrance at the East
Gate. Solution: turn your book sideways so that west appears at the
top of the map.

according to the principles of geomancy, a concept derived from India. At the centre of the Tibetan Buddhist universe lies a mythical palace on top of Mount Meru, which at Samye is symbolised by the main temple (Utse). Surrounding this is a great 'ocean', with four great island-continents, and eight sub-continents. If the colour-coded chortens look a bit out of place in this scheme of things, it's because they were razed during the Cultural Revolution, and were only reconstructed in the early 1990s, in new brick, with synthetic paints, and without much finesse. Renovation and reconstruction of other parts within the walls is on-going.

The complex is bounded by an oval wall (the original wall was a zig-zag design), pierced by four gates and topped by 1,008 small chortens that represent Chakravala, a ring of mountains that surrounds the universe. The wall itself has been hastily restored, using a large amount of concrete – the favourite material of the Chinese.

There are currently about 100 monks attached to the main temple. The monastery was built long before the rise of the different sects in Tibet. In the late 8th century, Trisong Detsen presided over a debate at Samye between Indian Buddhists and Chinese Zen Buddhists concerning which type of Buddhism should prevail in Tibet. The Indians won. Since that time, the monastery has came under the influence of various sects, such as the Nyingma, Sakya and Geluk traditions. Even today, influences are eclectic.

Samye Utse The three-storey temple faces to the east. The upper storeys were removed during the Cultural Revolution, but the gleaming roof was restored in 1989. To the left of the main entrance is a 5m-high stone obelisk; erected by King Songtsen Gampo, it proclaims the Indian school of Buddhism to be the state religion. Inside the main assembly hall of the Utse are statues of the early kings, and images of Padmasambhava and Atisha. The inner sanctum contains a beautiful Sakyamuni image. To the right side of the assembly hall is a Gonkhang or tantric protector chapel with odds and ends like a stuffed snake and an old musket. To the left of the assembly hall is the Avalokitesvara Chapel, with a fine bas-relief portrait of the bodhisattva.

Upstairs, you can access several chapels and might even be allowed to view the former quarters of the Dalai Lama.

On the second floor is an open gallery with a long string of murals, some depicting the history of Tibet; there is also a damaged mural of the fabled land of Shambhala here.

North of the Utse temple lies the Chapel of the Moon, and to the south, the Chapel of the Sun. Four chortens are positioned respectively to the northeast (green), southeast (white), southwest (red) and northwest (black).

Ling Chapels While Meru is connected with the realms of the gods, humanoids are supposed to live on the four island-continents (*ling*) across a vast ocean, flanked by satellite islands or sub-continents (*ling-tren*). These are all symbolised by one or two-storey chapels at Samye, some lined with murals, and graced with pleasant courtyards with gardens and potted plants, others lying in a decayed state, awaiting restoration.

Jamphel Ling, at the east side, is dedicated to Manjughosa. It the 1980s it was a commune office. At the southern end, Aryalpo Ling, dedicated to Hayagriva, was where Indian scholars lived during the great debate of the 8th century. It has undergone some restoration of its murals; on the upper storey are strange murals depicting creatures riding scorpions, dragons and bears. The chapel immediately west of this is worth a visit: it has been renovated with a full set of murals.

Jampa Ling, the chapel near the west gate, is dedicated to Maitreya (*Champa* or *Jampa* in Tibetan) and is where the Chinese monks resided during the 8th century. At the entrance hall is a mural showing Samye at it once was. Jangchub Semkye Ling, at the north, was dedicated to Prajnaparamita. Inside is a 3-D scale model of Samye. This building is undergoing restoration – it was previously used for wood storage.

Just east of Jangchub Semkye Ling is a north-facing red-walled building – Pehar Kordzoling, a protector chapel. Samye's Sanskrit texts were once stored here in the care of the protector deity Pehar. Pehar's mandate was to watch over the monastery's treasures: among these was a leather mask that was believed to come alive, with rolling of bulging eyes. After several centuries at Samye, Pehar was removed to Nechung Monastery in Lhasa, and became the protective deity of the state oracle. There was also an oracle at Samye: Pehar's job at Samye was taken over by Tsemar, the red protector, who sat in judgement of the souls of men once a year: evil-doers were chopped to shreds. Pehar Kordzoling is adorned with unusual mural work featuring skulls; though under renovation, the chapel appears to be a site where special rituals are carried out.

Following Chinese occupation, villagers were encouraged to treat the walled sanctuary of Samye as just another part of the village, so pigs, cows, braying donkeys and sheep were herded through the muddy wasteland. Along with a large band of dogs that hung out on the flagstones near the Utse, this gave Samye a somewhat earthy and surreal air – you would round a corner looking for a sacred temple, and instead stray across a pig wallowing in the mud. Although the dogs still lounge around, the animals have been pushed back outside the walls again (although herders occasionally bring their flocks through).

Hiking at Samye

To the east of Samye you can hike to a ridge called **Mount Hepori**, which offers a terrific bird's-eye view of the town. To get there, walk out of the east gate, go to the end of the village, and then veer right to find the trails that lead up the foothills to the ridge-top temple. The hike takes about 30 to 40 minutes. If there are pilgrims around, you can follow them: they make offerings at the ridge-top temple shrine, festooned with prayer flags. From this vantage point, you can see the elliptical shape of Samye's walled enclosure and something of its cosmic plan. The walls used to be circular (apparently before 1959), but were rebuilt as elliptical. About 500m south of the south gate you can see a grey, three-storey building enclosed by a high wall: this used to be one of the three queens' residences, but there's no access to the place (the other two residences were apparently destroyed).

To the far northeast of Samye is **Chimphu**, which is riddled with hermitage caves (there are said to be 108 of them). Monks and nuns come for retreat here: if visiting, take some tsampa and candles as donations. It takes about 40 minutes on a walking-tractor to reach the general area, then a three-hour hike (round trip), so you'd have to allow five or six hours for the visit. If arriving by walking-tractor, make sure the driver waits to take you back to Samye.

There is a five-day trek between Samye and Ganden monasteries. See the Ganden section, page 149, for details.

Tsedang

Tsetang, Zedang, Nedong; elevation 3,600m; capital of Shannan Prefecture; area code: 0893

Tsedang is a Chinese town – or to put it more bluntly, a Chinese eyesore. This is the shape of things to come, as more Chinese settlers move in. The town functions as a Chinese hub in Central Tibet. In contrast to traditional Tibetan architecture, which

blends into the mountain and desert environment, Chinese structures here look totally jarring, with bland concrete blocks finished in bathroom tiling and blue-tinted glass. Although there was an ancient Tibetan town at Tsedang, it has been marginalised – remnants of an old Tibetan quarter exist to the east of the market area with an active gompa and a nunnery. Due to a military presence, there is a surfeit of karaoke bars and bars stocked with young women.

Tsedang is mostly used as a stepping-stone to destinations like Yumbulagang Fortress. There are a few hikes on the eastern side of Tsedang that are of middling interest. A four-hour hike takes you up a mountain trail to Gangpo Ri monkey cave. This cave is revered as the mythical site where a monkey (an emanation of Avalokitesvara) consorted with a demoness (an emanation of Tara) to give birth to the six children, later leaders of the Tibetan clans. The monkey then instructed them how to cultivate grains in the fertile valley, so Tibet's first cultivated field is supposed to be in the Tsedang area. This tale of the origin of the Tibetan race, involving descent from a monkey, has an oddly Darwinian touch.

Getting there
Tsedang is 196km from Lhasa and 97km from Gongkar Airport. There are buses running to Tsedang from Lhasa, and you might consider taking a taxi and sharing the ride with others. Since the road is smooth, paved and flat, you can get there in record time – three hours should suffice, or less for a taxi-ride. The PSB office in Tsedang here seems bent on restricting your movements. They may do spot checks on travellers, asking for permits for the Yarlung valley destinations. It's unclear if Tsedang, as prefecture capital, is open with permit or without permit.

Getting around
The choice is between regular VW taxis, motorised three-wheel contraptions (seating two) or bicycle trishaws (also seating two).

Facilities and shopping
For trip supplies, try the department store near the main crossroads, and also the street markets nearby. For artefact shopping, the west end of the street markets offer tankas and Qinghai carpets. The post office/telecom building is at the main crossroads: the Tsedang area code is 0893. One street south is the Xinhua Bookstore (on the second floor – don't expect much – you might find some posters or maps). There doesn't seem to be a bank that deals in foreign exchange: your best bet is to try Tsedang Hotel.

Lodging and food
A strange cat-and-mouse game goes on with hotel, guesthouses and restaurants in Tsedang. Tsedang seems to be a PSB-Mafia-dominated monopoly. Travellers

who have tried to stay in non-Chinese-operated guesthouses or restaurants have been visited by Tsedang PSB officers and told to move along. Some Chinese hotels refuse to accept foreigners, including the high-end Golden Crane Hotel. Restaurant owners, intimidated by the PSB, may inform Westerners they cannot eat in the restaurant. PSB officers have been seen trailing travellers around the town. Travellers should make deliberate efforts to break this stranglehold when it comes to restaurants (try drinks only at a Tibetan teahouse to annoy the Beijing Boys), but there doesn't seem to be a way round for hotels, as the PSB can easily close down Tibetan-run guesthouses. That means there may be no low-end hotels available for travellers, and there could be permit hassles. In fact, it is much cheaper to take a taxi back to either the truckstop compound at the Samye ferry (KM155 marker) or the guesthouses in the Gongkar Airport vicinity (KM95 marker).

The rough centre of Tsedang is a dusty traffic roundabout with a golden flying horse statue in the middle. Most activity takes place on Naidong Road, the street running south of the roundabout. Arrayed along here are the following hotels:

Postal House Naidong Rd; tel: 782 1888; quotes Y220 minimum for a room, although rates for Chinese guests posted are Y40-80.

Shannan Hotel Naidong Rd; tel: 782 6168; has 53 rooms going for Y280 economy, Y380 standard, Y680 suite and Y80 for 'o'clock room' (a short-time room for Chinese military – and, presumably, prostitutes).

Tsedang Hotel Naidong Rd; tel: 782 1899; boasts 190 rooms for Y888 standard, Y1,212 triple and Y1,680-2,200 for a suite (all prices are subject to a 10% service charge). Group tours stay here. Facilities include email and internet access at the hotel business centre.

South of Tsedang

The main attraction south of Tsedang is **Yumbulagang Fortress**, 13km from town along a sealed road. A pilgrim bus runs out to the fortress, or you could hire a taxi for a few hours and see several sites en route, like Trandruk. Yumbulagang fortress crowns a hilltop; it is set in a valley with a village below. Now you see it, now you don't. Yumbulagang is in the RRDCR-CR category (reduced to rubble during the Cultural Revolution and completely rebuilt). Pictures taken in the late 1970s show nothing left of the fortress – it was shorn from the rock. Pictures taken in the 1980s show the entire fortress again. The present building, reconstructed in 1982, is a pretty good copy of the original, though not quite as big. The architecture is rare and distinctive: Yumbulagang Fortress is believed to have been built by the Yarlung dynasty kings in the 7th or 8th century. Later it was converted into a monastery. Now it is a museum of sorts, looked after by some Geluk monks. You can clamber up through several storeys to the two-tiered chapel at the top. From this eyrie, there are fine views of the patchwork of fields in the village below.

On the way out to Yumbulagang, or on the return trip, you can visit **Trandruk Gompa (Falcon-Dragon Temple)**, originally built by King Songtsen Gampo in the 7th century. The monastery is 7km from Tsedang, reached by a good road. The monastery is a warren of chapels: in an upstairs chapel right at the back is the monastery's treasure. Locked in a dusty glass case is a precious tanka depicting Avalokitesvara, whose ghost-like image is reputed to be composed of 30,000 pearls sewn into a red tapestry.

A different fork from Tsedang leads 17km south to **Tangboche Monastery**, which, though in a sorry state, is worth checking out for the murals covering the walls of the assembly hall. These murals were commissioned in 1915 by the 13th

Dalai Lama (whose image naturally appears among the murals). A further 13km southwards brings you to Chongye, where the tombs of all the Yarlung dynasty kings are located. **Chongye Royal Tombs** consist of massive earth mounds, which all look pretty much the same except for their size. This has led to much confusion over who is actually entombed within. The largest tomb is believed to be that of the 7th-century warrior-king, Songtsen Gampo. On top of this tomb is a small chapel, reached by a flight of stairs – it features a statue of Songtsen Gampo, flanked by two of his wives and two important ministers.

To the east of Tsedang, approached from Tsangri, an arduous hike leads to **Lhamo Latso**, the oracle lake. In former times, high lamas would venture out to Lhamo Latso and contemplate the lake to induce visions used in divinations. In the early 1930s, visions conjured up here helped direct Reting Rinpoche's search for the 14th Dalai Lama. The trek into Lhamo Latso is very tough, going over several high passes. Having a guide would be a good idea; you might want to take camping gear and make a two-day trip out of it – that would leave time to contemplate the lake.

Samye monastery

Lhasa to Kathmandu Route

THE GREATEST ROAD ROUTE IN HIGH ASIA

The Lhasa to Kathmandu route ranks, in my mind, as the finest in High Asia, not in terms of road surface, but because of the ethereal views. You are motoring across the roof the world, powering over five passes – festooned with prayer-flags – all above 4,500m. If you take the Gyantse route, winding up to Khamba La pass, you come to stunning views of the Turquoise Lake (Yamdrok Tso) with snowcaps on the Bhutanese border. Three great monasteries – at Gyantse, Shigatse and Sakya – lie along the road route. If you have arranged it with the driver and guide, you can drive all the way to Everest base camp – a magical spot that will (almost literally) blow you away. Even without the base camp trip, on a clear day you can see some 8,000m peaks right from the roadway, including Cho Oyu (8,153m), near Tingri. And then there's a fantastic drop right off the Tibetan plateau – from high-altitude desert, switchbacking down to tropical Nepalese jungle. There is nothing in High Asia that can compare to this roadshow. Lhasa to Kathmandu is an excellent adventure. Nobody said the trip would be easy, though...

Logistics

On your own, you can catch a bus running to Shigatse from Lhasa, but no buses run on the southern route to Gyantse (the buses go to Shigatse first, and then from Shigatse back to Gyantse). There is an intermittent service to Lhatse and Sakya also, as well as pilgrim trucks headed in this direction. Some backpackers have managed to negotiate rides all the way to the Nepalese border. Three backpackers I met paid for a ride on a CITS bus that was heading from Shigatse to Zhangmu to pick up a group at the border, but there was no stopping or sightseeing.

If you want to stop where you like, the best option is to club together with other travellers and rent a Landcruiser with driver and guide (or several Landcruisers). There are a number of options here: take the Landcruiser to Zhangmu and cross the border into Nepal, or go to Zhangmu, turn around, and come back to Lhasa. You might want to arrange a mixture: drop some passengers at Zhangmu, and then return to Lhasa. Landcruiser travel gives you flexibility. A factor you have to consider when planning this trip is where to overnight. Apart from the places mentioned in this text, the driver and guide can ferret out small restaurants or places to stay overnight if you are stuck somewhere at nightfall. There's always a guesthouse or teahouse tucked away somewhere.

In theory, the Lhasa to Kathmandu route (the actual highway) is open without permits. However, if you stop anywhere or overnight, the only place that appears to be quite open is Shigatse. You are supposed to have permits for places like Gyantse, Sakya, Everest, Shegar and so on. The guide with a Landcruiser can

LHASA TO KATHMANDU

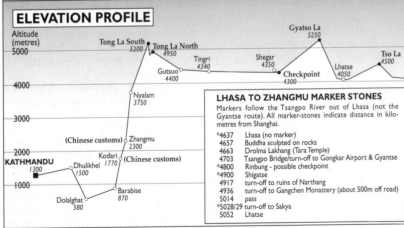

0 _____ 50km
0 _____ 30 miles

Bradt

N

Ali (Shiquanhe),
Kailash (north route)

Kailash
(south route)

Raga   Gyatro   Sangsang

Saga   Yarlung Tsangpo   Pabai Dzong   Ngamring

Car
ferry   Napshi   Lhatse   Tso
La

Paiko Tso   Gyatso La   Renda

Gutsuo   Shegar Lulu   Klako Kangri
6482m   Sakya

Tong La   Friendship Highway   Bailar
Tingri   Lungja   Military
checkpoint
Pang La

Shishapangma
8012m   Zamukh   Rongbuk
Monastery
Everest
base camp

Lönpo Gang
7083m   Nyalam   Milarepa's Cave   Cho Oyu
8153m   Karta

Zhangmu   Gauri   Everest
8848m   Makalu
8475m

Kodari   Shankar
7146m   Namche
Bazaar

KATHMANDU   Barabise
Lamosangu

BHAKTAPUR   Dolalghat
Dhulikhel

N E P A L

T   i

ELEVATION PROFILE

Altitude
(metres)   Gyatso La
                                                  5250
5000   Tong La South Tong La North   Tso La
        5200   4950   4500
                        Tingri   Shegar   Checkpoint Lhatse
                        4340   4350   4300   4050
        Gutsuo
        4400

4000

        Nyalam
        3750

3000

        (Chinese customs) Zhangmu
                           2300

2000
KATHMANDU Kodari
        1300   Dhulikhel 1770 (Chinese customs)
                1500
                                Barabise
1000   870
        Dolalghat
        580

LHASA TO ZHANGMU MARKER STONES

Markers follow the Tsangpo River out of Lhasa (not the
Gyantse route). All marker-stones indicate distance in kilometres from Shanghai.

*4637	Lhasa (no marker)
4657	Buddha sculpted on rocks
4663	Drolma Lakhang (Tara Temple)
4703	Tsangpo Bridge/turn-off to Gongkar Airport & Gyantse
*4800	Rinbung - possible checkpoint
*4900	Shigatse
4917	turn-off to ruins of Narthang
4936	turn-off to Gangchen Monastery (about 500m off road)
5014	pass
*5028/29	turn-off to Sakya
5052	Lhatse

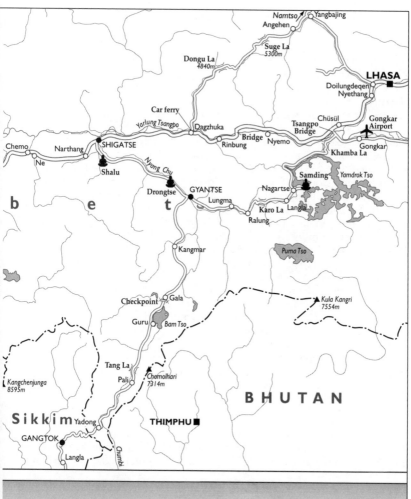

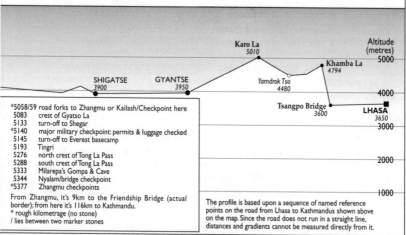

*5058/59 road forks to Zhangmu or Kailash/Checkpoint here
5083   crest of Gyatso La
5133   turn-off to Shegar
*5140   major military checkpoint: permits & luggage checked
5145   turn-off to Everest basecamp
5193   Tingri
5276   north crest of Tong La Pass
5288   south crest of Tong La Pass
5333   Milarepa's Gompa & Cave
5344   Nyalam/bridge checkpoint
*5377   Zhangmu checkpoints

From Zhangmu, it's 9km to the Friendship Bridge (actual border); from here it's 116km to Kathmandu.
* rough kilometrage (no stone)
/ lies between two marker stones

The profile is based upon a sequence of named reference points on the road from Lhasa to Kathmandu shown above on the map. Since the road does not run in a straight line, distances and gradients cannot be measured directly from it.

arrange these. On your own, you may be able to pick up permits for onward destinations at Shigatse PSB – ask other travellers about the current situation. Permits from Shigatse PSB are usually valid up to seven days, cost Y50 and require a Y200 deposit. Most destinations in this chapter fall under the jurisdiction of Shigatse Prefecture (area code 0892).

Timing
A lot of navigation information is carried in the Lhasa to Kathmandu Route map in this book. You can work out turn-offs and where you are by a system of kilometre marker-stones by the roadside. This is the best way, for example, to find Milarepa's Cave (which is not visible from the road). The entire route from Lhasa to Kathmandu is 938km if you go via Gyantse, but 865km if you take the direct Lhasa-Shigatse route. If you take sidetrips to Shegar and Sakya (highly recommended), you add 56km to the kilometrage, since Sakya lies 21km off the main route. There's a major detour of 70km off the main route to reach Everest base camp (refer to the *Star Treks* chapter, page 198).

Without stops or obstacles, fast drivers can make the run from Lhasa to Zhangmu in two days, overnighting at Tingri. With stops, the trip would require a minimum of four days. It's recommended you allow six to seven days, depending on sidetrips. If you include Everest base camp, allow more time. Approximate driving time along the route: Lhasa to Shigatse, 6 to 10 hrs (depending on route taken); Shigatse to Lhatse, 3¹/₂ hrs; Lhatse to Tingri, 4 hrs; Tingri to Nyalam, 4¹/₂ hrs; Nyalam to Zhangmu, 2¹/₂ hrs; Zhangmu to Kodari, 1¹/₂ hrs (includes checkposts); Kodari to Kathmandu, 4 hrs.

Sample itinerary
A sample itinerary for an eight-day foray from Lhasa to Kathmandu (via southern route through Gyantse) might look like this:

Day 1   Drive from Lhasa to Gyantse via Nagartse (Samding), overnight Gyantse.
Day 2   Hiking in Gyantse, overnight Gyantse.
Day 3   Morning in Gyantse, drive to Shigatse, hike kora, overnight Shigatse.
Day 4   Morning in Shigatse, drive to Sakya, hike around Sakya, overnight in Sakya.
Day 5   Drive from Sakya to Shegar, hike at Shegar; overnight at either Shegar or at guesthouses at crossroads near Shegar, or continue to Tingri.
Day 6   Drive from Shegar/Tingri to Nyalam, overnight Nyalam.
Day 7   Drive to Friendship Bridge. Cross into Nepal, pick up transport to Kodari and maybe on to Dhulikhel. Overnight at either Kodari or Dhulikhel.
Day 8   Arrive Kathmandu.

Reverse trip
The description here follows the Lhasa to Kathmandu route for the very good reason that it's more approachable in that direction due to both the altitude acclimatisation factor and the visa/permit situation. It is possible to do the route in reverse, but bear in mind the following words of caution: once you enter Tibet at Zhangmu, you do not have an Alien Travel Permit. Technically, the road from Zhangmu to Lhasa is open without permit, but this could be sticky. Really, you are at the mercy of CITS in Zhangmu, who arrange Landcruiser rides to Lhasa for US$100–150 a person. You're in a poor bargaining position, as CITS is a transport

monopoly. Coming in from Kathmandu, be careful what you bring in your baggage – suspect literature, such as that about the Dalai Lama, may cause big problems. Guidebooks are not usually targeted. Going up from 1,300m in Kathmandu to a 5,200m pass, you may be in no mood or condition for sightseeing, as you may have trouble with altitude sickness. Some Landcruiser drivers carry a small tank of oxygen in the vehicle for this reason.

Lhasa to Shigatse routes

There are three routes from Lhasa to Shigatse. If on a round-trip from Lhasa, you can combine routes. For example, for a long loop, you could motor via Yamdrok Tso to Gyantse, and then return to Lhasa via Yangbajing, stopping at various monasteries along the routes.

Northern route

The northern route via Yangbajing is the least-travelled way of getting from Lhasa to Shigatse, but it makes sense if you've been off to Lake Namtso. The route is sometimes used if for some reason the main westward route is blocked. Yangbajing supplies geothermal power to Lhasa; there is a hot-spring pool here. Heading southwards from Yangbajing you motor across two high passes – Suge La and Dongu La. On the north banks of the Yarlung Tsangpo you can detour along a rough road to Menri Gompa, a small Bon monastery. You cross the Yarlung Tsangpo by car ferry to Dagzhuka, and join the main western route to Shigatse. Approximate driving time (no stops) on this route is: Lhasa to Yangbajing, 2 hrs; Yangbajing to Suge La, 2½ hrs; Suge La to Dagzhuka ferry crossing, 2½ hrs; Dagzhuza to Shigatse, 2 hrs.

Western route

This road follows a canyon running along the Yarlung Tsangpo – it is used by Chinese military and supply trucks to get from Lhasa to Shigatse in the fastest time. It thus sees the heaviest traffic, with convoys of military trucks heading through. The road runs beneath steep canyon walls: rockfalls may block the road entirely. Slabs of roadway have also been known to disappear into the Yarlung Tsangpo, because engineering skills haven't quite been perfected. The bridge spanning the Yarlung Tsangpo near Rinbung is one-way, meaning that there can be traffic line-ups when the flow is against you. Driving time on this Lhasa to Shigatse route is about 5 to 6 hours if there are no delays or problems.

Southern route

This route via Gyantse to Shigatse is much more dramatic, taking in the beautiful lake of Yamdrok Tso. This route is longer, more winding and rougher, so it is not used by supply trucks. This means minimal traffic and far superior views. On the southern route, exiting Lhasa, you cross the Tsangpo Bridge and wind up to Khamba La, with stunning views. Down the other side of Khamba La you reach Nagartse, a village with a small restaurant, plus a guesthouse. If you can, arrange a sidetrip to Samding Monastery. From Nagartse, the road climbs over Karo La and heads for Gyantse. Approximate driving time on this route: Lhasa to Khamba La, 1½ hrs; Khamba La to Karo La, 3 hrs; Karo La to Gyantse, 2½ hrs; Gyantse to Shigatse, 2 hours.

Southern route to Gyantse
Drolma Lakhang

Exiting Lhasa on either the western route or the southern route, you can visit this well-preserved temple, about 25km from Lhasa. See *Exploring Central Tibet* chapter for details.

Yamdrok Tso

From Khamba La, where prayer flags are buffeted by the winds, you get a magnificent view of Yamdrok Tso (the Turquoise Lake), with the large snowcap on the horizon being Kula Kangri (7,554m) on the Bhutanese border. From this vantage point you can see why the Tibetans consider Yamdrok Tso to be a sacred lake. It is Tibet's largest freshwater body of water.

Winding down from Khamba La toward the shore of Yamdrok Tso, you can see a hydropower plant, with Austrian-built turbines. This plant is part of a hare-brained Chinese scheme that drains the lakewater to produce electricity for Lhasa during peak demand. The plant is designed as a pumped storage plant with a 90MW capacity. The project has been a total disaster since its inception in 1985. In 1986, due to vigorous objections from Tibetans headed by the 10th Panchen Lama, work was halted, but was resumed after the Panchen Lama's death in 1989. Overriding international campaigns, the Chinese went ahead with construction, and reports filtered through of leaking and collapsed tunnels leading from the lake to the turbines. The plant started generating power in mid-1997.

Western environmentalists are concerned that the water level at Yamdrok Tso could drop significantly – or, in a worst-case scenario, that the lake might completely drain away. Authorities in Lhasa insist this is not the case: they say they will pump water back from the Yarlung Tsangpo to replenish the lakewater. But even if this were true, it means snow-fed lakewater would be replaced with muddy river flow, with uncertain ecological results. Pumping water back up into Yamdrok Tso requires a separate power source: a new dam, under construction on the Nyang River, 30km east of Gyantse, is said to be that source. The building of this dam has spawned an entire town of corrugated roofing, housing Chinese construction workers and engineers.

Nagartse and Samding Monastery

Nagartse is the only sizeable village near Yamdrok Tso: Landcruiser drivers headed for Gyantse may break up the long day with a rest stop here. Nagartse has a few restaurants (Holy Lake Restaurant, Lhasa Restaurant) and several guesthouses. Technically a permit is required to stay overnight: Nagartse and Yamdrok Tso are under the jurisdiction of Shannan Prefecture.

Yamdrok Tso is shaped like the pincers of a crab: in the grip of the pincers lies the monastery of Samding, about 8km from Nagartse. You can reach it by Landcruiser from Nagartse, or hike in. Nagartse PSB does not seem to like travellers visiting this one, so be discreet when visiting. The monastery is on a hilltop, reached by a set of switchbacks; a few dozen monks are in residence. There are expansive views across the valley from Samding.

Samding Monastery has an odd history. The monastery was probably founded in the 13th century, and was associated with the Bodong sect, initiated by Bodong Chokle Namgyel (1306–86). The Bodong sect never gained much prominence, although a number of temples within radius of Samding followed its precepts.

At one time, Samding appears to have had both monks and nuns in residence, and was run by an abbess, one of the only female incarnations in Tibet. The lineage goes back to the 18th century. In 1717, legend has it, the abbess (venerated as Dorje Phagmo, or the 'Thunderbolt Sow', believed to be a reincarnation of Tara) transformed herself and her cohorts into pigs to save them from a Dzungar (Mongol) attack. For centuries, the lineage continued uneventfully, until the year 1937. That year the acting Regent of Tibet announced that the 6th Dorje Phagmo had been recognised in a young girl, even though the 5th was still at large. He argued that the transference of souls actually took place in this case before death. The 5th Dorje Phagmo died the following year, but the Tibetans would not accept the 6th as the true incarnation and three other candidates were put forward. The matter was hotly disputed by the nominated 6th's father, and a costly legal battle drained the funds of Samding and tore its monks and nuns apart with internal strife.

The 6th Dorje Phagmo (the girl selected in 1937), it appears, hardly took up residence at Samding, since the legal wrangle carried over into the 1950s. In 1959, she fled to India, but the same year decided to return to Tibet by way of China. She then sided with the Chinese in her loyalties and made it clear she did not wish to be a Living Buddha anymore. She married and had three children, and held a high government position in Lhasa. When last heard of, however, she had resumed her role as head of Samding and was said to be again giving initiations.

If a community of nuns and monks with an abbess at their head sounds like good material for a novel, there is one that draws inspiration from Samding. In his suspense novel *The Rose of Tibet*, author Lionel Davidson combines Yamdrok Tso and Samding to create a place called Yamdring Monastery.

GYANTSE
Gyangtse, Gyangze; elevation 3,950m

Gyantse was established as the personal fiefdom of King Pelden Sangpo, in the 14th century. His successor, Rabten Kunsang Phapa (1389–1442), extended the fiefdom's range, and constructed Palkor Choide Lamasery and the mighty Kumbum, both of which are still standing today.

In later centuries, Gyantse developed as an important centre of the wool trade in Tibet, and a bustling caravan stop on the trade-route from Lhasa to India. That route – leading to Sikkim and Bhutan – was closed by the Chinese after they took over in 1950. Gyantse has since fallen into obscurity, its role usurped by Lhasa under the Chinese. This situation, however, has left Gyantse intact as a Tibetan architectural entity, which is something quite rare amid all the Chinese destruction and reconstruction. Gyantse has a largely Tibetan population – perhaps around 15,000. There is a huge fort at one end of town, a walled-in monastery-grounds at the other end, and a ramshackle market-place with older buildings and alley-ways between fort and monastery.

In the late 1940s, Italian photographer Francesco Mele passed through Gyantse. Here's his description of the market:

> Its market is rich, due to the wool trade and the Indian and Chinese imported objects sold there. The shops are near to the main street, and many of them are simply tents. Here women wearing silver and turquoise jewellery sell clothing and household articles... There are even some Nepalese and Bhutanese salesmen, and a few Muslims who have taken the few weeks' journey from Ladak in order to sell their products in Gyantse. Muslims are often employed as butchers of yak and goat here, since the Buddhist religion forbids Tibetans to kill animals. Fresh and dried beef and mutton hang in every part of the market, giving it an oddly surrealist appearance.

Gyantse market appears to have died: there isn't a whole lot happening around the old quarter anymore. Instead, various smaller street markets are scattered around the town. Nevertheless, Gyantse is a great place to visit, and will give some idea of what an intact Tibetan town must have looked like.

Buildings in Gyantse date back as far as the 14th century. One of these is the massive *dzong* (fort), occupying a strategic hilltop at the southern end of town. The dzong guarded the road to Lhasa, and the invading British expedition of 1903 found it a formidable obstacle. The British eventually stormed the dzong, the Tibetan defenders capitulated, and there was no further resistance on the road to Lhasa.

Although the last of the British forces withdrew in 1908, several vestiges of British presence remained in Gyantse, in the form of a British Trade Agent, a British wool-agent station, a British post office (with a telegraph line running to India), and later a British-run school for upper-crust Tibetan children. By the 1940s, a great deal of Gyantse's sheep-wool production was slated for export to British India. There was little interest in yak-wool, which was too harsh in quality, although in the pre-synthetic era, the beards worn by Santa Clauses in US department stores were made from yak-tail hair. Gyantse became a funnel for the export of wool due to its location, and wool was brought here from outlying areas of Tibet.

The 1950s saw a period of severe dislocation in Gyantse. In 1954, the town was nearly destroyed by flooding; in 1959 the local industries were virtually dismantled with the exodus of artisans from Tibet, and the removal of others to workcamps. After putting down the 1959 revolt, the Chinese imprisoned 400 monks and laymen at the monastery of Gyantse. During the Cultural Revolution, the monastery itself was ransacked and dismantled – items of value were either destroyed or shipped back to China. Gyantse Kumbum, however, was spared. Since 1980, the Chinese have attempted to stimulate the handicraft production for which Gyantse was so famous. But if there has been any stimulation, there is little evidence of it in Gyantse's present-day market-place.

In the late 1990s, Chinese authorities embarked on a propaganda blitz in Gyantse, naming it 'Heroic City' in praise of valiant Tibetan resistance to British troops in 1904. In Chinese terms, the logic runs thus: 'Tibetan patriotic soldiers safeguarded state sovereignty and territorial integrity – defending the Tibet-China Motherland.' These propaganda efforts were most likely tied in with a round of Brit-bashing after the 1997 hand-over of Hong Kong. First there was the 1997 release of *Red River Valley*, a Shanghai-made epic movie about the British in Tibet, with on-location filming at Gyantse. This was followed by renaming the main street of Gyantse 'Hero Street', and the erection of a huge obelisk as a monument to heroic Tibetan fighters. The monument makes a convenient navigation landmark, right near the town's central roundabout.

Gyantse basics
Getting there and away
Motoring over several stunning passes on the back route from Lhasa is the best way to get to Gyantse. This trip should take about six hours or so – longer if you stop en route. If arriving by Landcruiser and overnighting, park the vehicle within your hotel grounds. Buses to Gyantse are routed through Shigatse. The cost is Y35 for the Lhasa–Shigatse run and Y25 for Shigatse–Gyantse. There are larger luxury buses used on the Lhasa to Shigatse run. Sometimes drivers in Shigatse refuse to take foreigners, even if they have permits for Gyantse. An alternative might be to hire a taxi in Shigatse for the run. The 90km from Shigatse to Gyantse should be covered in three hours or less. Twenty-seat minibuses congregate at the central roundabout of Gyantse early in the morning for departures to Shigatse. You can also try your luck hitching – walk part of the way in the direction you want to travel, and then wave like a windmill.

Getting around
You can mostly get around Gyantse on foot, though it's a long walk out to destinations like Pala Manor. If you're with a Landcruiser driver and want to speed

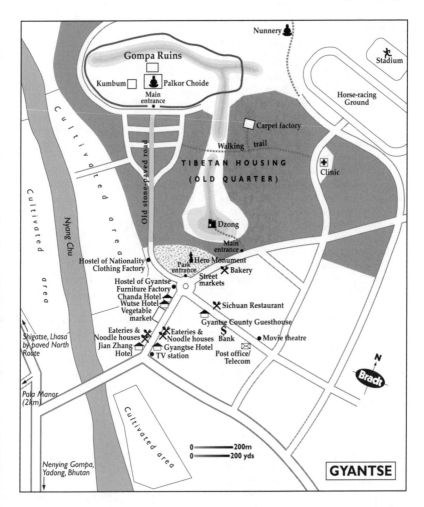

things up, get him to drive you around to sites like the main monastery, Pala Manor or Ani Gompa. These destinations would be easy to get to by bicycle if you can lay your hands on one. Gyangtse Hotel has a few bikes, but only for their guests, and they are expensive at Y5 an hour, or Y50 a day. An alternative is hiring a bicycle trishaw driver in town.

Facilities

Facilities in Gyantse are limited, but include a half-hearted attempt at a department store (shelves bare) and a half-hearted attempt at a bank (staffed by Chinese who appear to have perfected the art of camouflaging themselves as non-bank workers). Further down the street is the post office, with long-distance telecom capabilities if you goad the staff. Try and avoid the clinic at the northeast side of town – it's unsanitary. Gyantse at night is subject to the occasional tuneless wailing from karaoke bars or the sound of kung-fu epics emanating from video salons or Tibetan teahouses; there's also a movie theatre with an antiquated sound system.

Lodging

Some hotels in Gyantse appear to be only for Chinese guests. For exact hotel locations, see the Gyantse map.

Hostel of Gyantse Town Furniture Factory Located right at the central roundabout. Comfortable, with dorm beds for Y35 each, including TV. There are no showers in the rooms, but hot water is provided in the public shower at certain hours if there are enough guests.

Hostel of Nationality Clothing Factory Located a little north of central roundabout on the monastery road; another truckstop compound with drive-in courtyard and basic dorm-type rooms: a tap in the yard provides the plumbing.

Gyantse County Guesthouse Located southeast of roundabout; tel: 817 2247. No English sign at front, so hard to recognise. It's a Chinese blockhouse with softer beds than elsewhere, but the plumbing, though it may look impressive, fails to perform. Charges Y80-100 for room and Y25-30 for a bed in 3-bed dorms.

Jian Zhang Hotel Located southwest of roundabout; tel: 817 3720; fax: 817 3910. Has 17 rooms for Y200 apiece, and caters mostly for a Chinese clientele.

Wutse Hotel Located southwest of roundabout; tel: 817 2999. This recommended hotel is popular with travellers and groups seeking to avoid snooty Gyangtse Hotel. This hotel is cosy and has a drive-in courtyard. It has forty standard rooms for Y300 each; half a dozen single rooms for Y250; and 2 suites. The hotel has 11 dorm beds for Y40 apiece with 24-hour hot showers available.

Gyangtse Hotel: Located towards the river at the southwest edge of town; 8 Yingxiong Rd; tel 817 222; fax 817 2366. The most expensive hotel in town (the plumbing actually does work), complete with snooty staff. This is the place for group tours, with a dining hall and a souvenir shop. Amenities include hot water; oxygen pillows can be requested. StarTV viewing may be possible. The hotel rents bikes for Y5 an hour or Y50 a day, but only to guests. The 120 standard and deluxe rooms here are expensive, going for around Y500 and up.

Food

Scattered around town are small eateries, some with only two or three tables. For real Tibetan atmosphere try Tashi Restaurant, near the central roundabout (on the second floor), a Tibetan-style teahouse serving palatable food. There's a string of small restaurants along the street southwest of central roundabout – Muslim, Tibetan and Chinese styles on offer. Along the same strip (set back off the road) is a small fruit and vegetable market where you can even buy peaches and bananas. In the mornings, try the tiny bakery just east of the main roundabout for hot baked goods. Stores in Gyantse are not well-stocked like they are in Shigatse.

What to see
Orientation

Gyantse cleaves into several distinct zones. To the northern end of town is the old quarter, with Tibetan housing. To the southern end of town, south of the central roundabout, are newer Chinese concrete blocks and Chinese facilities like the bank, post office, cinema and so on. At all compass points around the town are cultivated fields. There are stupendous views of Gyantse from the topmost ramparts of the fort.

Horse-racing festival

The time when Gyantse really comes to life is during the horse racing festival, held in the first week of the eighth lunar month (usually sometime in late July or early

August). The horse-racing ground is to the northeast side of town. Festivities last for about five days. The jockeys are young boys: the winners (both boy and horse) are festooned with white ceremonial scarves. Large parades, with dancers and singers, and monks in full regalia, accompany the opening and closing ceremonies.

Old Quarter

Gyantse is a great town to walk around. The Tibetan part of town, toward the gates of Gyantse Gompa, is a fascinating medieval jumble of alleyways, with the odd cow roaming through. Gyantse market used to be located along the stone-paved road close to the main monastery. There's no plumbing in the old quarter – water comes from street taps – and little electrical supply. However, solar cookers have been introduced by the Chinese: these concave-shaped reflectors are found on the flat roofs in the old quarter – they can bring a kettle of water to the boil in a few minutes.

There is a walking trail through from the monastery toward the horse-racing ground – it cuts through a cleft in a high ridge (see map). Along the way is **Gyantse Carpet Factory**, where all work is done by hand – carding the wool, spinning, dyeing and weaving. This small operation is a shadow of what Gyantse once was. There's also a clothing factory in Gyantse. A worthy destination to the northeast side of town is **Ani Gompa**, a nunnery with 30 nuns in residence. A tiny chapel here contains a large wooden prayer-wheel and some life-size frescos, including one that shows the 10th Panchen Lama (a mural near this used to show the current Dalai Lama, but, under orders, the head was repainted in the likeness of the 5th Dalai Lama). Behind the nunnery is a cliff face with hermit caves; there's a sky burial site in the vicinity.

The monastery

Pictures taken by Leslie Weir on a visit in 1930 show a complex of 16 monasteries within the high walls at the north end of Gyantse (Weir was a British Trade Agent at Gyantse). The monastic town has been razed with the exception of a few of the larger buildings.

Access

The monastery is only accessible by the south gate, where an entry fee is charged. The Kumbum appears to only be open in the mornings – in any case, this is the best time to visit. Chapels can be dark, so bring a flashlight.

The Kumbum

The main sight of Gyantse is the immense chorten or Kumbum in the grounds of the walled monastery at the north end. It was built in the 14th century by Rapten Kunsang Phapa. Kumbum means 'having 100,000 images', and Gyantse Kumbum may well live up to that description. The chorten is a deluxe model and quite innovative in its architecture – there is nothing like it elsewhere in Tibet. It has 70 small interlocking chapels that you visit as you spiral your way to the golden plume at the top. Each chapel contains fine statuary, and murals painted in the 15th century by Newari artists.

In aerial perspective, the chorten is shaped like a mandala, the embodiment of the Lamaist universe. Pilgrims circumambulate this giant wedding-cake structure: the inner spiralling circuit of the chorten is a meditational aid, with the top canopied section representing the highest plane of wisdom. How far you can ascend depends on how adept you are at convincing the caretaker monks to allow you to proceed. The best strategy is to try and follow pilgrims, since entrances to upper regions are hidden behind statues and in dark alcoves (some may be locked). Right near the top you come out below the large all-seeing eyes of Buddha, painted on the upper walls. The chapels here are larger and contain intricate tantric murals and mandalas. Although it may appear you cannot go higher, in fact there are ladders leading above the all-seeing eyes through a trapdoor to an open wooden turret, under the top umbrella-like structure. From here there are panoramic views of Gyantse.

Palkor Choide Lamasery

This monastery is believed to have been constructed 1418–25 by Rapten Kunsang Phapa. Though in the past it served the Sakya and Geluk orders, it is presently looked after by Gelukpa monks. The monastery has miraculously survived with some original statuary intact. More interesting than the ground floor assembly hall are the chapels on the second floor. On the third or topmost floor is a shrine to Sakyamuni Buddha, with huge tantric wheel murals of Sakya deities.

Hero monument

Facing the central roundabout is a huge three-sided obelisk, with text or characters on each side in Chinese, Tibetan and English. The English side reads: 'Gyangtse Mount Dzong Monument to Heroes'. The monument is set in a large park, and a token entry-fee is charged. The Chinese-style monolith is made of concrete and finished in marble: it sits on a dais similar to one at the Temple of Heaven in Beijing, with Chinese imperial lions – not Tibetan snow-lions – standing guard.

Around the base of the obelisk are bas-reliefs which are faded but fascinating. The front section shows the battle of 1904 with Tibetans throwing down rocks, British troops (easily identified by pith helmets and guns) and what appears to be characters with Chinese dress and swords (not historically correct, asthere were no Chinese soldiers or advisers at Gyantse in 1904). A side panel shows the British with heavy machinery, and the back panel shows PLA troops waving Chinese flags and people holding portraits of Mao Zedong.

The fort

This brooding 500-year-old colossus crowns a hilltop at the southern end of Gyantse. The fort's foundations are of 14th-century vintage, while the thick walls were probably constructed later. Access to the dzong is only from steps at the southeast side – there's a path leading from a roadway bridge here, through village housing, to the outer door. You may need to find the gatekeeper to open the dzong's huge doors, but if those are open, proceed to a ticket gate higher up, where you pay the Y25 entry-fee. Other buildings in the dzong complex may be locked, too. You can climb right to the top battlements, which offer a superb view of Gyantse town and make a great photo perch. Within the dzong, there's actually little to see. Various buildings and battlements were blown to smithereens by Nepalese invaders, then British invaders, and again by the favourite cohorts of Mao Zedong (the Red Guards), leaving a lot of rubble lying around. Even so, it is one of the best-preserved forts in Tibet. Two restored sections include a chapel with some dark murals and newish Buddhist statuary, and an anti-British museum.

Anti-British museum

'Memorial Hall of the Anti-British' is the name of a two-room museum exhibit at Gyantse Dzong. The museum charges another fee to get in. There are pictures; explanations in Tibetan, English and Chinese; a couple of small cannons; and a heroic statue of Tibetans fighting the imperialist British 'to safeguard the

Motherland' (meaning the Chinese motherland). There are other howlers: a guide who was shepherding along some group tourists seemed to think that the Tibetans won the battle at the fort in 1904, an assertion which my (British) companion loudly called into question. Later on, we were intercepted by a Chinese official who arrived to question us about the questions we'd asked the guide, at which point we feigned ignorance. History, it seems, undergoes constant revision within the PRC. Oddly, a Chinese movie crew making a movie in 1996 about the British invasion of Tibet did not use Gyantse Dzong as a set.

Toiling on upwards, you come to a viewable room labelled 'Dungeon', which contains a tableau with life-sized figures, one a Tibetan aristocrat (as judge) and four others involved in flogging a prisoner. This is meant to show the harsher side of the feudal serf system in old Tibet. Other descriptions of these nasty feudal times include binding a prisoner in cowhide and throwing him in the river, and scooping out eyeballs or intestines. The Chinese may have overlooked the fact that similar penalties (if not worse) were meted out in Imperial China during this era.

A set of (Chinese-built) concrete steps leads straight up from here to the top of the fort. The top turret is about four square metres and offers breathtaking views (in all senses of the word – you are actually over 200m higher than the town). This makes an excellent vantage point for orientation and photography.

Pala Manor

Over a bridge, on the west side of Nyang River, is a junction with several turn-offs. To the west you can drive or walk 3km to Pala Manor, which is an old noble's house in the middle of a small village. The manor belongs to the 'feudal' days when an aristocrat ruled the village and surrounding lands. The walled three-storey manor – mostly constructed of wood – features the former tearoom and stables.

Pala fled Tibet in 1959 and lived out his days in exile. A tableau upstairs shows Pala and his cronies (one the abbot of Palkor Choide monastery) indulging in the game of mahjong, drinking tea and taking the occasional shot of whiskey. This is meant to show decadence but in today's China, half the population is addicted to mahjong. You are shepherded around and shown three or four rooms on the uppermost floor. The first is likely to be one with personal effects of Pala on display – stocks of Kraft cheese, Britannia biscuits and Diamond Jubilee confectionery. Next is a lounge room of sorts, with an ancient gramophone and snow-leopard or monkey-fur covers on the cushions. A meditation room features stained-glass imported from India.

Downstairs is a room that looks like a shop, with glass cases showing imported wines and goods from France, the US, the UK, Australia and India. There's a wardrobe crammed with boots, ceremonial wear and fur hats, while another case shows rollerskates, soccer boots and a soccer ball (very progressive for Tibet – soccer, introduced by the British, was banned by the monastic authorities in the 1940s). On the wall is a picture of Pala in the late 1940s and another picture taken in 1956 in India – also in the line-up is the young Dalai Lama, Ling Rinpoche (his tutor), and Ngawang Jigme (who was later to betray the Tibetans).

The extensively restored manor is a showpiece on how the people of Gyantse were exploited by Tibetan nobles – that's before all the major buildings of Gyantse were blown up by the Chinese. To drive this point home, you are escorted across the street from Pala manor to some dark hovels where servants used to live. The captions all tell the same story: life is far better under Chinese rule. One caption describes a carpet maker who used to live in a 10m^2 hovel with dirt floors at Pala Manor, but after Chinese liberation was able to shift to a 400m^2, two-storey home with three cows, a horse, 23 sheep and a colour TV.

Sidetrips from Gyantse

A turn-off on the west side of Gyantse leads directly south to **Nenying Gompa**, about 20km from Gyantse. This is an active monastery set in a small village. The monastery was nearly destroyed by the invading British in 1903, and later rebuilt, only to be destroyed again during the Cultural Revolution (and then rebuilt). The road here leads southward all the way to **Yadong**, at the border of Sikkim. There's a military checkpoint at Gala, beyond which you are most unlikely to be allowed to proceed (after that, there are views of Mount Chomolhari from the road).

The main turn-off from Gyantse is the one leading to Shigatse. It's a fast, flat run from Gyantse to Shigatse – the ground can be covered in a matter of several hours. There are two monastery stops you can make. The first is at **Drongtse Monastery**, a small place famed for its slate bas-relief carvings. Drongtse is about 9km from the junction in Gyantse. A second possibility is **Shalu Gompa**, which is reached by a turn-off 18km short of Shigatse. The gompa is 4km off the main route (you can also visit Shalu on a day-trip from Shigatse – see page 183).

SHIGATSE

Xigaze, Zhigatse; elevation 3,900m; capital of Shigatse Prefecture; area code: 0892
Shigatse, the second largest town in Tibet, has a population of around 60,000. The massive monastery of Tashilhunpo dates from the mid-15th century. Shigatse was the power-base of the King of Tsang in the 16th century: he was defeated in battle in 1642 by the Mongol leader, Gushri Khan. In 1652, the 5th Dalai Lama bestowed the title of Panchen Lama on the abbot of Tashilhunpo Monastery. From that time on, the authority of the Panchen Lama outweighed that of the Lhasa-appointed

WAX SEALS AND POSTAL RUNNERS
Geoffrey Flack

After invading in 1903, the British negotiated the right to set up telegraph and post offices in Tibet. This gave the Tibetans access to the international postal system. There were a handful of British post offices, the earliest starting around 1906. The British were not permitted to establish a post office in Lhasa, but three British post offices linked the main trading corridor from Tibet to India: at Gyantse, Phari and Yadong. The mail then went on to Kalimpong, in India.

The postal system for external mail in Tibet was primarily used by Nepalese and Indian traders. Delivery was accomplished by runners; the monasteries, for instance, had their own runners. Ponies were also used, and in the 1930s a Dodge truck operated on part of the route to India. The runners, like most Tibetans, were illiterate and could only identify traders' mail by handmarked symbols on the envelopes. The mail could be delivered in a fairly short time: officials in Lhasa used to subscribe to newspapers in Calcutta, which might arrive a week or so later. Considering the altitude of the passes along the route, the runners did a remarkable job.

In 1910 the 13th Dalai Lama, who had fled to India, asked the British company of Waterlow to design a Tibetan stamp. Waterlow produced some proofs with a snow-lion on them, the symbol of the Dalai Lama. These were rejected by the Tibetans, but they kept the proofs, and the Waterlow design was copied for the first Tibetan stamp issue of 1912. Tibetan stamps were a very haphazard affair. The 1912 issue, done in five different *trangka* values, was printed off woodblocks of 12 stamps. Stamp colour largely depended on what inks were available in the market-place. Tibetan cancels never bore dates, and district governor, who occupied the defeated king's castle (the present-day ruined dzong) in town.

Apart from Tashilhunpo Monastery and a small Tibetan quarter, Shigatse is heavily Chinese in character, by which I mean an ugly concrete sprawl. There's a weird wind blowing through Shigatse. It's the wind from Beijing, the dusty wind of the Gobi. Look at a Chinese map of Shigatse and you can get some idea of what has transpired. A Chinese map I picked up barely mentions any Tibetan features, except for an entry that says 'Trashilhunpo Temple' (can't even get that one right). Apart from the usual 'No 1 Bus Team', 'No 2 Guesthouse', is this curious entry: 'Building for Overseas Tibetans'. Could this be the fabled shop where Tibetans from Nepal come to buy their souvenirs?

Some glaring omissions on the map are the large army bases that ring the town. Shigatse is something of a glorified army base, with huge barracks punctuating the landscape. The arrival of the PLA *en masse* was not auspicious. In 1960, the PLA surrounded Tashilhunpo Monastery (which had hitherto escaped reforms) and seized all 4,000 monks within. Some were later executed, some committed suicide, and large numbers were taken to labour camps. Only 200 monks remained at the Tashilhunpo.

Because of the status of the Panchen Lama and Chinese attempts to manipulate the High Lama, Tashilhunpo Monastery was largely spared Red Guard destruction. By the 1980s, the number of monks in residence crept back up to around 800. In 1995, another major showdown took place at Tashilhunpo Monastery between the monks and Chinese authorities. The dispute erupted over the unfortunate Chinese choice of 11th Panchen Lama, resulting in tremendous upheaval. Many monks were

the random print-runs were never announced – the 1914 issue of stamps was not discovered by the West until 1942.

If you were living in Lhasa in the 1930s and you wanted to get a letter to England, life got complicated. There was no British post office in Lhasa, and Tibet was not a member of the International Postal Union. So you needed two sets of stamps on an envelope – Tibetan and Indian. In Lhasa, they'd cancel the Tibetan postage and forward the item to the Tibetan post office in Gyantse. Somehow the letter would make it across town to Gyantse's British post office, and then go on to Yadong and India, where it entered the international postal system.

Incoming mail was virtually impossible to orchestrate unless sent care of a trader in Gyantse or Phari, who would affix the Tibetan postage and forward the letter. In the process, the actual stamps would be dwarfed by a selection of wax seals, handstamps, chops and registration-marks. Red wax seals could only be used by Incarnate Lamas. Few of the Dalai Lama's letters went beyond Sikkim. They were carried by private runners, and enclosed ceremonial silk scarves and perhaps a small bag of gold-dust. They could only leave the Potala on auspicious dates.

By the early 1950s, stamp collectors were rushing to buy Tibetan postage. The majority of fake Tibetan stamps and covers started to appear at this time, though the hobby goes back to 1920. Buyers who are offered earlier Tibetan stamps in Kathmandu will probably be shown forgeries nine times out of ten. Covers are now forged so well that only a handful of world experts can tell the difference.

Geoffrey Flack (web: www.tibetanpost.com) is a recognised expert on stamps, resident in Canada imprisoned or ousted, to be replaced by pro-Chinese monks or those more timid. The head abbot was later sentenced to six years in jail for his part in the proceedings.

Shigatse basics
Getting there and away
Buses and minibuses ply the route from Lhasa to Shigatse – the ride is Y35. The buses have more comfortable seating. You can also cover the ground by taxi (from either Lhasa or Shigatse) or hired Landcruiser. The transport company to the southeast side of Shigatse runs buses and minibuses to Lhasa and to Gyantse.

Getting around
To get around Shigatse, you can walk to most places. It's possible to rent a bicycle from Tenzin Hotel. Prowling the streets are bicycle trishaws, motorised trishaws, and regular VW taxis – negotiate before setting out. You can also flag down a walking tractor for a ride across town – just jump on the back and pay when you arrive. CITS Shigatse has a few Landcruisers and minibuses in its stable, but these could be expensive to hire.

Permits
If you need onward permits, the PSB office to the east of Tashilhunpo Monastery may oblige. Shigastse PSB is open 09.00–13.00 and 16.00–19.00. There have been cases where, on the same day, the PSB office has given permits to some individuals but refused to give permits to others. Normally, you should be able to get ATPs for all destinations on the highway to Nepal, including Everest base camp. You can also get permits for Gyantse here, and for Shalu Gompa, but not for Samye. Permits cost Y50 plus a Y200 deposit, and are valid 5 to 7 days. If you are exiting Tibet into Nepal, you should be able to skip the Y200 deposit. Otherwise, you must come back to Shigatse PSB to collect the deposit (and they will keep the permit, so photocopy it if you want a souvenir). Note that for the Nepal border point (Zhangmu) there might be written in Chinese on your permit 'Zhangmu Back' (returning to Lhasa) or 'Zhangmu Through' (one-way trip to Kathmandu). Zhangmu on the permit seems to include Nyalam, while Tingri seems to include Shegar.

Information and services
Shigatse Hotel and Shandong Mansion Hotel have giftshops with a good supply of maps and books, and may even stock film. The Xinhua Bookstore up the street is fairly useless, though you might stray across a map or poster here. There are some photoshops downtown that can develop print film.

Email and internet
China Telecom Internet Bar is a large cybercafé run by Chinapost – it is located next door to the main post office. Further south along the same street is a cybercafé. Several smaller places are found opposite the Xinhua bookstore and vicinity. High-end hotels have internet access in the business centre.

Banking
The Bank of China is near Shigatse Hotel – this is the main branch where you can change travellers' cheques. Smaller branch offices of the BOC downtown only deal in cash.

Medical
There are two hospitals in town, but neither is of much use to travellers.

SHIGATSE

Tibetan Quarter

Dzong ruins

Hiking trail

Old Quarter

Freemarket (souvenirs/meat)

Market (hardware/ clothing)

Pilgrim circuit

Carpets
Tienfu

Tenzin Hotel

Dry goods market

Greasy Joe's Café
Zhengxian
Gongkar Tibetan

Hotel Manasarovar

Photo-shops

Handicraft stores

PSB

Samdrutse

Tashilhunpo Monastery (see plan below)

Xinhua Bookstore (2nd floor)

Lhasa

Holyland Hotel
TV station

Hospital of Tibetan Medicine

Shigatse People's Hospital

Bank of China
CAAC (ticket office)

Red Cross office

Shandong Mansion

Yarlong Tibetan

Department store

Lhatse, Sakya

Fruit Orchard

Carpet factory

Post office/Telecom
China Telecom
Internet Bar

Bowling alley

Transport Company: (buses to Gyantse & Lhasa)
Xing Yue

River

Shigatse
Bank of China
CITS Shigatse

Cybercafé

New Panchen Palace

Park

N

Bradt

0 ——————— 300m
0 ——————— 300 yds

Shalu Gompa, Gyantse

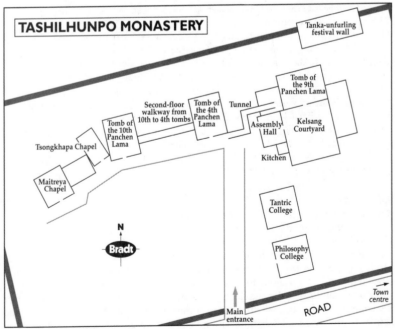

TASHILHUNPO MONASTERY

Tanka-unfurling festival wall

Tomb of the 9th Panchen Lama

Second-floor walkway from 10th to 4th tombs

Tomb of the 4th Panchen Lama

Tunnel

Tomb of the 10th Panchen Lama

Assembly Hall

Kelsang Courtyard

Tsongkhapa Chapel

Kitchen

Maitreya Chapel

Tantric College

N

Bradt

Philosophy College

Town centre

Main entrance

ROAD

Shopping and supplies

Shigatse is one of the best places in Tibet to replenish your stocks or add to them. It is second only to Lhasa. For trip supplies, check out the department stores first, as these carry canned and packaged goods. Shopping for Tibetan artefacts is best in the Tenzin Hotel area – at the freemarket, and further east for carpets and handcrafted items. There are also several handicraft shops in town, and a gift shop at Shigatse Hotel. Shigatse is so big it even has its own bowling alley (the only other place like this in Tibet is in Lhasa).

Lodging

There's a lot of accommodation in Shigatse, but not much in the budget range. Dark horses (possibly for Chinese only) include the River Hotel. The following hotels are arranged starting with budget and progressing through mid-range to high-end.

Tenzin Hotel Overlooking the market; tel: 882 2018. The best choice for a lower-priced hotel in Shigatse, run by a friendly Tibetan family. This 20-room place has lots of character. It's several stories high, with rooftop views and a Tibetan teahouse. It has an intermittent hot shower powered by rooftop solar panels (attempt a shower in the afternoon, not the morning). Rooms range from dormitory-style to two-, three- or four-person rooms. Doubles go for Y40–Y60.

Fruit Orchard Hotel Near Tashilhunpo Monastery; tel: 882 2282. A large Chinese-run concrete block (you have to resist the temptation to call it 'the Fruit Palace') which is functional but boring. The name comes from the Ganggyen Fruit Orchard, which is behind the hotel. Has over 25 rooms: Y15–25 a bed in 4-bed dorm; Y80 double; Y90 triple.

Friendship Hotel (Zhufeng GH) Close to the Fruit Orchard Hotel, with similar prices.

Samdrutse Hotel, 2 Gongjueling Rd; tel: 882 2280; fax 882 1135. A featureless blockhouse hotel that seems to host Tibetan guests. Has 70 rooms for Y200 double.

Hotel Manasarovar 20 Qingdao Donglu; tel: 883 9999; fax 882 8111; e-mail: mnsrvr@public.ls.xz.cn. Good mid-range hotel, comfortable, with 42 standard doubles for Y370 each, and 20 economy rooms with common bathroom for Y180 each.

Holyland Hotel 3 Beijing North Rd; tel: 882 2922; fax 882 1990. Fancier hotel with elevators; has 90 rooms, ranging from Y360 standard to Y780–1180 a suite.

Shigatse Hotel To the southeast side of town; tel: 882 2525; fax: 882 1900. Group tour or expedition hotel: the 120 rooms here are Y400 double, Y450 triple and Y980–1,540 deluxe suites. This hotel has a dining hall, exchange counter, small business center, gift shop and bar.

Shandong Mansion Hotel 5 Shandong Rd; tel: 882 6138; fax: 882 6124. White-tiled building with green windows: at nine floors, it's the highest building in Shigatse. Has 110 rooms, with in-house movies; some rooms have oxygen machines. A number of restaurants lurk within the hotel. The lobby bookstore selection is good. Foreigner rates are posted in US dollars: US$65–75 double (Y558) and US$200–322 for a deluxe suite. Chinese rates posted range from Y358 to Y400 for a standard room and from Y888 to Y1,580 for a suite.

Dining out

One positive thing the Chinese brought to Shigatse is stir-fried food. The best place to get fresh food is at a strip of small restaurants around the corner from the Tenzin Hotel. Several places have English menus, or you can simply point out the vegetables you want, and the chef will stir-fry them. Another tactic is to shop for fresh vegetables at the small market near Sangzhuzi Hotel and take these to the restaurant, where, for a fee, they will cook it all up. Greasy Joe's Café is good, as are Zhengxian Restaurant and Tienfu Restaurant. For breakfast, these places offer excellent fresh yoghurt, which you can combine with fruit. More dubious cuisine comes from Gongkar Tibetan Restaurant down the road on the corner. This place

MIDNIGHT RAID

It was close to midnight and Jane (not her real name) was cocooned in her sleeping bag. A loud banging on the door shattered her dreams. Her midnight visitors were six men from the Shigatse constabulary – they burst in, shouting: 'We know who you are!' and 'Where is your Swiss friend?!'

Jane could not determine what she had done to incur their wrath, but she was quite shaken by the experience. The men demanded passport and papers – which she handed over – and interrogated her for several hours. Meanwhile, soundly snoring away on the other side of town, in a deluxe hotel, were the real targets of the raid: Andy (from the US) and Marie (from Switzerland). After staying in a string of spartan hotels, they'd decided to splurge and clean up.

Shigatse police had been looking in the wrong place. They should have been looking for an American male, not a female. Andy's crime was that he had slipped through and made it to Kailash. This was shortly after September 11, and everything in west Tibet had closed down due to massive military movements in the west by Chinese troops racing to seal off the Afghan corridor and crack down on the Muslim population in Xinjiang. Andy and Marie, determined to see the mountain of their dreams, hitched rides, hid under blankets in the back of trucks and made it through to Ali after an epic trip on dusty backroads, dodging police and walking around checkpoints at night.

In Ali, they were arrested, fined, and told if they wanted to go to Kailash, it was possible, but only on a high-paying Landcruiser tour. The tour would be one-way Ali to Kailash, and then on to the Nepal border, where they would have to leave Tibet. The problem was, Andy and Marie both had air-tickets from Lhasa to Chengdu, and luggage in Lhasa, with precious film in it. However, seeing no way out of the situation, they paid up for the exorbitant Landcruiser deal, got to Kailash and walked the *kora* of their dreams.

But a funny thing happened on the way to the Nepal border: at four in the morning, Andy and Marie slipped out of the hotel in Nyalam, and started hitching towards Lhasa. They got as far as Shigatse that day, and took an expensive hotel room. The furious Landcruiser chaperones phoned Shigatse police, but somewhere along the line the genders got mixed up, and Shigatse police thought they were looking for an American female in a low-end guesthouse. Andy and Marie made it back to Lhasa, where they were briefly interrogated and then promptly put on a flight to Chengdu.

sells fish from the Yarlung Tsangpo, but most Tibetans avoid eating fish due to their religious beliefs. Near the TV station is another Tibetan place, Yarlong Tibetan Restaurant. Across town near Shigatse Hotel is Ying Yue Restaurant, which is an expensive Chinese restaurant with classier décor.

What to see
Pilgrim circuit
Just as interesting as Tashilhunpo Monastery is the cross-section of pilgrims who come from far and wide to pay homage. Pilgrims follow a circuit that starts at the monastery gates and circles clockwise around Tashilhunpo Monastery. Off to the northwest side of the circuit is a sky burial site. Instead of completely looping around Tashilhunpo, most pilgrims continue on a path eastward that finishes at the

market in Shigatse's old quarter. There are lots of prayer flags and *mani* stones that mark the route – just follow the pilgrims, and keep an eye out for dogs. The entire circuit takes about an hour and a half.

This hike is good orientation for surveying Shigatse from an aerial-type perspective. A good touring plan would be to spend the morning at Tashilhunpo Lamasery, visit the carpet factory and new Panchen Palace in this vicinity, and then hike the kora to the destroyed dzong at the east side of Shigatse in the afternoon.

Old quarter, freemarket and dzong

The Tibetan quarter, near the dzong ruins, is quite lively, with a skein of alleys to wander around. There's an extensive freemarket selling all kinds of souvenirs, such as Tibetan boots, stirrups, hats, bolts of cloth, and dried legs of lamb. The target audience is Tibetans (legs of lamb) and tourists (souvenirs). Nearby are several Tibetan teahouses and chang-drinking hangouts.

Photos from the 1930s show Shigatse Dzong looking like a mini-Potala, with the same classic lines. The fort continued to function as the offices of the dzongpon (district governor) until 1950; it was dynamited to rubble during the Cultural Revolution and has not been rebuilt. You can climb up and clamber around the ruins for good views overlooking the old quarter rooftops.

Carpet factory

A short walk from the front gate of Tashilhunpo Monastery is Ganggyen Carpet Factory, which first started operations in 1987 as a project initiated by the 10th Panchen Lama. To get the project off the ground, he invited the same Tibetan businessman who started up the highly successful Tibetan carpet-weaving venture in Kathmandu to get involved. The factory is part-owned by Tashilhunpo Monastery, and a slice of the profits is donated each year to the monastery. Ganggyen Carpet Factory employs several hundred Tibetans, most of them women. If work is in progress, you can drop in and walk around, and see hand-looming at work. Women weavers often sing as they work – most of the weaving is done from memory, which is quite a feat considering the intricate designs. In addition to carpets, the factory sells wool jackets, sweaters, belts, scarves, bags and blankets. Tibetan horsemen use carpeting as a saddle base: these horse carpets are made here. For carpet purchases, shipping can be arranged right at the factory.

New Panchen Palace

South of Tashilhunpo Monastery is a compound with a high wall where the Panchen Lama supposedly stays when in Shigatse. The compound hosts Tibetan-style palatial buildings enclosing a garden courtyard. The main three-storey structure is larger than the Dalai Lama's summer palace in Lhasa. Rooms are bare of furniture, but you will see chandeliers and stained glass imported from India. You may be shown a room on the second floor with some personal effects of the 10th Panchen Lama – his writing desk and so on. The most startling exhibit is the stuffed dog of the 10th Panchen Lama, which looks like a large Alsatian. The dog apparently survived its master by a ten years, which begs the question: if the Panchen Lama was reincarnated, did the dog recognise its former master as the 11th Panchen Lama, or reject him as a fake? (speaking, in this case, of the enforced Chinese choice of 11th Panchen Lama).

Tashilhunpo Monastery

The Tashilhunpo is the seat of the Panchen Lama, a topic that raises blood pressures on all sides. The monastery is highly sensitive because of the controversy surrounding the 11th Panchen Lama. Pictures of the Chinese-appointed 11th Panchen Lama abound as icons at the monastery. There are monk-stooges hanging about: take care what you do or say here. Tashilhunpo is immense, a monastic city with temples, assembly halls, living quarters and administrative offices. At its height, it housed up to 5,000 monks. Today, the figure is probably closer to 700.

Access

The grounds are only fully accessible in the morning. In the afternoon you may be able to see some of the chapels. Although there are a number of gates (including one at the northeast wall), only one is sanctioned for entry and exit – you pay a foreigner's entry fee. Pilgrims follow an internal temple circuit which is described here, and also an external circuit around the monastery walls.

Main structures

As you look northward from the front gates of Tashilhunpo Monastery (see plan page 177), you will see several buildings that stand out as taller than the rest. You can roughly identify these off the plan in this book. At the back right wall is an enormous tanka-unfurling wall the height of a nine-storey building. This is where massive tankas of Buddha are unfurled during summer festivities. To the left of the grounds, the largest building is the Maitreya Chapel: it is here that pilgrims begin their tour of the monastery.

The **Maitreya Chapel** houses a 26m-high statue of Maitreya, the Buddha of the Future (*Champa* in Tibetan), seated on a lotus throne with the right hand in a symbolic teaching pose (which looks like the 'OK' gesture, in which forefinger and thumb are pressed together in a circle). The statue is gold-plated: the structure is made of tons of copper and brass, moulded on a wooden frame. Tibetans believe that Champa will return to preside over the world when all human beings have earned deliverance from suffering. Pilgrims crowd in to make offerings and murmur mantras as they make an inner circuit around the statue itself. The fortress-style building that houses the Maitreya was built from 1914–18 by the 9th Panchen Lama.

The newest building at the Tashilhunpo is the **Tomb of the 10th Panchen Lama**. It was completed in 1993 and is similar in design to that of the 9th Panchen Lama. The Chinese government is reported to have donated 500kg of gold for use in the 10th Panchen Lama's tomb construction, which may explain the Chinese-style roof. A gilded, jewel-encrusted stupa encloses the embalmed body of the 10th Panchen Lama, who died in 1989. A life-sized statue of the Panchen Lama is shown at the front of the tomb. Surrounding the stupa are intricate murals. Above the tomb are other sections. You can reach the top floor by a staircase to the left (west side) of the building. Up a few flights of stairs, you reach a room with a gigantic 3-D Kalachakra mandalic sculpture (see box, page 218, for an explanation of 'mandalic') and impressive mandala murals on the walls.

Finding the next part is a bit tricky: your best bet is to follow the pilgrims. On the second floor, at the southwest side of the building, is the entry to a dim corridor-walkway lined with small, dark chapels heading east. This corridor is lined with Buddhas large and small, Tibetan scriptures, tankas, and with side chapels displaying statues of Tsongkhapa and the Kalachakra deity. The corridor leads from the Tomb of the 10th to the **Tomb of the 4th Panchen Lama**. This tall, russet gold-roofed building houses a large silver stupa, enclosing the embalmed body of Losang Chokyi Gyeltsen, the 4th Panchen Lama.

Moving along, through a tunnel, you come to the gold-roofed **Tomb of the**

THE RENEGADE LAMA

The Panchen Lama, Tibet's second highest incarnate, traditionally has a seat at Tashilhunpo Monastery in Shigatse. The Panchen Lama (literally 'Precious Scholar') was also known as the Tashi Lama. There is considerable confusion over the number of Panchen Lamas in the lineage. This is because, in the 16th century, the 5th Dalai Lama declared Losang Chokyi Gyeltsen (then the abbot of Tashilhunpo Monastery) to be the 4th reincarnate in a line that retroactively dated to the 14th century. He also declared him to be a manifestation of the Buddha Amitabha. From this time on, the elder of either the Panchen Lama or the Dalai Lama served as tutor for the other.

The Tibetan people have never recognised the Panchen Lama's authority to rule over the country of Tibet: his jurisdiction was always restricted to the Shigatse area. However, the Chinese have seen fit to promote rivalry between the Panchen Lamas and the Dalai Lamas.

The 10th Panchen Lama was born in 1938 in the Koko Nor region (Amdo). He fell into communist hands and was certified in Xining in 1949; his qualifications as an incarnate were accepted under duress by Lhasa. He was then brought to Shigatse in 1952 by the PLA as the Chinese were determined to belittle the Dalai Lama's authority. After the Dalai Lama fled Tibet in 1959, the 10th Panchen Lama developed, by early accounts, as a mouthpiece for the Chinese. However, after the PLA raided Tashilhunpo Monastery in 1960 and disbanded the monks, the Panchen Lama changed tack and started to openly support the Dalai Lama. In 1961, when asked to move to the Potala to replace the Dalai Lama, the Panchen Lama flatly refused to do so, and dropped out of public view. In May 1962, he delivered a blistering 70,000-character report on conditions in Tibet to Mao Zedong, and demanded that mass arrests be halted and religious freedom restored. This document was kept secret for three decades until an anonymous source turned it over to Tibet Information Network in London. TIN had it translated and issued in book form in London in 1998

9th Panchen Lama. It was completed in 1988 and was consecrated by the 10th Panchen Lama only a week before his own death. During the Cultural Revolution, the bodies of the 5th through to the 9th Panchen Lamas were hidden and their identities were confused, so eventually all the remains were placed in a single tomb.

This tomb is attached to an elaborate complex that is the oldest part of Tashilhunpo Monastery, **Kelsang Courtyard**. The courtyard is enclosed by multi-storey galleries. Strolling around the different galleries gives you an idea of what the place looked like in centuries past. On the east side of the complex is a printing studio where scriptures are made from woodblocks. To the west side at the mid-levels is a large **Assembly Hall** where monks congregate for sutra chanting. Leading off this is a medieval kitchen with mammoth copper cauldrons, giant implements, and fires burning away on a scale that would've had Macbeth's witches cackling. This is where food for all the monks is prepared. Debating between monks may take place in Kelsang Courtyard.

Heading back southward, you come to the Tantric College, where, if your timing is right, prayer ceremonies may be in progress in the assembly hall. In the courtyard of the **Philosophy College**, monks gather in the mornings to debate the finer points of Buddhist philosophy, vigorously emphasising points with their unique, overarm slapping technique.

under the title *A Poisoned Arrow*, which is what Mao Zedong called the report.

In 1964, the Panchen Lama was asked to denounce the Dalai Lama at the height of the Monlam prayer-festival in Lhasa. A crowd of 40,000 gathered outside the Jokhang, and the Panchen Lama delivered a stunning speech of solidarity with the Dalai Lama, and in favour of Tibetan independence. He was promptly placed under house-arrest, denounced as a reactionary and brought to trial. After being beaten to induce confessions, the Panchen Lama disappeared, along with his parents and entourage.

The Panchen Lama was taken to Beijing and sentenced to ten years in prison in 1967, much of it spent in solitary confinement. From time to time he was taken out for 'struggle sessions' in a Beijing sports stadium, where he was humiliated in front of thousands of people. In 1978 he was set free again, supposedly a fully reformed man. He lived in Beijing, where he held an important government post. He was married to a Chinese woman and had a daughter: while he was alive, his wife pretended to be his personal secretary to preserve the Panchen Lama's spiritual standing among Tibetans, since none of the Panchen Lama lineage holders had married.

Eventually the 10th Panchen Lama managed to return to Lhasa and Shigatse for extended visits, during which he again became increasingly critical of Chinese policy in Tibet. In 1989 he was found dead of a heart attack in Shigatse, at the age of 50. Although seriously overweight and a prime candidate for a heart attack, many Tibetans believe he was poisoned. When he died, the Chinese infuriated his wife by trying to bar her from memorial ceremonies at Tashilhunpo Monastery. She obstinately continued to live in Panchen Lama's Palace in Beihai Park, Beijing, in a building that is destined for the Chinese-sanctioned incarnate, the 11th Panchen. The 11th Panchen Lama is one of the most hotly disputed reincarnates in the history of Tibet. To read more about the missing 11th Panchen Lama, refer to the *Tibetan Buddhism* entry in the *Background Information* chapter.

Sidetrip to Shalu Gompa

To the south of Shigatse (18km away, then an extra 4km off the road) is Shalu Gompa. Shalu is most associated with 14th-century scholar Buton, a prolific translator and writer of sacred texts. During the Cultural Revolution, these precious texts were destroyed. The upper part of the monastery was also destroyed – donations from Chinese patrons account for the present-day green-glazed tiling on the Mongolian-style roof. Parts of the monastery lie derelict, with faded murals, due to lack of funds to renovate. There are about 60 monks living here. Technically, you need a permit to visit Shalu Gompa (obtainable from Shigatse PSB, so if getting permits for places along the road to Kathmandu, add Shalu as well). In practice, if you just take a day-trip to Shalu Gompa, the chances are nobody will check for permits.

SHIGATSE TO TINGRI

About 15km west of Shigatse you pass the ruins of **Narthang Monastery**, formerly one of Tibet's three great woodblock printing lamaseries. The other two were at Kumbum (Amdo) and Derge (Kham) – only Derge Monastery survives as a large-scale printing works for sacred texts. The high crumbling walls of Narthang are visible behind a roadside village: a few monks have returned to the lamasery and several minor buildings have been restored. Further westward, you cross Tso

La; shortly after this, at a place between KM5028 and KM5029 marker-stones is a turn-off to Sakya, a highly recommended detour of 21km.

Then you can motor on to **Lhatse** (aka Lhaze or Lhartse), elevation 4,050m. Lhatse could be renamed 'Karaoke-ville.' Everything in Lhatse is strung out along the highway – karaoke bars, eateries, a few truck-stop hotels, a theatre and a gas station. Options for hotels range from Lazi Highway Hotel (Y15 a bed, west end of town) to Lhatse Hotel in the middle of town (tel: 832 2208) which has rooms for Y150–200, but offers dorm-rooms as well. Finding a restaurant in lovely Lhatse is never a problem – there are over 40 of them lining the main drag, catering to truck drivers that come through. There are some hotsprings located 11km from Lhatse; they're a bit derelict, with springs channelled into concrete pools, and an entry fee of Y25. At the western edge of Lhatse is a Tibetan gompa.

The road forks just west of Lhatse, with a branch heading northwest to Kailash, and southwest to Kathmandu. There may be a checkpoint near the junction. After crossing Gyatso La – at 5,250m the highest pass on this route – you reach the Shegar area.

Sakya
Sagya, Sag'ya; elevation 4,000m

Sakya ('Grey Earth'), 21km off the main Shigatse to Tingri route, was once the base of the Sakyapa sect which rose to power in the 13th century. The founder of the Sakyapa was Drokmi, who set up a monastery in Sakya in the 11th century. The Sakyapa were strong on magic and sorcery, and permitted their abbots to marry and to drink liquor. This led to hereditary rank (the post alternates between two families), and to a rather unsavoury reputation for worldliness among the monks. Although rank is hereditary, it is believed that seven incarnations of the Buddha of Wisdom (Manjushri) have appeared in the lineage of the Sakyapa.

The rise of the Sakyapa was largely due to 'the Mongol connection'. In the mid-13th century, Mongol warlord Godan Khan invited the leader of the Sakya sect, Sakya Pandita, to educate his people spiritually. Sakya Pandita accepted the task and under Mongol overlordship, the Sakya school gained great political influence. The Mongol link continued with the succession of Phagpa (nephew of Sakya Pandita) and Kublai Khan. The power of the Sakyapa declined in the late 14th century as the fortunes of the Geluk tradition rose, but Sakya retained its links with Mongolia over the centuries.

In 1959, at the age of 14, Sakya Dagtri Rinpoche was enthroned at Sakya Gompa, becoming the 41st Patriarch (his title is also the Sakya Trizin, or throne-holder). Almost immediately after the event, he and his entourage of teachers and personal staff fled to India. It took Chinese soldiers several months to get to Sakya after the 1959 uprising in Lhasa. The Chinese told the 500 monks at Sakya Gompa that they had supported the Khampa rebels, so the monastery was seized, grain-stocks confiscated, and monks and nuns were submitted to *thamzing* (struggle-sessions – self-criticism and public-criticism sessions where those accused are humiliated and beaten up in front of a crowd of locals).

After getting used to such strange phenomena as trains, cars, buses and airplanes, the Sakya Trizin set up a base in exile at Dehra Dun, in Uttar Pradesh, with a Sakya centre and college established in the 1960s. Today there are Sakya centres all over the world, and the throne-holder has toured extensively, teaching in Europe, America and Asia.

Meanwhile, back in Sakya, the bathroom-tiling school of architecture is honing in on the south bank. A huge boulevard with street lighting was

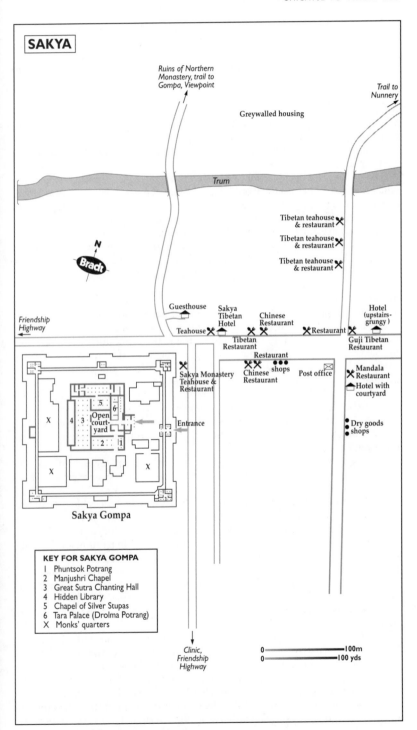

SAKYA

Ruins of Northern
Monastery, trail to
Gompa, Viewpoint

Trail to
Nunnery

Greywalled housing

Trum

Tibetan teahouse
& restaurant

Tibetan teahouse
& restaurant

Tibetan teahouse
& restaurant

Guesthouse

Sakya
Tibetan
Hotel

Chinese
Restaurant

Hotel
(upstairs-
grungy)

Friendship
Highway

Teahouse

Restaurant

Tibetan
Restaurant

Guji Tibetan
Restaurant

Restaurant

Sakya Monastery
Teahouse &
Restaurant

Chinese
Restaurant

shops

Post office

Mandala
Restaurant

Hotel with
courtyard

Entrance

Dry goods
shops

Open
court-
yard

Sakya Gompa

KEY FOR SAKYA GOMPA
1 Phuntsok Potrang
2 Manjushri Chapel
3 Great Sutra Chanting Hall
4 Hidden Library
5 Chapel of Silver Stupas
6 Tara Palace (Drolma Potrang)
X Monks' quarters

Clinic,
Friendship
Highway

0 ——— 100m
0 ——— 100 yds

constructed at the east side, leading right into the village. Videobars screening noisy Chinese kung-fu movies are sprouting up. When the dust settles, this transformation will mean a largely Chinese urban style on the south bank except for the monastery and a cluster of nearby buildings, but the north bank is still Tibetan in character.

Sakya basics

Sakya is reached by a dirt road – it is 21km from the main Lhasa-to-Kathmandu highway. You might find a pilgrim truck running on this route from Shigatse. Minibuses sometimes make the trip to Lhasa also. Sakya has a small bus station and a post office.

There's not a lot of choice for lodging; there are three Tibetan truck-stop hotels with – I almost choke on the word – 'beds.' More popular is Sakya Tibetan Hotel, which is close to the gompa. A second truck-stop is just a little west, and the third place is near the post office. Dorm-type beds go for around Y15–20.

There are hole-in-the-wall eating houses around Sakya: the monastery teahouse is a good place to hang out, but food supply is minimal. For more substantial fare, try some Chinese-style restaurants that are close by – pick out what you want from the kitchen and have it stirfried. Some tiny shops can also be unearthed.

Sakya Gompa

The immense Mongolian-style outer walls of Sakya Gompa dwarf any other structure in the town. At the corners of the gompa walls are corner-turrets and watchtowers. The monastery is thought to date to the 13th century, at which time the Sakyapa were powerful enough to employ not only large numbers of Tibetan works and artisans, but also artisans from India, Nepal and central China to decorate the monastery.

Access is only by the east gate, where an entry fee is charged. You cross a courtyard to gain entry to the inner temple, which surrounds another open courtyard. From this courtyard, try to find a staircase that leads to the upper deck of the monastery, overlooking the central courtyard. You can also walk along the outer parapets for good town views.

Getting into the monastery chapels often requires finding the right monk with the right key. You can tour the main structures here in a clockwise circuit, keyed to the map in this text.

At Phuntsok Potrang, only an upstairs chapel may be accessible, containing fine murals and statues. Phuntsok Potrang (Palace) is the former residence of one of the principal lamas of Sakya. The post of leadership in the Sakya sect alternates between two families, one formerly occupying Phuntsok Potrang, the other occupying Drolma Potrang opposite. The next in line for Phuntsok Palace lives in exile in Seattle, USA. Manjushri Chapel is a large chamber once used for important rituals. It contains a number of bookcases, and glass cases enshrining several thousand bronze statues. The statues of Manjushri and Sakyamuni Buddha here were rescued from the rubble of Sakya's northern monasteries.

The Great Sutra Chanting Hall is lofty and spacious – the roof is supported by four rows of pillars, with 10 pillars in each row. At the base of the massive tree-trunk pillars are lotus-patterned stone pedestals; between the pillars are low carpeted benches with seating for some 400 monks. If you're lucky, Sakya monks may be conducting a sutra-chanting session, in which case you'll experience the acoustics of the hall. The main visual focus of the hall is the row of massive gilded Buddha statuary at the west wall. These statues are

SAKYA'S HIDDEN LIBRARY

At the back of the Great Sutra Chanting Hall is a library that runs the entire length of the north-south wall, with shelves of sacred texts reaching from floor to ceiling. The library is hidden from view and access to it may not be possible – to get in, you need to find someone to unlock a small wooden door that allows you to go around the back of all the statues on display. It's pretty dark so a flashlight is needed. The musty atmosphere is positively medieval, evoking the fabled lost library of Alexandria. The library shelving here is about 60m long, 10m high and one metre deep, and filled with thousands of dusty Buddhist scriptures, many hand-copied by Tibetan calligraphers and illuminated in gold or silver ink. Near the northwest corner is a huge manuscript illuminated in gold called the *Prajnaparamita Sutra*. This is an 8,000-line basic scripture of all schools of Mahayana Buddhism, setting forth the Bodhisattva path to enlightenment in conversations between the Buddha and three of his disciples. The book is so large it requires its own special rack: the pages are 1.75m wide. Apparently Sakya's library survived the ravages of the Cultural Revolution because the books were hidden underground. Above the portico leading to the monastery's central courtyard is another room housing rare Sanskrit palm-leaf manuscripts, but this section is out of bounds.

surrounded by thousands of artefacts, seals, ceremonial props, ritual vessels and books amassed from all over Tibet. A small doorway leads to a large hidden library behind the statues.

Continuing the clockwise circuit, you come to the Chapel of the Silver Stupas which contains 11 silver stupas enclosing the remains of the past throneholders of the Sakya lineage. Six more stupas (enclosing the remains of important past abbots of Sakya) are found in a small chapel just to the north. In the Tara Palace are five stupas of important throne-holders from this family branch. The Tara Palace or Drolma Potrang is the former residence of the current Sakya throneholder, now living in Dehra Dun, India. Only the upstairs chapel is open, displaying superb murals; the altar has images depicting the longevity triad of Amitayus, Vijaya and White Tara.

Hiking at Sakya North

On the north side of the river there used to be a monastic complex of 108 chapels. Most were destroyed during the 1960s, but some were converted into Tibetan housing. Today, the north side is mostly composed of grim, grey-walled Tibetan housing, with brushwood and yak-dung lining the ramparts of dwellings, and livestock living in the courtyards. You can hike on the northwest slope up to a small restored gompa and viewpoint (you need to find a monk to open the doors here). A precipitous path leads from the monastery along the northeast ridge to Rinchen Gang Labrang, an active nunnery rebuilt in 1988, and currently home to about 30 nuns. You can also do the reverse route – go directly from Sakya town up to the nunnery and find the back-route to the monastery. Sakya is right off the main road, so it lies in a completely rural area, and there are other directions you can walk into the countryside. Or the countryside may come to you, asherders and traders propel yaks, donkeys or sheep right through Sakya town.

Shegar
Shekar, Shelkar, Xegar, Xin Tingri, New Tingri; elevation 4,350m

Shegar, set back 7km off the main road, is a small Tibetan settlement with an active monastery at the northern end, at the base of a peak. Right up the rock peak are the imposing ruins of Shining Crystal Dzong. The castle was formerly the residence of the governor of Shegar. In 1924, a member of the British Everest expedition marvelled at the fantastic castle, perched on the 5,000m mountaintop, appearing to be fused to the rock. Today barely a single piece stands upright – it was destroyed during the Cultural Revolution.

At around the same time, the extensive monastery of Shegar was also destroyed. It once housed 300 Geluk monks, but today there are only a few reconstructed buildings, with a handful of monks in residence. It's worth visiting the monastery building at the base of the mountain, and then hiking up through the ruins toward the peak (watch out for the nettles). There is a path to the summit, but it's difficult to find – take along a local kid as a guide. The path starts about halfway up, to the left of the ruined fort, and winds around the back of the mountain to the prayer flags at the very top, where, on a clear day, you are rewarded with views of Everest. The old quarter of Shegar is the village clustered closer to the gompa. The Chinese section is further southwest, in the vicinity of the post office.

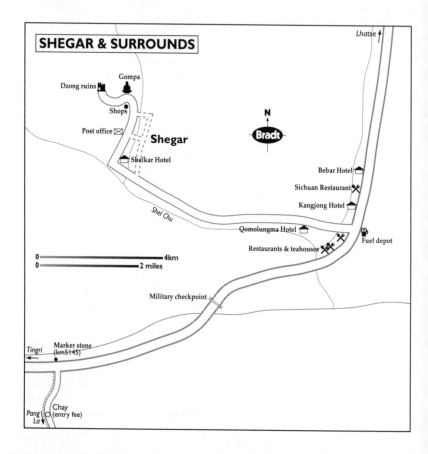

Basics

Shelkar Hotel is a Chinese concrete compound with a lack of plumbing, overpriced rooms and surly staff. The alternatives to this dismal place are low-priced truck-stop hotels near the main highway and the higher-priced Qomolungma Hotel (see the following entries). For food in Shegar, there's a Chinese restaurant opposite Shelkar Hotel, and there are several shops with small, low-quality selections of consumer goods. The post office in Shegar is said to be the highest in Tibet.

Shegar to Tingri
Checkpoint: major military checkpoint 7km west of Shegar junction
At the turn-off to Shegar is a busy junction with truck-stop hotels and a few restaurants. A number of travellers opt to stay here and visit Shegar on a day trip. The junction is also the launching point for the ride to Everest base camp.

There are at least four truck-stop inns at the junction: the coziest is Kangjong Hotel, with a Tibetan teahouse serving food. Rooms are Y50 each, with no showers. Others include the Bebar Hotel for Y40 a room. A major hotel lies about 600m from the Shegar turn-off. It's called the Qomolungma Hotel (aka Dingri Zhufeng Hotel; tel: 826 2268) and is a large Chinese-run operation with a glitzy restaurant, bar and giftshop. Group tours stay here before heading off to Everest base camp. The 60-odd rooms here are expensive, but there are some cheaper dormitory-type rooms. The majority of the rooms here are standard doubles at Y350. There are also 3-bed rooms for Y460, and a suite for Y865. There are 12 rooms that act as dorms, of sorts: Y240 for a 6-bed room with no toilet or shower (so Y40 a bed), and Y320 for a 4-bed room with toilet but no shower (so Y80 a bed). You can use an outside shower for these rooms. And finally, there is a Y50 'hour' room, with shower. It's not clear who uses a room like this, the Chinese military or filthy Everest returnees.

Travellers tend to settle for the food offered in the hotels and guesthouses, though this is pricey for what you get. There are some restaurants at the Shegar junction: one called Zhuang Yuan Sichuan Restaurant offers a 10-page English menu, but again it's pricey.

Seven km west of the junction is a military checkpoint (at roughly the KM5140 marker-stone). This is the most important checkpoint on the Lhasa to Kathmandu Route – your documents will be checked, and your luggage may be searched. Have your passport and papers ready. From here, it's 5km west to the Everest turn-off at the KM5145 marker-stone. See the *Star Treks* chapter for more details on this major sidetrip.

Tingri
Tinggri, Dingri, Dengre, Old Tingri, Lao Tingri, Tingri West; elevation 4,340m
Tingri is a Tibetan village arrayed over a hillside. It was once a Tibetan-Nepali trading centre for grain, goods, wool and livestock. This trade largely died out after 1959 but you can still see the odd Nepali trader in Tingri – they occasionally saunter in with a few yaks over Nangpa La pass.

Tingri is essentially one big army base disguised as a village. Tibetan housing hugs the hillside, but at the north end are walled army compounds and an army telecommunications centre; at the south end are more army compounds. The compounds at the south end are curious – at first sight they appear to be Tibetan buildings. Closer inspection reveals they are Chinese – could this be a new form of camouflage?

Tingri lies at the edge of a vast plain. There are great views of the Himalayan giants to the south, assuming there's no cloud cover. Everest, or the topmost part of it, is visible to the far left, but from this distance it doesn't look like a mammoth. However, Cho Oyu, straight ahead, looks stunning. It's worth taking a short hike to the south of Tingri for better views; another viewpoint is from the top of the hill above the village, where there are some old fort ruins. And here's something to think about as you gaze across the plains: the area was once full of gazelles, blue sheep, antelopes, and wild asses, which were remarked upon by Everest expedition members in the 1920s and 1930s. This fabulous wildlife sanctuary has completely disappeared – now all you can see are the odd herds of domesticated sheep, goats or yaks.

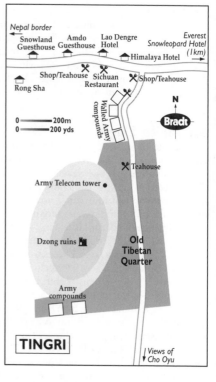

Basics

Facilities in Tingri are strung out along the highway. There are half a dozen Tibetan inns, including the Himalaya Hotel, Amdo Guesthouse, Tingri Snowland, Lao Dengre Guesthouse and Rong Sha Hotel. The best of the bunch (Himalaya Hotel and Amdo Guesthouse) have cozy Tibetan teahouses with carpeted seating low on the floor. You can order *momos* (meat dumplings) and potatoes here. The spartan rooms are around Y25–30 a bed. Both Amdo Guesthouse and Tingri Snowland claim to offer hot showers at certain hours for Y10 if you're a guest, or Y15 if you're an outsider.

A kilometre east of Tingri along the main road (KM3193 marker-stone) is Everest Snowleopard Hotel, a huge compound used by group tours. It contains over 50 rooms, priced at Y160 a double, but try bargaining – you might be able to cut that price in half, so Y120 for a 4-bed room would be more reasonable. The hotel is clean and has a large central courtyard with secure parking for vehicles. There are generator lights for a few hours a night, and televisions in the rooms. There is a small teahouse to one side, and even an 'Everest View' room (on the second floor, in the centre).

Apart from hotel eateries, there are several restaurants along the road – notably the Sichuan Restaurant, offering stirfried dishes. A few small shops complete the 'strip' here. Further into Tingri village, there's very little, although you might stray across a Tibetan teahouse or a tiny shop.

TINGRI TO KATHMANDU

From Tingri westward, in clear weather, you get spectacular views of Himalayan peaks, especially from passes. Tong La is a double pass, with its north crest at 4,950m and its south crest at 5,200m. You may be able to glimpse the 8,000m hulk of Shishapangma from this vicinity. After this, it's downhill all the way to Nyalam, and on to Nepal. There are two more checkpoints en route: the first is on the west side of the bridge spanning the Matsang River at Nyalam (strategically placed: you must go across the bridge); the second checkpoint is just above Zhangmu.

Milarepa's cave

Nearing Nyalam, close to the KM5333 marker-stone, is Milarepa's gompa and cave. The gompa is hidden from view at the roadside, but your guide should know where it is. If not, find some local kids to show you the way. You need to find a caretaker with keys to the cave and gompa, which might require some funds. Milarepa, the 11th-century sage who enlightened his students through music and poetry, never founded any monasteries. He lived a mostly itinerant existence in remote areas, living in caves and dining on nettle soup. The mystic is easily recognised in pictures and statuary due to his greenish skin and having his right hand cocked to his ear. Milarepa's cave is set inside a tiny gompa, which was destroyed during the Cultural Revolution but rebuilt in the early 1980s with the help of the Nepalese. In the cave you can see handprints made by Milarepa, illustrating the time when he employed his mystical powers to prevent a huge overhanging rock from falling while a disciple moved a smaller rock in place as a support pillar. Although the cave first belonged to the Kagyu sect, it was taken over by the Geluk order centuries ago.

Nyalam
Elevation 3,750m; checkpoint: on west side of bridge spanning Matsang River
Nyalam is a truck-stop on the Lhasa to Kathmandu route, with a fair range of hotels and small restaurants. The centre of town is a large parking lot for trucks and other vehicles; there's another truck parking area on the southeast side of town, next to a large karaoke complex. Because the town is easily supplied from Zhangmu, there is a much greater range of food and goods available here. Along the main road, commerce is mostly operated by Chinese or Nepali merchants, although some shops are run by Tibetans. Take a sidestreet to the west to find the old Tibetan quarter, with traditional-style stone buildings and yaks lounging in doorways. There is a small gompa at the northern end of this street.

Further afield, Nyalam is the base for trekking to Shishapangma base camp (see the *Star Treks* chapter). Even if you have no intention of trekking to the base camp, the initial part of this route – accessed from the northwest end of Nyalam – is well worth a day-hike, or an overnight hike if you take a tent and sleeping bag.

If you're coming from Lhasa, a highly unusual treat in Nyalam is...trees. Stacks of wood are piled up, used as a fuel source. Nyalam is low enough for poplar trees to grow, and other wood is brought in from forested slopes lower down.

Basics
Nyalam is well supplied with hotels, small restaurants and shops. The Tibetan-style Snowland Hotel is one of the best choices here, but is often full as expeditions often use it. Rooms are Y60 a double. The hotel has a rooftop deck. Among the other hotels and guesthouses are Nyalam Hotel (Y20 a room), Nga Dom (Y30 a room), Nielamu County Guesthouse (Y60 a room – recommended) and the bland-looking Post Hotel. A string of restaurants lines the main road near the truck parking area. The Nepali Restaurant is good, serving large silver platters with *dhal* and lots of sidedishes. Also try Snowland Restaurant, located on the third floor of the building opposite Snowland Hotel. For real atmosphere, nearby Amdo Tash Restaurant is the best – you can choose between Tibetan low couches or Western-style seating. On the breakfast menu is apple muesli and chocolate pancakes.

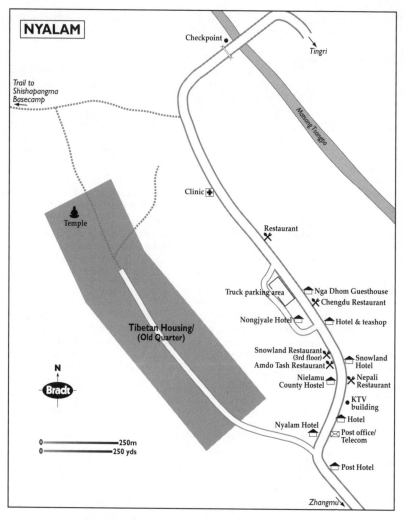

NYALAM

Checkpoint

Tingri

Trail to
Shishapangma
Basecamp

Mangeng Tsangpo

Clinic

Temple

Restaurant

Truck parking area

Nga Dhom Guesthouse
Chengdu Restaurant

Nongjyale Hotel

Hotel & teashop

Tibetan Housing/
(Old Quarter)

Snowland Restaurant
(3rd floor)
Amdo Tash Restaurant

Snowland
Hotel

N

Nielamu
County Hostel

Nepali
Restaurant

Bradt

KTV
building

Hotel

Nyalam Hotel

Post office/
Telecom

0 ————————— 250m
0 ————————— 250 yds

Post Hotel

Zhangmu

Nyalam to Zhangmu

From Nyalam, there's an amazing drop off the plateau, down through lush jungle
terrain with gushing waterfalls and singing birds all the way to Zhangmu. It's a
'gorge-ous' ride – this is one altitude shift you'll remember for some time to come.
Because of cascading water (sometimes springing straight over the cliffsides near
the road) the route here is prone to rockfalls and landslides, especially in the
monsoon season. Because it is at a much lower elevation, Zhangmu is prone to
much heavier monsoon rains than, say, Nyalam.

The Chinese name for the entire route between Lhasa and Kathmandu is the
'Friendship Highway'. The Chinese name a lot of border features into
neighbouring countries like this: Friendship Gate (*Youyi Guan*, the border crossing
into Vietnam) and Friendship Bridge (*Youyi Qiao*, the border crossing into Nepal).
It's not clear whether the Chinese constructed the Friendship Highway as a
military route into Nepal, but the Chinese designed and built the road on the

Nepalese side all the way into Kathmandu. The two countries remain on very good terms – for the moment.

Zhangmu
Dram, Khasa; elevation 2,300m; checkpoint: at top of hill above Zhangmu
There's little to see in the border town of Zhangmu (pronounced Jang-moo) unless you like watching Nepalis, Tibetans and Chinese unload and reload goods and haggle over currency exchange rates. Hair stylists, karaoke bars and loose women abound. Zhangmu is no longer Tibet – it's more like a Nepali trading town, with Nepali products everywhere, Nepali moneychangers, Nepali merchants and scores of Nepali porters. The town is arrayed along some steep switchbacks that snake down to the Chinese customs and immigration post. Half the town appears to be a construction zone, so things may well have changed from the description here.

Out of synch
Nepal is two and a quarter hours behind Tibet, which operates on Beijing time. Thus when it's 12.00 (noon) in Zhangmu (Chinese immigration post), it's 09.45 in Kodari (Nepalese immigration). Bear this in mind when considering banking hours and immigration post hours of opening. Sunday can be a non-working day in Zhangmu, although the main bank is still open.

Customs, immigration, money
If exiting Tibet, you can change residual Chinese yuan back into US dollars (with original bank receipts). A much better deal is to change Chinese yuan into Nepalese rupees. Change either at the Bank of China (BOC, two branches) or with moneychangers close by. It's preferable to do these transactions inside a shop rather than on the street: always carefully count the money offered before presenting your part of the deal. The BOC is in theory open from 09.00–12.00 and 15.00–18.00, running on Tibetan time.

In Zhangmu you can pay for goods in either Chinese yuan or Nepalese rupees, but once out of Zhangmu, Chinese yuan are useless anywhere in Nepal (you can, however, trade them with travellers at guesthouses in Kathmandu). On exit, Chinese customs may search baggage looking for 'antiques', which means anything older than 1959. Immigration checks are simple – you are stamped out.

Those entering Tibet at Zhangmu are usually in an arranged group headed for Lhasa. There are several hurdles here. The first is clearing immigration and being stamped in. The second is the baggage check: customs may be thorough and they will be looking for pro-Tibetan material that is available in Kathmandu. Then you set about changing money, and proceed northward. Lone travellers have managed to slip through this border, but will most likely be waylaid by a man from CITS (who have an office in the nearby Zhangmu Hotel) demanding that the loner joins a group (four travellers) to take a CITS Landcruiser to Lhasa.

Lodging and food
At the mid-levels of Zhangmu are some budget guesthouses. Ask to see a room before putting any money down: rooms can be more basic than you might imagine. Lower down, right near the customs post, is the main group tour hotel, the cavernous Zhangmu Hotel, which is in cahoots with CITS. If entering or exiting, you can use the ground-floor bar at the Zhangmu Hotel to take a breather, or to clean up. Landcruiser drivers linked to CITS lie in wait near the customs post, ready to prey on travellers coming through from Kathmandu. Although the rooms at Zhangmu Hotel are expensive (Y400 for a double), you can talk your way into cheaper dorm rooms

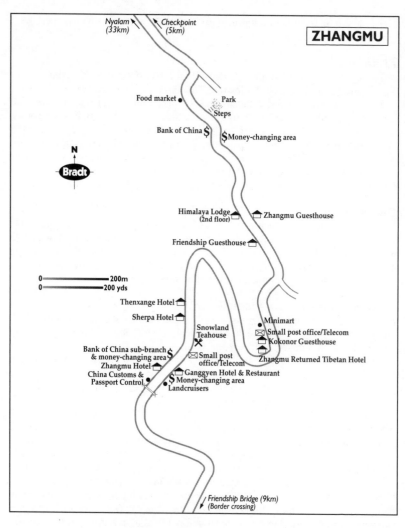

downstairs at Y50 a bed. Ganggyen Hotel, opposite, has similarly priced dorm beds, and cheaper doubles at Y150. The further north you are in Zhangmu, the cheaper the hotels, or so it seems. Rooms at Kokonor Guesthouse go for Y50, and further up the hill is the Friendship Guesthouse. Intriguing for its name is Zhangmu Returned Tibetan Hotel, also in this area.

In the food line, you can rifle through the shops in lower Zhangmu, bearing good stocks of Indian and Nepalese goods such as mango fruit drinks and biscuits from Kathmandu. The town has several mini-marts with a good range of chocolate and other delicacies for the deprived. Near the customs checkpost is Ganggyen Restaurant and Snowland Teahouse. Group tours eat in the dining hall at Zhangmu Hotel.

Zhangmu to Kodari

Once you leave Chinese customs, you head 9km down to the Friendship Bridge. If you have a Landcruiser driver, he will be charged for permission to drive past the

Chinese customs post. The bridge is the real border crossing, with the Bhotekosi river delineating the border. It has been washed away several times in the past. Halfway across the bridge is a dividing line – one half of the bridge belongs to Nepal, the other half to China. At exactly this point, it seems, you should switch sides of the road – from right-hand drive (China) to left-hand drive (Nepal). Nepal immigration is in Kodari, 2km from the Friendship Bridge. Your passport is checked here – if you have no visa, you will be stamped in. You just provide US$15 in US cash for a 15-day visa, or US$30 for a 30-day visa, plus a passport photo. Nepal customs is a bit further down the line near Tatopani.

Kathmandu

A ride of 114km along a paved road from Kodari brings you into the bazaars of Asan Tole, in old Kathmandu – in former times the trading crossroads of the empires of India, China and Tibet. You'll find more Mars bars, apple pie, fresh croissants, shampoo and English newspapers in a 200m stretch of a street in Thamel than you will in all of Tibet. The trick is not to go berserk when faced with such myriad choices. The sudden change of diet can wreak havoc on your system: switching to steaks, apple pie and ice cream after months of living off biscuits in Tibet can be traumatic. Still, hot showers, clean white sheets, Swedish massage and other luxuries won't hurt. They may even be therapeutic.

Kathmandu has great resources for things Tibetan: there are Tibetan monasteries scattered around the valley; there are Tibetan-run hotels, shops and travel agents in Kathmandu's Thamel district. If you are incoming from Tibet, Kathmandu has all the forbidden and seditious material on Tibet that Chinese officials so diligently search baggage for. Kathmandu has one of the highest concentrations of English bookstores of any place in the Indian sub-continent. Lots of second-hand books are available as well. You can find Free Tibet T-shirts, flags, and many handcrafted Tibetan items that are superior in quality to those found in Tibet – carpets, for instance.

However, Nepal has become increasingly unstable due to Maoist insurgency, and travel there may be risky. Over 3,000 people have been killed since Maoist insurgents began their campaign to overthrow the monarchy in 1996. Their aim is to set up a one-party communist republic. In late 2001, the Nepalese government declared a state of emergency and deployed the army for the first time in an attempt to crush Maoist insurgency. Maoists have issued threats targeting the tourist industry in Nepal – specifically hotels, airlines, buses and travel businesses owned by prominent Nepalese. Kathmandu has been hit by a string of small explosions blamed on Maoists. It's wise to keep an eye on internet media to find out just how ugly the current situation is in Kathmandu, and to keep a watch on which areas of Nepal might be trouble hotspots.

Everest: north facing, with monastery

Star Treks

HIGH-ALTITUDE FORAYS TO EVEREST, KAILASH AND BEYOND

This section describes some treks in western Tibet that individuals have successfully tackled, but which are highly challenging, both in terms of physical effort and dodging demands for permits. The rewards? We're talking about a backdrop of the highest peaks on earth here – moonscapes, star treks and stellar vistas! Trekking in Tibet is expeditionary in nature. If you go with an organised group, then yaks and porters will ferry in supplies. This is one of the few places in the world where trekking is assisted by behemoths, in the form of sturdy yaks. If you plan to go on your own, you need good equipment and supplies – trekking here is fraught with all kinds of logistical problems. You have to be self-sufficient, and that includes food.

If trekking with a group, ask in advance about conditions for porters. It is the responsibility of the operator to ensure adequate equipment and safety for porters, so by all means press the operator on these concerns. Are the porters properly clothed and equipped for the rigours of mountain travel? In Nepal, there have been a number of accidents – and deaths – involving porters, due to lack of adequate footwear, clothing and gear, poor medical care, and neglect and mistreatment by trek leaders. This situation has raised the hackles of Maoist guerrillas in Nepal, who have stopped trekking groups to inspect conditions for porters. A porter should not be setting out with a 50-kilo load to tackle a high snowbound pass in tattered running shoes, but this has happened. Such neglect can result in frostbite. The International Porter Protection Group (IPPG) is lobbying trekking companies to ensure that porters have adequate equipment and that they are provided with the same standard of medical care as trekkers and leaders would themselves enjoy. This means that in the event of illness, a porter is not simply paid off and sent back down a mountain alone – which has resulted in deaths from altitude sickness in Nepal in the past. In Tibet, altitude sickness should not be an issue for porters as Tibetans are well acclimatised. However, some Nepalese trekking outfitters bring in their own porters from Nepal who could be from lowland areas, rather than Sherpa porters, who are from highland areas. In Tibet, porters are more commonly used on large expeditions. Organised trekking trips in Tibet are more likely to be yak-supported, or with combinations of porters and yak-caravans.

There are three excellent guidebooks that cover trekking routes in Tibet in detail: Gary McCue's *Trekking in Tibet,* Kotan Publishing's *Mapping the Tibetan World,* and Victor Chan's *Tibet Handbook* (with 60 detailed pilgrimage and trekking itineraries). A handful of classic Tibet treks – enough to keep you busy for quite some time – are described in the following section. The approaches and trailheads are all reachable by Landcruiser.

TREKKING IN THE EVEREST REGION

There are three main targets in the Everest area: Rongbuk (Everest north base camp), Karta (Everest east base camp), and Cho Oyu base camp. You can reach Rongbuk by Landcruiser. Two staging-points to bear in mind are: Shegar in the east, and Tingri to the west. Refer to the Lhasa to Kathmandu route map in that chapter (see pages 162–3) for locations.

Everest is not in the same class as Kailash when it comes to being a sacred peak. For one thing, the monastery at Everest was only established early in the 20th century (the shrines at Kailash go back to the 13th century). More importantly, Kailash has always been off-limits for climbers, and there are no throngs of Tibetan pilgrims headed for Everest because you can't circumambulate the mountain. Nevertheless, Everest is known to the Tibetans as Chomolangma, which transliterates as Queen (*Jhomo*) on an Ox (*glangma*), otherwise more prosaically rendered as 'Mother Goddess of the World'. Tibetans believe that the goddess was Miyo Langsangma (one of the five Tsering sisters; according to legend, each of these five goddesses inhabits a high peak in the Himalayan region) resides at Mount Everest: her mount is an ox, although other images show her astride a tiger.

The goddess is not one to tangle with lightly. Witness what happened to the first expeditions. In 1921, Tibet opened expedition attempts on Everest to British climbers. The monks at Rongbuk were none too keen on the idea of climbers wending their way up a sacred peak: they predicted dire things would come to pass – which, in the case of Mallory and Irvine, they did. The monastery practice of blessing climbers rather than cursing them appears to have started in the late 1920s or 1930s when Nepali Sherpas were employed by the British as porters and cooks. Because Sherpas are Tibetan Buddhist, monasteries started dispensing blessings for safe passage on the mountain. Sherpas climbing from both sides visit monasteries before going to base camp, where they light butter lamps in supplication of various deities. At base camp itself, Sherpas make offerings of tsampa and chang to the goddess Chomolangma in the belief that the wrathful goddess will turn a blind eye and allow them passage. Tsampa is thrown skyward; ice axes and other gear also get a ritual blessing before climbers go higher.

Driving to Rongbuk

Everest base camp is remarkable in that it's a drive-in approach. The rough road to the base camp at the north side of Everest was engineered in 1960 for Chinese mountaineering attempts on the summit. The common approach by road is from the Shegar end, though it's also possible to drive in on a rougher route from Tingri. You can commandeer a Landcruiser in Lhasa and drive right to Rongbuk Monastery, which is about 12km short of Everest base camp. You can also try hitching in on this route, picking up a supply truck of some sort. There's primitive lodging at Rongbuk. Landcruisers can cover the distance from Shegar to Rongbuk in about seven or so hours if there are no holdups like flooding.

If arriving from Shegar, there are two major checkpoints on the way to Everest. The first is the military checkpoint close to the Shegar turn-off. There are cursory checks of passports and baggage here. At the village of Chay, each passenger must pay a fee of US$8 for entry into what is billed as being Chomolangma Nature Reserve. There is also a vehicle entry charge.

From the Rongbuk area you can also drive further to Everest base camp and have a poke around. There are great day hikes around Rongbuk: you can clamber around and get fantastic views of the north face of Everest. The Big E will blow you away – literally, if a wind comes howling down the valley. Everest does not

Above North face of Mount Everest, with Rongbuk Monastery
in foreground

Below left Monks debating at Tashilhunpo Monastery, Shigatse.
In the bowls is yak-butter tea.

Below right View of Gyantse, central Tibet

Above North face of the sacred Mount Kailash
Right Pack yak unloaded at Darchen, west Tibet
Below Pilgrims getting off a truck at the start of the Kailash circuit

always co-operate – it might be obscured by low cloud. But if the sun is out and it's clear, Everest will take your breath away. In the north face of Everest, you are looking at the highest mountain face on earth.

Trekking to Rongbuk

There are two routes into Rongbuk on foot – from the Shegar end, or from the Tingri end. Trekkers tend to favour the walk in from the Tingri end because there's no checkpoint to contend with and it's easier to hire pack animals in Tingri. However, there's zero chance of hitching a ride from the Tingri end – if your equipment is not so good, or your intention is to get a ride in and trek back, then you should stick to the Shegar route, which has more in the way of lodging and teahouse support. You can combine the routes by taking one route in and the other route out (and consider a sidetrip to Cho Oyu base camp on the Tingri route). You might want to think about hiring a donkey (or yak) and handler to carry supplies and food. The handler will also act as a guide. Animals are scarce when harvesting is in progress; if you're only going one-way with a pack animal, the handler may want compensation for the return journey.

From Tingri

The walk into Rongbuk takes about four days. The first day's target is not particularly strenuous: the village of Lungjhang (4,500m), with beds available. The next day *is* strenuous – it's best to work your way toward the base of Lanma La and camp out near a herder's camp. The next day, you can trek over Lanma La (5,150m) and make it to the village of Zhommug, where basic lodging awaits. Zhommug is not far from the jeep road that winds in from Shegar: you should be able to reach Rongbuk by the end of the fourth day of trekking.

From Shegar

You essentially walk along the jeep track to Rongbuk. The trek takes three to four days; there are enough lodges along the way to qualify this as Tibet's first 'teahouse trekking' route. Starting out from the Tibetan truck-stop at the KM5133 marker-stone, you can hitch or walk to the Everest turn-off at the KM5145 marker-stone. If you're on foot, you may have to pay an entry-fee at the Chay checkpoint, but you're in a better position to bargain than those in Landcruisers because the fee is supposed to be collected for road maintenance. You can negotiate the hire of a donkey at Chay for the trip as far as Peruche, where there is a Tibetan-run lodge – albeit a filthy one – and also a few shops. On the next leg of the journey, between Peruche and Chosang, are two villages where you can stay: Tashizom and Passum. Both have teahouse-lodges with cheap beds. These places are at around 4,100m in elevation. The last place with beds is Chosang, but trekkers have found the folk here particularly light-fingered and cold-hearted, so you may want to skip this place. From here it is a steady climb to Rongbuk.

Trek alert

Tibetan villagers in the Everest region are notoriously prone to thievery. You have to consider that there are not a lot of shops out this way: taking things from visitors is somehow considered fair game. Even hosts at village inns will brazenly take small items, and when confronted, think it is no big deal. Keep an eye on gear that you can't do without – watch those waterbottles. Always negotiate carefully and establish prices before consuming any food or drink at teahouses in the area – there have been problems. Another alarming problem is: innkeepers in the Everest region have been known to beat up their wives. So what do you do – ignore this

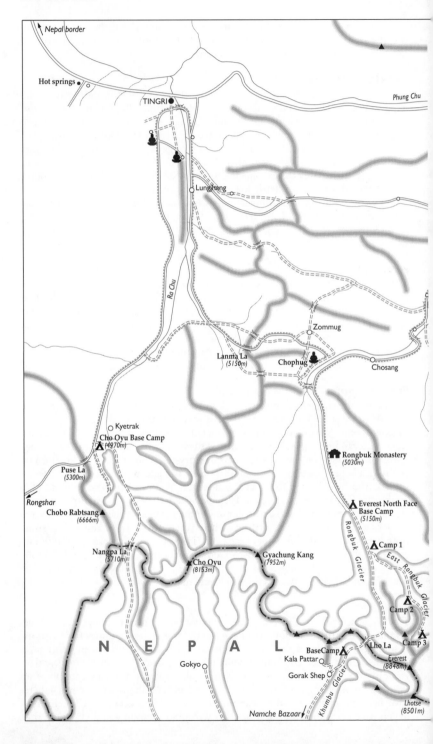

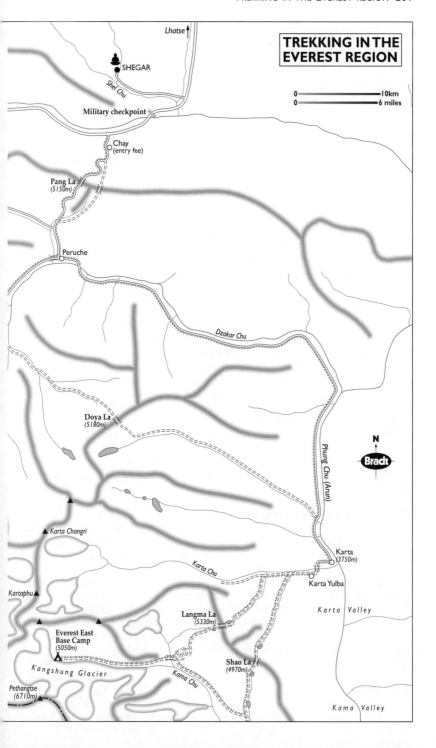

late at night, or try to step in? It's a tough call. Donkey and yak handlers can be hard to get along with and argumentative – this has little to do with language, and more to do with temperament.

Rongbuk
Dza Rongphu, elevation 5,030m
Rongbuk Gompa, the highest monastery in the world, was established some time in the early part of the 20th century, under the Nyingmapa sect. Its history is sketchy. Rongbuk Valley was known as the 'sanctuary of the birds.' There was a strict ban on killing any animal in the area. Domestic animals could be eaten as long as they were slaughtered outside the valley. The British Everest reconnaissance party, arriving at Rongbuk in 1921, found the animals of the valley extraordinarily tame: wild blue sheep would come down to the monastery. There were hundreds of lamas and pilgrims engaged in meditation in a cluster of brightly coloured buildings. The British did not meet the Head Lama as he was off doing a year's 'time' in a cave. It was common for hermits to go on meditation retreats in caves in the valley, subsisting on water and barley passed to them once a day.

The monastery was razed in the 1960s. At the instigation of Red Guards, Tibetans were encouraged to disassemble the buildings for raw materials, such as precious wood beams. The monastery's stupa was split in two and ransacked of its treasures. The abbot of Rongbuk fled over the Himalaya and established a new monastery at Junbesi in Nepal.

In the late 1980s and early 1990s, rebuilding took place at Rongbuk and its monastery has been resurrected, along with the stupa that figures prominently in tourist photography of the scene. A dozen monks and 30 or so nuns live at Rongbuk Gompa. Surrounding the monastery is a village; further up the valley is a nunnery, and there are cave-retreats scattered around the hilltops. You can stay at a simple 20-room guesthouse attached to Rongbuk Monastery. There's an outhouse, and hot water in thermoses can be obtained for a payment from the monastery, but don't expect luxuries here – nights can be very cold, and there's no electricity.

Due for completion in 2003 at Rongbuk is a 'tourist centre'—a building complex with an emergency room, oxygen room, plus 16 hotel-style rooms. There are also plans for building an environmental monitoring centre and a mini-museum showing wildlife of the area, as part of the proposed Qomolongma Nature Reserve.

North Face base camp
From Rongbuk, you can drive or walk the final 12km out to the North Face base camp, at an elevation of 5,150m. Base camp is marked by a single concrete building, and possibly by a lot of expedition tents, depending on the season. The area is a glacial moraine – a bleak and desolate place – but awe-inspiring because it is so close to the Big E. Beyond base camp lies a trek described by Gary McCue (*Trekking in Tibet*) as 'the Highest Trek in the World . ..an incredible journey to Camp III (6,340m) and to the base of the North Col via the East Rongphu Glacier'. McCue says that the ascent is possible without climbing gear, though it would be advisable to have items like crampons when traversing the glacier. You need excellent back-up and considerable logistics to undertake such a strenuous – and potentially hazardous – journey.

The big E
At higher elevations, Everest is scoured by 100km/h winds: the constant threat of avalanche, being crushed by an ice *serac* (a pinnacle of ice on the surface of a

glacier), falling down a crevasse, or succumbing to altitude make it a deadly peak to climb.

In 1921, the Tibetan government opened the Himalaya to the British. The first nine expedition attempts on Everest were made from the Tibetan side in the 1920s and 1930s, because Nepal was inaccessible to Europeans at the time. None of these teams succeeded. Early expedition climbers wore woollens, thick tweeds, Norfolk jackets and studded leather boots. The only hardware was ice axes and primitive crampons, but oxygen tanks were also lugged along. On the third expedition attempt, in 1924, George Mallory and Andrew Irvine were making good time for the summit when they were enveloped in cloud and never seen again. Whether they succeeded in gaining the summit remains one of mountaineering's great mysteries. Another mystery concerns Eric Shipton, who, connected with these British attempts, photographed footprints left by the Yeti (known as *migyu* in Tibetan). Given to practical jokes, it seems likely that Shipton faked the footprints. Failing to summit Everest, Shipton and his climbing cronies set about bagging a host of first ascents on lesser peaks around Everest.

Since the 19th century, Tibet has attracted more than its fair share of visionaries and eccentric travellers: with Everest, spectacularly so. In 1934, British ex-army officer Maurice Wilson announced that he was going to crash-land a Tiger Moth on the slopes of the mountain and climb from there to plant the Union Jack on the summit. Incredibly, Wilson got financial backing, learned how to fly and flew all the way to India, where officials promptly seized his plane. Spurred on by his megalomaniacal brand of divine faith, Wilson found his way through Tibet disguised as a deaf and dumb monk. At Rongbuk, he got on famously with the head lama. Wilson apparently believed that earlier British expeditions had cut an ice stairway straight up the mountain – he thought he would simply climb this staircase and pray his way to the top. He had little equipment, no warm clothing and no mountaineering experience. Another British expedition of 1935 (under Eric Shipton) found his frozen body at around 6,700 metres.

In 1947, Canadian climber Earl Denman sneaked into Rongbuk to assault the mountain: he got above Camp 3, but turned back. This was the last attempt from the Tibetan side for some time, as the Tibetans banned the issue of travel permits to Tibet. In 1950, after the Chinese invasion, no foreign climbers were allowed in. Western attention had already shifted to Nepal, which had become accessible after 1949. In May 1953, New Zealander Edmund Hillary and Sherpa Tenzing Norgay 'knocked the bastard off' (as Hillary put it), summiting from Nepal as part of a British expedition.

Meanwhile, from the Tibetan side, the Chinese would not allow climbers to attempt the route until they had succeeded in putting Chinese mountaineers on top first. In 1959, the Chinese and the Russians undertook a joint reconnaissance. With the rift between China and Russia in 1960, China carried on the work alone, and then stepped into the Everest spotlight in a big way. In March 1960, the Chinese claimed that all of Everest, as well as an 8km stretch south to Namche Bazaar, belonged to China. At the time, China was busy testing the limits of Indian and Nepalese patience in border disputes. The Everest claim did not sit well with the Nepalese Prime Minister, who made a counterclaim that all of Everest belonged to Nepal, including parts of Rongbuk Glacier. The same month, a 214-man Chinese expedition arrived at Rongbuk base camp for a summit attempt. A Chinese and Tibetan climbing team reached the summit, but there were no photos as the summit attempt took place at night. In 1975 (by which time the border between Tibet and Nepal had been firmly delineated as running across the summit) the Chinese mounted another huge expedition. One

Chinese and eight Tibetans gained the summit and left a tripod there as definite proof of their ascent.

In 1980, the Chinese, satisfied that their claim had been accepted, opened the north side again to foreigners. In August, 1980, in contrast to the huge Chinese teams, came a team of two – Italian climber Reinhold Messner and his girlfriend. In one of mountaineering's most extraordinary feats, he made it to the top of Everest, solo and without oxygen, on a variation of the route pioneered by Mallory and Irvine. Two years earlier, climbing from the South Col, Messner and Habeler had been the first to climb the mountain without oxygen. Until they attempted this feat, it was unknown if a climber would survive reaching the top without oxygen, as past 7,000m is known as the Death Zone (no further acclimatisation is possible). At Everest's peak, a climber without oxygen could suffer debilitating physical and mental problems. Messner did not go in entirely blind – he was a passenger on an unpressurised plane flying at high altitudes, and tested himself without oxygen for short periods. Other climbers have since reached the top of Everest without oxygen, including a female climber, Lydia Bradey from New Zealand, who summited in 1988.

In 1986 Messner claimed another record – the ascent of all 14 peaks over 8,000m, including ascents of Everest and Shishapangma in Tibet. To date, only a handful of climbers have repeated the feat. Messner also narrowly missed being the first in the race to bag the highest peak on all seven continents. This record fell to Canadian climber Patrick Morrow, who added Carstensz Pyramid (in West Irian/Papua New Guinea) to the equation. New Zealander Rob Hall raised the bar by bagging the Seven Summits in seven months. Others have gone on to bag the Seven Summits plus the two poles. Where will it end? Well, there's still the snowboarding record up for grabs: climb the Seven Summits and snowboard down. In 2001, Marco Siffredi snowboarded from the summit of Everest to Advance Base Camp, while a year earlier, Davo Karnicar made the first true ski descent from the summit via the South Col. Another Everest descent record: in September 1988, French climber Jean Marc Boivin paraglided from the summit, landing at Camp 2 (Nepalese side) in 11 minutes. But the most incredible feat of all is the man who did – quite literally – go in blind: Erik Weihenmayer, a blind climber from the US, reached the summit in May 2001.

Almost 90% of Everest climbers fail to reach the summit. Nevertheless, at the last count, over 1,500 ascents of Everest have been successfully made (including repeat summiteers), the majority from the Nepalese side (the year 2001 alone saw 182 summit ascents). Meanwhile, over 170 deaths have been recorded in climbing attempts on Everest and, grisly but true, most of the bodies still lie where they fell. Roughly a third of the deaths recorded are of Sherpas. Many of the Sherpas act as porters, but others have developed reputations as fine climbers – Apa Sherpa has summited Everest 12 times, and Ang Rita Sherpa has summited the peak ten times without oxygen.

But there's politics at the top: Everest is the only place in Tibet where the Tibetan flag can be flown without interference. Sherpa climbers tackling Everest from the Nepalese side are prone to leaving small Tibetan flags fluttering from the summit; they also leave an image of the Dalai Lama in the snow at the summit. When he summited in 1996, Jamling Norgay (son of Tenzing Norgay, who summited in 1953) left an ice-axe with the flags of Tibet, Nepal, India, the USA and the UN flying from it.

In May 1999, a remarkable discovery was made by climber Conrad Anker on the upper slopes of Everest. He found George. After going missing for close on 75 years, George Mallory turned up on the internet, of all places: a photo of his

MOUNTAIN BURIAL

One of Everest's less salubrious records is being the highest rubbish dump in the world. Some expeditions have been undertaken solely to clear out the hundreds of oxygen bottles and canisters strewn at the highest camp, about 900 metres below the summit. Something that cannot be so easily removed, however, are the bodies of dead climbers. Because of the weight, carrying back dead alpinists from this zone – at these high altitudes – is exceedingly difficult. Instead, if possible, bodies of climbers are simply pushed into crevasses, a method of dispatch known as 'mountain burial.'

That's indeed if there's still a body left. Macabre sightings at high elevations include partial cadavers. These act as grim landmarks, and reminders of how thin the line is between life and death up here. The area above 7,000m is called the Death Zone because the body cannot acclimatise here. Climbers have to move quickly in this zone before their strength is sapped by dehydration, cold and high altitude.

It is said there is no morality above 8,000m. If climbers stop to help another climber at this elevation, they will most likely have to abandon their own summit attempt. In a 1996 summit attempt, two Japanese climbers on the Tibetan side were heading for the top when they came across three Ladakhi climbers from an Indian expedition. The Ladakhis had summited but had been forced to spend the night out – though horribly frostbitten they were still alive, and moaning unintelligibly. Not wanting to jeopardise their ascent, the Japanese climbers simply sidestepped the Ladakhis – not offering food, water or oxygen – and carried on to the summit. On the way down from the summit they again passed two of the Ladakhis, who were left to die where they had fallen. Interviewed soon after their descent, one Japanese climber explained that the Ladakhis looked 'dangerous'; the other Japanese climber said, 'We were too tired to help. Above 8,000m is not a place where people can afford morality.'

bleached torso was posted by expedition members to their website (www.mountainzone.com). This did not sit well with descendants of the Mallory family (including Mallory's grandson, George, who summited Everest in 1995), and nor did other media exposure of the body, including a cover-photo for Outside Magazine. Those selling the pictures claimed that the photos were proof that Mallory had been found. Edmund Hillary said it was disgusting to expose the body in such a fashion, that the dead should be given some respect.

For Edmund Hillary, there were some terse moments: in Mallory's pockets were notes that showed he was toting more oxygen cannisters than previously thought, which means he and Irvine might have been able to make the summit. But no camera was found on Mallory's body. So who got to the top first? Edmund Hillary let slip in his autobiography that he could lay claim to being first, a few steps ahead of Tenzing Norgay. Meanwhile, it was discovered that Tenzing Norgay was not Nepalese at all, but of Tibetan blood, so one of the premier summiteers, fittingly, is Tibetan. He grew up in the village of Moyun, in the Karta Valley, in the shadow of Everest. Seeking a better life, his parents left Tibet and walked over to the Nepalese side. Tenzing Norgay kept his real origins obscure, and finally took out Indian citizenship under the patronage of Prime Minister Nehru. Tenzing Norgay never lied about his origins, but he didn't quite tell the truth, either: it was not until after his death in 1986 that the full story emerged. Here's an intriguing link: Norgay and Mallory may have actually met. Mallory's 1921 expedition passed through Moyun, the village where young Tenzing Norgay lived, and spent the day there. Tenzing Norgay was seven years old at the time.

And here's another conundrum: is climbing in the genes? Edmund Hillary's son Peter summited Everest, Mallory's grandson George did too, and both the son of Tenzing Norgay (Jamling) and his grandson (Tashi Tenzing) have summited, making that a three-generation affair.

Karta

Everest East Base Camp, elevation 5,050m

This arduous ten-day loop takes you through the Kama and Karta valleys with views of Everest's Kangshung Face. Of the three faces of Everest, this is the one rated the most daunting to climb, and the one rarely viewed by Westerners. The 1921 British expedition, exploring the Karta Valley on its reconnaissance of Everest, decided the approach was out of the question. It was not until 1981 that an American team tried to summit the Kangshung Face. They failed, but another expedition with some of the same members succeeded in 1983.

Of the treks described so far, the Karta loop is the most taxing, requiring considerable logistical support. Several outfitters can arrange trips, starting from Kathmandu, stopping to trek at Karta and moving on to Lhasa. If you are very determined and well supplied with food and camping gear, you should be able to put together your own trek.

CAVEAT Porters and yak-handlers in the Karta area have a notorious reputation for being unreliable and reluctant companions. On group tours, histrionic scenes have included porters getting drunk on *chang* at breakfast and not getting under way with the yaks until mid-day, thus throwing out the daily trekking targets. Furious arguments can erupt over what loads are to be carried on the yaks, porters can be rough in handling duffle bags, and yak handlers may stop and demand extra money before continuing. So it goes on. They are also known to be fond of pilfering loose items.

Kangshung Trek

To save time and conserve energy, it would be advisable to get a ride to the trailhead village of Karta. The approach by road is initially the same as for Rongbuk, with a turn-off at Peruche. From Peruche to Karta is about six bone-jarring hours by Landcruiser, with repeated river fords. You could trek in – the scenic 90km from Peruche to Karta would take three or four days (a donkey and guide can be hired in Peruche to assist).

Everest East Face base camp can be reached by several routes: a ten-day loop takes in several of these. There are two high passes en route: trekkers pick the lower one (Shao La, 4970m) to go over first as this allows more chance to acclimatise. At the base of Shao La are two glacial lakes, where good campsites are found. If the weather is clear, there are good views of Everest, Makalu and Lhotse from the top of Shao La. Shao La leads into the beautiful Kama Valley which is surprisingly coated with meadows full of rhododendrons, and, further on, forests of pine and fir. Westward along the Kama Valley there are many streams to cross, and meadows with wildflowers. From this vantage point, there may be views of Chomo Lonzo. The trek continues to Everest East base camp, at a site called Pethang Ringmo by British climber George Mallory. If the weather is co-operative, there are unparalleled views of the Kangshung Face and Kangshung Glacier.

The return trek is made via Langma La, at 5,330m, with steep rocky sections giving way to more gentle pastures. At the Kama River is the medieval village of Lundrubling, with solid houses of stone and timber. With a few hours' trekking to the east, you return to Karta Yulba.

Cho Oyu base camp

Lesser-known than Everest – but no less spectacular – is Cho Oyu, an 8,153m behemoth. You can see the peak quite clearly from Tingri. The walk out (or drive) to its base camp crosses the plains of Tingri in the same direction as the Rongbuk trail. Cho Oyu base camp is nestled at 4,970m. You can take a day-hike from here toward Puse La for good views. Near Cho Oyu base camp is Kyetrak, with the ruins of a salt depot on the old trading route from Nepal, crossing Nangpa La. The glaciated route is still used by the odd Nepali trader, and as an escape route by Tibetan refugees, which might explain Chinese military manoeuvres in the area.

SHISHAPANGMA BASE-CAMP TREK

Shishapangma is the only 8,000m peak totally within Tibet (the others – Everest, Lhotse, Cho Oyu and Makalu – lie on the Tibet-Nepal border). For a long time it was not a question of climbing Shishapangma, but getting to see it. It was not until 1951 that Peter Aufschnaiter (the Austrian who escaped with Heinrich Harrer to Tibet) was able to get within 10km of Shishapangma to photograph it. This was only the second photo taken of the mountain, the first being an aerial one taken in 1950. Shishapangma was the last of the 8,000m giants to fall to climbers.

The first ascent of Shishapangma (Xixabangma) was achieved in 1964. In March of that year, an army of over 200 Chinese support personnel and climbers gathered at the north base camp. Climbers swore to plant the five-starred red flag on the summit 'for the honour of the party and the socialist construction of the Motherland' (as described in the magazine *China's Sports*). The climbers not only put the red flag on the summit, they also deposited a bust of Chairman Mao. The summit was reached by four Tibetan and six Chinese climbers, one of whom, Wang Fuchou, had climbed Everest four years earlier. In 1980, a German climbing team summited the peak; in 1982, British climbers Doug Scott and Alex MacIntyre reached the top via the southwest face. French climber Didier Givois and two companions not only summited Shishapangma, they telemark-skied back down it.

Ironically, since the Lhasa-to-Kathmandu route opened to tourism in the 1980s, Shishapangma has become the most accessible of the 8,000m peaks. There are two approaches to Shishapangma. You can drive to Shishapangma north base camp by heading north out of Nyalam, and taking a fork to the west that leads to Lake Paiku Tso. Heading along this road is another fork to the south, leading to the village of Serlung. Here you can hire yaks and handlers if you want to trek in, or just motor on for the last 15km from Serlung to the north base camp at 4,900m.

Shishapangma south base camp, at 4,980m, can be reached by an in-and-out trail from Nyalam, taking about four or five days for the round trip. You head out northwest of Nyalam, following a river through alpine valleys. Because Shishapangma is a conglomerate peak (with several possible summits), it's difficult to determine where the real summit lies.

WEST TIBET

There are two main targets in west Tibet, both taking about a week to reach from Lhasa. The main focus of interest – for both pilgrim and trekker – is Mount Kailash. A second spectacular site is the ruins of the Guge Kingdom near Zanda. You can visit both if you have lots of time and money, and luck on the road.

Another variable here is that you may not want to return to Lhasa, or even start from Lhasa. Kailash can also be approached or left from the road going down to Kathmandu. There is a shortcut around the south side of (Lake) Paiku Tso, which skirts close to Shishapangma north base camp. Group tent-trekking tours from Kathmandu either drive up through Nyalam, or use another five-day walk-in route from Simikot (far western Nepal) to Burang. However, these Sherpa-escorted trekking trips were disrupted by guerrilla activity, when Maoists in the area starting demanding a 'tax' from trekkers.

Indian pilgrims arrive as part of a lottery system: they come over the Lipu Lek pass to Burang, then on to Kailash. Some Western group tours have been allowed to follow this same route, trekking in through the Garhwal Himalaya and over Lipu Lek pass.

Routes from Lhasa

Travel to Kailash is like one of those epic Marco Polo diary entries: 'Five or six days' hard journey to the west, you come to a great snow-covered mountain which is considered very holy by the Tibetans, who leave articles of clothing as proof of their pilgrimage to it…' The pilgrimage to Kailash has long been considered the most difficult in Asia, due to the sheer distance, harsh weather conditions, the high altitude and lack of any supply points. No matter which way you go, the trip is arduous and you need good planning. Timing is everything at Kailash. It's snowed-in for much of the year, but June and July are generally good months to go. August is not good – monsoon rains can wash away roads and bridges leading in. September is possible. Treks at Kailash start and finish at Darchen, an encampment on the south side of the peak. There are half a dozen routes to Kailash, all of them arduous and time-consuming. Consult the Tibetan Autonomous Region map at the front of this book for an overview of routing.

Hiring vehicles

A Landcruiser driver would be most reluctant to travel alone on any of the Kailash routes. If he gets stuck in mud or trapped while fording a river, there's no way out. You have some options: arrange to hire two Landcruisers, or, better yet, hire a Landcruiser and a truck. The Landcruiser can seat four paying passengers plus guide and driver; the truck seats two paying passengers in the front cabin, plus driver. The truck acts as a tow vehicle if the going gets rough – it can haul the Landcruiser to the next town for repairs. In the back of the truck are all the supplies for the trip: food, gasoline, camping gear and so on. You can rotate passengers through the two vehicles. A Landcruiser and truck combination might work out at around US$4,500 for six people for 25 days. That means about US$750 a person, including permits, gasoline, driver and guide fees, but not food. Take as much food and water with you as you can manage from Lhasa: potatoes, vegetables, dried fruit, roasted walnuts – anything that will last the distance. Some take along lots of liquid supplies too.

Another good transport configuration here is one truck and two Landcruisers, if you can find enough people for the journey. This makes more efficient use of the truck by sharing it between two Landcruisers. The full circuit of Lhasa via the north route to Kailash and back to Lhasa on the south route is just over 3,000km – a major road trip.

A far cheaper way to go (about US$250 a person) is with ten people in the back of a truck (guide and driver in the cabin, plus one passenger on a rotation basis). Chinese Dongfeng trucks are not known for their shock-absorbers: you'll be thrown around like a sack of potatoes, showered in dust, and have your kidneys messed with. There are periodic clamp-downs by authorities on this kind of truck transport – sometimes they turn a blind eye, other times they say foreigners can't use trucks. All transport hire is done from Lhasa, and rarely from other places unless taxis. There is a short listing of operators in the *Lhasa* chapter (page 100), but in any case, you may be restricted to TTB-run agencies.

Permits

Visiting the region of West Tibet requires more than usual in the way of permits. Apart from the regular ATP listing Ali, Darchen and so on, you need special permits to visit the Guge Kingdom. This paperwork starts in Lhasa, continues in Ali or Darchen, and then requires more work in Zanda.

North route

The longest way to Kailash is from Lhasa via Lhatse and Gertse to Ali, then south to Darchen. En route, you could make a sidetrip to Zanda and Tsaparang. Lhasa to Kailash by this route is around 1,900km (the Ali to Darchen stretch is 330km). A return to Lhasa would probably be made on the south route via Huore and Zongba to Saga. From here you either continue onward to Lhasa, or cross the Yarlung Tsangpo by ferry at Saga, detour around the south side of Paiku Tso and head for Zhangmu on the Kathmandu route. The north route – though long – has the advantage of roads that are in reasonable shape. Some parts need no roads at all – the trucks forge their own route across grassland.

There are some horrible, polluted, soul-destroying truck-stop towns en route. No-name hotels have rough and tumble facilities, if any at all – hot water supply comes in thermoses. Some towns like Tsochen and Gertse have a few small restaurants hidden away. This is the main Lhasa-Ali-Kashgar truck and military supply route, so truck-stops cater to the driving crews. Among the truck-stops are Sangsang (4,520m), Raga (4,800m), Tsochen (4,650m), Dongco (4,400m), Gertse (4,400m), Tsaka (Yanhu) and Gakyi (4,450m). There are some high passes of 5,000m and 5,200m north of Tsochen. The wild terrain in between truck-stops makes the journey more than worthwhile: you might see wild asses, antelopes and even black-necked cranes. There are a few hot springs along the way, too.

Kashgar route

Connecting from Ali through Yecheng to Kashgar is this route, the wildest of all. Some have managed to hitch from Kashgar to Ali – the stumbling block is Yecheng, 250km south of Kashgar, where PSB men are prone to sending travellers back to where they came from. The route crosses some very high passes and there are no supply points along it. Kashgar is in a remote corner of the PRC, but the Karakoram Highway to Islamabad provides a convenient exit or entry (open May to November, with a valid Pakistan visa).

South route

Although the south route to Kailash from Lhasa, via Lhatse and Paryang, is more direct (a total of 1,200km), it is also more prone to flooding, washed-out roads and downed bridges. There are some high passes on the south route: Paryang and Huore both sit at 4,500m, and between them is a pass of 5,100m. Some travellers take the south route up to Darchen and retrace their passage the same way. If heading for Kathmandu, there is a shortcut – you can cut from Saga (4,500m) around the south side of Paiku Tso to the Tong La pass, and on to Nyalam on the Kathmandu route (see the *Lhasa to Kathmandu route* map on pages 162–3 for details).

Ali

Shiquanhe, elevation 4,220m; capital of Ngari Prefecture; area code: 0897

Ali is a Chinese concrete monstrosity of a town, with some of the ugliest post-Mao proletarian-monolithic socialist-realist architecture in Tibet. It's composed of concrete cubicles and wooden kiosks, with garbage all over the place. Still, at least there's a Lion statue in the middle, not a Mao statue. The town is Chinese to its rotten core – no Tibetan towns existed out this way except for the old capital of Gartok (a nomad tent encampment which has disappeared without trace). Although it is commonly called Ali, the town is also referred to by the river it is located along, the Indus, which the Chinese refer to as Shiquanhe and the Tibetans call Sengghe Tsangpo ('River issuing from the Lion's Mouth'; hence Sengghe Drong, or 'Lion Village,' is the Tibetan name for Ali).

Ali is easily the largest town in western Tibet, with the largest military garrison of the region. Army platoons jog around the streets in formation at six in the morning, and again around sunset. After sunset the top brass head for the karaoke bars and help themselves to the women. Otherwise, there's not a whole lot to see in Ali, apart from a place called the Cultural Relics Bureau, which has a display centre. The main reason for visiting Ali is shopping – for food and for permits.

Permits

A glance at the map will show Ali is strategically sited at the junction of the north route from Lhasa, the south route from Kashgar, and onward routes to Zanda and Kailash. PSB men will be on the lookout for travellers who don't have their papers in order: the PSB office will most likely want to check your permits if you are spotted. Some backpackers who have hitched out this far have been able to turn themselves in at Ali, pay a fine, and be issued with permits for Kailash. This policy can easily change. If you want to finalise paperwork for visiting Zanda, you must visit both the PSB office and the Cultural Relics Bureau, to the south end of town, to get the right papers.

Facilities

You can stock up on supplies like shampoo here. The kiosks around town are the best bet; there's not much in the 'department stores'. Facilities to the western side

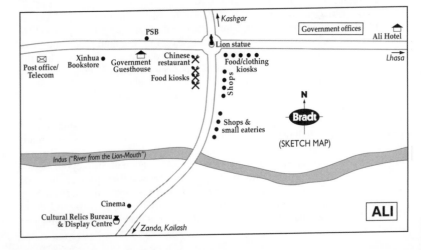

of town include a small Xinhua bookstore, a PO/telecom office, and just west of this, a bank. There's also a hospital in Ali.

Lodging and food
Ali Hotel at the east end of town is a concrete wasteland where little seems to work. Rooms downstairs are cheaper than the ones upstairs. Yyou might be able to get a hot water thermos and basin together to clean up. A cleaner place to stay is the Government Guesthouse, opposite the PSB office; the price difference is minimal. To the southwest side of the Lion statue is a Chinese restaurant with quite palatable Sichuan food. There are also eateries on the road to the south. Food kiosks in this vicinity may have little nuggets hidden away, including chocolate bars, pineapple in jars, crackers and candles.

Zanda
Tsanda, Tsada, Zada, Thöling, Toling; elevation 3,660m
From Ali, the road to Zanda traverses an entire mountain range – a breathtaking trip, with snowy passes as high as 5,200m and 5,500m – before dropping down to a canyon with ghostly shapes. You drive through this canyon along a dry riverbed to reach Zanda. With such a spectacular route, allow an entire day to motor by Landcruiser from Ali to Zanda, with frequent stops en route. The canyons, with hues of yellow, red and copper, are extraordinary for their phantasmagoric sculpted forms, which appear at times to be like the outlines of dream castles or cathedrals, at other times like gigantic guardian statues or mythical animals.

Zanda is the Chinese name for an ancient Tibetan town of Toling, once the capital of Ngari (west Tibet). Remnants of this capital are scattered around town and the surrounding hills; there are dozens of chorten-like structures toward the Sutlej River.

Permits
If you want to visit Toling Gompa in Zanda or the ruins of the Guge Kingdom in Tsaparang, you need permits from the Cultural Relics Bureau, located near the bank. Tsaparang requires separate permits from Lhasa, Ali and Zanda – put them all together and you are allowed to visit. With one of those permits missing, there could be problems.

Lodging and food
Zanda is a glorified army garrison – facilities are for the military, not for the stray tourist. There's a big army base at the southern end of town, and an old Tibetan quarter at the northwest end. In between is a main drag with two guesthouses, one of which belongs to military. The one near Toling Gompa is preferable – there are balcony rooms upstairs, and there's a tap in the courtyard with running water. Several small Chinese restaurants line the main strip, and some tent-shops (selling supplies out of tents); there's also a post office (with telephone) and the Agrarian Bank.

Toling Gompa
The main sight in town is the largely abandoned Toling Gompa. Toling dates back to the 11th century when a structure was built by Yeshe O, the king of Guge. Assisted by scholar Rinchen Zangpo, he led a revival of Buddhism in western Tibet. Buddhism was snuffed out in a few short years in central Tibet by King Langdarma (who ruled AD838–842), a staunch supporter of the Bon faith: upon the assassination of Langdarma, Tibet was broken up into lay and monastic pockets of influence. The Guge Kingdom became an enclave that was vital for the survival of

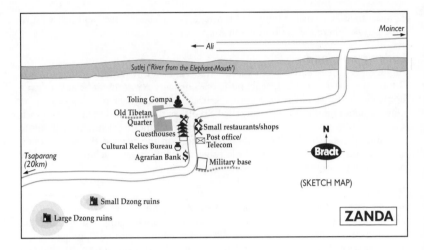

Buddhism. King Yeshe O and Rinchen Zangpo promoted cultural exchanges with Indian Buddhists. Although over a hundred monasteries were built in the western region (which at that time encompassed Ladakh), Toling became the most important centre of Buddhist study, and its reputation grew with the arrival of 11th-century scholar Atisha from India. Eventually the kingdom was sacked in the 17th century. In the mid-1960s, Red Guards trashed Toling Gompa.

The main draw at Toling today are the fine murals in the few chapels remaining. In addition to destruction by Red Guards, murals in the White Temple have suffered water damage. Similar to those at Tsaparang, the murals are in early Newari and Kashmiri styles, both rarely seen in Tibet. You need a powerful flashlight to view them, and considerable perseverance to persuade the caretaker-monk to open the chapels in the first place. You may have to bribe your way through, even if you've already paid up through the Cultural Relics Bureau.

Out of town
On ridge-tops to the southwest of Zanda are two *dzongs* (citadels) made of clay. This is the most peculiar hiking you'll ever do: scrambling over sand and dealing with crevasses of clay. Access to the larger dzong (the one to the west) is via a steep trail, and then through a sloping tunnel carved out of clay. Above the tunnel are former cave-dwellings and dangerous crevasses. From here you continue climbing, and reach a vantage point with a magnificent view of the Sutlej valley.

Tsaparang
Located 26km west of Zanda (a one-hour drive) are the extensive ruins of Tsaparang, the once-powerful capital of the 10th-century Guge Kingdom (pronounced *Goo-gay*). The main building material is not stone, but clay, with walls, buildings, secret tunnels and escape exits all fashioned from this material. Thousands of people lived here in cave-dwellings in this kingdom of clay, which appears to have been operational in the 10th and 11th centuries. Little is known of the history of the Guge Kingdom, but some of the exceptional murals at Tsaparang portray realistic scenes with courtiers and visiting dignitaries, and give some idea of how people lived.

To access temples at Tsaparang, you need the caretaker to open the doors. The Tibetan caretaker lives in a small house near the main gate: if he's not at home, he's probably in the tiny village visible not far away from the ruins. The caretaker may want to see your paperwork, and may insist that no photos be taken inside the temple structures. Interior photography of the site is a very sensitive point; official permits for photography are complex to obtain, and expensive if you do manage to get them.

Tsaparang is built tier-on-tier up a clay ridge. The best-preserved parts are the lower ramparts; at the very top are excellent views of the area from the dzong. As you go through the gate into Tsaparang, the first thing you see is the Rust-coloured Chapel, thus designated because its function is not clear – it bears murals of Tsongkhapa, Sakyamuni and Atisha. The White Temple suffered extensive damage to its statuary, but its murals remain intact. Some murals portray Avalokitesvara, the 11-headed, thousand-armed bodhisattva of compassion. The mural style is Kashmiri. The Red Temple was destroyed and left open to water damage, but even so, its murals are striking, with beautiful large Tara frescos. Engrossing here are murals apparently depicting scenes from daily life at Guge – in one section envoys are arriving by donkey at the court; another part shows a high lama giving teachings. The Yamantaka Chapel is dedicated to its resident tantric deity Dorje Jigje: the walls bear murals of deities locked in tantric *yabyum* embraces (see *Glossary*, page 272) with their consorts.

From here, wend your way up clay steps, passing through a fantastic winding tunnel to the top-most ruins. There's an entire ruined citadel at the top. Once past the tunnel, there is a complex of chambers and passageways: the citadel had its own water supply in times of siege, and the king had an escape route tunnel that lead off the rear of the ridge.

At the top, the most impressive structure is Tsaparang Dzong – the king's simple summer palace – with expansive views over the valley. There are several temple complexes at the top: the most important is the tiny Demchok Mandala Chapel. This chapel is usually locked – if you manage to get in, you can view the remains of a large 3-D mandala, which was smashed in the Cultural Revolution. The chapel is a *gonkhang* or protector temple, and the site of initiation rites. It is thought that in times of crisis, the king and ministers would come to this chapel to ask for protection or direction. The chapel is dedicated to the protector deity Demchok, who is depicted in murals with his consort Dorje Phagmo. Fascinating tantric murals cover the walls: a flashlight is needed to view them. Depicted are

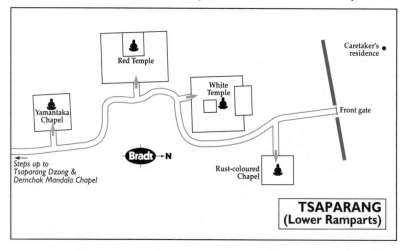

TSAPARANG
(Lower Ramparts)

rows of dancing *dakinis*, the female deities who personify the wisdom of enlightenment; below these are gory scenes of disembodiment from hell realms.

Tirtapuri

While Kailash is the main sacred site of western Tibet, there are a number of others on the pilgrim's 'wish-list.' After Lake Manasarovar, the most revered site is Tirtapuri, a yellow-streaked rocky landscape with hot springs. After encircling Kailash and Manasarovar, Tibetan pilgrims come to Tirtapuri for a relaxing circuit – the *kora* is only an hour, and there are grassy meadows for picnicking as well as hot water for soothing tired limbs. Tirtapuri lies 10km southwest of Moincer (which has a basic guesthouse), approachable by Landcruiser or truck. There is a short circuit in the Tirtapuri region – you can follow the pilgrims as they walk past elaborate mani walls and sacred caves, and pay their respects at a small monastery. The entire Tirtapuri circuit takes an hour, but you should allow several hours to stop and drink in the atmosphere and the landscape. At the site, pilgrims bathe – or dip their feet – in several sulphurous hot-spring pools, which can accommodate three or four people. The hot springs are reputed to have healing powers, and Tibetans search the waters for pellets of lime, for medicinal purposes. Just being able to feel hot water is therapeutic enough for Western visitors.

The Kailash Region

Kailash is the centre of the universe – or at least the Tibetan Buddhist universe. In the Tibetan worldview, at the cosmic axis of the universe lies Mount Meru, the abode of the gods. Mount Kailash is thought to be an earthly manifestation of the mythical Meru. Things are not as simple as this, however, as the Tibetan worldview incorporates existence in multiple dimensions. The Tibetan name for Kailash is 'Kang Rinpoche' – Precious Jewel of Snows: the dome-shaped peak is symmetrical like an uncut diamond, with a permanent cap of ice and snow. At 6,714m, the mountain is modest by Himalayan standards, but nevertheless impressive to view. The peak is sacred to Tibetan Buddhist and Bon adherents, and to the Hindus and Jains of India.

In the late 19th century and early 20th century, Kailash assumed mythical dimensions among western geographers and explorers. For the longest time there was reputed to be a high mountain that was the source of the great rivers of India. But Tibet was inaccessible, so geographers were unsure if this was myth or fact. Finding the source of India's great rivers was a prime geographer's puzzle, on a par to finding the source of the Nile. The British employed Indian pundits, who, disguised as pilgrims, measured distances with prayer-beads, and tossed marked logs into rivers to find out where they would pop up further down the line in India.

Eventually, it was discovered that the headwaters of four of Asia's mightiest rivers lay within 100km of Kailash – the Indus, the Yarlung Tsangpo (which later emerges in India as the Brahmaputra), the Karnali (a major tributary of the Ganges), and the Sutlej. Remarkably, the mouths of same rivers end up as far as 3,000km apart. The Tibetans know the rivers by more prosaic names, identified with the four cardinal directions and four legendary animals. Thus the Indus becomes the 'River issuing from the Lion's Mouth' (Sengghe Tsangpo or Sengghe Khambab, at the north), the Yarlung Tsangpo becomes the 'River from the Horse-Mouth' (Tamchok Khambab, to the east), the Karnali becomes the 'River from the Peacock-Mouth' (Mabchu Khambab, to the south), and the Sutlej is the 'River from the Elephant-Mouth' (Langchan Khambab, situated in the west).

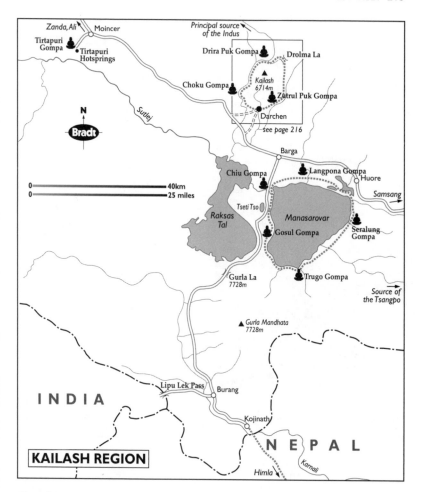

Principal source of the Indus

Zanda, Ali — Moincer
Tirtapuri Gompa
Tirtapuri Hotsprings

Drira Puk Gompa — Drolma La

Choku Gompa

Kailash 6714m

Zutrul Puk Gompa

N

Sutlej

Darchen
see page 216

Bradt

0 ——— 40km
0 ——— 25 miles

Barga

Chiu Gompa — Langpona Gompa
Huore

Samsang

Tseti Tso

Raksas Tal

Manasarovar

Gosul Gompa

Seralung Gompa

Gurla La 7728m — Trugo Gompa

Source of the Tsangpo

Gurla Mandhata 7728m

Lipu Lek Pass — Burang

INDIA

Kojinath

NEPAL

KAILASH REGION

Himla — Karnali

Darchen

Also known as Tarchen or Dharchen (elevation 4,620m), Darchen can best be described as a cross between a Tibetan tent encampment and a Chinese truck-stop depot. A few tents and adobe hutches dispense noodles and tea, and there are some shops by the river on the eastern side of Darchen. There's not a lot of choice when it comes to places to stay – most travellers opt for a room at a Chinese-run Gangdishi Guesthouse, a truck-stop compound with a large parking area. Prices tend to be high for what you get (which is little more than a rock-hard bed), so you may have to bargain. Also useful to know is that you can leave your gear here when trekking, in a locked storeroom. There's similar-priced lodging at another compound run by the PSB. It's a good idea to hang around Darchen for a day or two to acclimatise, perhaps taking a day hike up to Serlung Gompa.

There is a small clinic in Darchen with oxygen supply, where altitude sickness can be treated. Group tours are also known to use the military hospital in Burang, and may also race clients (patients) over the pass into Nepal to Himla, where helicopter evacuation can possibly be arranged. Note, though, that individual travellers may not cross the border at this point.

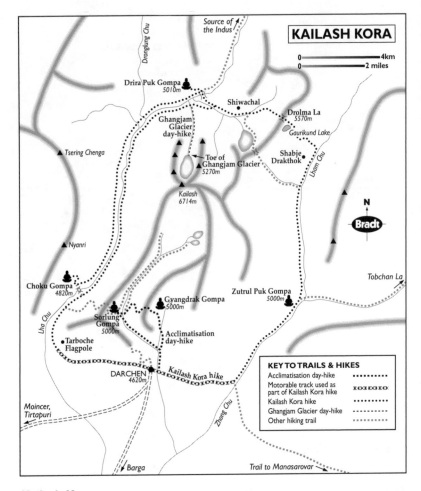

KAILASH KORA

Source of the Indus

Dronglung Chu

Drira Puk Gompa
5010m

Shiwachal

Drolma La
5570m

Gaurikund Lake

Ghangjam
Glacier
day-hike

▲ Tsering Chenga

Shabje
Drakthok

Toe of
Ghangjam Glacier
5270m

Lham Chu

Kailash
6714m

N

Bradt

▲ Nyanri

Tobchan La

Choku Gompa
4820m

Gyangdrak Gompa
5000m

Zutrul Puk Gompa
5000m

Sorlung
Gompa
5000m

Acclimatisation
day-hike

Lha Chu

• Tarboche
Flagpole

DARCHEN
4620m

Kailash Kora hike

KEY TO TRAILS & HIKES
Acclimatisation day-hike ● ● ● ● ● ●
Motorable track used as
part of Kailash Kora hike ꞮOꞮOꞮO
Kailash Kora hike ▬▬▬▬
Ghangjam Glacier day-hike ─ ─ ─ ─
Other hiking trail ∙∙∙∙∙∙∙∙

Moincer,
Tirtapuri

Zhong Chu

✦ Barga

Trail to Manasarovar

Kailash Kora

The circuit around the sacred mountain is known as the Kailash *kora*. Tibetans complete the circuit in one long day, starting before dawn, and finishing after nightfall. Unless you are super-humanoid, don't attempt this at altitude. The minimum time for most Westerners to complete the circuit would be two days. Most allow three to four days. If you have a tent and want to dawdle, taking in the landscape at a leisurely pace, plan on five days or more.

You can head out of Darchen carrying your own backpack with food supplies, or you can hire a porter in Darchen to carry gear. Group tours often hire yaks in Darchen to carry camping gear and duffle bags on the kora. As an individual, you probably won't need to camp out (you can stay at two monastery guesthouses along the route), but if planning a more leisurely kora, you'll need camping gear so you can stop where you want. Don't expect much in the way of food on the circuit, although there may be some teahouse tents along the way, if you're lucky. Sometimes the gompa guesthouses sell noodles. A clean water supply is essential – take water bottles and filtering devices (water can also be boiled). It is not advisable to trek around Kailash alone – there are too many variables at stake. Walk with at least one companion.

Fellow hikers at Kailash are mainly Indian and Tibetan pilgrims. The Tibetans come from as far away as Kham, usually arriving by 'pilgrim truck.' Tibetan pilgrims comprise many different nomad groups with a fascinating array of costumes – particularly the women. Women coat their faces in *tocha* – a cosmetic made of concentrated buttermilk or roots – to protect the skin from dryness and UV rays. Indian pilgrims come as part of a lottery system run by the Delhi government, in operation since the early 1980s. Each year, up to 10,000 Hindus from all parts of India apply. About 700 finalists are chosen: after fitness tests, this number is whittled down to about 400. Hindu pilgrims are allowed ten days in Tibet. Travelling in groups of around 35, the lucky lottery winners walk across Lipu Lek Pass where they are met by Chinese guides and the sacred circuit of their dreams gets under way.

Acclimatisation hike

Strongly recommended is a day trip up to Gyangdrak and Serlung gompas, due north of Darchen. These gompas are situated at 5,000m: you can complete a triangular loop in about six or seven hours, returning to Darchen by nightfall. This hike serves several functions: you can adapt to the altitude somewhat (by hiking high but sleeping low) and you can find out how to pace yourself at altitude. If intending to trek around Kailash with your own backpack, you might want to take the full load with you on the day hike to find out just how heavy it is.

POWERING UP AT KAILASH

In Darchen, you can stock up on last-minute supplies, and get your pilgrim supplies too. At tents and shops at the northeast side of Darchen, pilgrims purchase prayer-flags (to drape at the passes), small squares of paper with windhorses embossed on them (to fling around at the main pass), and for good measure, prayer-beads (to mumble mantras with, to get over the high passes). The windhorse (lungta) is a beautiful steed that brings good fortune (symbolised by the jewel on its back) wherever it goes. It is also painted on prayer-flags – the wind sets the horse in motion, carrying good fortune in all directions.

In their lifetime, all Tibetans aspire to make the sacred pilgrimage to Kailash – some travel enormous distances in the backs of open trucks to get there. Pilgrimage is considered healthy and holy – the most popular time to attempt Kailash is after the annual harvest. When it comes to the Kailash kora, there's a kind of merit point system involved: the more you suffer, the greater the merit earned. Some pilgrims attempt not one circuit, but three (often on consecutive days in one season) or 13 circuits, or 108 circuits (spread over a number of years), which assures entry into nirvana. Prostrators, who proceed with inchworm-like motions, flinging themselves to the ground, take 15 to 25 days to complete the Kailash circuit, and must prostrate through anything in their path, be it snow, slush, mud, or whatever. If you see a prostrator going in an anticlockwise direction, it must be a Bon adherent. For Bon believers, Kailash is the spiritual centre of the Shang-Shung ancient Bon empire of western Tibet.

Punctuating the Kailash circuit are sacred markers in stone – carved chortens, carved mani-stones and cairns with prayer-flags. Offerings made by pilgrims at these sites might include pins (said to sharpen mental faculties), discarded clothing (as proof the pilgrim has been there) or tsampa (thrown in the air as protection against evil).

SHAMBHALA AND SHANGRI-LA

As earthly paradises go, Tibet's vision is a bit different. Most Tibetans haven't heard of Shangri-La, but James Hilton (the author of *Lost Horizons*, 1933) probably based his story about Shangri-La on the Tibetan legend of Shambhala, which most Westerners haven't heard about.

The Shambhala legend was first heard by Jesuit and Capuchin missionaries who stumbled into Tibet, and who probably served as models for Hilton's characters. In *Lost Horizon*, a Capuchin monk called Perrault had made his way into the valley of Shangri-La and attempted to convert the residents. Instead, he was converted to Buddhism, and some 200 years later, as High Lama, this wizened gentleman was still alive to tell new recruits the rules. The main luxury at Shangri-La was Time, that slippery gift that often eludes Westerners. Shangri-La was a repository of the best of eastern and western knowledge, preserved for:

> a time when men, exultant in the technique of homicide, would rage so hotly over the world that every precious thing would be in danger, every book and picture and harmony, every treasure gathered through two millenniums, the small, the delicate, the defenseless – all would be lost...

Hilton set his story in a Tibetan monastery high in the mountains. The location is not revealed – the Western visitors arrive in a plane that crash-landed. This world has led Westerners to confuse Tibet with a mythical realm and not a real place. The phenomenon has been dubbed 'The Shangri-La Syndrome' by Tibetan intellectuals.

There are several Tibetan versions of the legend of Shambhala, but they run in the same pattern. Somewhere to the north of Tibet is a kingdom ringed by impenetrable snowcapped mountains and cloaked in mist. In this sanctuary, poverty, hunger, crime and sickness are unknown, and people live a hundred years. In the city of Kalapa there is a glittering palace where the sacred Kalachakra teachings are kept. According to the legend, about 300 years from now, when Lhasa lies under water, the world will erupt in chaotic warfare. When the last barbarian thinks he has conquered the world, the mists will lift from Shambhala and the King of Shambhala will ride forth to destroy the forces of evil. The King will establish a new Golden Age of a thousand years.

The Shambhala theme is often depicted in Tibetan temple murals, sometimes in mandalic form. There are large Shambhala murals in the Potala and the Norbulingka in Lhasa, and also at Samye. Many other monastic frescos portray the Kalachakra deity. Tsongkhapa and other great Tibetan wizards and sages are thought to have visited Shambhala in the past. When the Golden Age dawns, it is said that the tomb of Tsongkhapa at Ganden will open up, and he will live again to teach true wisdom. A number of ancient, surrealistic Tibetan texts have been written on how to get to Shambhala. Some say Shambhala lies in west Tibet, near the Guge Kingdom; others think it is in the north, in Changtang, or much further north in the Kunlun range, or even in Mongolia. Yet others think it lies at the North Pole. Some Tibetans believe Shambhala is a mystical nirvana of the gods; others believe it is real, but that the journey is not external but internal – and that the war with ignorance is in your own heart.

Day one The target of the first day's walk is usually Drira Phuk Gompa, about 8 to 10 hours from Darchen, including stops. Leaving Darchen, you head west: you'll know you're on the right trail when you come across a cairn adorned with prayer-flags, and with discarded clothing left by pilgrims – tattered shirts, sweaters, worn-out runners, old socks, yak heads and goat horns. Further on is Tarboche, a large flagpole from which flutter long lines of prayer-flags. Every year, at Saka Dawa (full moon day in May or June), thousands of Tibetans gather to celebrate: the flagpole is taken down, and new prayer-flags are placed on it, replacing the tattered ones from the previous year. If the pole tilts after it is raised again, it is considered a very bad omen. Pilgrim trucks can reach this site by dirt track, so this is often where Tibetans start the kora.

Beyond Tarboche, high on a ridge – a 20-minute climb up from the trail – is Choku Gompa, which was originally set up in the 13th century as a shrine. The current building was reconstructed after the Cultural Revolution, and is looked after by monks from the Drukpa Kagyu sect (as are the other two monasteries on the kora route). Shiny-eyed pilgrims crowd in to see the monastery's famed treasures: a white stone statue of the Buddha Opame, and a sacred silver-embossed conch shell, said to have been Milarepa's. From Choku, there's a choice of hiking up either side of Lha Chu (River of the gods), though a canyon with impressive rock peaks, such as Nyanri. At Drira Phuk Gompa, there is a simple concrete building with a few rooms where you can stay – or you can camp out in the grassy fields nearby.

Day two This is a rest day, with a possible half-day hike up to Ghangjam Glacier and back. Building in a rest day at Drira Phuk gives your body a chance to recover, and will help you acclimatise for the arduous walk over Drolma La. Drira Phuk offers the chance to get quite close to Kailash, on a half-day hike to the toe of Ghangjam Glacier at 5,270m. Assuming clear conditions, there are awesome views of the glistening icy walls of Kailash's north face from this vantage point. You begin to understand why the Tibetans call the peak Kang Rinpoche (Precious Jewel of Snows), and why it is said that a wish made in front of the north face will definitely come true – one day.

Day three Heading out of Drira Phuk, you begin the tough ascent to Drolma La. This is the longest haul on the circuit – it takes about 10 to 12 hours to walk to Zutrul Phuk. Out of Drira Phuk is a bizarre sight: a field littered with discarded clothing. The place is Shiwachal, named after a cremation ground in Bodhgaya, India (Shiva-tsal). In this symbolic field of death, pilgrims must leave behind a personal item – clothing, a lock of hair, or even a few drops of blood – as proof of being there. A rock pillar in the middle of Siwachal is covered with scraps of cloth and bracelets.

Toiling upward, you reach Drolma La, which is the focus of the entire kora. Drolma La means 'Pass of Tara': a large boulder depicting Tara is festooned with prayer flags. Tibetans attach their own prayer flag, and leave coins, locks of hair or other mementoes of their passage; they fling windhorse squares into the air and shout *Tso tso tso! Lha Gyalo!* (Victory to the gods!). Down the other side of the pass is a beautiful greenish tarn, Gaurikund Lake – Hindus are supposed to take a dip here, but ice skating might be more appropriate. You continue down, down, down – on a descent that is taxing on the knees – to meadows where Tibetans picnic. Eventually, you reach Zutrul Phuk Gompa, which has a basic concrete guesthouse attached.

Day four Around the Kailash kora are relics left by the great cave-dwelling ascetic Milarepa, who engaged in a competition with sorcerer Naro Bon Chun. At Zutrul

Puk Gompa, the reconstructed monastery encloses a cave that Milarepa fashioned with his bare hands – there's a statue of him within. The caretaker monk will show you around, although you may need a flashlight. The final showdown between Milarepa and Naro Bon Chun is said to have taken place on the peak of Kailash: in the ensuing duel, Naro Bon Chun fell, and in so doing, is said to have carved a long vertical cleft in the mountain's south face.

And so, totally wasted, totally knackered, you head back to Darchen to complete the Kailash circuit. Fortunately it's a level or downhill walk to Darchen, and it doesn't take that long to dribble back into town.

Chiu Gompa

South of Darchen is a scene that frequently appears in photographs of Kailash: a monastery crowning a hill in the foreground and Kailash poking up in the background. The monastery is Chiu Gompa, the most impressive of the gompas encircling Lake Manasarovar. It's an easy drive from Darchen. The ancient monastery is thought to have been the last resting place of sage Padmasambhava. You can work your way up to the top chapel, with views of the entire area. A family-run guesthouse is located near Chiu Gompa, and close to this are some sulphurous hot springs channelled into a pool, where it's possible to wash your hair.

Manasarovar

Tibetans undertake several koras in the Kailash region: the first of Kailash itself, the second of Lake Manasarovar, and then a visit to Tirtapuri (some pilgrims tackle Lake Manasarovar first). Lake Manasarovar draws Hindu pilgrims who come for ritual bathing in the icy waters: full submersion in the waters is claimed to ensure enlightenment (Tibetan Buddhists, by contrast, settle for a sip and a splash over the head). Indian pilgrims pick up pebbles from the lakeside and fill containers with holy water when returning home. A 90km walking circuit around the lake takes about four to five days. The route is perfectly flat and lies at 4,560m in altitude.

Eight monasteries encircling the shores of the lake were once so sited to represent the Dharma wheel with its eightfold path. They were destroyed during the Cultural Revolution, but some have been partially restored and remain active. Even if you don't attempt a circuit of Manasarovar, it's well worth driving past Chiu Gompa as far as Gurla La for a glimpse of magnificent Gurla Mandhata. If you can, try and continue as far as Burang.

If contemplating the Manasarovar circuit, you would probably need a pony or donkey assistant to carry camping gear and food; bring sunscreen and insect repellent. You can start and end the circuit at Chiu Gompa, where there are places to stay. An alternate starting point is the town of Huore (where horses can be hired), ending at Chiu Gompa again (not a complete circuit, but close) – this will cut down the walking time. Foreigners rarely undertake the Manasarovar circuit (usually they are spent after the Kailash trek) but the lake offers pristine hiking, with bird-life visible at certain parts, and a slew of monasteries or ruins along the way. The route usually proceeds from Chiu Gompa past Langpona and Serlung gompas to Trugo and Gosul gompas, passing by the small lake of Tseti Tso, and continuing north back to Chiu Gompa.

Raksas Tal

While Manasarovar is identified with the positive forces of light (the sun), the lake next door, Raksas Tal, is aligned with the forces of darkness (the moon). For this reason, Raksas Tal is shunned by pilgrims – its waters are rumoured to be poisonous (actually, they're not), as opposed to the healing waters of Manasarovar.

The road to Burang

Right down south, close to the Nepal-India border, is the old trading town of Burang – also known as Purang or Taklakot. Burang lies at 3,900m in elevation. The distance from Darchen to Burang is around 110km, or a three-hour drive. Indian pilgrims enter via Lipu Lek Pass and Burang to get to Darchen; Western trekkers are permitted to take a five-day hike from Simikot (in Nepal) to Burang (or over the Lipu Lek Pass), and take a Landcruiser to Kailash. However, since this area is a Maoist stronghold, Western tour operators will probably avoid it altogether. As an individual, you won't be able to cross here, but regardless of this, Burang makes a great drive from Darchen, passing between Lake Manasarovar and Lake Raksas Tal, and driving right by Mount Gurla Mandhata.

Gurla Mandhata, though 7,728m high, appears to be quite low from this perspective, and the summit appears so close you almost imagine you could get out and start walking up it. Which is exactly what a couple of American climbers once did (unofficially), telling their startled driver to come and fetch them in a few weeks, after they'd bagged the peak! Gurla La, a pass of 4,600m, offers spectacular vistas, as does Ara La (4,200m): continuing southward are the pretty villages of Garu and Topa, with handsome, hand-crafted houses.

Burang is an old caravan stop on the banks of the Karnali River. Today it functions as a military outpost, with lots of men in green running around. It is aligned along a north-south road: at the north side is a military checkpost (your documents will be scrutinised); toward the southern side are some small restaurants and shops, an expensive guesthouse, and the post office, bank and PSB office. Staying in Burang is a problem as the sanctioned guesthouse is an overpriced dump. It's difficult to find an alternative. While restaurants are mediocre, you may be able to buy fresh vegetables at a street market and take them to a restaurant to be stirfried. Stocks of canned fruit and other items are quite good.

There's good hiking and a few things to see in Burang – you can combine several options by taking a western fork out of town. Head toward a bridge that spans the Karnali at the northern end of Burang. There's a small bazaar selling clothing, and some food (a small eatery here) with a few snooker tables. Continue west on a trail that leads up a steep hillside. Set into the cliff face is a remarkable cave-temple, Gokung Gompa. The caretaker monk will show you around for a token fee – the monastery ranges over three storeys, set within caves. Cave-dwellings are used as houses in this area. If you carry on over the top of a crest, you'll come to the Nepalese Bazaar, where Nepalese goods are sold in exchange for Tibetan wool, which is rolled into huge balls. Concrete shopfronts offer Nepalese and Indian goods, portered in from the Nepalese town of Darchula.

To the northwest of Burang, on a hilltop, you can make out the ruins of Shembaling Gompa. Once the largest monastery in the region, it housed several hundred monks, but was completely destroyed in the Cultural Revolution. Today the biggest active monastery in the region is at the pretty village of Kojinath (Korja or Kojarnath), situated 15km southeast of Burang, on the Karnali River right near the Nepalese border.

Kumbum, Amdo

Amdo, Kham and East Tibet

TIBET OUTSIDE THE TAR

Tibetans are today found scattered through areas of
western China bordering the TAR. In fact,
according to Chinese statistics, there are more
Tibetans in the Chinese provinces adjoining the
TAR than there are within the TAR itself.

Vast tracts of what were formerly the Tibetan
territories of Kham (east of Lhasa) and Amdo (northeast of Lhasa) were carved off
by the Chinese into four neighbouring provinces of the TAR. Tibetans referred to
this area as 'Four Rivers, Six Ranges' – later used as the name of a Khampa guerrilla
resistance movement. The Chinese christened the new slabs of territory 'Tibetan
Autonomous Prefectures' (TAPs). The process started under the Chinese KMT
regime before 1949, and continued under the communist government from 1950
into the 1980s. The historic Tibetan region of Amdo falls into present-day western
Gansu and Qinghai provinces, while the historic region of Kham falls into present-
day western Yunnan and Sichuan provinces. Some of the TAPs are enormous:
Ganzi TAP in Sichuan, for instance, covers about one-third of Sichuan's land area.
On the fringes of the plateau are a number of smaller areas called Tibetan
Autonomous Counties (TACs), where Tibetans and other nationalities live in
mixed communities. Some TAPs are also occupied by Tibetan-related minority
groups, such as the Qiang people of northern Sichuan. The ethnic Tibetan area can
be roughly correlated with the Tibetan plateau. On the plateau, the Tibetan nomad
culture is still present: where the plateau drops off, the descent is made to Chinese
towns. However, there has been lots of Chinese infiltration since the 1950s.

Major overland routes

The descriptions in this chapter are route-based for the simple reason that Amdo
and Kham cover vast areas. Few foreigners visit the Tibetan communities in these
parts, but travel is easy enough because these areas are not classed as 'Tibet', so
stringent travel restrictions imposed by the Chinese don't apply here. There is
much to explore here – enough to keep you busy for months. If you exited Tibet
via Golmud, for instance, you could make your way to Xining, and then follow a
great route southward via the Aba grasslands to Chengdu, passing through ethnic
Tibetan areas (travel through Gansu and Sichuan is far more pleasant than travel
through barren Qinghai province, which is known as the black hole of China, with
many prison camps). And from Chengdu, you could spend another month taking
the high route through Litang and Zhongdian to Kunming, and then exit overland
into Vietnam. None of this requires permits. However, deeper in, toward the TAR
borders, the policies of PSB offices vary – some turn a blind eye, while others jump
on travellers and turn them back if they appear to be headed overland toward Lhasa
(which they invariably are).

Key destinations in Kham and Amdo are the larger monasteries, the objective of pilgrims who travel great distances to see them: Kumbum, Labrang, Tongren, Derge and Jyekundo.

Following up

There are 2,700 pages of further reading, along with photos, maps, charts and other data on the CD-ROM *Tibet Outside the TAR* (produced 1997, available through ICT, Washington). ICT also distributes a separate map of Kham and Amdo, titled *The Eastern Regions of Tibet*, with cartography by Academica Tibetica (available through the ICT website at www.savetibet.org/). An excellent website for finding out about travel in Kham is www.khamaid.org/travel/.

ROUTES THROUGH AMDO
with Bradley Rowe
Route 1: Lanzhou, Xining, Kokonor and the route to Golmud
Lanzhou to Xining

The Tsong Chu Valley flows through Xining and then down off the Tibetan plateau to join the Yellow River near Lanzhou. This route has for many centuries been the main access to northern Amdo and formed an important part of the Silk Road. Old explorers had difficulties in the gorges but now the road and rail link between Lanzhou and Xining only takes half a day.

Coming from Lanzhou the first county of note is **Minhe**, which has a large smelting industry and is generally unattractive. However, in the surrounding mountains are branches of the Tusu (Mongour) people, a Turko-Mongol tribe who held administrative posts during the Mongol Dynasty in China. They have their own language, costumes and customs but their written language was only developed last century. They have long been Tibetan Buddhists and several of the tiny monasteries in this region were established by Tibetan (Karmapa and Sakyapa) lamas on visits to the Chinese courts, although most have since been taken over by the Gelukpa sect. The only one of note to survive is Qutansi, 20km south of the county town of Ledu. Qutansi has some unique murals and is based on the forbidden city in Beijing.

Further upstream, the county town of **Pingan** is at a crossroads 30km before Xining, and a road leads north 55km to the main Tusu county of Hodru. The large monastery of Gonlung is located in a side-valley before the county town and can easily be reached from Xining within a couple of hours. At festival time you can see Tu embroidery, but for most of the time these people wear Chinese clothes. A short walk across the river from Pingan brings you to White Horse Temple (*Beimasi* in Chinese). It is connected with three monks who fled Central Tibet in the 9th century to maintain the Buddhist lineage.

To the south of Pingan the road leads to Hualong and Tongren (see *Route 2* description, page 228). **Taktser**, the birthplace of the present Dalai Lama, is about 20km southwest of the county town, and about 7km from the small attractive monastery of Shadzong. Tsongkhapa spent some years here, and nowadays this small forested zone is popular with picnickers at weekends. Taktser itself is situated on a ridge above the valley: the Dalai Lama's house was reconstructed in 1986. The easiest way to visit these sites is to hire transport for a day in Xining or try your luck hitching at the turn-off. A little-used side-road leads through the hills from Taktser to Kumbum.

Xining

Xining and Lanzhou are the twin transport hubs of the Amdo (Qinghai and Gansu) region. They are both large, ugly, commercial Chinese cities with little to see. Xining has a strong Islamic presence, with many Hui Muslims living here. You can use Xining as a springboard for day trips to the nearby Kumbum monastery, birthplace of Tsongkhapa, or to Taktser, birthplace of the Dalai Lama.

Like Lanzhou, Xining is well connected by air, rail and road. Flights on a variety of domestic carriers connect the city with Beijing, Shanghai, Guangzhou, Chengdu, Urumqi, Xian and Lhasa. There are frequent rail connections east on the Lanzhou-Xian line (which carries on to Beijing and Shanghai), and to the west to Golmud. Buy tickets at least a day in advance. The long-distance bus station, just south of the train station, handles routes to various points within Qinghai Province, though service to some points is not daily. From this bus station, and also from the main railway station, there are overnight buses leaving for Golmud. There's also a through bus to Lhasa, but foreigners will most likely be forced off it in Golmud and told to buy the exorbitant foreigner-priced ticket from Golmud to Lhasa.

Xining PSB is located on Bei Dajie: you might be able to get a visa extension of one month here. Xining and Golmud are the only cities where you can be sure of changing foreign currency, so stock up at the Bank of China (there are two branches in Xining). Right near the BOC on Bei Dajie is the main post office.

A good place to stay is Xining Binguan, to the west side of the city, which has comfortable dormitory beds in 3-bed rooms for around Y50 each, including hot shower. A double with satellite TV will run around Y240. Several travel companies and CITS have offices at Xining Binguan. Opposite the bus station is the cheap and popular Yongfu Hotel, but it is noisy, and sneak thieves abound in this area. A 15-minute walk, or a short minibus or taxi ride on the main road south of the train station, is the upgraded Xining Dasha, with rooms from Y180. High-end hotels include Qinghai Binguan.

Food in Xining ranges from Sichuan and Cantonese styles to Uighur-style kebabs and Muslim restaurants. You can find night markets with cheap fare: try the area opposite Xining Dasha (hotel) or south of Xining Binguan for foodstalls and small eateries.

Kumbum

A 40-minute bus ride west of Xining covers the 27km to Kumbum (Taersi in Chinese), the most famous monastery in Amdo and one of the six great Geluk monasteries of the Tibetan plateau. In its prime, Kumbum once housed 3,000 monks, but under Chinese rule it was closed down for a period: since it reopened in 1979, the monastery has housed about 400 monks, with half the buildings functioning in museum mode. The former abbot, Ajia Rinpoche, fled in 1998 to seek asylum in the US: he was the highest-ranking monk in the Chinese Communist Party. Situated in the largely Muslim county of Huangzhong, the temples here were protected during the Cultural Revolution and contain some of the greatest artworks of Amdo. However, Kumbum is a major Chinese destination, and the monks are tightly controlled, which affects the atmosphere. There is a guesthouse here with rooms ranging from US$5 to US$15, though you can base yourself in Xining and visit for the day by public bus or minibus taxi.

Kumbum is the birthplace of Tsongkhapa, founder of the Gelukpa sect in the early 15th century. Inside a spectacular green-tiled building is a silver pagoda containing the earthly belongings of Tsongkhapa. The monastery is thought to have been built (in the 16th century) around a legendary pipal tree, said to bear a Buddha-like image on every leaf. The tree is accredited with magical powers. The temple is famed, too, for its elaborate yak-butter sculptures – in the shapes of animals, landscapes and religious figures – which can reach 15m in length.

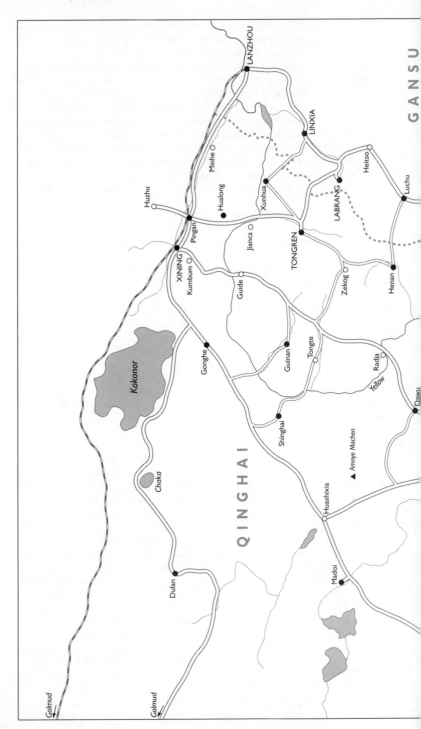

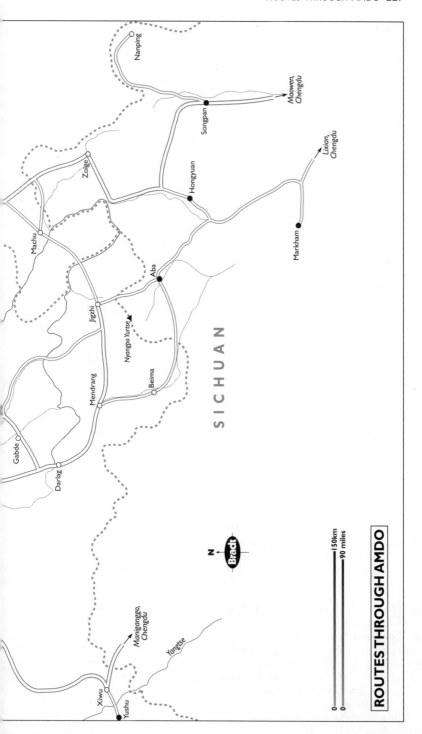

ROUTES THROUGH AMDO

Festivals at Kumbum attract large numbers of Tibetan pilgrims. Because Kumbum is easily accessed (being so close to Xining) it unfortunately also attracts large numbers of Chinese tourists, who stand next to cardboard cutouts to have pictures taken. The monastery has a disturbingly commercialised air about it. The best times to visit are at festival times (tour agents in the Xining hotels can tell you of any up and coming festivals).

Kokonor to Golmud

From Kumbum, the main road continues west to the Sun Moon pass (about three hours by bus from Xining) from where a main road leads south to Gonghe and Yushu (see *Route 4, Xining–Madoi route*) while a very good tarmac road continues west to Kokonor Lake. The Sun Moon pass was made famous in the 7th century, when the Chinese Princess Wencheng, en route to meet her intended husband, King Songtsen Gampo in Lhasa, wept here. Her tears are said to have formed a river flowing east to west into the lake.

Kokonor, or Blue Lake, which gives Qinghai province its name (in Chinese), is a huge freshwater lake with excellent pastureland in the surrounding hills. The rail link goes north of the lake but the road continues for over 100km on the south side through fields of yellow rape and wheat. Many of the farmers are recent Muslim immigrants, and there are some tensions with the Tibetan herdsmen, whose winter pasture they have taken over.

By the side of the lake is Qinghai Lake Guesthouse, built in mock-Tibetan style. This is quite popular with tour groups, though expensive for budget travellers. The tour boat to the small island in the middle of the lake has a capacity of around 60 people and costs US$200 to hire for the day, so casual visitors must hope to join a pre-existing tour. On the western side of the lake, 53km from the cheap guesthouses at Heimahe, is Niao Dao, a bird sanctuary inhabited by cormorants, and, in spring, by bar-headed geese, gulls, terns and even an occasional black-necked crane.

Further east is **Chaka**, a large, heavily-mined salt-lake in a Mongol county. Then the road descends into the Tsaidam, where the Kunlun mountains are found to the south and a marshy desert lies to the north. The only town of note is Dulan, currently the site of a major immigration project. The road continues endlessly past Lao Gai prison settlements which appear neat and well-maintained, before finally reaching **Golmud**, 780km from Xining. Golmud has grown into a huge metropolis to service the nearby mining industries: when British writer, Peter Fleming, visited in the 1930s, he found barely a dozen houses. Sleeper-bus tickets to Lhasa, costing an exorbitant Y2,000 each for foreigners (including permits and three-day Lhasa tour) can be purchased at Golmud Binguan, about 15 minutes' walk from the train station. You could also try your luck for cheaper rates at the bus station. Construction is under way on a controversial rail link to Lhasa (see pages 14–15).

Route 2: Xining/Lanzhou via Labrang and Songpan to Chengdu
Lanzhou to Labrang

Buses, minibuses and shared taxis run regularly from Lanzhou to Linxia (170km), and a further 98km to Labrang, taking five to nine hours for the entire journey, at a cost of US$4–15 per head. Local insurance is compulsory in Gansu and should be purchased at the hotel tour agencies before buying a bus ticket.

Linxia is a large, old Muslim county town in an agricultural region where villages specialise in single products, such as garlic or watermelons. Just south of here, a side-road leads east, over a pass, 80km to **Xunhua**, a county town on the banks of the Yellow River. Xunhua is the home of the Salar Muslims who settled here from Central Asia six centuries ago. There are some small Tibetan monasteries in the hills around, and the road continues to Tongren.

From Linxia the main road goes south to Heitso and Sichuan. Shortly before the turn-off to Labrang is a white chorten which marks the traditional border of Labrang's influence and the gateway to Amdo.

Xining to Tongren

From Pingan, the road heads south out of the Tsong Chu valley and then slowly descends towards the Yellow River. After 30km, the road leaves Tsong Chu Valley and descends towards the gorges of the Yellow River. A short way after the pass is a turn-off, which after 30km leads to the important, stunningly located, monastery of Shachung. Built on a precipice overlooking the Yellow River, this monastery is where Tsongkhapa 'cut his hair' (that is, took his vows). Tractor taxis are usually found at the turn-off and will take you down to the monastery for under a dollar. Further along the main road, a side-road leads down to Liujiaxia, a modern town with a reasonable guesthouse built to serve the nearby hydro-electric dam. The resulting lake can be crossed by ferry into a provincial nature park containing the important Nyingma monastery of Achung Nam Dzong, and a nearby nunnery. This wooded region contains imposing mud stacks, one of which is a retreat centre.

The main road turns east toward Hualong before descending to the Yellow River, where it continues eastwards along the northern bank. Shortly before the turn-off to Tongren is another bridge to the small and rarely visited county of Jianca (Jentsa in Tibetan), which is 75km from Pingan. There are several monasteries in the hills and villages around, the most important of which is Lhamo Dechen, a reconstructed Geluk gompa set in the hills 25km away. Several small Nyingma temples are in the villages on the rough roads to Liujiaxia on the south bank. Jianca's county guesthouse is cheap and reasonably clean.

Thirty kilometres further on, the main road crosses a bridge over the Yellow River and continues up the gorges of the Gu Chu, or Nine River Valley. After 20km the valley broadens into a rich agricultural district, in which is found the prefectural capital of Tongren (known as Repkong to the Tibetans).

Tongren to Labrang

Tongren itself is not particularly attractive, but the 600-year-old monastery of Rongwo Gongchen is worth a look. The main attraction of the area are the two small art schools Yangoo and Mangoo (known as Wutun to the Chinese), which are located 6km north of town. These schools have provided mural and tanka painters for all of Amdo's monasteries. Opposite them is a remarkably gaudy but impressive chorten. It's easy to hitch a ride or walk out to the art schools. Back in Tongren, the county guesthouse, close to the bus station, costs US$4–12 a person.

Several other monasteries are found in the hills and 25km south of town is a hotspring where you can bathe. Shortly before the hotspring, a side valley west leads past an important Bonpo gompa toward the holy mountain of Amnye Shachung (Jakhyung).

The road past the hotsprings continues, through patches of forest, on to the grasslands proper, and the wild west town of **Zekog**, 100km from Tongren. This is true nomad country, and roads lead south to Henan and west to Tongte (see *Central Amdo*, page 233). Henan, only 40km south, is a Mongol county where yurts are used in the rich pastureland rather than the black yak-hair tents of the Tibetans. A side-road from here leads back to the main Sichuan route near Luchu.

Fifteen kilometres north of Mangoo, a side-road leads east, soon splitting towards Xunhua (75km from Tongren) and Labrang (135km from Tongren). On this stretch, before reaching the grasslands proper, there are several small monasteries, the most important of which is Tashi Chi, set on a ridge high above the village of Shongpongsi. Once over the pass there are thousands of yaks and dozens of tents, and the road slowly descends to the village of Ganja, in Gansu. Five kilometres north of town is a small gompa, Draka, where deep caves are an important part of the pilgrim's circuit. It is important to have a monk as guide, and a good torch (flashlight). This is a great trekking area: several small lakes can be visited on a three-day kora in the mountains, but beware of nomad dogs. After one more pass, the road continues 27km to Xiahe, the county town in which the large and important Geluk monastery of Labrang is found.

Labrang

Labrang is currently the largest monastery on the Tibetan plateau and is a major destination for tourists. It is incorporated into the Chinese county town of Xiahe, on a turn-off from the good road between Linxia and Lanzhou to Heitso, or a poor road over the mountains west to Tongren.

The main bus station, at the bottom of the single main street, is 20 minutes' walk from the monastery, and a large number of hotels, restaurants and tourist shops have been built on this stretch. Some minibuses to Linxia and Heitso use a small depot near the top of town. Drivers will pester you to use their taxis or motorised trishaws along this street, but this is only worthwhile if you intend to stay at Labrang Binguan (see below) or have a great deal of luggage. Otherwise, the best advice is to walk past the department stores, post office and foreign police office to the main restaurant area. Leave your luggage with a companion, and check out the hotels at your leisure.

Most hotels are in the Chinese fashion, with concrete corridors and shared toilets (Daxia and Minzu, for example) and beds at US$3–8, although some of the newer ones (such as the White Conch) have en-suite facilities at US$30–50. Individuals often choose to stay at Tashi's (on the left just before reaching the gompa) which has shower facilities, or even the cheaper monastery guesthouse further on, which is very basic. However, the best (and quietest) hotel is the binguan (a major hotel) some 45 minutes' walk out of town, built in the old summer palace. This place has luxury chalets, standard rooms with bathroom, and a few dormitory rooms, at prices from US$7–60. The major disadvantage here is the distance from the restaurants, if you do not wish to use the somewhat overpriced dining room at the binguan.

Labrang was founded in 1709 and rapidly grew to become one of the six great Gelukpa monasteries. The main Assembly Hall was rebuilt after being destroyed by fire in 1985, but most of the other halls survived the Cultural Revolution relatively intact, and contain beautiful works of art. The monks' quarters have been rebuilt in recent years and some are spacious and comfortable. A kora lined with prayer wheels surrounds the complex and is well worth the hour-long walk. The temples and colleges of Labrang can only be visited on a morning or afternoon official tour, priced at around US$4. Labrang acts as a major teaching centre and monks come from not only the 108 satellite gompas scattered throughout nearby counties, but also from central Tibet and Mongolia. Thus the number of monks is somewhat fluid, although there are likely to be around 2,000 here at any one time. There is also a small nunnery and Nyingma temple on the far side of the complex.

You can be sure that with such a large contingent of monks, the Chinese keep a close eye on proceedings. The town cleaves into three distinct populations: Tibetan, Hui Muslim, and Chinese. Strangely enough, Tibetan devotional items like prayer wheels and katas are mostly sold by Hui Muslims (who are Chinese except for their religion).

At a cool 2,900m, Xiahe makes an excellent place for hiking. Foreigners tend to stay longer than intended at Labrang, not only because of the monastery and Western food, but also because of the opportunity to see the surrounding hills and grasslands. Bikes can be hired to reach the Sangke grasslands region, where picnics are available in Tibetan-style tents, and where horses can be hired. The nearby hills offer good opportunities for day walks, and you may be offered butter tea and yoghurt if you reach the nomad camps higher up, but beware of dogs! The most vicious dogs are chained up, but some of the others do present a serious danger if you enter their territory unbidden. Carry a walking stick, some stones, or a 'gokor' (a lump of lead on a string) if you plan to visit these areas. The dogs around the monastery are generally very docile, but still should not be approached.

Labrang to Zoige

Twenty-eight kilometres downstream of Labrang, the road joins the main Lanzhou-to-Sichuan route. About 35km south is the large prefectural capital town of **Heitso** (Tzu in Tibetan). There are several cheap guesthouses in and near the two bus stations. On the outskirts of town is a nine-storey Tibetan tower built to commemorate the labours of Tibetan poet Milarepa. Heitso is a major bus centre, and roads lead east to the Tibetan outpost of Chone, but the main road continues south to Luchu and Lamosi on the border of Sichuan.

Passing through a mainly agricultural district, the road continues 90km south to Luchu (a side-road leads to Henan from here) and on to Taksang Lhamo (Lamosi in Chinese), 175km from Heitso. There are two large Geluk gompas here, situated in an attractive mountain setting 4km off the main road. Tourist facilities are still basic and cheap, but this is a popular destination for many independent travellers. The main road crosses a pass into Sichuan and descends to the flat grasslands around Zoige, 85km from the turn-off to Taksang Lhamo.

Zoige to Songpan

Zoige (elevation 3,470m) is a small county town in the heart of Amdo's grasslands. It has a wild west feel to it: shaggy nomads ride in on their dreadlocked yaks, Tibetan horsemen with sheepskin coats trimmed in leopard skin roam the streets, along with yaks and cows, and in the middle of it all are Tibetan monks, calmly playing billiards at open-air tables. You may be forced to stay in the county guesthouse here as the cheaper (and dirtier) bus station accommodation is closed to tourists. Since all buses leave in the early hours of the morning this means a ten-minute walk in the dark. The monastery on the edge of town has an important medical school but the temples contain little of interest.

From Zoige a road bears west and then south towards Hongyuan and then Markham (see *Central Amdo*, page 233), but the route to Songpan heads through a shallow valley to the south. Leaving the grasslands, the road descends into the still-wooded section of the Min valley just north of Songpan. The road up the Min valley continues to Jiuzhaiguo and Nanping county (see below), but south through some recently constructed villages lies the old trading town of Songpan, 175km from Zoige.

Songpan to Chengdu

Songpan has long been an important trading town for tea, musk, furs and gold. It is an ancient Chinese garrison town with drum towers and walls. Qiang and Tibetan women visiting the market wear elaborate headdresses of amber and coral.

Songpan has become a major tourist destination due to the impressive nearby national parks. New guesthouses and budget hotels are built every year, so the best place to stay would usually be the newest as it has not had time to acquire a coat of filth from the spittle-happy Chinese. The best advice is to leave your luggage at one of the restaurants and wander down the single main street checking places out. Basic accommodation costs around US$2, but en-suite rooms with tiles and granite veneers will run at US$20 a night or more.

Small taxis, minibuses or jeeps can be hired for journeys to the national parks of **Huanglong** or **Jiuzhaiguo**. Expect to pay around US$10 for the 105km journey to Jiuzhaiguo if sharing a taxi with three others, or try joining an existing group.

En route to Jiuzhaiguo is a large Bonpo monastery called Gamal Gonchen, with over 400 monks and a nearby nunnery. Once over the pass out of the Min Valley, there are numerous guesthouses near the park entrance but, along with park fees, guide fees, food and accommodation, you are unlikely to see much change from US$20 a day. Horses are available to ride up the two main valleys, which contain numerous and vibrantly coloured pools connected by small waterfalls on the valley bottom, while the forest extends to the snow peaks above. The scenery is stunning but, although it is a panda park, you are unlikely to see any black-and-white furries – or indeed any wildlife – most probably because the animal populations have been decimated by poachers.

Huanglong park is closer to Songpan, lying on the eastern side of Shar Dungri, a Bon holy mountain, and is cheaper and less visited than Jiuzhaiguo. Many tourists, however, simply negotiate horses and guide for other treks in the mountains around. The most popular currently is a one to three-day journey into the Niao Me (Nyenyul) valley. In this valley lie several Bonpo monasteries, including the important Gyagar Mandi (which is built on an Indian model) and the Sakya monastery of Jara, as well as a famous waterfall called Zaga Pubu and a set of hotsprings. It is also possible to reach this valley by road from a turn-off 30km to the south of Songpan. Be sure to check out the guide and precisely what services you are paying for before parting with any money.

The bus ride to Chengdu takes at least a full day, and delays are frequent after summer rains due to landslides and heavy traffic. The Min valley is a well-forested gorge (where it hasn't been deforested) and many of the villages are set high above the road. The area is the home of the Qiang people, who are believed to be descendants of the ancient Ch'iang tribe that ranged widely across the north of the plateau before the period of the Tibetan kings. Nowadays they are principally agriculturalists, with wheat and maize as their main crops, although many keep a few domestic animals stabled in large courtyards or on the ground floor of their three-storey stone and timber houses.

Maowen, 140km from Songpan, is a very small town around which are many Qiang villages, and is a good place to observe the intricate embroidery and chunky amber jewellery of the Qiang women. Two rivers combine here, and the eastern tributary – the Heishui – can be followed in a loop past Murge Gompa to rejoin the Min further upstream. This monastery is an important Geluk institution and was visited by Mao Zedong during the Long March in 1934–35, when Communist troops were escaping the Nationalist Chinese. Until the late 1990s, this river was used to float logs downstream. The massive deforestation since the fifties halved the area's forest cover but, after flooding in central China, a logging ban was imposed, and there are now tentative signs of replanting.

Further south, the major town of **Wenchuan** is architecturally uninspiring; apart from its attractive setting, there is only a colourful market to recommend it. An important bridge crosses the Min here and a rugged road leads west to

Markham. Further south, a side-road leads west to the Wulong Panda Reserve and Danba in southern Gyarong.

Finally, the Min valley opens onto the vast red basin of Sichuan at the town of **Guanxian**, 140km from Maowen. This is the site of an extensive two-thousand-year-old waterworks project to divert the Min river into irrigation canals and reduce flooding. A few kilometres from the town is the Daoist holy mountain of Chingcheng Shan, which takes around four hours to climb. It is possible to sleep at Shangqing Gong temple and rise early to see the dawn from the summit. A final 57 kilometres across the red basin brings you to Chengdu.

Route 3: Central Amdo: Xining to Golok, Markham and Chengdu
Xining to Guide and Dawu
Close to Kumbum, the main road heads south over the mountains and down to the Yellow River at Guide, 75km from Xining. Guide is a poor, largely Muslim county town, and there is little reason to stop here, apart perhaps for the hotsprings fed into bathhouses some 15km southwest of town. There are several monasteries in the nearby side-valleys, but all are poorly appointed and there are very few monks.

The main road south has been substantially upgraded and is now the main route to Golok. It by-passes the small counties of Guinan and Tongte. Roads west lead to bridges over the Yellow River from either of these two towns to link up with the Xining-to-Yushu route. Guinan was closed at the time of writing, but Tongte is open, and though it's hardly ever visited, it's worth a day or two if you have the time. All monasteries are outside town – the most important is Serlag, but the muddy track that leads to it may be impassable.

After Tongte, the road leads down again to the Yellow River at Radja Gompa, 220km from Guide, which is an enclave of Golok and has long been important in Amdo's history. Truck-stops and basic restaurants are available on the south side of the bridge and the monastery is at the foot of the holy mountain Khyunggon, which takes half a day to circumambulate.

Golok
Two hours (70km) further south on the grasslands is the prefectural capital of Golok, **Dawu** (or Machen), 210km from Huashixia on the Yushu Road. This is an entirely new town with a single very long high street, although all facilities are concentrated near the crossroads. The county guesthouse, which you may be forced to stay in, is a little more expensive than the others, but offers occasional hot showers.

From here, it is possible to arrange for guided tours of the seven-day **Amnye Machen circuit**, though this can be very expensive. Roads west lead to Xueshan, the traditional starting-point of the seven-day circuit. In trekking terms, this is a fairly easy walk, with two gradual passes of 4,500–4,900m, and is best done in May to October, when pilgrims abound and nomads will have their flocks in the area. Although the trek can be completed in seven days at normal walking pace (around five hours a day), complications could arise with the weather, making it longer. Camping gear is essential. Winter is extremely cold in Golok, with temperatures often below –30°C, and summer rainfall is relatively light and bearable.

From Dawu, a road leads southeast 80km toward the small county town of **Gabde**, which, although officially closed, doesn't appear to offer any problems to those staying a night or two. The side-valleys down to the Yellow River from Gabde shelter several important monasteries of the Geluk, Nyingma and Jonang sects. A small monastery 12km along the main road to Darlag holds frequent festivals attended by thousands of Golok.

Darlag (aka Dari or Jumi) itself is also still semi-closed and can be reached in under two hours (50km) from Gabde or directly from Huashixia (195km) on the main Xining to Yushu road. It is beside the Yellow River and the most important nearby monastery is 15km west of town – a large Nyingma monastery called Traling (Chalangsi in Chinese).

From Darlag, the road goes 105km southeast to **Mendrang** (Manzhang in Chinese) village on an upper tributary of the Yangtse. A rough road leads from Mendrang for a distance of 65km to the Nyingma monastery of Tartang, one of the largest in Golok (a number of festivals are held here each year, particularly a winter festival). Sixty kilometres south of Mendrang is Beima county, one of the most attractive areas of Golok, lying between the rolling grasslands of the Yellow River and the forested gorges of southern Amdo. It is similar in landscape to Serthar, Zamthang and Aba counties in Sichuan and, like these, it possesses many monasteries. Unfortunately, all of these counties are currently closed and visitors to the towns themselves are liable to be sent packing. There are numerous large monasteries in these four counties, particularly Aba, where Kirti gompa houses over 1,000 monks.

From Mendrang the road heads east past the Golok's other holy mountain, **Nyangpo Yurtse** (5,369m), set in a remarkably pristine environment of craggy peaks and lakes, an area not used for grazing. The road continues to the tiny county town of Jigzhi (260km from Darlag), a truly remote nomad town. As before, the main road down to Aba is closed, but there is a very infrequent bus service which crosses the Yellow River twice to reach the county town of Machu in Gansu, from where roads lead to Lamosi and Gahe near Luchu on the main Labrang-to-Zoige Road. If you travel this roundabout route from Xining to Machu, be sure to allow extra days for bus problems or sight-seeing.

This route then joins the Labrang-Songpan route as far as Zoige. Then it heads east back to the elbow of the Yellow River and south 135km to the grasslands county town of Hongyuan (which can also be reached from Songpan in 180km). Hongyuan is a small, modern county set in a broad grassy valley. The large monastery of Mewa lies in a side-valley nearby, and houses over 1,000 monks.

Fifty kilometres south is a turn-off to the county town of **Aba**, one of the richest regions in Amdo, but most likely closed to foreign visitors. Traders from this region, including monks working for the many large monasteries, can be found all over Tibet.

Leaving the grasslands over a pass, the road enters Gyarong, a series of forested gorges where small kingdoms of the Qiang survived until early last century. The dialect and costumes here are distinct from other areas of Amdo. At Sonmalu the main road heads southeast through the county of Lixian to Wenchuan and thence Chengdu (328km from Sonmalu). Around 60km west of Sonmalu lies the prefectural capital of Markham (Barkham in Tibetan), a large administrative centre of little interest to travellers (Markham is 200km from Hongyuan). Villages nearby, however, both on the valley floor and on small plateaus set on steep slopes, are worth a visit. Further west, the road joins the Do Chu river, which can be followed south to Kangding, while further west lie the remote counties of Sertar and Zamtang.

Route 4: Xining to Madoi, Ganze and Chengdu

From the Sun Moon pass, a good road heads south toward Yushu. Buses take two days to reach this prefectural capital, which is part of Kham in Qinghai, and which separates Amdo from the Tibet Autonomous Region.

The early part of the journey is through a fairly desert-like landscape to the agricultural settlements around **Gonghe**, 150km from Xining. This is quite a large, unattractive town, mostly populated by Muslims and Chinese. Most buses stop here for lunch: there is little other reason to visit the place. Further south, the road crosses a mountain range to enter the more Tibetan grasslands in the county of **Shinghai**. This small county town is 17km off the main road, and a road continues across the Yellow River to link up with Tongte. Some 15km south of town, over a small river, is the remarkably attractive monastery of Drakar Treldzong, or White Rock Monkey Fortress Temple. There is a half-day kora around its craggy peaks and several retreat caves in the interior, some of which are associated with Guru Rinpoche and the important Amdo scholar Shabkar. A few nuns and long-haired Nyingma lamas are usually in attendance at the caves; the monastery itself houses about 400 Geluk monks.

Further on down the main road, 165km from Gonghe, the small town of Wenchuan contains little more than truckstop inns and restaurants, with a nearby undeveloped hotspring. At **Huashixia**, a further 75km along, is a similar settlement, where one route heads down to Dawu and Darlag, while the main road continues south toward Yushu. From Huashixia, it's possible to hitch the 40 kilometres to the western side of the Amnye Machen circuit at Xiao Dawu, where there is a small gompa.

Eighty kilometres beyond Huashixia is **Madoi** (almost 500km from Xining), a county town on the western edge of Golok where the grasslands are now diminishing and turning into a sparse vegetation zone more typical of the Changtang. Madoi is slightly off the main road, and from here it's possible to hire – for around US$20 per person – a jeep to take you to the two lakes, Ngoring and Gyaring, which are the traditional sources of the Yellow River. Purists, however, will point to the feeder streams much further west as the true source.

After Madoi there is a stretch of semi-desert dotted with small lakes before the 4,800m pass into the headwaters of the Yarlung, a major tributary of the Yangtse. This is the end of Amdo and the start of Yushu prefecture, the largest and least populated in Qinghai. Qumarleb, Zadoi and Zhidoi counties are in the far west where the upper Yangtse and Mekong fade into the barren Changtang, while the southernmost county, Nangchen, still retains some of the old-growth forest on a rough road down to Riwoche.

It is 330km from Madoi to **Yushu**, through attractive high grassland valleys. The town of Yushu, two (or often three) long days' bus-ride from Xining, actually falls in the region of Kham: it is in the middle of nowhere, near the convergence of the TAR-Sichuan-Qinghai borders, but still outside the TAR. Yushu (known as Jyekundo in Tibetan) was once a busy trading centre for wool and tea; its rich grasslands supported great herds of yaks and sheep. The town's Dondrubling temple complex was totally destroyed during the Cultural Revolution, and then rebuilt. An unusual feature of the temple is the grey-walled, cell-like housing of the monks, of the Sakya sect. Yushu, the only open part of this vast region, lies at 3,700 metres by a river in a pretty valley surrounded by high peaks, with dzong ruins occupying one hilltop. A horse-riding festival is held every year in Yushu around late July and early August.

Fifty kilometres before reaching Yushu on the Xining road lies Xiwu, from where a road heads southeast through fertile grasslands 100km to Serchu county, and on to join the main Derge-Ganze-Chengdu road at Manigango (a further 220km).

ROUTES THROUGH EAST TIBET

This section is very sketchy, and serves only as a brief link between the TAR and routes described outside the TAR in Kham and Amdo. Very few travellers venture into east Tibet because of its lack of key attractions, because transport is difficult, and because getting permits is very difficult (many parts of east Tibet remain closed, probably due to military presence). If you want to get right off the track, east Tibet is the place to go.

These routes are more likely to succeed if leaving the TAR, as fewer PSB problems will arise in this direction (PSB is not likely to order you back to Lhasa). Long overland routes snake from Lhasa eastward through the TAR to Derge (Sichuan) or Deqin (Yunnan). Landcruisers from Lhasa are prone to dropping passengers here because both Derge and Deqin lie just outside the borders of the TAR, and the permit brouhaha stops here. Once in Derge or Deqin, you can do what you like, and nobody will bat an eyelid.

Permits are complicated for the Lhasa to Derge or Deqin routes and permission may be refused outright. You are largely restricted to expensive Landcruiser deals. There are no major monasteries along these routes, but excellent scenic spots and many high passes. Lhasa to Derge or Deqin takes about 14 days, allowing time for sightseeing. With three to four passengers plus guide, the tariff for Lhasa to Derge or Deqin is Y15,000 or around US$1,800 (which is roughly US$450 a person if split between four passengers). A slightly cheaper way would be to get two Landcruisers together with only one guide for the group, but it's still cheaper to fly from Lhasa to Chengdu for that price, or to fly from Lhasa to Zhongdian (near Deqin).

Lhasa to Chengdu is 2,400km via Chamdo (north route), and 2,080km via Litang (south route). On the first part of the route, you could undertake a tour to Samye and Yumbulagang, and then kick off from Tsedang (see the *Central Tibet* section, page 157). Here you enter Nyingchi Prefecture. Highlights of this region include the sacred lake of Basong Tso; the sacred peak of Mount Bonri; Mount Namche Barwa; and visits to Monpa, Lhoba and Tengpa villages. However, most of these places remain closed (possibly due to military presence in these areas) and permits are hard to come by.

Heading out of Lhasa, 48km east of Kongpo Gyamda is a turn-off northward another 47km to **Basong Tso** (aka Basum Tso). This ethereal lake is associated with the legend of King Gesar of Ling, Tibet's epic poem. You can visit enchanting Tsosum Gompa, on an island reached by boat. This small gompa was rebuilt by Dudjom Rinpoche, who was the highest-ranking Nyingmapa lama from the Kongpo area (he lives in exile). There is a two-day pilgrim circuit around the lake. About 10km south of Nyingchi town is sacred **Mount Bonri**, which, as the name suggests, is an important pilgrimage spot for *Bonpos* (followers of the ancient Tibetan Bon faith). Bonpos circle the mountain anti-clockwise, taking two days, but if attempting this, you should allow three days.

An unusual feature of Nyingchi Prefecture is that the altitude can dip quite low, with lush forest and monsoonal weather, and that means that Namche Barwa may be obscured by cloud. At 7,756m, **Namche Barwa** is the highest peak in eastern Tibet: the Yarlung Tsangpo stages a dramatic U-turn around Namche Barwa, cutting through the world's deepest gorge (for more on the Tsangpo Gorges, see the *Geography* section under *Background Information*, pages 4–5). From the area close to Baxoi, the road splits. The more interesting option is to head on the north route via Chamdo to Derge.

Chamdo (3,240m) is the only major town in east Tibet and the capital of Chamdo Prefecture. It's an administrative town of 25,000 people, with a fair sprinkling of highrises and the usual Chinese concrete-and-karaoke mayhem layered on top of dilapidated Tibetan structures. Foreigners who make it through the permit hoops are expected to stay at Chamdo Hotel, which is right next door to the PSB office. Overlooking Chamdo is the Geluk monastery of Jampaling, with close on a thousand monks in residence. The gompa dates to the 15th century. About 100km

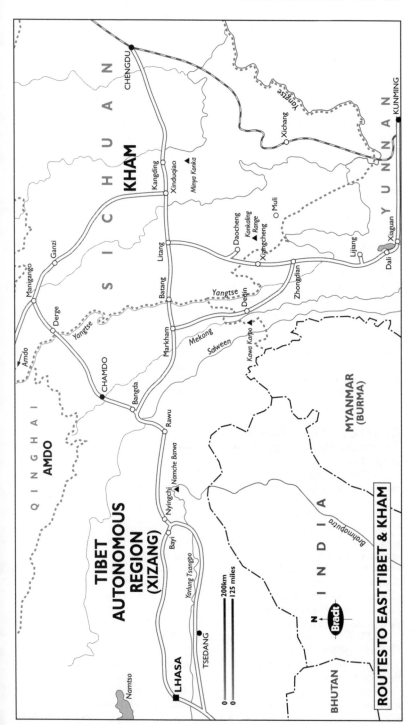

ROUTES TO EAST TIBET & KHAM

south of Chamdo is Bangda (aka Bamda, Pomda or Changdu) Airport, a military airport which now functions as a civil airport as well. Commercial flights from Lhasa to Bangda were tested out in 1999 on Boeing 757s, and there are chartered flights from Chengdu to Bangda. Bangda Airport, at elevation 4334m, is the highest commercial airport in the world. One slight problem for individual travellers here is: both Chamdo and Bangda are officially closed.

Just east of Chamdo is **Derge** Monastery, the star attraction on the long-haul Lhasa to Chengdu northern route. Once you get to Derge, permit problems vanish. The dividing line for the TAR is the Yangtse River, and Derge lies east of that. There are even privately-run guesthouses to choose from in Derge.

Derge (3,220m) is the largest woodblock printing monastery left in the Tibetan world (two others were destroyed, in Narthang and Shol). There are two kinds of ink used here – black for religious texts and red for medical text. Some 300 workers under the direction of the abbot assemble texts by hand for shipment to temples in Qinghai, Gansu or Sichuan provinces, as well as to the TAR itself. The monastery possesses several hundred thousand woodblock plates, and a library with rare Sanskrit editions. Some travellers go all the way to Derge from the Chengdu side and then double back, which may seem like a long detour, but Derge can be viewed as a destination in its own right, with excellent trekking in the area. Detailed itineraries can be downloaded from the www.khamaid.org website.

Linked to the former kingdom of Derge are two other obscure monasteries to the southeast of Derge. Only reachable by horseback (about six hours from the nearest road) is Palpung Gompa, a fortress-style monastery with a complex design, like a mini-Potala. The monastery is a base of the Kagyu sect; the gompa has been adopted by the New York-based World Monuments Fund, and placed on its highly endangered list. Four hours away is the Sakya-sect monastery of Baiya, with rare murals. To the northeast of Derge lies Dzogchen Gompa, one of the most influential monasteries in eastern Tibet. It follows the Dzogchen teachings from the Nyingma order.

ROUTES THROUGH KHAM
Chengdu via Litang, Daocheng and Zhongdian to Kunming and Hanoi

From Chengdu there is a spectacular high-alpine route along the eastern edge of the Tibetan plateau and on to Kunming. This route traverses the area known to the Tibetans as Kham, which was carved off by the Chinese and donated to Sichuan and Yunnan provinces.

You could cobble several routes together: exit by plane from Lhasa to Chengdu, proceed to Kunming, then exit overland to Vietnam. Or you could drop in half-way along the following route by taking a Landcruiser from Lhasa to Zhongdian, or by flying from Lhasa to Zhongdian (same flight as the one from Lhasa to Kunming). Another overland route would be from Lhasa by Landcruiser via Chamdo to Derge, where the Landcruiser drops you, and you proceed by bus to join the following route just west of Kangding. And if you have lots of time on your hands but little money, there's an epic (and perfectly legal) journey by bus from Lhasa to Golmud, on to Xining, and down via Xiahe and Songpan to Chengdu (follow the Route 2 description in the Amdo section). All of which puts you at the starting position for the following route – if you have any kidneys left at that point.

Most of the Chengdu–Kunming route described here can be covered by regular bus. The trip takes two to four weeks, depending on road conditions, the weather, side trips and mode of transport. The route is impassable in winter because of snow, and not advisable in summer when heavy rain can wash out bridges or cause landslides. The best times to tackle the route are April–June and September–November. High altitude can be a factor to deal with: much of the route tops 4,000m and one pass is 4,700m.

In contrast to Tibet proper, there are no problems with permits or police in Kham, as long as you do not cross into the TAR. The whole of Ganzi Tibetan Autonomous Prefecture in Sichuan is open, and all of Yunnan Province is open, including Diqing Tibetan Autonomous Region. Both Ganzi TAP (covering some 150,000km²) and Diqing TAP (almost 24,000km²) border the TAR, and the route described here goes through these regions.

The Khampas

The Tibetan Autonomous Prefectures in Sichuan and Yunnan have a lot more freedom than in Tibet: people appear much more prosperous, with Tibetan entrepreneurs often living in castellated structures (complete with satellite dish on the roof) and driving jeeps. And you will see large Dalai Lama pictures in monasteries in Kham, something that would not be tolerated by Chinese authorities in Tibet itself.

Historically, the Kham region was beyond the reach of the central Lhasa government and was dominated by heads of powerful clans prior to Chinese invasion. The tall brawny Khampas have a reputation as the fierce warriors of Tibet: in the 1950s, Khampa guerrillas engaged in stubborn resistance to Chinese incursions, and protected the Dalai Lama on his 1959 flight into exile. Though considerably subdued under Chinese rule, the Khampas are nonetheless not intimidated by the Chinese, and are aggressive traders who can be encountered as far off as Nepal and India.

Chengdu to Kangding

The bus to Kangding leaves from Xinanmen bus station, which is right next door to the Jiaotong (Traffic) Hotel. So if you stay at the Jiaotong, that would be a head start: the hotel offers a range of options, from three-bed dorms to doubles, and has a cybercafé. Right opposite the hotel, on the other side of the river, is Paul's Oasis, a small bar where travellers get together. You probably need to purchase insurance before being issued a ticket on the route toward Kangding, the first destination along this route.

The road starts out as a super-highway, so you can make fast progress. It's 370km from Chengdu to Kangding – the trip takes a day by bus. Two remarkable pieces of engineering lie en route: about 130km before Kangding, the road bores through the extra-long Erlang Tunnel (which opened in early 2001 and considerably reduced travel time up to Kangding); and at the town of Luding, about 50km before Kangding, there's a fortified suspension bridge first built in 1706, spanning the Dadu River.

Kangding (elevation 2,500m) sits at the dividing line between Chinese and Tibetan influences. It is an old trading town sited alongside a fast-flowing river – a bit of urban sprawl mostly Chinese in character and architecture. However, at Kangding you cross into the vast Ganzi Tibetan Autonomous Prefecture, of which Kangding is the capital. Ganzi TAP is vast – it covers 150,000km², or about one-third of the area of Sichuan. There are a few Tibetan monasteries in the region surrounding Kangding, and right in town is Ngachu Monastery (Anjuesi is a Chinese variant spelling of the monastery name). A good place to stay is the guesthouse nearby, called Gonggashan Lushe, which is run by Tibetans. Up the hill from here is another option, Kangding Binguan which, although expensive,

DOC ROCK GOES EXPLORING

The first Westerner to explore this remote terrain was eccentric American plant-collector, Doctor Joseph Rock. A number of explorers had tried to penetrate the region but failed, partly due to brutal weather conditions, but mainly due to the threat of Tibetan bandits, who were in the habit of robbing pilgrims coming to pay homage to the peaks. These bandits included 400 monks from Konkaling Gompa (Snow Mountain Monastery) who used to rob pilgrims blind and then return to their quiet meditations – apparently not a contradiction in these parts.

In mid-1928, the resourceful Dr Rock enlisted the help of the King of Muli (aka the Head Lama of Muli Monastery) who dispatched stern missives to the bandit chiefs and monks telling them to back off at least long enough for Rock to photograph and write a National Geographic article and to collect flora and fauna samples: the region of Sichuan and Yunnan provided a treasure trove of unusual species for Western collectors, especially for plant hunters such as Dr Rock (the title 'Doctor' seems to have been self-given: Rock never formally studied botany).

Rock rode into the region with a posse of Naxi and Tibetan bodyguards, armed to the hilt. Rock carried two Colt-45 pistols and a rifle himself – a bit of a cowboy. They visited twice during the monsoon season, experiencing torrential rain, which meant the peaks were obscured by cloud. Rock bided his time, lingering to get the photos he needed. When the clouds finally parted, the panorama knocked him out: 'In a cloudless sky before me rose the peerless pyramid of Jambeyang, the finest mountain my eyes ever beheld,' he crooned in the National Geographic article. Of course, Rock was pumping it up for his audience: there are plenty of snowcaps that rival Jambeyang in Bhutan, Tibet or Nepal.

Rock planned a third visit to the region in the dry season, but never made it: the area's robber chief bluntly said next time round he would murder Rock and

has cheaper dorm rooms available. A sidetrip south from Kangding leads to the Minya Konka area. Minya Konka, at 7,556m, is the highest peak in Sichuan.

Kangding to Daocheng

If you catch a very early bus, it's possible to get from Kangding to Daocheng the same day (albeit a long one). Another option is to overnight at Litang. Scenery along this route is stunning, with neat, three-storey stone farmhouses, herds of yaks and mountain vistas. Litang (elevation 4,200m) is a drab town, but it comes alive in August, with a five-day horseracing festival, held on the grasslands nearby. A tented town pops up: foodstalls, games, competitions, folk dances and visiting high lamas draw in nomads from surrounding areas.

Daocheng

Daocheng is the transport hub for this southern border region of Sichuan province. It's a small, bland town, the gateway to Yading Nature Reserve and other sites. There are a handful of guesthouses. The Blue Moon Valley Hotel (triples for Y120) even offers hot showers (there are also some hotsprings near Daocheng). But the best lodging option is a delightful Tibetan B&B called Tenzu Guesthouse (tel: 0836 572 8181). This is a three-storey castellated structure run by a Tibetan family, who can help arrange jeeps for further travels.

his escorts. Rock explains: 'His reason was the obvious displeasure of the gods. Shortly after our last trip around the peaks the wrath of the deities was aroused and hailstones descended in such size and quantity as to destroy the entire barley crop of the Tonyi Besi outlaws.' Rock took the hint and stayed away: he knew when to quit.

But even so, Rock had gathered a 'mountain' of material – enough to fill a whopping 60 pages of the July 1931 issue of *National Geographic*. That issue is said to have inspired James Hilton in writing *Lost Horizon*, a link that has never been proven, but one that brochure writers in Sichuan and Yunnan harp upon. A lot of the *National Geographic* page count was taken up with superb colour photos. Rock was a pioneer in the use of natural colour photography, dragging along heavy plates and developing the pictures on the spot. He would've marvelled at present-day Chinese tourists with their featherweight digital cameras, video-cams, and collapsible tripods.

Rock described Mount Chenrezig thus: 'The peak resembles a huge white throne, such as Living Buddhas use when meditating – a worthy seat for a Tibetan deity!' This is an oblique reference to the Tibetan naming of the three major peaks of the region after deities thought to reside atop the peaks. Depicted in Tibetan tankas (religious paintings), the trinity of deities are: Chenrezig (the Bodhisattva of Compassion), Chanadorje (a wrathful deity, the Holder of the Thunderbolt), and Jambeyang (deity of learning, shown wielding the Sword of Knowledge). The three peaks lie close to each other, arrayed in a rough triangle.

To mountaineers, the three lofty main peaks provide a tantalising challenge. Chenrezig (6,032m), Chanadorje and Jambeyang (both just under 6,000m) are all virgin peaks: they have never been scaled, though a number of expedition attempts have been mounted. There's something to be said, however, for keeping the mountains pristine, with the summit snows untrampled by the boots of mountaineers.

There's a big Tibetan monastery 20km from Daocheng called Yungten Gompa (Xiongdeng Gompa in Chinese), located at the top of a winding switchback route. It can be reached by car from Daocheng in about 30 minutes.

Yading Nature Reserve

Sichuan's Konkaling range has never been easy to get to, or trek around. Yading Nature Reserve is only accessible about six months of the year. You can rule out the winter – when the area is snowed in – and write off the monsoon period, when heavy rains reduce the trails to mud. The best times to tackle the route are April–June and September–November. The sole access route to Yading snakes in over some high passes from the town of Daocheng. It's about 90km from Daocheng to Yading village, at the trailhead. The road is exceedingly rough and is best attempted with a hired jeep, taking about six hours.

The only accommodation in the Yading area is in tented camps. The nearest hotel is in the town of Riwa (the nearest larger village to Yading). On the way into or out of Yading, make a point of stopping at Gongaling Monastery, located west of Riwa. This Gelukpa monastery is the largest in southern Sichuan, housing over 500 monks. In the morning, they're all seated in the lofty main prayer hall, which reverberates with the sound of chanting.

Yading Nature Reserve is a kind of paradise for well-heeled Chinese tourists coming from as far afield as industrial Shenzhen or Shanghai. It embraces a realm of crystal-clear gurgling streams, and luxuriant forests of larch, pine, cypress, fir and oak, and majestic snowcaps with cascading glaciers and odd-coloured glacial lakes.

Human habitation is minimal: there are no permanent residents inside the reserve apart from roving Tibetan shepherds. The nature reserve, first designated in the late 1990s, is pristine and pollution-free; the superb mountain vistas are a tonic for the senses. Shielded by the mountain range, the region has created its own micro-climate, with an ever-changing show of clouds dispersing over the snowpeaks, and a great interplay of lighting conditions revealing new colours.

If all that doesn't take your breath away, the altitude will: it's over 4,000m up here. Chinese tourists come armed with oxygen pillows, oxygen canisters and traditional herbal remedies to counter the debilitating effects of high-alpine air. Touted by Sichuan spin doctors as the 'Last Shangri-La', the region attracts lots of well-heeled Chinese tourists, but remains largely unknown to Westerners.

Horsing around in Shangri-La

Tourists can either hike into the area or opt, as most do, for a horseback ride for the 14km to Luorong pasture. Tourists are led by Khampa wranglers, and seated on woven Tibetan carpeted saddles. The first photo-op stop is near tiny Tsengu Gompa, the only temple in the area. Within a few hours by horse, you reach a view-spot known as Luorong Pasture, 14km from the trailhead, where overnight camping is provided in rudimentary tents. From this spot, it's possible to hike up toward a 4,700m pass to see pristine tarns, including one magical lake where, it is said, the future can be divined. If you have more time, attempt the kora.

To the Tibetans, the area is sacred ground: it is thought to be among the two dozen legendary hidden valleys scattered through the Himalaya, as described in Buddhist scriptures. Each hidden valley is said to have been consecrated by a great Tibetan guru. Clues are contained in Tibetan guidebooks on how to find them, but they are very dangerous and difficult to reach.

Tibetans dream of making a kora of Mount Chenrezig at least once during their lifetime. Assuming no snow or other weather obstacles, a kora can take one to two days to complete. Fifteen koras is said to be equal to the accumulated virtues of 100 million murmurings of the sacred mantra *Om Mani Padme Hum*, so some very strenuous hiking could save considerable wear and tear on the voicebox.

Daocheng to Zhongdian

Daocheng to Zhongdian by road is a stupendous winding high-alpine route: you cross a pass of 4,700m and head for the town of Xiangcheng (elevation 3,000m). Transport may be scarce between Daocheng and Xiangcheng, but Xiangcheng to Zhongdian presents no problem. From Xiangcheng, the road dips through dense forest – a rare sight in China today.

You have now arrived in Shangri-La, according to Yunnan spin doctors, and for the second time if you went to Yading. When you cross from Sichuan to Yunnan, you actually arrive in Shangri-La County (formerly Zhongdian County), which is one of three counties that make up Diqing Tibetan Autonomous Region (the other two counties are Weixi and Deqin). Diqing TAP covers a grand 23,870km? and is sparsely populated, with around 400,000 people, of whom perhaps 30% are Khampa, or ethnic Tibetan. The percentage rises in Deqin County (population 60,000, of which perhaps 75% belong to Tibetan or Tibetan-related minority groups).

The main sight of Zhongdian is Sungtseling Monastery, 5km north of the town. This is a monastic citadel, founded in the 17th century by the 5th Dalai Lama. The

SHANGRI-LA

Nobody with marbles intact would mistake Zhongdian for Shangri-La: it's a bland Chinese city full of concrete and karaoke, which doesn't fit the bill. But Zhongdian is being marketed as the gateway to Shangri-La, in rivalry with other candidates like Yading and Lijiang. This time, all of Diqing Tibetan Autonomous Prefecture is being pushed as a composite – large monastery in one part, classic pyramidal mountain in another – which helps explain the 2002 name-change from Zhongdian County to Shangri-La County. And this will also explain Diqing Shangri-La Airport, the official name of Zhongdian's airport, on the outskirts of town, with flights to Chengdu, Kunming and Lhasa. The Kunming-Zhongdian-Lhasa flights are not likely to run in winter (December to May), but the Kunming-Zhongdian flights probably will. A number of businesses in Zhongdian blithely use the Shangri-La logo without rhyme or reason: Shangri-La Online Tea Bar, Xiangerila Mini-mart, and so on. It's just another day in Shangri-La.

Due to all the regional dogfights in these parts over which place is the real Shangri-La, Chinese authorities came up with a novel solution. In late 2002, they announced the creation of a huge zone to be developed for tourism in western Yunnan and Sichuan, to be called the 'China Shangri-La Ecological Tourist Zone'. Development investment could run to billions of dollars. This drew howls of protest from exiled Tibetans, who say this is yet another marketing ploy to exploit the Tibetans, and that there can be nothing remotely resembling the utopia of Shangri-La if it falls under Chinese domination.

monastery has a spectacular setting and is worth half a day of roaming around.

Zhongdian (known as Gyalthang in Tibetan) rests at 3,275m. With a population of around 15,000, it is the largest town in Diqing TAP, with the most facilities. Various agencies around town claim to be able to organise trips by air or Landcruiser to Lhasa (the plane originates in Kunming, stops in Zhongdian and continues to Lhasa). They seem to go through the TTB Yunnan office, located in room 306 at Kangba Hotel. There are a number of places with email and internet access, like Tibet Café, Traveller Bar and Tibet Hotel.

For accommodation, travellers tend to favour Tibet Hotel (Yongsheng Luguan) at the southern end of town, with rooms for Y50 and up and dorms for Y20. A good alternative is right at the other end of town, a wonderful Tibetan B&B called the Buddhist Guesthouse (tel: 0887 822 7505), with rooms for around Y50 and some dorm beds. It is located at the northern end of town, along the road leading to Sungtseling Gompa. There is no shortage of low- and mid-range hotels in Zhongdian. In the centre of town is a four-star monstrosity called the Holy Palace Hotel (tel: 0887 822 9788), which claims to take its name – and its architectural inspiration – from the Potala Palace. Except that the Potala does not have a karaoke-nightclub warren on the rooftop. The Holy Palace has a mock-Tibetan-style, six-floor exterior and a grand European-style lobby. The 220 rooms go for Y530–700 each.

Deqin

Deqin is a frontier town of about 5,000 souls, and is the capital of the county of the same name. It sits at 3,280m, and is reached by a spectacular ten-hour bus ride from Zhongdian, covering close on 200km. Ten kilometres outside Deqin is

Feilaisi viewpoint, where the rising sun lights up a string of 6,000m peaks like candles. At centre-stage is Mount Kawa Karpo (aka Mount Kawagebo in Tibetan or Meili Xueshan in Chinese), which at 6,740m is Yunnan's highest peak. At Feilaisi's white chortens, Chinese photographers indulge in strange Tibet Chic rituals – chanting *Om Mani Padme Hum*, throwing rice in the air, and tying on prayer flags. The peak of Kawa Karpo is sacred to the Tibetans: there is a small temple at the base of the mountain, on the glacier trail.

Transport is scarce here: it's best to club together with other travellers and rent a taxi or vehicle to get to Feilaisi at dawn and then motor on across the Mekong to the Mount Kagebo glacier trail. A hike or horseback ride takes you to the toe of Minyong Glacier. Another option is to hitch the distance, since these are popular tourist sites.

There is accommodation in Tibetan-style guesthouses near the base of the Mount Kagebo glacier trail, and also a fine small guesthouse at Feilaisi viewpoint. In Deqin itself there are a number of guesthouses: the one with the most character is Dexin Tibetan Hotel (tel: 0887 841 2031) to the southeast side of town, with rooms for Y50 or so. More creature comforts can be had at the Meili or Adunzi hotels; you can bargain for half the posted prices – generally a double is around Y150.

Deqin is the end of the road: it's the furthest point in Yunnan you can access without crossing into the TAR. That means you have to double back to Zhongdian, unless you have arranged permits to cross into the TAR, or unless you are particularly sneaky.

Zhongdian to Kunming

From Zhongdian, heading south, you drop off the the Tibetan plateau, which means you also leave Tibetan ethnic groups behind. However, there are Tibetan-related ethnic groups in lowland areas: the Mosuo at Lugu Lake, and the Naxi at Lijiang. Both groups are matrilineal.

Roads have improved dramatically on the Zhongdian to Kunming route, slashing travel time considerably. The super-luxury express buses can whisk you from Zhongdian to Kunming in 11 hours. But you would be missing a lot by going straight through – it's better to break the journey at Lijiang. From Zhongdian, it's a 200km ride to Lijiang – downhill. **Lijiang** lies at 2,600m: near the town is an Italian-built cable-car that runs almost 3km up the flank of Jade Dragon Snow Mountain, reaching 4,500m at the top of the lift. The rapid ascent can easily cause altitude sickness: Chinese tourists not only rent parkas, they purchase oxygen canisters.

Lijiang is divided into two sections: old Lijiang (Naxi end of town, closed to motor traffic) and new, modern Lijiang (the Chinese end of town). Lijiang's wonderful old quarter is a UNESCO World Heritage Site, but is unfortunately overrun by legions of Chinese tourists who ramble through in unruly groups, ransacking the shops. There are lots of Naxi-style courtyard inns in the old quarter to suit all budgets, and the food is a brilliant selection of European, Chinese, Naxi and Tibetan – quite an eye-opener if you've spent time up Zhongdian way. You can while away time in pleasant cafés and bistros in Lijiang's bustling old town, and sample the local Naxi home-made wine, which tastes similar to port. The old quarter is actually the safest place to be: in 1996, an earthquake levelled the modern part of Lijiang, but left the old wood and stone Naxi buildings mostly intact, which speaks volumes about modern Chinese construction techniques.

The Naxi are an intriguing group. Their ancient pictograph script is thought to derive from *shamans*: Naxi shamans conduct rituals similar to Tibetan oracles. The Naxi not only lay claim to the world's oldest dance score, they lay claim to the oldest orchestra, the oldest musical instruments, and the oldest musicians. Naxi orchestra performers average around 80 years old in Lijiang. That's because they're the only ones who can remember the music, which was banned during the Cultural Revolution and revived in the 1990s. The elderly musicians are now passing on their skills to a new generation of performers.

Northwest of Lijiang lies **Lugu Lake** (2,688m), the centre of the fascinating Mosuo ethnic group. Mosuo women do not marry: they instead take on lovers for the length of time that suits them. Children belong to the household of the woman. Getting to Lugu Lake is a time-consuming, two- or three-step process: you may have to overnight at Ninglang, which is itself of great interest as a market town with minority groups. At Lugu Lake you can stay with a Mosuo family at Luoshui.

About three hours south from Lijiang lies the partly walled town of **Dali**, former capital of the Bai culture, and from here, it's an easy six-hour ride into Kunming by express bus. The best lodging option for Kunming is the Camellia Hotel known in Chinese as Chahua Binguan (tel: 316 2918), which offers dorm (Y30) and mid-range accommodation (Y100-170 double), rents bicycles, and has a great travellers' café called Chamabar. Building 3 hosts the consulates of Laos and Myanmar, and also hosts the office of Mr Chen, who can arrange air tickets to Lhasa and possibly other deals.

Kunming to Hanoi

Kunming is well-connected by air, for both domestic and international routes. You can fly direct to a number of Asian hubs like Bangkok, Hong Kong, Kuala Lumpur, Singapore, Vientiane, or Hanoi. But a cheaper and far more scenic option is to take the old French railway line from Kunming to Hanoi. This depends, however, on whether you are able to get a Vietnamese visa: it should be possible to obtain this in Kunming, but could take time – try through the Vietnam Airlines office. If the Vietnamese visa is not forthcoming, another choice would be to get a visa for Laos in Kunming, go by sleeper bus (or fly) to Jinghong and cross the Laos border at Ban Boten, reaching Luang Namtha.

If you're heading for the Vietnamese border crossing, you can take an overnight train from Kunming (north station) to Hekou at the border. Parts of the route are traversed in daylight: the track runs along sheer cliffs and tunnels through mountain-sides. Kunming to Hekou is one of the world's great train journeys: a marvel of engineering. At Hekou, you clear customs and cross over to the Vietnamese town of Lao Cai.

A highly recommended sidetrip is as follows: take a bus or hire a mini-van for the 30km uphill drive to the old French hill station of Sapa. This region is worth three days to a week of exploring. There are many hilltribes in the vicinity and fascinating weekend markets within reach of Sapa – at Bac Ha, Muong Hum and other places. After a rest in Sapa, you can take another overnight train to Hanoi, or rent a jeep with others and take a five-day jaunt through the Vietnamese highlands to Hanoi. And here, in Vietnam, I hand you over to two more fine books: *Vietnam, Cambodia and Laos* by Michael Buckley (Moon Handbooks, 2002), and *Cambodia: the Bradt Travel Guide* by Anita Sach. Bon Voyage!

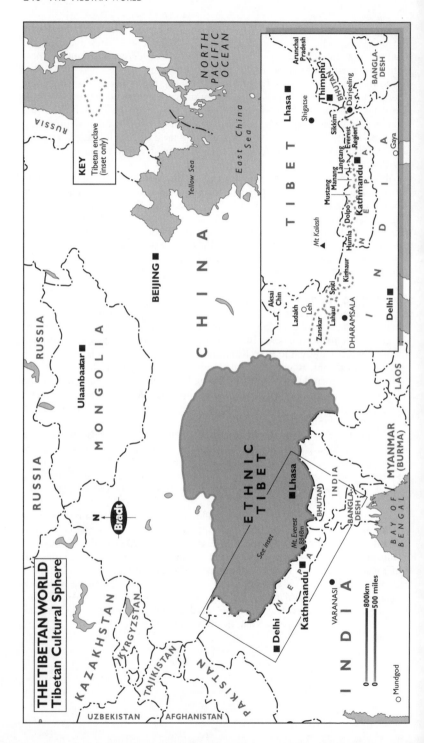

The Tibetan World

A prophecy attributed to the great sage Padmasambhava (8th century AD): 'When the iron bird flies and horses run on wheels, the Tibetan people will be scattered like ants across the face of the earth, and the Dharma will come to the land of the redskins.' Whether this is what he actually said, or whether somebody made it up later to suit the situation, the

Tibetans are certainly widely scattered, but not across the face of the earth. They are mostly scattered across the Himalaya. In the old Tibetan flat-earth worldview, however, they would be at the edges of the earth as the Tibetans knew it (which did not much extend beyond the Asian/Indian continent). Of the following destinations, the most rewarding trips are those to the high Himalayan regions inhabited by Tibetans. Journeys to these places can be stymied by formidable obstacles, both physical and bureaucratic, but if you make it you are rewarded with glimpses of the traditional way of life and festivals no longer seen in Tibet itself.

Probably the most surprising thing you learn as you visit different parts of the Tibetan world is the fact that the Tibetans are not really unified, except in their common beliefs. Tibetans are a very tribal people. Historically, different groups, while they recognised the power of the Dalai Lama (centred in Lhasa), were never obligated to the central Tibetan government, and were beyond its control. Centuries ago, rivalry between sects of Tibetan Buddhism openly took place with, in some cases, battles fought. Tension between 'clans' and rival sects is on-going, even in exile.

For a great overview of these diverse Tibetan regions, a remarkable guidebook is *Mapping the Tibetan World* (Kotan Publishing, 2000). This book is a very ambitious project, covering the entire Tibetosphere in 420 pages, with over 280 maps. Check out the www.kotan.org website for more details. And in the travel narrative line is my own book, *Heartlands: Travels in the Tibetan World* (Summersdale Publishing, 2002). This book is based on a series of trips to different parts of the plateau, from Ladakh to Bhutan, taking in such phenomena as flying hats, giant phalluses and healing oracles.

TIBET IN EXILE

Until the mid-20th century, there was little motivation for Tibetans to leave the sanctuary of Tibet: some Buddhist masters travelled back and forth to India, and certain groups like the Sherpas migrated southward over the Himalaya. The exodus of Tibetans from their homeland really began in earnest with the escape of the Dalai Lama in 1959, who was soon followed by some 60,000 of his people. Today, Tibetan refugees continue to escape, dodging Chinese bullets and biting snowstorms to negotiate high passes when crossing from Tibet into Nepal.

In exile, the Dalai Lama has established nearly 200 monasteries, with over 15,000 monks. There are estimated to be about 140,000 Tibetan refugees living in exile, mostly in India (100,000) and Nepal (perhaps 20,000). The West has been very reluctant to accept Tibetan refugees, although occasionally the doors have opened a crack, allowing 2,000 to settle in Switzerland, 2,500 in the US, and 700 in Canada. In pockets of the Himalaya in India and Nepal, you can see Tibetan culture in a more pristine environment, without Chinese troops and police. Traditions disrupted in Tibet, or festivals that are no longer permitted in the TAR, can be seen in places like Dharamsala. The main Tibetan exile location is India. A rough breakdown of where they live is as follows: in northwest India, about 21,000 in Himachal Pradesh, 6,500 in Uttar Pradesh, and 5,000 in Ladakh; in central India, about 8,000; in south India, approximately 30,000; in northeast India, an estimated 8,000; while 14,300 live in West Bengal and Sikkim.

India's relations with China are cool, perhaps even cold – as in Cold War. Although India was quick to recognise the PRC when it came to power in 1949, tempers flared over border disputes, with a major showdown in 1962. China considers parts of Sikkim and Arunachal Pradesh to be its territory, as it has never recognized the India-China border drawn up by the colonial British in 1914. China lays claim to 90,000km^2 of territory in Arunachal Pradesh. In late 1962, the PLA invaded, humiliating the Indian defenders: their artillery and trucks failed to work in the high-altitude conditions and many Indian soldiers fled. Thousands of Indian soldiers were killed. The PLA were within a few days' march of Calcutta when the US airlifted military supplies to India, at which point the PLA abruptly turned around and left, withdrawing to the old border-line. A few months later, Pakistan ceded 25,000km^2 of disputed Kashmiri territory under its control to China, which enabled the Chinese to build a strategic mountain road connecting Xinjiang to Tibet through the zone of 25,000km^2 of ceded territory (known as Aksai Chin).

In the late 1960s and 1970s China openly armed and trained separatist militants in northeastern India. Since the 1970s, China has given military support to Pakistan, and is believed to be the source of Pakistan's supply of Silkworm missiles – capable of striking Indian cities – and there are strong suspicions that China provided critical expertise and components to enable Pakistan's nuclear testing in 1998. China has given military support and training to three nations surrounding India: to Pakistan, Burma and Bangladesh.

India sees both Pakistan and China as border threats. In 1998, India's Defence Minister, George Fernandes, accused Beijing of stockpiling nuclear weapons and extending military airfields in Tibet. In May 1998, India went nuclear: it shocked the world by conducting a series of nuclear tests in Rajasthan. This resulted in economic sanctions by the US, which are hypocritical considering America's nuclear arsenal. Beijing got the message loud and clear: China is not the only nuclear power in the region. A few weeks later, Pakistan exploded a series of nuclear devices, raising the stakes of destabilisation dramatically. The spectre of three nuclear-capable nations facing off in the Himalaya is all too real, with Indian and Pakistan becoming very confrontational.

Dharamsala

Arriving in India in 1959, exiled Tibetans did not fare well in the hot and humid conditions, and were susceptible to diseases and viruses not found on the Tibetan plateau. Where they could, Tibetans gravitated to mountain zones with cooler climates – to places like Manali, Mussoorie, Bir and Dehra Dun – which are all located in the mountain regions north of Delhi. There is a cluster of Tibetan settlements scattered throughout this area.

The base of the Tibetan government-in-exile is Dharamsala, a former British hill station in Himachal Pradesh, 495km north of Delhi. India tolerates this government-in-exile, but does not officially recognise it: India does not allow Tibetans to engage in political work, but as one exile put it, 'everything we do here is political'. Tibetans do not belong to India either. Most Tibetans are barred from taking out Indian citizenship, so they remain stateless – most just have Indian resident certificates. Even Tibetans born in India – who have never been to Tibet – may choose to remain stateless, although they have the option to take out Indian citizenship. This is due to their determination to one day see their homeland, independent as it once was.

Dharamsala is the lifeline for Tibetan culture. The Dalai Lama resides here, along with the ministers and cabinet of the government-in-exile, and the oracle of Tibet. At Gangchen Kyishong are the offices of the Central Tibetan Administration, with various ministries and information centres, as well as the Tibetan Computer Resource Centre and the Library of Tibetan Works and Archives (LTWA). The LTWA acts as a repository for ancient books and manuscripts from Tibet; a team of Tibetan scholars is engaged in translation, research, and publication of books. Among other educational centres around Dharamsala is the Amnye Machen Institute, a small centre for advanced Tibetan studies; the institute also endeavours to expose Tibetans to western literature and culture through translations. Among their publications is a fine map of Lhasa City.

Knowledge of Tibetan medicine is continued through the Tibetan Medical and Astro Institute, the only one of its kind in the world. It dispenses herbal medicines and trains students in Tibetan medical practices; research on new herbal medicines is also carried out here. The Tibetan arts have been revived through the Norbulingka Institute (for Tibetan artisans) and TIPA (Tibetan Institute of Performing Arts). The Tibetan Children's Village, mainly looking after orphans, is operated by the Dalai Lama's sister Jetsun Pema. In Dharamsala you can see festivals celebrated in full fashion, and Tibetan Buddhist ceremonies that carry real meaning (since they're not restricted, as they are in Tibet itself). Among the bigger celebrations are Losar (new year) and Monlam.

The Tibetan community-in-exile is not as cohesive as you might think. There are various points-of-view on Tibetan independence – some believe in full independence, others in limited autonomy. Some favour the use of force, by fighting a guerrilla war. When it comes to the government-in-exile, the Dalai Lama has tried to establish a quasi-democratic set-up, but this doesn't always work as few would like to oppose him in public. This is where people get confused: opposing a point-of-view of the Dalai Lama is taken as a mark of disrespect.

Educated Tibetans say not enough steps have been taken for ushering the Tibetan community into the modern world – for example, translating modern literature into the Tibetan language. Nor is the faith of Tibetan Buddhism unified. Apart from the four main schools of Tibetan Buddhism, there are a number of off-shoots or sub-sects. A major rift in the community developed in 1997 over a wrathful spirit with three bloodshot eyes, wreathed in the smoke of burning human flesh. Known as Dorje Shugden (Powerful Thunderbolt), this spirit seems to have originated in the 17th century: he is regarded by some as a protector deity, and by others as a murderous demon. The Dalai Lama, beginning in 1976, discouraged the propitiation of Shugden worship on the advice of the state oracle. In 1996, the Dalai Lama prohibited Shugden services in state offices and in government-in-exile-run monasteries, on the grounds that it is damaging to Buddhism. The subject is arcane and complex: several Dalai Lamas – the 5th and 13th in particular – tried to stop the practice and teaching of Dorje Shugden worship. The controversy is on-going: the Chinese, happy at any exile strife, have seized upon the rift to restore Shugden temples in occupied Tibet.

High points Dharamsala is divided into two very different parts: Kotwali Bazaar and lower Dharamsala, and McLeod Ganj in upper Dharamsala. The centre of activity for the Tibetan exile community is McLeod Ganj, set in forested mountain slopes. This laid-back town of perhaps 7,000 has lots of small restaurants and cafés where travellers hang out. There are numerous attractions related to Tibetan culture. As well as seeing the temples, you can visit the Tibet Museum – near the Dalai Lama's residence—offering two floors of displays. Apart from these attractions and the opportunity to take meditation classes, there is excellent trekking in the Dharamsala region, with camping trips of up to a week possible. Other activities include paragliding.

Low points During peak tourist seasons (June and November), the tiny town of McLeod Ganj gets so crowded that it's difficult to find a room in a hotel or guesthouse. People find the place so relaxing they just stay on: there's a very real danger of lingering over apple pie or chocolate cake in the cafés of McLeod Ganj and completely losing track of time.

Bizarre notes Nechung Monastery – the former Lhasa seat of the state oracle – was rebuilt in Dharamsala, with 70 monks studying the sacred rituals surrounding the oracle. The oracle is a man who acts as a medium to convey messages to the Dalai Lama from Dorje Drakten, a protector-deity. The messages are used in important decision-making. Ceremonies where the oracle goes into a trance are secret: the oracle is dressed in a traditional brocade costume and a heavy headdress of precious metals. The ceremonial headdress is thought to weigh 20 kilograms: normally it is too heavy to be worn without support. However, when in a trance, the oracle's strength increases considerably, and attendants quickly strap on the headdress. During the trance, the oracle is said to dance around as if the headdress weighs nothing.

Best time to go March to the end of June, plus October to November. Watch out for the monsoon (July to mid-September). Winters can be very cold in Dharamsala, but February is when Losar (new year) is usually celebrated.

Getting in Indian visas are valid for up to six months (and longer is possible); multiple-entry visas are also available.

Getting there You can reach McLeod Ganj by day or overnight bus from Delhi, taking about 12 to 15 hours for the 495km drive. The closest railway station is Pathankot. There's an airfield at Gaggal, connecting to Delhi, Kulu and Simla, but this airfield does not appear to be much used, and flights are erratic.

Following up A slew of mini-guides to Dharamsala appear on the site dharamsalanet.com (click on 'Holiday and Travel Guides').

Bodhgaya, Sarnath and South India
Bodhgaya, in Bihar state (in north-central India, due south of Kathmandu, and 15km from the town of Gaya), is the place where the Buddha attained enlightenment under a Bodhi tree. The original Bodhi tree was destroyed, but a sapling taken from it was introduced back from Sri Lanka and this exercise was then repeated half a dozen times. The present tree is part of the grounds of Mahabodhi Temple. Bodhgaya is today a site of special significance because the Dalai Lama has conducted Kalachakra initiations there. These esoteric initiations

were once highly secret and exclusive, and were only conducted in Tibet. In the ceremony, the initiator would harmonise inner elements of the body and mind to bring about harmony and peace in the outer world. In an attempt to counter humankind's destructive forces, the Dalai Lama has dispensed with exclusivity, conducting Kalachakra initiations around the world: up to 150,000 devotees have attended initiations in Bodhgaya.

Another Kalachakra empowerment site and Indian pilgrimage site visited by the Dalai Lama is Sarnath, 10km from Varanasi. Sarnath is the site of the Buddha's first sermon at Deer Park, 'Setting in Motion the Wheel of the Law'. Symbolising this sermon is the golden sculpture of the wheel with two deer that sits over the entrance of most temples in Tibet and is the national emblem of Tibet.

Like neighbouring countries, the Indians are not keen on large groups of Tibetans amassing, which explains scattered settlements in central India (8,000 Tibetans) and south India (30,000 Tibetans) where frontier-type settlements were hacked out of humid jungle, and the temples of Sera, Ganden, Drepung and Tashilhunpo were built anew at Mundgod, Mysore and Bylakuppe.

TIBETAN KINGDOMS AND FIEFDOMS

Apart from the Tibetan realms already mentioned in this book (Tibet proper, Tibet outside the TAR, Tibet in exile), there is another realm: a fourth Tibet. It is largely composed of kingdoms and fiefdoms that broke away from Tibet centuries ago, when Tibet itself still had ruling kings. The people in these places speak and read Tibetan, and follow Tibetan cultural practices, but otherwise have developed their own worlds. They do not identify with Tibetan exiles, nor do they particularly want to attract them.

India
Ladakh and Zanskar

The kingdoms of Ladakh and Zanskar (northwest India) originally splintered from West Tibet. Tibetans settled in Ladakh between AD500 and 600. Upon the death of the King of Ngari (western Tibet) around AD930, his kingdom was split between his three sons, one taking Guge and Burang, another Ladakh, and the third Zanskar and Spiti. The kingdoms of Ladakh and Zanskar changed hands numerous times. The most famous king of Ladakh, Senge Namgyal (1616–42), overran the kingdom of Guge in west Tibet, and even threatened central Tibet. By the end of the 17th century, Ladakh's power was in decline, leaving it vulnerable to Muslim incursions.

Due to its strategic location, Leh (the capital of Ladakh) once hosted a busy trading bazaar, attracting caravans from Kashgar, Khotan, Yarkand, Lhasa and Rawalpindi. With India's independence in 1947, Ladakh was absorbed into the Indian state of Jammu and Kashmir. Pakistan contested the borders and seized Baltistan, plus a part of Ladakh and a part of Kashmir. In 1962, the Chinese attacked Ladakh and took over the region east of Nubra, effectively ending any trade. There's now a heavy Indian military presence in Ladakh, to counter potential threats from Pakistan and China.

High points Dominating Leh is a derelict palace, built in the same monumental style as the Potala. There are many monasteries within easy driving range of Leh: some, such as Hemis Gompa, host traditional festivals and monastic dances. Most imposing of the lamaseries is Tikse Gompa, a fantastic complex that occupies a whole hillside 17km upstream along the Indus River from Leh; the main hall houses a 15m-high seated gold image of Maitreya. Another real high point is

Khardung La, a pass 40km north of Leh that sits at 5,606m and lays claim to being the world's highest motorable roadway. There are excellent trekking and mountaineering opportunities in Ladakh and Zanskar – you can put your own small group together and head out with a guide and donkey to carry gear.

Low points In snow-blocked months, the only way in is to fly to Leh from Delhi, and flights are often overbooked or cancelled, or both. Travellers have experienced the opposite – they've made it into remote Zanskar but then have been unable to get out due to heavy snowfall. Faced with the prospect of being trapped in Shangri-La for six months till summer, there are two ways out: radio for an Indian helicopter airlift (expensive), or hike out along the ice on the frozen Zanskar River (slippery).

Bizarre notes Although royalty has largely disappeared from Ladakh, Zanskar still has two kings. The King of Zanskar lives in Padam, and the King of Zangla controls one castle and four villages.

Getting in No special permits are required to visit – an Indian visa suffices. However, certain areas are out of bounds to tourists.

Routes/logistics Due to sporadic fighting between the Indian army and Kashmiri militants, the Srinagar to Leh route is not recommended (although you can travel from Leh to Lamayuru and back to Leh). Travellers use the Manali to Leh route to enter or exit Ladakh and Zanskar (you should also be aware that foreigners have gone missing in the Kulu Valley near Manali under mysterious circumstances – do not trek alone in this region). Although buses have been known to wheeze over the high passes on the 475km Manali–Leh route, it is best negotiated by a 4WD vehicle like a jeep. Along the route lies Tanglang La – at 5,330m, one of the highest road crossings in the world. The Manali–Leh road is generally open from July to October.

Following up Andrew Harvey's *A Journey in Ladakh* (1983) is the classic travelogue about the region based on his 1981 trip. You can access Ladakh information from Rough Guides at their www.roughguides.com website, which also divulges data on other regions of India.

Lahaul, Spiti and Kinnaur

The little-visited valleys of Lahaul and Spiti, accessed from Manali, are very Tibetan in character. No special permits are needed to enter Lahaul, but permits are required for parts of Spiti. Lahaul is reached over the 3,980m Rohtang Pass, while access to Spiti is via the 4,550m Kunzum La pass. Long ago, both Lahaul and Spiti were ruled by the kingdom of Guge in far west Tibet. This is reflected in the now-rare Kashmiri style of artwork found at Tabo Gompa in Spiti, which is similar to that of Tsaparang (Guge Kingdom) in west Tibet. Tabo Gompa houses one of the Tibetan world's finest collections of Buddhist arts, with seven chapels bearing frescos and a number of Guge-style chortens. May to June is the best time to visit these areas. Getting around is possible by bus, hired taxi or trekking. You might consider hiring a Landcruiser for the journey, splitting the cost with several others.

Southeast of Spiti is the Kinnaur region, where local people wear green felt hats. Like Lahaul and Spiti, Kinnaur was once part of the Guge Kingdom. The main focus of pilgrims to Kinnaur is the sacred mountain of Kinnaur Kailash (6,050m), which Hindus set out to circle clockwise. It is thought that Shiva comes from Mount Kailash in west Tibet to winter at Kinnaur Kailash – and to smoke hashish. Kinnaur can be accessed from Shimla; there is also a route leading from Kinnaur to Spiti.

Darjeeling, Kalimpong and Sikkim

Darjeeling and Kalimpong in northeast India were once controlled by Sikkim, but in the 18th century Kalimpong was lost to the Bhutanese while Darjeeling fell to the Nepalese. Eventually, the lands fell into the hands of the British East India Company, which developed the region as a tea-growing centre. Darjeeling is a former British hill station – a cool place at 2,100m, and the base for trekking in the area. From Darjeeling there are views of Kangchenjunga, at 8,595m the third highest peak in the world. There are several Tibetan monasteries around Darjeeling; great places to visit are the zoo – featuring rare Himalayan animals like the red panda and the snow leopard – and the HMA (Himalayan Mountaineering Institute) which was run by Tenzing Norgay until his death in 1986, and now houses a climbing museum and climbers' training centre. Apart from being a resort, Darjeeling is a major educational centre, attracting the children of wealthy Sikkimese and Bhutanese.

From Darjeeling you can take a bus, jeep or taxi to Kalimpong. In the days of British Raj, the main wool-trade route to Lhasa was via Kalimpong and Sikkim through Yadong to Gyantse. This trading route has been closed since 1962 as a result of border clashes between China and India, but there is talk of it opening up again. Kalimpong is a pleasant trading town – famed for its cheese – with several Tibetan monasteries. The town attracts Indian tourism.

Sikkim used to be a Tibetan kingdom – a kind of vassal state. Later, it was run by the Rajas of Sikkim; in 1975, it was annexed by India (China also claims the whole of Sikkim). The story of the demise of Sikkim has all the elements of a fairytale – with a bad ending. In Darjeeling in 1959 the crown prince of Sikkim, Palden Thondup Namgyal, met Hope Cooke, an American on a study trip in India. He married her in 1963 at a ceremony at Gangtok Monastery; two years later he became king and she was given the title of queen. But the match did not sit well with the people of Sikkim. Hope Cooke remained distant: she never converted to Buddhism and she made frequent trips to Europe and America with the couple's two children. In 1973 there was a wave of unrest in Sikkim, and Indian troops took advantage of the situation to place the royal family under house arrest. Hope Cooke eventually left the king, returned to New York with her children, and filed for divorce. In 1975, the Sikkim National Congress voted to incorporate Sikkim into India. The monarchy was abolished, and Sikkim was annexed as the 22nd federal state of India. The deposed king died in 1982 in a New York cancer clinic.

Gangtok, elevation 1,500m, is the capital of Sikkim. Here you can find the former royal palace, the royal chapel, and the Institute of Tibetology, with a fine collection of Buddhist literature. About 25km from Gangtok is Rumtek Monastery, built as a replica of Tsurphu Monastery (near Lhasa – see the *Exploring Central Tibet* chapter for more about Tsurphu) by the exiled head of the Kagyu sect, who fled Tibet in 1959. There are excellent treks north of Gangtok, usually arranged in small groups with permits, porters, and horses. The prize trek is up toward the base camp of mighty Kangchenjunga. Another highlight is the trip up to Nathu La on the Sikkim-Tibet border, to wave Tibetan flags at PLA border guards. There are indications that this border is porous – group tours may be permitted to cross into Tibet here, or exit Tibet.

When to go Best months are April–May (spring flowers in bloom) and October–November (post-monsoon). Winters are cold, with occasional snowfalls.

Getting in Darjeeling is open without permit. You can obtain a two-week permit for Sikkim in either Darjeeling or Siliguri, and an extension of two more weeks should be possible (longer permits for Sikkim may require booking a trek with an agency in advance).

Routes/logistics Half of the thrill is getting there: the 'toy train' – a narrow-gauge railway completed in 1881 – winds up from Siliguri for the 80km to Darjeeling, passing tea plantations and misty mountains. The closest airport to Darjeeling and Kalimpong is Bagdogra. You can overland from Darjeeling via the border town of Kakarbhitta to Kathmandu.

Following up A mixed photographic work and travel narrative is *Footsteps in the Clouds: Kangchenjunga a Century Later*, by Pat and Baiba Morrow (Raincoast, 2000).

Nepal

Nepal is a small country sitting on a border shared with an up-and-coming super-power. The Nepalese have no desire to confront the PLA, so the Nepalese government has worked closely with the Chinese since their invasion of Tibet, and fully supports the Chinese position in Tibet. In the late 1960s the Chinese requested help in snuffing out Khampa resistance operating from Nepalese territory, in the region of Mustang. After the Dalai Lama appealed to the Khampas to lay down their arms, the Nepalese Army surrounded the last guerrillas in Mustang and ambushed them. Most were killed; the rest were thrown in jail for lengthy periods.

Since the entire royal family was gunned down in mid-2001, Nepal has experienced great instability. Ferocious battles broke out with Maoist insurgents in border regions and in the west. It's best to keep up-dated on this situation through websites (see website listings in *Appendix 3*, pages 277–81).

Nepal is the main conduit for refugees escaping Tibet. They hike over high passes to the south of Tingri and Sakya. Refugees run a gauntlet through Nepal – Nepalese police routinely rob Tibetans and there have been cases of them raping Tibetan women. The Nepalese have in the past co-operated with the Chinese in handing over escaping Tibetans, although this policy seems to vary. Escaping Tibetans usually try to reach the safe haven of India, although there are refugee camps for Tibetans in Nepal.

About 20,000 Tibetan exiles live in Nepal, but no politicking is allowed – Nepali officials have sworn to cooperate with the Chinese and swear they will not allow any demonstrations by Tibetans in Nepal. In fact, demonstrations have taken place – on March 10, 1998, some 5,000 Tibetan refugees gathered at Bodnath Stupa to voice their protest, but were barred from walking to the Chinese Embassy by Nepali police in riot gear.

The Nepalese press is blatantly pro-Chinese, muzzling voices that support the Tibetan cause. Oddly, however, Kathmandu is the best place in Asia or the Indian sub-continent to buy materials on Tibet, such as Free Tibet stickers, Free Tibet T-shirts, books, magazines and tapes. It is this material that roadblock searches in Tibet are directed at if you head toward Lhasa by road from Kathmandu.

Two of Nepal's major foreign exchange earners centre around Tibetans: carpets and tourism. The flourishing Tibetan carpet industry – centred in Kathmandu – was initially set up by exiled Tibetans in the early 1960s as part of a Swiss aid project to benefit Tibetan refugees in Nepal. The venture became wildly successful and is a major foreign income earner in Nepal. Tourism in Nepal is largely connected with Tibetans: Kathmandu's most popular temples are Tibetan and the commonest trekking routes are through Sherpa or ethnic Tibetan regions.

Sherpas, a group that migrated from Tibet centuries ago, are directly involved in the tourist, trekking and mountaineering industries. They are often wealthy business people who run lodges, guide groups and so on. Sherpas speak a language similar to Tibetan – they can converse with Tibetans, but have no written language.

They are followers of Tibetan Buddhism. Sherpas have been sympathetic to the Tibetan cause, and have formed a kind of 'underground' to help arriving refugees in Nepal. There are probably around 20,000 Sherpas living in Nepal, with the strongest base around the Khumbu area. Sherpas are identified by their last name 'Sherpa' as in Jangbu Sherpa or Tashi Sherpa. Other Tibetan-related groups in Nepal are the Lhobas from Mustang and the Dolpopas from Dolpo.

High points In Kathmandu, Bodnath Stupa is the main Tibetan temple area, surrounded by Tibetan-run shops and businesses; further out from Kathmandu is the Monkey Temple in Swayambunath. Nepal is the most 'developed' of any of the trekking destinations in the Himalaya. Teahouse trekking is the easiest way to visit regions with Sherpa or Tibetan-related populations – places like Solo Khumbu, Langtang, and Annapurna. A visit to the restricted Mustang or Dolpo regions requires self-sufficient camping trips: usually only in groups, with a liaison officer and special permits worth US$700 per trekker. Both Dolpo and Mustang used to lie on old salt-trading routes from Tibet: Tibetans took salt and wool south to exchange for grains from India. Dolpo is a Maoist rebel stronghold, so is probably difficult to access.

Low points In peak seasons – October especially – popular trails can be jammed with trekkers, and lodges can be full. Near Namche Bazaar, Lukla Airstrip waiting-room can get pretty wild as trekkers and mountaineers duke it out to get on the overbooked light aircraft back to Kathmandu. Failure to make it onto a flight may mean a meaningless ten-day walk back.

Bizarre notes Mustang is a Himalayan kingdom with a real king – King Jigme Parbal Bista – who is the 24th monarch in a line stretching back to the 14th century. His wife, the queen of Mustang, is originally from Shigatse in Tibet. Trekkers take a week to reach the town of Lo Manthang, where the king lives. This is one of the rare Tibetan-style citadels with walls still intact. If the king is around, trekkers can most likely drop in for a quick audience over a cup of butter tea. Not having the time or the stamina to trek for a week, Nepalese dignitaries have been known to drop in for tea by helicopter, landing in a wheatfield next door to the king's humble palace. The king himself, if he goes out to Jomosom, relies on neither of these transport options. He rides one of his horses out, escorted by a mounted bodyguard. The king breeds the best horses in Mustang: one of his horses can fetch several thousand dollars.

Best time to go Go in the October–early December or March–April trekking seasons. Avoid the mid-June to late-September monsoon season – trails are slippery, and roads can be washed out, with frequent landslides and mudslides.

Getting in One-month visas are available on arrival at Kathmandu airport, or when coming in by road from Tibet. Visas are easily extendable. If you go trekking, you need a permit for each region to be visited – these are obtained in Kathmandu.

Routes/logistics Most trips have a start or end point (or both) in Kathmandu. Good trekking equipment can be bought in Kathmandu – a lot is left behind by expeditions.

Inspiration *The Snow Leopard* (Penguin USA, 1996 – reprint of 1978 edition) by Peter Matthiessen is a finely wrought account of a journey to Dolpo. Matthiessen also wrote text for *East of Lo Monthang* (Shambhala Publications, 1995), a photobook featuring pictures of Mustang by Thomas Laird. In the fiction line, *Escape from Kathmandu* (St Martin's Press, 2000, reprint of 1989 edition) by Kim Stanley Robinson takes the reader on a wild ride, with some hilarious excursions to the Tibetan side. Taking a mystical tack on snowboarding is *Surfing the Himalaya*

(St Martin's Press, 1997) by Frederick Lenz. On the net, a website with many links is run by Amaa Consultants at www.catmando.com/nepal.htm. If you go to the news section you can access items like the Kathmandu Post, but be aware that newspapers in Nepal are subject to heavy-handed censorship.

Bhutan

In the Himalaya, of the vast area that was once the spirited domain of the Tibetan religion and culture – stretching from Ladakh to Yunnan – only the tiny enclave of Bhutan survives as a self-governing entity, with Tibetan Buddhism as its state religion (Outer Mongolia, far to the north, is also independent and follows Tibetan Buddhism, but its people and language are Mongolian). With an area of 47,000km², Bhutan is roughly the size of Switzerland, and seeks to be as neutral. It allows India to control its foreign policy in exchange for military protection from China. To protect itself from a take-over by India, Bhutan has held a seat at the UN since 1971.

Although Bhutan was self-governing since the 17th century in a kind of theocracy, the Bhutanese monarchy is a hereditary dynasty started in the early 20th century. Ugyen Wangchuck, previously the governor of Bhutan, was crowned hereditary monarch of Bhutan in 1907 with British support, after his role as intermediary between the British and the Tibetans during the Younghusband expedition of 1903.

The present monarch, King Jigme Singye Wangchuck, has been in power since 1972. He is married to four daughters of a Bhutanese nobleman. Through his efforts, Bhutan has entered the international community, establishing diplomatic relations with many countries. King Jigme Wangchuck has fostered the traditional culture of Bhutan to the point of strong-arming other ethnic cultures. The predominant ethnic groups in Bhutan – the Drukpas and Monbas – migrated from Tibet centuries ago. Bhutan, however, is not a safe haven for refugee Tibetans, whom the Bhutanese fear will build up in greater numbers and power (there are several thousand currently living in Bhutan). Nor are they keen on a large Nepalese presence. The southern lowlands are mostly occupied by people of Nepali origin.

Figures on population in Bhutan vary wildly from 600,000 to 1.8 million. How you can lose a million people on a census is hard to fathom, but it seems that in a 1988 census ethnic Nepalis may have actually outnumbered Drukpas in Bhutan, so the government could have rearranged the population figures to suit. The government banned the speaking of Nepalese, and has an on-going program to boot as many ethnic Nepalis as possible back to Nepal, citing their failure to assimilate to Bhutanese culture and learn the language as the reason for marching orders. Numbers of these people languish in refugee camps in southeast Nepal.

The official faith of Bhutan is Drukya Kagyu, a tantric form of Tibetan Buddhism (and a subsect of the Kagyu order); also practiced is Buddhism of the Nyingma school; in Nepali areas, the faith is Indian and Nepali-influenced Hinduism. Bhutan's national language, called Dzongkha, is related to Tibetan but is quite different from the Lhasa dialect. Dzongkha is a compulsory subject at school, although the medium of instruction is English.

High points Bhutan has a pristine environment, untouched by industrial development, or in fact any kind of development. The best way to see this beautiful land is by trekking or jeep safari; more recently, whitewater rafting and mountain-biking have been introduced. Top treks include the one north toward Mount Chomolhari on the Tibetan border. Bhutan is famed for its traditional festivals, elaborate affairs with parades, Cham sacred dances and archery contests.

Low points The crippling cost of getting into Bhutan may prove hazardous to your wallet, but it's also the factor that keeps the tourist masses at bay.

Bizarre notes The king is so intent on preserving the traditional way of life that it is an offence not to wear the wear the national robe (*kho* for men, and *kira* for women) – a fine can be levied. In addition to the national dress, men or women may wear a ceremonial scarf, and men often wear argyle socks.

Best time to go Best seasons are autumn (November) or spring (April/May). Avoid the June–October monsoon.

Getting in Access is restricted – visitors are allowed only in a group-tour or by personal invitation from a party in Bhutan. This policy keeps the numbers down to around 7,000 visitors a year. They either fly into Paro (west of the capital of Thimphu), or come overland through Phuntsoling. With advance clearance, visas are issued on arrival at either location. On group tours a set fee of US$120–230 a day is levied on each visitor, depending on the kind of trip. This may sound very high, but it includes all the bills (accommodation, food, trekking equipment and transport). Paperwork can take several months to complete if going through an agent outside Asia; in Kathmandu, the red tape can be completed in a week.

Following up Barbara Crossette's book *So Close to Heaven* (Vintage Books, 1996) explores the vanishing Buddhist kingdoms of the Himalaya. Jamie Zeppa's travel narrative, *Beyond the Sky and the Earth* (Riverhead Books, 1999) is an excellent personal take on the kingdom. For up-to-date information and news snippets on Bhutan, check these websites: www.kuenselonline.com (national weekly English newspaper) and www.bootan.com (online outfitter with a lot of information provided about Bhutan – the domain name bhutan.com is reserved by a cyber-squatter).

Mongolia

Apart from a few monastic visitors, there is no Tibetan presence in the independent nation of (Outer) Mongolia. It is not a Tibetan kingdom or fiefdom, but the country is mentioned here because it preserves Tibetan Buddhist practices: the national faith of Mongolia is Tibetan Buddhism. Mongolia makes an interesting case study: it was a Tibetan Buddhist nation under Communist (Russian) domination and then regained its independence soon after the collapse of the Soviet Union in 1991. In the 1996 election, the Mongolian Democratic Coalition garnered most of the seats, ending 75 years of communist rule. This is the scenario that intrigues Tibetans most – the Fall of the Chinese Empire (with breakaway slabs being Tibet, Xinjiang and Inner Mongolia).

In the Stalin era, 700 larger and 1,000 smaller monasteries were destroyed in Mongolia, and thousands of monks were executed by the Russians in an attempt to wipe out Tibetan Buddhism, the predominant faith in Mongolia. A handful of larger monasteries survived (such as the one at Karakorum), and now, out on the grasslands, felt tents (*gers*) are converted for use as temples as Tibetan Buddhism enjoys a comeback. Also staging a comeback is Mongolian military hero Genghis Khan. After the last Russian troops left in 1992, Genghis rode back in, appearing larger than life, on the screen in a four-hour epic movie, playing at cinemas in Ulaanbaatar. Genghis' fat bearded face also popped up on banknotes, and on the label of Chinggis Khan Vodka, a twist for the national Russian beverage.

All of which makes the Chinese very nervous – they're not keen on Genghis nationalism spilling over the border into their zone of Inner Mongolia (Genghis Khan's tomb is located in Inner Mongolia). Genghis brings back bad ancestral memories for the Chinese – in the early 13th century his hordes of horsemen surged with ease over the Great Wall, which was designed to keep them out. The Mongols weren't in any hurry to leave, either – the sons and grandsons of Genghis (particularly Kublai Khan) hung around China for the rest of the 13th century. Thus relations with Chinese-controlled Inner Mongolia are testy. There are hardly any Mongolians left in Inner Mongolia anyhow – out of a population of 20 million, perhaps only two million are reckoned to be Mongolians (the rest are Han Chinese settlers). This is what the Dalai Lama points his finger at: Inner Mongolia has been swamped by Han Chinese and has totally lost its identity.

Relations between Tibetans and (Outer) Mongolians, by contrast, are good. The Sakya sect established relations with the court of Godan Khan in the 1240s – an on-going link. At the court of Kublai Khan in the 13th century, a great contest took place to see which philosophy had the greatest power – Islam, Nestorian Christianity, Confucianism, Taoism or Tibetan Buddhism. The latter prevailed, but it was not until the 16th century, under Altan Khan, that Tibetan Buddhism really took hold in Mongolia. Altan Khan conferred the Mongolian title Dalai Lama (meaning 'Ocean of Wisdom') on Sonam Gyatso (the third Dalai Lama). Despite Chinese protests, the current Dalai Lama has visited Mongolia a number of times since 1990, drawing huge crowds. He has established teachings there through his own monks. With the revival of Tibetan Buddhism in Mongolia, the Dalai Lama has a new ally. Buddhism is also rejuvenating in the Mongolian-populated areas of Russia – Buryatia and Tuva – on China's sensitive border zones.

High points Ulaanbaatar is a dump, with Soviet-style apartment blocks blotting the skyline, but it has an incredible Fine Arts Museum, with intricate bronze statuary and stunning woven or painted tankas, some showing scenes of Lhasa and the Potala. The beautiful statuary in this museum is largely the work of 17th-century master sculptor Zanabazar, who studied in Tibet and returned to Mongolia to spread Tibetan Buddhism.

There are more animals in Mongolia than people – many more – with animal husbandry the mainstay of the economy. With a population of 2.3 million spread over an area of 1.56 million km², Mongolia is very sparsely inhabited and largely untouched – it's one big wildlife sanctuary in a sense, with herds of gazelles, wild camels, wild asses and bighorn sheep roaming the wilderness. That's what is most surprising about a visit to the Gobi Desert – the unexpected amount of wildlife. This is probably the way Tibet used to be. To see this kind of pure environment, go to the mountainous Lake Hovsgol region in the northwest, or to the Gobi in the southwest.

Low points Food in Mongolia – at least supplementary food, aside from the main course – is hard to find, and revolves around meat. Bring your own in the form of freeze-dried soups or meals to supplement the Mongolian meat-based staples.

Bizarre notes Large, whimsical postage stamps feature subjects like a Mongolian cosmonaut (sent into space on a Russian craft), Mickey Mouse, and Fred Flintstone riding a dinosaur past some *gers*. Also featured on stamps are Taras (Tara is the goddess of compassion), and tantric deities locked in *yabyum* (see *Glossary*, pages 271–2) embraces. On the 1-tugrig banknote, the snow lion appears, as it used to on pre-1950 Tibetan money (the watermark on this bill is an image of Genghis Khan).

Best time to go Winter is severe with possible heavy snowfall and sub-zero temperatures, made even more sub-zero by howling winds! In other words, go in the summer, from June to September. The Nadam Fair – featuring horse racing, wrestling and archery – takes place in July.

Getting in Individual travel restrictions have eased up since the 1990s. The easiest way to get into Mongolia is to extend your stay off the TransMongolian Express. Some long-term visas are available direct from embassies from places like London (UK) or Vientiane (Laos). It's hit-and-miss: some embassies issue them, others don't. Monkey Business (aka Monkey Star), a Belgian travel agent with offices in Hong Kong and Beijing, seems adept at getting these visas on short notice – they run tours to Outer Mongolia. You can also get Outer Mongolian visas in Ulan Ude (on the TransMongolian, near Lake Baikal), and in Hohhot, the capital of Inner Mongolia.

Routes/logistics Journeys to Mongolia invariably start and end in Ulaanbaatar. A single passenger rail-line traverses the country from north to south, linking Moscow to Beijing via Ulaanbaatar. There are few roads in Mongolia, but a jeep can go almost anywhere on the grasslands in the summer, so no road is required. As an individual, you'll most likely have to get together with other travellers to rent a jeep. The trick is to find a jeep that has gasoline, as there's a severe shortage of the precious stuff. Mongolia is one of the few countries left where ancient Russian turboprop jets are still in use, on domestic runs. And you may even stray across an old AN-2 biplane parked at an airfield – it may be on display as a vintage aircraft, or it might actually still be in service.

Following up Tim Severin's book *In Search of Genghis Khan* (Atheneum, 1991); on the net, www.mongoliaonline.mn carries limited information in English, while the site www.ulaanbaatar.net tells you more than you'd want to know about the capital.

Snow leopard

Tibet

Appendix

TIBETAN LANGUAGE

Any attempt you make at speaking Tibetan, however awkward, will be greatly appreciated in a place where the language has such a low profile compared to the use of Chinese. It's worthwhile carrying two phrasebooks to handle situations: one Tibetan, the other Mandarin Chinese. Many Tibetans – particularly in the towns – understand some Mandarin, but will most likely not appreciate attempts to communicate with them in Chinese. Phrasebooks become doubly useful if they have Tibetan script: you can point to phrases if the pronunciation is not getting through (this is limited by a literacy factor, however). Good non-verbal communication can be achieved through use of pictures. Examination of pictorial subjects can lead to long dialogue – carry a book with pictures of Tibet, or brochures about Tibet, and carry photos of your family and your city. You can derive a lot of dialogue from learning numbers in Tibetan, and not just for pricing. Numbers can be used in other creative ways: how many children do you have? How many yaks?

Tibetan is a difficult language to speak, with a number of different dialects. Lhasa dialect (the standard dialect) employs a series of rising and falling tones – up to eight of them. Tonal usage increases with talking in a polite manner. There are also letters that are retroflex, glottal, aspirated or non-aspirated. Unfortunately, there is no accurate way to render these complexities in English phonetics, so what follows is a rough attempt, and one that you should polish by reviewing with a Tibetan speaker.

Tibetan is an ancient language which borrows modern words like 'post office,' 'fax machine' or 'airport' from the nearest language. Within Tibet, these terms may be taken from Chinese, while in India the word might come from English or Hindi, which all leads to a standardisation headache. But consider this: it's sometimes possible to use an English word (with a twisted accent) and be understood – the Tibetan for 'jeep' is *jip*, and the Tibetan for 'Landcruiser' is *landkrusa*. It's difficult to find Tibetans to practise with in the West. You can attune your ear by listening to Tibetan-language radio broadcasts (see the internet resources listing that follows).

Tibetan terms used in this book can be put to good use as speaking vocabulary. A yak is a yak, and tsampa is tsampa (nobody else in the world eats the stuff). Also usable are things like *dzong* (castle), *gompa* (monastery) and *tsangpo* (river). For more vocabulary, check the *Glossary* (see pages 271–2; some terms are Sanskrit, not Tibetan).

Useful phrases

Here are a few useful phrases for pidgin Tibetan speakers: *tashi delek!* is an all-purpose opener, meaning: greetings! how are you? congratulations! best wishes! *Yapodu* or *yabadoo* means 'good'(thumbs up) while *yapo mindu!* means 'bad!'(thumbs down). Vital to your survival is the phrase *kale kale*, which means 'slow down,' when spoken to a maniacal driver. Etiquette when you reach the prayer flags on top of passes in Tibet requires you to shout, at the top of your lungs *Sso-so-so-so-so! Lha Gyalo!*, which means 'Victory to the gods!'

Phrasebooks and tapes

Cheap Tibetan/English phrasebooks can be found in Kathmandu, along with Tibetans who will give lessons. In a handy format are two books on the market: Snow Lion Publications' *Learning Practical Tibetan* (book and two audio cassettes – see www.snowlionpub.com) and Lonely Planet's *Tibetan Phrasebook*. Phrasebooks are only as good as the sounds you can elicit from them. If you don't have a tape, go over the sounds with a Tibetan speaker, or have a native speaker help you record your own English-Tibetan tape.

Giving access to a much wider range of spoken Tibetan are CD-ROM packages which cost around US$50 each, like *Learning Tibetan* (Eurotalk Interactive) with innovative games and quizzes, and *Fluent Tibetan*, with 26 hours of tape compressed into a single CD-ROM. Both CD-ROM packages are available through Snow Lion Publications – consult their www.snowlionpub.com website.

Internet resources

Two sites give access to simple phrases spoken in Tibetan in RealAudio: these are downloadable. Take a look at www.wordbridge.com and at www.tibetlink.com; the latter site has Tibetan singing samples, and you can access Tibetan script and language software. More advanced tuning of the ear can be achieved by listening to radio broadcasts in Tibetan on the web, at three sites: www.vot.org, www.rfa.org and www.voa.gov. These sites are blocked in China: Radio Free Asia and Voice of America are both Washington-based, with part of the broadcast in Tibetan. Voice of Tibet is the only dedicated radio station broadcasting in the Tibetan language, and was established in 1996. From the Dharamsala site www.tibet.net, Tibetans can download Tibetan keyboard and language software, and use the world's first web-based Tibetan language e-mail service (tibetmail.net).

Openers

greetings (good fortune)	*tashi delek*
goodbye	*kaleshu* (spoken to the person staying)
	kalepay (spoken to the person leaving)
pleased to meet you	*kerang tukpa gapo chung*
how are you?	*kerang debo yinbe?*
I'm fine	*nga debo yin*
where are you going?	*kerang kawa droga?*
what's your name?	*kerangi mingla karey re?*
my name is ...	*nge mingla ... min*
I only speak a little Tibetan	*nga perkay teets teets shingi yur*
I don't understand	*nga hako masong*
Do you understand?	*kerang hakosong eh?*

Getting personal

where are you from?	*kerang lungpa kane yin?*
I am from X	*nga X ne yin*
UK/Canada/Australia	*injilungpa/kanada/ostrelia*
America/France	*ahri/farenci*
Tibetan/Chinese/Nepalese	*perpa/gyami/pelpo*
How old are you?	*kerang lo katsay yin?*
nomad/farmer	*drokpa/shingpa*
monk/pilgrim	*trapa/nekorpa*
married/single	*changsa/migyang*
husband/wife	*kyoka/gyemen*
mother/father	*ama/apa*
children/son/daughter	*puku/pu/pumo*

younger brother/younger sister	*pingya ohma pu/pingya ohma pumo*
older brother/older sister	*jojo/aja*

Flattery

good/very good	*yapo du/yapo shedra re*	very interesting	*nangwa dropo shedra re*
The food is great!	*kala shimpo du!*	I feel happy	*gyipo du*
I love this place!	*nga sacha dila gapo yur!*	we had a good time!	*ngantso gyipo chung!*
beautiful	*nying jepo du*	good luck	*lamdro yongbar shok*

Negatives, questions, requests

yes, that's it	*re*	can I take a photo?	*nga par gyapna digi rebay?*
yes, OK	*digi re*	what's this called in	*perke nangla di kandres*
no problem	*kay chegi mare*	Tibetan?	*lab gire?*
no	*mare (mindu)*	what does this mean?	*di terntak karey re?*
not okay, no good	*yapo mindu*	where/where is?	*kapa/kaba du?*
thank you	*tujeche*	what?	*karey?*
that's enough	*dik song*	when?	*kadu?*
need	*gerh*	who?/why?/how?	*su?/karey jeni?/kandres?*
don't want (don't like)	*mo gerh*	how much	*katsey?*
I don't know	*nga shingi meh*	(how many)?	
sorry, excuse me	*gohnda*	how far?	*ta ringpo rebay?*

Red tape

passport	*chi tern lakteb*	tourist	*takorwa*
permit	*lakyer (chokchen)*	I need a translator	*nga la gegyur cheken*
PSB office	*gonganju*		*chik gerh*
	(Chinese word)	what's the problem?	*gang ngel karey tresong?*
	sangwe nyen tokbe lekung		
	(Tibetan)		

Medical

sick/very sick	*nagi du/shedra nagi du*	I need a doctor right	*nga gyokpo amchi laten*
altitude sickness	*zatuki natsa*	away	*gerh gi du*
headache/fever	*gonagi du/tsawa pargi du*	oxygen	*kabu*
diarrhoea/	*troko shegi du/troko*	emergency	*zatrak netsul du*
stomach ache	*nagi du*	hospital	*menkhang*
cold/cough	*champa nagi du/lo*	pharmacy	*men tsongkhang*
	gyabgi du	medicine	*men*
feel dizzy	*goyu korgi du*		
I was bitten by a dog	*khi chik sogyab song*		

Transport

ticket	*pasey*	Do you rent bicycles?	*gangkor laya yurbe?*
	(Indian-Tibetan word)	how much for an	*chutsu chik la katsey re?*
	zinyik (Tibetan)	hour?	
plane	*namdru*	how much for a day?	*nyima chik la katsey re?*
motor vehicle	*mota* (Indian-Tibetan)	what time is the bus?	*jijger lun korte chutsu*
	noomkor (Tibetan)		*katser la drogi re?*
bicycle	*gangkor*	guide	*lamtriken*
horse	*ta*	driver	*siji* (Chinese word)
I'd like to hire a jeep	*nga jip chik lander yur*		*kalowa* (Tibetan)
I'd like to hire a	*nga landkrusa chik*	go slowly please	*kale kale drorok nang*
Landcruiser	*lander yur*	please stop here	*tuk rok nang*

Trekking

tent	*kur*	porter	*jalak kyerken*
sleeping bag	*nyeche*	is this the trail to X?	*di X droya ki lamka rebay?*
stove	*tapga*		
I want to hire a yak	*nga yak chik lander yur*	how many hours will it take to reach X?	*X pardu chutsu katsey gorgi re?*

Places

I want to go to X	*X la dronder yur*	temple	*lakhang*
airport	*namtang*	market	*trom*
post office	*drakhang*	photo shop	*barkhang*
bank	*ngukhang*	bookshop	*teb tsongkhang*
PSB office	*gonganju*	museum	*dem tonkhang*

Lodging

hotel	*drukhang*	telephone	*kapa*
guesthouse	*dronkhang*	key	*deymi*
room	*khangpa*	blanket	*nyejay*
bed	*nyetri*	candle	*yangla*
can I see the room?	*khangpa la migtana digi rebay?*	toilet/paper	*sangcher/sangcher shuku*
		shower/hot shower	*trukhang/trukhang tsapo*
do you have a room with private toilet?	*khang panang lola sangcher yur rebay?*	towel	*ajo*
where can I leave luggage?	*nge jalak dintso kawar shakka?*	thermos of hot water	*chadam chu tsapo*

Food

hungry	*trokok toki du*	meat	*sha*
thirsty	*kha komgi du*	yoghurt	*sho*
restaurant	*sakhang*	water	*chu*
let's eat!	*kalak soh!*	boiled water	*chu kolma*
tearoom	*jakhang*	hot Indian tea	*cha ohma*
can you bring me ...?	*... chikyer yong roknang?*	yak butter tea	*cha suma*
bowl of noodles	*thukpa*	homebrewed beer	*chang*
meat dumplings	*momo*	salt	*tsa*
stir-fried vegetables	*tsema ngowa*	sugar	*che makara*

Bargaining

how much is this?	*gong katsey re?*	too expensive	*di gong chenpo shedra du*
do you have any ...?	*kerang-la ... yurbe?*	can you give me a better price?	*gong jak tupki rebe?*
big/small	*chenpo/chung chung*		
old/new	*nyingpa/saba*	discount	*gong jakya yurbe*

Time

today	*tering*	Monday	*sa dawa*
now	*tanda*	Tuesday	*sa migma*
tonight	*togong*	Wednesday	*sa lhakba*
yesterday/tomorrow	*kesa/sangyin*	Thursday	*sa pubu*
morning/afternoon/evening	*shoke/chitro/gongtak*	Friday	*sa pasang*
		Saturday	*sa pemba*
year/month/week/day/hour	*lo/dawa/zankor/nyima/chutsu*	Sunday	*sa nyima*

THE TIBETAN SCRIPT

The elegance of Tibetan calligraphy is shown in this haiku-like poem. It was written by Tsangyang Gyatso, the 6th Dalai Lama – who is considered among Tibet's most accomplished poets.

In the short walk of this life
We have had our share of joys
Let us hope to meet again
In the youth of the next life

For the country name 'Tibet' in Tibetan script, see page 260.

Numbers

0	*lekor*	15	*jo nga*
1	*chik*	20	*nyi shu*
2	*nyi*	30	*sum ju*
3	*sum*	40	*shib ju*
4	*shi*	50	*ngab ju*
5	*nga*	60	*druk chu*
6	*druk*	70	*dun ju*
7	*dun*	80	*gyeb ju*
8	*gye*	90	*gub ju*
9	*gu*	one hundred	*gya tamba*
10	*ju*	five hundred	*nyab gya*
11	*ju chik*	one thousand	*chik tong*
12	*ju nyi*	two thousand	*tong-trak nyi*
13	*jok sum*	one million	*sayachik* (or: *bumju*)
14	*jub shi*		

Geographical terms, map features

river	*gyuk chu*	rain	*charpa*
	(also: *tsangpo*)	pass	*la*
spring	*chumi*	hill, mountain	*ri*
hotspring	*chukerl*	plain, plateau	*tang*
village	*trongsep*	lake	*tso*
town	*trongte*		(also: *yumco, caka, nor*)
fort	*dzong*	map	*sabtra*
monastery	*gompa*	compass points:	*chang* (N), *lho* (S),
ice/snow	*kyakpa/kang*		*shar* (E), *nub* (W)

CHINESE LANGUAGE

Such is the dominance of Mandarin Chinese in Tibet that, in order to get hotel rooms, obtain food in restaurants, talk with truck drivers or deal with officialdom, you need some knowledge of Chinese. However, if you are talking with a Tibetan, it's far preferable to stay with Tibetan language.

Though there are eight major dialects in China, the standard version is Mandarin, or Beijing dialect. Mandarin is a tonal language – it takes a musical ear to get the hang of the tones. Without mastery of the tones, your efforts at Chinese will be unintelligible, reducing you to a gibbering curiosity. Written Mandarin Chinese is no easier: it draws on a fund of about 50,000 characters (originally pictographs), although literate Chinese need only knowledge of about 5,000 characters.

Pinyin is the romanisation system used for rendering Chinese sounds into approximate English. There are several quirks in pinyin pronunciation. The vowels are rather tricky, and some consonants are pronounced differently: pinyin 'c' is pronounced 'ts', pinyin 'q' sounds like 'ch', pinyin 'x' comes out as 'sh', and pinyin 'zh' is pronounced 'j'. Thus on Chinese maps you may see the place-names 'Xigaze' (Shigatse), 'Qamdo' (Chamdo) and 'Zhangmu' (Jangmu). Pinyin romanisation, in addition, uses accents over the letters to indicate tones (these are not employed in this book). The word *ma* for example, can have four different meanings depending on whether the tone is flat, rising, fall-rising or falling ('mother', 'hemp', 'horse' or 'swear'). Thus you could be trying to rent a horse and end up with a bag of hemp. For tones, accented pinyin is of limited help: the best thing is to go over phrases with a Chinese native speaker to get the sounds right.

Useful phrases

Good all-purpose words are *keyi* (okay, yes, agreed), *mei wenti* (no problem) and *hen hao* (thumbs up, very good). Another form of 'yes' in agreement is *dui*, which is often used in a rapid-fire sequence, as in *dui-dui-dui-dui-dui*. A catchy idiomatic phrase for 'so-so' is *mama-huhu*, which literally means 'horse-horse-tiger-tiger.'

Phrasebooks and tapes

Phrasebooks become doubly useful if they have Chinese characters next to them: you can point to the characters if the pronunciation is not getting through. Another feature to look for is a mini-dictionary at the back of the phrasebook. There are a number of pocket-sized phrasebooks on the market, including those in the Rough Guides, Berlitz, BBC, and Eyewitness series. Because Mandarin Chinese derives its meaning from tones, it's well worth chasing cassette tapes, audio CDs or CD-ROM language-learning versions to get the sounds right. Worth checking out are CD-ROM packages authored by Edward Chang, titled *Early Chinese Tutor (Mandarin)*, and CD-ROM interactive material from the Rosetta Stone Language group (web: www.rosettastone.com), whose clients include the Peace Corps and NASA.

Internet resources

The Rosetta Stone Language group offers online language learning for a monthly fee: this is like having your own language instructor available to suit your schedule. For more advanced stages, attune your ear to Mandarin by listening to radio broadcasts in Chinese at www.rfa.org (Radio Free Asia) and www.voa.gov (Voice of America).

Openers

hello	*ni hao*
goodbye	*zaijian*
pleased to meet you	*hen gaoxing renshi ni*
how are you?	*ni hao ma?*
very well, thank you	*wo hen hao, xiexie*
where are you going?	*ni dao nali?*
what's your name?	*ni jiao shenme?*
my name is ...	*wo jiao ...*
I only speak a little Chinese	*wo ju dongde idiendien hanyu*
I don't understand	*wo budong*
do you understand?	*dong ma?*

Getting personal

where are you from?	*ni cong nali lai?*
I am from Britain/Canada/Australia	*wo cong yingguo/jianada/oadaliya ... lai*
America/France	*meiguo/faguo*
Tibet/China/Nepal	*xizang/zhongguo/niboer*
how old are you?	*ni ji sui?*
my job is ...	*wode gong zhuo shi ...*
I'm married/single	*wo jiehunle/wo shi danshen*
husband/wife	*zhangfu/qizi*
mother/father	*mama/baba*
children/son/daughter	*haizi/erzi/nuer*
brother/sister	*xiongdi/jiemei*

Flattery

good/very good	*hao/hen hao*	beautiful	*piaoliang*
terrific food!	*hen hao chi!*	that's great!	*haojile!*
cheers! (toasting)	*ganbei!*	I had a great time!	*wo hen kaixin!*
I love this place!	*wo hen xihuan zhege difang!*	good luck!	*zhu ni hao yun!*

Negatives, questions, requests

yes	*shi*	I want to take a photo	*wo yao zhao ge xiang*
OK/no problem	*hao*	what's this called in Chinese?	*zhege zhongwen jiao shenme?*
no	*bu*		
no (don't have)	*mei you*	please write it down for me	*qing ni bang wo xiexialai*
not okay/no good	*bu hao*		
please/thank you	*qing/xiexie*	what does that mean?	*shenme yisi?*
enough, thank you	*goule, xiexie*	where/where is X?	*nali?/X zai nali?*
I want/need	*wo yao*	when?/who?/	*shenme shihou?/shui?/*
don't want/don't like	*bu yao*	why?/how?	*weishenme?/ zenme?*
sorry, excuse me	*duibuqi*	how much/many?	*duoshao?*
I don't know	*wo bu zhidao*	how many kilometres?	*duoshao gongli?*

Red tape

passport	*huzhao*	tourist	*lu-ke*
visa	*qianzheng*	I need a translator	*wo xuyao fangyuan*
travel permit	*tong xing zheng*	what's the problem?	*yo shenme wenti?*
PSB office	*gonganju*		

Medical

sick/very sick	*sheng bingle/bingde hen zhong*	doctor	*yisheng*
altitude sickness	*gao shan bing*	need a doctor	*jao ge yisheng*
I feel dizzy	*wo touyun*	please help	*qing bang mang*
headache/fever	*touteng/fashao*	emergency	*jinji qingkuang*
diarrhoea	*laduzi*	hospital	*yiyuan*
stomach ache	*xiaohua bu liang*	oxygen	*yangqi*
cold/sore throat	*ganmao/hou-long teng*	pharmacy	*yaodian*
		medicine	*yao*

Transport

ticket	*piao*	let's go!	*zouba!*
plane	*feiji*	for a whole day?	*yitian duoshao qian*
taxi	*chuzuche*	we want to hire a jeep	*women yao yiliang jipu*
jeep	*jipu*	where is the bus station?	*qichezhan zai nar?*
truck	*kache*	what time is the bus to X?	*dao X de gongche shenme shihou kai?*
bus	*gonggong qiche*	driver	*siji*
bicycle	*zixingche*	guide	*daoyou*
I want to hire a bicycle	*wo yao zu yiliang zixingche*	slow down please	*qing ni man idien*
how much for an hour?	*yige xiao shi duoshao qian?*	stop here!	*qing zai zheli ting!*

Trekking

tent	*zhangpeng*	where can I hire yaks?	*wo sheme difang keyi gu yitou mao niu*
sleeping bag	*shuidai*	how much a day?	*yitian duoshao qian?*

Places

I want to go to X	*wo yao qu X*	PSB office/foreign affairs branch	*gonganju/waishi ke*
airport	*feijichang*	Buddhist temple	*fo si*
bus station	*qichezhan*	market	*shichang*
railway station	*huochezhan*	bookshop	*shudian*
post office	*youju*	museum	*bowuguan*
cybercafé	*wang ka*		
Bank of China (foreign exchange)	*zhongguo yinhang*		

Lodging

main tourist hotel	*binguan*	room	*fangjian*
smaller hotel	*fandian*	dormitory	*duorenfang*
guesthouse	*zhaodaisuo*	single room	*danrenfang*
can I see the room?	*wo keyi kan fangjian ma?*	double room	*shuangrenfang*
		room with bath	*dai yushi de fangjian*
where can I leave luggage?	*wo xingli fang narli?*	toilet/paper	*cesuo/shouzhi*
		shower/hot shower	*linyu/re linyu*
telephone	*dianhua*	towel	*maojin*
key	*yaoshi*	thermos of hot water	*yo re kaishui de shuiping*

Food

hungry	*duzi e*	meat	*rou*
thirsty	*kouke*	water	*shui*
restaurant/café	*fandian/kafeiguan*	boiled water	*kaishui*
let's eat!	*chi fanba!*	mineral water	*kuangquan shui*
do you have ...?	*ni you .... ma?*	tea	*cha*
noodles	*miantiao*	black tea	*hong cha*
rice	*mifan*	green tea	*lu cha*
biscuits	*binggan*	coffee	*kafei*
soup	*tang*	beer	*pijiu*
stir-fried vegetables	*chao shucai*		

Bargaining

how much is this?	*duoshao qian?*	too expensive	*taigui*
do you have ...?	*ni you ... ma?*	do you have anything cheaper?	*yo pianyi yidian de ma?*
big/small	*da/xiao*		
old/new	*jiu/xin*		

Time

today	*jintian*	Monday	*xingqi-yi*
now	*xianzai*	Tuesday	*xingqi-er*
tonight	*jinwan*	Wednesday	*xingqi-san*
yesterday/tomorrow	*zuotian/mingtian*	Thursday	*xingqi-si*
morning/afternoon/ evening	*zaoshang/xiawu/ wanshang*	Friday	*xingqi-wu*
		Saturday	*xingqi-liu*
year/month/day/hour	*nian/yue/zhi/xiaoshi*	Sunday	*xingqi-tian*

Numbers

0	*ling*	15	*shiwu*
1	*yi*	20	*ershi*
2	*er*	30	*sanshi*
3	*san*	40	*sishi*
4	*si*	50	*wushi*
5	*wu*	60	*liushi*
6	*liu*	70	*qishi*
7	*qi*	80	*bashi*
8	*ba*	90	*jiushi*
9	*jiu*	one hundred	*yi-bai*
10	*shi*	five hundred	*wu-bai*
11	*shiyi*	one thousand	*yiqian*
12	*shier*	two thousand	*liangqian*
13	*shisan*	one million	*yi baiwan*
14	*shisi*		

Geographical terms, map features

river	*he* (also: *jiang*)	province	*sheng*
lake	*hu*	snow	*xue*
mountain	*shan*	map	*ditu*
summit, peak	*feng*	compass points:	*bei* (N), *nan* (S),
pass	*shankou*		*dong* (E), *xi* (W)
valley	*shangu*		

Takin

Appendix

GLOSSARY

For details on popular icons, refer to the Jokhang section of the *Lhasa* chapter (see page 120).

ani	nun
Bon	pre-Buddhist religion of Tibet
chang	fermented barley-beer, a potent milky liquid
chorten	inverted bell-shaped shrine containing relics, or the ashes or embalmed body of a high lama (*stupa* in Sanskrit)
dharma	the word of the Buddha and his teachings
dorje	'thunderbolt.'A sceptre-like ritual object, made of brass and used against the powers of darkness
dzong	castle or fort, usually grafted onto a high ridge
gompa	active monastery
gonkhang	protector chapel at a monastery
kata	white greeting scarf, made of cotton or silk, presented on ceremonial occasions or offered at monasteries
kora	clockwise circuit of a sacred temple, lake or mountain
lakhang	chapel or inner sanctuary
lama	master spiritual teacher or guru
Losar	Tibetan New Year, usually celebrated around February
mandala	mystical circle (often enclosing a square) representing the Buddhist cosmos and used as a meditational aid (*chilkor* in Tibetan)
mani stone	stone tablet inscribed with a mantra, often included as part of a mani-wall, composed of many such stones
mantra	sacred syllables repeated many times as part of spiritual practice, such as *om mani padme hum* ('hail to the jewel in the lotus heart,' a phrase addressed to the Buddha)
momo	Tibetan meat dumpling
Monlam	the Great Prayer Festival, around the time of Losar
nirvana	release from the cycle of mortal existence and rebirths
potrang	palace
prayer-flag	small flag printed with sacred prayers, activated by the power of the wind
prayer-wheel	large fixed wheel or small hand-held wheel containing mantras and activated by the spinning of the wheel
prostrator	pilgrim who measures the distance to a sacred destination with the length of his or her body, flung prone along the ground
rinpoche	'precious one'. A reincarnate lama, also known when young as a *tulku*
Saka Dawa	day of Buddha's enlightenment, celebrated around June
sutra	sacred text, the written or spoken teachings of the Buddha
tanka	painted portable scroll, usually depicting a deity, on fine cotton or silk; can be used as a teaching aid

tantra	the 'web of life', or *vajrayana*, is the form of Buddhism most often associated with Tibet. It employs radical steps to seek enlightenment within a single lifetime
torma	ritual 'cake' sculpted from tsampa and yak-butter
tsampa	ground barley-flour, a Tibetan staple food
tulku	reincarnate lama
yak	hairy high-altitude cattle, or 'cow with a skirt'
yabyum	tantric sexual pose of deity and consort, symbolising fusion of opposites, and often misconstrued by Westerners as sexual activity without any tantric significance.

Chinaspeak

Chinese rhetoric on Tibet is an odd mix of the irrational and the predictable. This quote is taken from the magazine *Beijing Review*, 1983, describing the Lhasa uprising of 1959:

> The imperialists and a small number of reactionary elements in Tibet's upper ruling clique could not reconcile themselves to the peaceful liberation of Tibet and its return to the embrace of the motherland. The reactionary elements were intent upon launching an armed rebellion, negating the agreement and detaching Tibet from China. Abetted by the imperialists, they continued to sabotage and create disturbances. Despite the central government's consistent persuasion and education, they finally launched an armed rebellion on March 10, 1959. But, contrary to their desires, this rebellion accelerated the destruction of Tibet's reactionary forces and brought Tibet onto the bright, democratic, socialist road sooner than expected.

This puts forward the standard Beijing bafflegab on Tibet, unchanged for the last 40 years. For maximum effect, try and listen to this stuff spoken out loud, with a shrill Chinese accent and lots of static.

China's Tibet To reinforce the idea that Tibet is not a separate country, attach the word 'China' to it. Chinese-produced tourist brochures and maps all specify 'Tibet, China,' or 'China-Tibet.' China branding is found all over: China Post, Chinapolice, China Mobile. There's even a book titled 'Chinese Tibetan Opera.'

counter-revolutionary Anyone who opposes official policy, an enemy of the state, or someone 'committed with the goal of overthrowing the political power of the dictatorship of the proletariat and the socialist system'. Despite an official Beijing repeal of this crime to placate international critics, those previously convicted of it still languish in prison. Now, prisoners continue to be convicted and are either held without charge or trial, or charged with being either a spy or a terrorist (the latter term more in vogue since September 11, 2001). Another term is 'reactionary'.

the Dalai In June 1998, when President Clinton went on national Chinese television to say he thought the Dalai Lama was 'an honest man', this must've been news to a billion Chinese, who are more used to hearing him cursed as a treasonous demon. In rhetoric, the Chinese often employ the abbreviated form 'the Dalai', which is considered insulting by the Tibetans. Followers of the Dalai Lama are called 'the Dalai clique'. Chinese news sources call the exiled leader a 'splittist' and even 'a major hindrance to the development of Tibetan Buddhism'.

Democratic Reform Chinaspeak for the period immediately after the 1959 Lhasa Uprising and the flight of the Dalai Lama, when authorities set about dismantling the Tibetan culture in earnest—wading in there with machine guns where necessary.

foreign imperialists General all-purpose scapegoats. It is never specified which country they're from, but the popular candidates are 'bad elements' from Taiwan, the USA, the UK and Germany. After the Dalai Lama received the Nobel Peace Prize, Norway was added to the blacklist.

hot topic a newish term to denote anything like taxes or price increases that dissidents (reactionaries) supposedly capitalise on to foment unrest and demonstrations. Tibetan independence is, of course, very hot. So is the Dalai Lama – when asked what they think of him, most Chinese squirm and try to drop the subject like a hot potato.

internal affairs Chinese shorthand for 'back off, it's a domestic dispute, it's no concern of yours what we do behind closed doors, so don't meddle in our affairs'.

minority nationality The minorities, or non-Hans, are viewed as being part of the big happy Han family, even if they don't speak the same language. A minority theme park outside Beijing presents them spending their time dancing and singing, rather like happy children. Within Tibet, however, the Tibetans are less politely referred to as 'barbarians.'

the Motherland As well as referring to mainland China, this term embraces any parts of Asia that China wants to occupy. A number of China's neighbours have had trouble with this concept, including Russia, India, Taiwan, Vietnam and the Philippines. *Love the Motherland* was the name of a campaign for Chinese schoolchildren in 1998. *Splitting the Motherland* is an all-embracing, heinous crime in Chinese eyes.

peaceful liberation A reference to the entry of the People's Liberation Army into Tibet in 1950. Some Chinese sources admit that the invasion was in fact not entirely peaceful – some Tibetans resisted, so the PLA was reluctantly forced to machine-gun the hapless Tibetans to clear them out of the way. Mostly, however, the people loved the PLA, according to official sources.

re-education Mainly for monks, teaching them to see that black is white, and white is black, to say the Dalai Lama is bad, and to say the Chinese-chosen Panchen Lama is good. Sometimes monasteries are closed to tourism while this is in progress. The authorities might as well hang out a sign: Closed For Revision.

serfdom The pre-1950 state of the ordinary Tibetan, locked into exploitation by Tibetan nobility and monastic overseers. The Chinese broke down this class system. How? By replacing the Tibetan masters with harsher Chinese ones.

Soul Boy The 11th Panchen Lama, a child into whose soul the 10th Panchen was reincarnated. The boy is the most hotly disputed reincarnate in Tibetan history. 'Soul Boy' is a translation of the Chinese term applied to reincarnations, 'Lingtong' (ling=soul, tong=boy/child). Tibetans find the translation annoying and misleading.

spiritual pollution An odd term for an atheist nation to develop but this refers to interference from outside sources, such as Westerners, in the form of books, tapes, videos and so on. Some of these are 'black' (political pollution), others 'yellow' (pornographic pollution).

splittists Favourite Chinese term for those advocating independence for Tibet, or separatists. The idea here is that the Motherland must stay whole—anybody that splits off a piece will ruin the symmetry. Other chunks where splittists seem to be hard at work include Xinjiang, Mongolia and Taiwan.

274

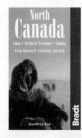

Appendix 3

FURTHER INFORMATION
Recommended reading

Some of the following books, multimedia materials and websites are frowned upon, restricted, or simply outlawed in China. Do not attempt to bring in risqué material if travelling to Tibet. Books with straight printed material should not be a problem, but visual material is different – customs and soldiers will flip through a book looking for artwork like the Tibetan flag or pictures of the Dalai Lama.

Kathmandu is the best place in the sub-continent to find materials on Tibet, especially books and maps. Mention of Tibetan or Taiwanese independence or criticism of Beijing's policies are in theory forbidden in Hong Kong SAR. In practice, however, books continue to circulate freely, and anti-China protests (such as the Falun Gong) are tolerated in the colony, although for how much longer is uncertain: some Falun Gong (a religious sect outlawed in China) members have been detained on arrival in Hong Kong and promptly sent packing. And authorities are not mad about Harry, either: Harry Wu, a prominent anti-China activist, was detained on arrival in early 2002 in Hong Kong and deported (no reason was given).

For such a little-visited place, Tibet has generated an extraordinary amount of literature. What's listed here is just the tip of the iceberg. You can glean lots more information from the websites of specialist publishers. These include:

www.snowlionpub.com (Snow Lion Publications, NY)
www.shambhala.com (Shambhala Publications, Massachusetts)
www.wisdompubs.org (Wisdom Publications, US and UK)
www.tricycle.com (Tricycle Books and quarterly magazine)
www.potala.com (Potala Publications, NY, part of the government-in-exile's office).

History, political intrigue

Avedon, Richard, *In Exile from the Land of Snows*, HarperCollins, NY, 1998. A classic that first appeared in 1984.
Hilton, Isobel, *The Search for the Panchen Lama*, Penguin Books, UK, 2000.
Shakya, Tsering, *The Dragon in the Land of Snows*, Columbia University Press, 1999. A definitive history from a Tibetan scholar.

Human rights, testimonials

Amnesty International, *Persistent Human Rights Violations in Tibet*, London, 1996.
Choedrak, Tenzin, *The Rainbow Palace*, Bantam, NY 2000.
Gyatso, Palden, *Fire Under the Snow*, Harvill Press, 1997 (published in the US as *The Autobiography of a Tibetan Monk*).

Buddhism

Batchelor, Stephen, *Buddhism without Beliefs*, Riverhead Books, NY, 1997.
Thurman, Robert, *Inside Tibetan Buddhism*, Collins, San Francisco, 1995.

The Dalai Lama (as author)

My Land and My People, Warner Books, 1997. A reprint of the 1962 edition of the autobiography of the Dalai Lama.

Freedom in Exile, Harper, San Francisco, 1991. Part two of the Dalai Lama's autobiography.

Ethics for the New Millennium, Riverhead, NY, 2001. The Dalai Lama delivers his timely message to a world sadly lacking in moral values.

Tibetan culture

Baker, Ian, and Romio Shrestha, *The Healing Arts of Tibet*, Thames & Hudson, London, 1997.

Goldstein, Melvyn and Cynthia Beall, *Nomads of Western Tibet: The Survival of a Way of Life*, UC Press, Berkeley, 1990.

Larsen, Knud, and Amund Sinding-Larsen, *The Lhasa Atlas: Traditional Tibetan Architecture and Townscape*, Serindia, 2001.

Exploration, mountaineering, adventure

Anker, Conrad, and David Roberts, *The Lost Explorer: Finding Mallory on Mt Everest*, Simon & Schuster, NY, 1999.

Berry, Scott, *A Stranger in Tibet*, Kodansha, NY, 1989.

Hammleb, Jochen, et al, *Ghosts of Everest: the Search for Mallory and Irvine*, the Mountaineers, 1999.

Harrer, Heinrich, *Seven Years in Tibet*, Putnam, 1997 (originally appeared in 1953).

Hopkirk, Peter, *Trespassers on the Roof of the World*, OUP, Oxford, 1982.

Norgay, Jamling Tenzing, *Finding My Father's Soul*, Harper, 2001 (written by the son of Everest's premier summiteer).

Peissel, Michel, *Barbarians at the Gate*, Henry Holt, NY, 1997.

Venables, Stephen, *Everest: Kangshung Face*, General Publishing, Toronto, 1989.

Travel narratives

Buckley, Michael, *Heartlands: Travels in the Tibetan World*, Summersdale, UK, 2002.

Kerr, Blake, *Sky Burial*, Snowlion Publications, 1997.

Le Sueur, Alec, *Running a Hotel on the Roof of the World*, Summersdale, UK, 1998.

Guidebooks

Batchelor, Stephen, *The Tibet Guide*, Wisdom Publications, 1998.

Chan, Victor, *Tibet Handbook*, Moon Publications, USA, 1994.

Dorje, Gyurme, *Tibet Handbook with Bhutan*, Footprint, UK, 1998.

Mapping the Tibetan World (joint authors), Kotan Publishing, 2001. A very ambitious project, and highly recommended.

McCue, Gary, *Trekking in Tibet*, the Mountaineers, Seattle, 1999.

Photobooks

Borges, Phil, *Tibetan Portrait*, Rizzoli, NY, 1996.

Harris, Brian, *Tibetan Voices*, Pomegranate, San Francisco, 1996.

Nomachi, Kazoyoshi, *Tibet*, Shambhala, Boston, 1997.

Rowell, Galen (photographer, with text by the Dalai Lama), *My Tibet*, UC Press, Berkeley, 1990.

Fiction

Davidson, Lionel, *The Rose of Tibet*, Gollancz, London 1962. A terrific read.

Hilton, James, *Lost Horizon*, William Morrow, NY, 1933 (reprinted many times since). The book that gave the world Shangri-La.

Mitchell, Ken, *Stones of the Dalai Lama*, Douglas & McIntyre, Vancouver, 1993.

Norbu, Jamyang, *Sherlock Holmes: the Missing Years*, Bloomsbury, London, 2001. Written by a Tibetan iconoclast and scholar.

Rampa, Lobsang T, *The Third Eye*, Corgi, London, 1956 (reprinted many times since). Masterful New Age hokum.

Tshe Ring Dbang Rgyal, *The Tale of the Incomparable Prince*, HarperCollins, NY, 1996. An 18th century classic revived in translation from the only novel in the Tibetan language.

Other media
CD-ROM
Tibet Outside the TAR: a 2,700-page report crammed onto a single CD-ROM by Steven Marshall and Susette Cooke (1997). Available through ICT, Washington; web: www.savetibet.org.

CD
Freedom Chants, Gyuto Monks: cerebral sacred music from India.
In a Distant Place; Quiet Mind: two albums of the many performed by Nawang Kechog.
Tibet Tibet; Coming Home: two albums by exiled female singer, Yungchen Lhamo.

DVD, film and video
The website www.tibet.com/films.html lists over 200 Tibet-related films and videos, with further links. Here are some major movies related to Tibet, in order of release date:

Lost Horizon, directed by Frank Capra, Columbia TriStar, 1937. The movie that spread the legend of James Hilton's Shangri-La far and wide.

Kundun, directed by Martin Scorsese, Touchstone Pictures, 1997. Superb biopic about the early years of the Dalai Lama.

Seven Years in Tibet, directed by Jean-Jacques Annaud, Columbia TriStar, 1997. Stars Brad Pitt and David Thewlis, and introduces Tibetan actress Lhakpa Tsamchoe (later to star in *Himalaya*).

Red Corner, directed by Jon Avnet, MGM, 1997. Set in Beijing, but concerned with the judicial system and human rights. Stars Richard Gere.

The Cup, directed by Khyentse Norbu, 1998. The first major movie ever directed by a Tibetan, a rinpoche resident in Bhutan. It's about soccer-crazed monks at a monastery in northern India. Filmed in Tibetan and Hindi languages.

Windhorse, directed by Paul Wagner, Paul Wagner Productions, 1998. Based partly on a true story about a singer who must flee Tibet: at great risk, the director took video of actors on location in Lhasa. This 'docudrama' was filmed in Tibetan and Chinese languages and stars Dadon, a famous Tibetan singer who escaped into exile in 1992 and now lives in the US.

Saltmen of Tibet, directed by Ulrike Koch, Switzerland, 1998. About the salt route caravans from Tibet to Nepal, a trade now mostly extinct. Filmed in Tibetan and in the secret salt language (with cryptic salt-language subtitles).

Himalaya, directed by Eric Valli, 1999. A stunning French-Nepalese co-production with an all-Tibetan cast, this was filmed in Dolpo, Nepal, in the Tibetan language. Stars Lhakpa Tsamchoe. The movie offers great insight into the nomadic way of life.

The Touch, directed by Hong Kong master cinematographer Peter Pau, 2002. Romantic action movie, with some scenes shot on location in Lhasa and central Tibet. Stars Michelle Yeoh and Ben Chaplin.

Website directory
Accessing the 'wrong' sites has landed Chinese surfers in jail. That probably wouldn't extend to foreign surfers, but it gives an idea of just how sensitive the internet is in the

Middle Kingdom. In late 2001, a purge of cybercafés in China resulted in 17,000 of them being closed down, and a further 28,000 ordered to install monitoring software (called 'Internet Police 110') which shields banned sites and flags local authorities when such sites are being accessed. Since 2002, networks in China are required to use domestically produced software. A number of the following sites are banned in China and are most likely firewalled. Some, like those listed in the section on Human Rights, are extremely sensitive. At the same time, it is surprising what is still accessible from within Tibet and China. Strangely enough, sites that were firewalled in Lhasa did not appear to be firewalled in Chengdu (and vice-versa for other sites). Maybe it's a case of different sensitivities in different places?

The net is your news lifeline in a place like Lhasa, where no foreign print news sources can be found. Staying up-to-date on current politics and travel conditions is very important. The following sites can assist with trip preparation, and give you the latest information.

Regional information
Cybercafés
www.netcafeguide.com Worldwide listing of cybercafés – use the search function.

Searching for it
www.google.com
www.metacrawler.com
www.amazon.com To use Amazon, go to travel and browse by subject.

Currency conversion
xe.com.ucc/full.shtml Universal currency converter, one among many such sites.

Weather
www.cnn.com/weather Five-day forecasts for Lhasa, Shiquanhe (Ali) and more.
weather.yahoo.com Go to 'Asia' for 5-day forecasts for Lhasa and other Asian cities.

Travel warnings
www.fco.gov.uk/travel
travel.state.gov/travel_warnings.html
www.dfait-maeci.gc.ca UK, US and Canadian official travel warning bulletins.

General news
www.worldnews.com
www.worldnewsasia.com
www.guardian.co.uk
www.globeandmail.ca
www.asiaobserver.com

Asia/India news
www.timeasia.com
www.timeasia.com/travel
asia.cnn.com
www.iht.com
www.bbc.co.uk/worldservice/eastasiatoday
asiaobserver.com
www.scmp.com
news.indiatimes.com

Regional travel information

www.pmgeiser.com Swiss-based site that covers China, Tibet and Indochina regions. Click on the relevant flag (but exercise caution here).
www.timeout.com/hongkong

Hotel listings and practical information for Hong Kong.

dharamsalanet.com Copious resources on visiting this corner of NW India.
www.nepalnews.net Excellent source of news from within Nepal (so government controlled): click on Kathmandu Post.
www.catmando.com/nepal.htm www.nepal-net.com/travel These two sites list hotels and travel agents.

Airport information

www.airportcitycodes.com Ever wondered where your bags are being routed to? This site can bring up many Chinese airport codings.

Banking

www.visa.com
www.mastercard.com Use the ATM locator to find a machine in Kathmandu or Chengdu.

Health

www.drwisetravel.com
www.cdc.gov/travel
www.tripprep.com
travelhealth.co.uk
www.internationalsos.com The sites listed here are excellent for pre-departure information.

Surfing Tibet

Some websites appear in other relevant parts of this book. For links on the Tibetan World (Bhutan, Nepal, NW India, Outer Mongolia) see the *Tibetan World* chapter. For links on Tibetan Language, see *Appendix 1*. For relevant publisher websites, see *Appendix 2*.

Gateway sites

www.kotan.org The website for the publishers of the book *Mapping the Tibetan World*. Click on 'Tibet Cultural Region Directory' for a host of links.
www.tibet.com Official site of the government-in-exile, offering loads of links.
www.tibetlink.com Links given on this site, based in Toronto, Canada, are angled more for the Tibetan community.

Current travel conditions in Tibet

www.savetibet.org Search for current travel and other information.
www.tibetinfo.net Search for travel information on this site.
www.atc.org.au/travel Excellent site by Tony Williams for the Australia Tibet Council.
www.khamaid.org/travel Excellent on travel to the Kham region.

Virtual Lhasa

www.tibetgame.com Cool interactive travellers' game (and it's free). You have limited money and three Dalai Lama pictures: the object is to give acquisitions away, thereby increasing your karma to attain bodhisattva-hood. This site, created by Sydney-based Peter

Danford, gives you the feeling of being on the ground, exploring Lhasa via 24 linked panoramas with some audio. You need some plug-ins to run this game.

Everest homepage
everestnews.com Every 8,000m peak should have one: this site has everything you need to know about the Big E and all the climbing trivia.

Tibet maps
www.tibetmap.com Cartography from the Tibet Map Institute, a French site.
www.tew.org Click on Geography for satellite maps and theme maps from Tibet Environmental Watch.

The airline
www.cswaad.com Minimal site for CSWA airlines, which flies the Lhasa routes: solicits ads for inflight magazine *Eagle*.

Chinese viewpoints
www.china-embassy.org From Washington, click on 'Tibet' for Chinese rhetoric.
www.tibet-tour.com Slick site from Tibet Tourism Bureau, Shanghai branch (TTBS).
www.goldenbridge.net/offices.htm This travel agency is affiliated with the Chinese military, which explains how they get permits sewn up.
chinasite.com A gateway site with many links, many in the Chinese language and a number banned in China.
www.cnd.org China News Digest, compiled by a group of Chinese scholars in New York (another banned site).

Tibet news sources
www.tibet.net Tibetan Bulletin, from Dharamsala, can be accessed from this site.
www.tibetpost.com 'Tibet Daily,' a virtual newspaper, compiled through Worldnews Network. **www.tibet.ca** Has World Tibet Network News archive, via CTC, Canada.
www.savetibet.org Click on Tibet Press Watch, the online newsletter of ICT—you need Acrobat Reader to decode it.
www.tibettimes.org Tibetan-language newspaper, established in 1996.
worldbridges.com/Tibet Collection of visuals (photo/video) from news sources.

Emailed news services (Listserves)
World Tibet Network News Send email request to: listserve@lists.mcgill.ca with message: subscribe WTN-L your name (WTN is also archived at www.tibet.ca)
TIN Newsletter To subscribe, send an email to: emma@tibetinfo.net with 'join' in the subject line.
The Oriental-List Author Peter Neville-Hadley's moderated discussion list about China and its near neighbours, including Tibet. To subscribe, send a blank email message to: subscribe-oriental-list@list.xianzai.com (you can specify digest format).

Activism
www.tibet.org/Resources/TSG Worldwide listing of support groups.
www.savetibet.org Site for ICT Washington and ICT Amsterdam.
www.freetibet.org UK organisation, Free Tibet Campaign.
www.tibet.org/sft Students for a Free Tibet.
www.tibetinfo.net Tibet Information Network, UK.
www.tibetjustice.org Tibet Justice Center, in the US.

Human rights

www.un.org/rights Gives the full text of the Universal Declaration of Human Rights.
www.dfn.org Digital Freedom Network, operating from New Jersey, gives lesser-known voices a chance to be heard.
www.hrw.org
www.hrichina.org Human rights in China are under scrutiny on these sites.
www.tchrd.org Dharamsala-based centre.
www.amnesty.org An organisation banned in China.

Tibetan Buddhist leaders

www.kagyu.org
www.karmapa.org Homepages (of sorts) for rival Karmapa candidates.
www.tibet.com/DL/index.html A kind of homepage for the Dalai Lama.
www.tibet.ca/panchenlama/index.html A cyberspace candle burns for the missing incarnate on a site set up for young viewers.

MEASUREMENTS AND CONVERSIONS

To convert	Multiply by
Inches to centimetres	2.54
Centimetres to inches	0.3937
Feet to metres	0.3048
Metres to feet	3.281
Yards to metres	0.9144
Metres to yards	1.094
Miles to kilometres	1.609
Kilometres to miles	0.6214
Acres to hectares	0.4047
Hectares to acres	2.471
Imperial gallons to litres	4.546
Litres to imperial gallons	0.22
US gallons to litres	3.785
Litres to US gallons	0.264
Ounces to grams	28.35
Grams to ounces	0.03527
Pounds to grams	453.6
Grams to pounds	0.002205
Pounds to kilograms	0.4536
Kilograms to pounds	2.205
British tons to kilograms	1016.0
Kilograms to British tons	0.0009812
US tons to kilograms	907.0
Kilograms to US tons	0.000907

5 imperial gallons are equal to 6 US gallons
A British ton is 2,240 lbs. A US ton is 2,000 lbs.

Temperature conversion table
The bold figures in the central columns can be read as either centigrade or fahrenheit.

°C		°F	°C		°F
−18	**0**	32	10	**50**	122
−15	**5**	41	13	**55**	131
−12	**10**	50	16	**60**	140
−9	**15**	59	18	**65**	149
−7	**20**	68	21	**70**	158
−4	**25**	77	24	**75**	167
−1	**30**	86	27	**80**	176
2	**35**	95	32	**90**	194
4	**40**	104	38	**100**	212
7	**45**	113	40	**104**	219

Black-necked cranes

KEY TO STANDARD SYMBOLS

—·—·—	International boundary		🏛	Historic building
······	District boundary		✝	Church or cathedral
——————	National park boundary		♣	Buddhist temple/monastery
✈	Airport (international)		♠	Hindu temple
✈	Airport (other)		☾	Mosque
✈	Airstrip		▶	Golf course
🚁	Helicopter service		🏃	Stadium
🚂	Railway		▲	Summit
··········	Footpath		△	Boundary beacon
—🚢—	Car ferry		⊚	Outpost
—🚢—	Passenger ferry		✕—✕	Border post
⌘	Petrol station or garage		⌂	Rock shelter
P	Car park		⌐◦⌐	Cable car, funicular
🚌	Bus station etc		⌣	Mountain pass
🚲	Cycle hire		○	Waterhole
M	Underground station		☼	Scenic viewpoint
⌂	Hotel, inn etc		✿	Botanical site
🏕	Campsite		⌘	Specific woodland feature
♦	Hut		⚓	Lighthouse
♇	Bar		~	Marsh
✕	Restaurant, café etc			
⊠	Post office			
ℓ	Telephone			
e	Internet café			
✚	Hospital, clinic etc			
⚱	Museum			
🐘	Zoo			
i	Tourist information			
$	Bank			
⚲	Statue or monument			
∴	Archaeological or historic site			

Other map symbols are sometimes shown in separate key boxes with individual explanations for their meanings.

Index

Around the back of the Barkor, Makye Ame restaurant's rooftop on the third floor has great views over the parade of pilgrims. From various hotel rooftops, you can also get good views of Lhasa, and see paper kites launched from other rooftops. Some hotels like the Kecho may have rooftop cafés.

Entertainment and nightlife

Lhasa's handful of hotels and restaurants are nightlife and entertainment venues by default: they are gathering points for information exchange. Source and sauce: other travellers provide the latest information, and you digest it over a steaming bowl of noodles. Snowland, Tashi I, Dunya, and Kailash restaurants function as traveller cafés. This is how travellers mostly pass their nights. Chinese nightlife consists of crooning, carousing and chasing Sichuan women around in karaoke bars or places like Top View Disco (some Westerners venture in here too). Other night-time Chinese endeavours include dwarf-tossing contests. Tibetan nightlife consists of crowding into tiny video salons where sound distortion and flasks of chang are the big things.

Dinner-dance venues

The Mad Yak restaurant, inside the Kirey Hotel, and the Crazy Yak restaurant, located next door to the Kirey (off the road a bit) may stage dinner-dance events. The cost is Y50 including dinner, or you can probably get by on a beer for Y10 only. These places cater mostly to foreign group tours, but they don't mind if individuals show up. Dinner starts at 19.00 and the show takes place from 19.30 to 21.30. The show is a mix of traditional dance and music, with the highlight being the exuberant yak dance, performed by two Tibetans hidden inside a yak skin. It is traditionally performed as a welcome dance. The dancers roll on the floor, flick the tail around, and charge into the audience. There may be other Lhasa restaurants with dinner-dance shows. Check the Tibet Lhasa Kitchen restaurant.

Bars

Popular with foreigners is the upstairs bar at Dunya restaurant, next to the Yak Hotel. You can't miss the Heineken sign out the front – the bar was set up by a Dutchman.

Opposite the Yak Hotel is Ganghla Metok, a trendy Chinese-run restaurant and bar, with Chinese artwork on the walls masquerading as Tibetan. The food is bland, but the place is fine for drinks, and stays open late.

INFORMATION
Traveller network

Your best information source is other travellers, encountered at cafés or guesthouses. Make other contacts through the message boards at Snowland, Yak, Banakshol, Pentoc or Flora hotels – you can buy or sell medicines, sleeping bags, tents and freeze-dried foods. Assembling small groups for Landcruiser trips is often achieved through the boards.

Books and maps

You might dredge up the odd map, poster or Tibetan music cassette from the Xinhua Bookstore at the west end of Mi Mang Lam; otherwise, pickings are slim. Prices for maps and books can be absurdly low if produced by the Chinese government. There's a Xinhua bookstore branch out near Lhasa Hotel. Look for a sheet map called *Lhasa Tourist Map*, produced by Chengdu Cartographic

Publishing House, dated 2001 and sold for Y16. This large, double-sided map carries an impressive wealth of detail and a selection of mini-guide material.

The souvenir shops at Lhasa Hotel and Tibet Hotel are good for books, though more expensive. Also selling books and postcards are souvenir kiosks near the Potala ticket entrance and inside the Norbulingka. Rule of thumb: when you see something you really want, bargain and buy it – you might not see it again. Other Chinese bookstores are scattered around; there's one at the east side of Barkor Bazaar.

SERVICES
Banking
The main branch of the Bank of China is located just northeast of the Golden Yak roundabout. It provides full services, including credit card advances (although commissions can be high). The BOC is open 10.30 to 13.30, and 15.30 to 18.00 Monday to Friday; from 11.00 to 15.00 Saturdays; and it may be open on Sundays. There are sub-branches in a few other locations – notably one near the Banakshol hotel. Major hotels like Lhasa Hotel have their own exchange counter, but the rate is not as good. ATMs exist in Lhasa, but with instructions in Chinese you should not count on this option.

Medical
You're best off moving to a comfortable hotel in the event of a medical problem. High-end hotels usually supply oxygen pillows and may have a doctor on call. Hospitals in Lhasa cost a fortune for foreigners to stay in, and the medical attention is dubious anyway. Lhasa's finest is the Military Hospital at the north end of town, but that's not for foreigners. The People's Hospital is basic, although one unit is supported by an Italian NGO project for equipment and training and there's an X-ray unit there. The Emergency Centre (tel: 632 2200) at this hospital has a small ambulance.

Communications and media
The Potala post office awaits you: the main branch for telecommunications lies near the Potala, on Beijing Road. The sending of regular mail and parcels takes place here; bring along your own packing materials as few are supplied (for larger items, you might have to open your package for customs inspection). Some hotels handle mail too – they deliver to the post office. Part of the China Post complex on this block is a large store devoted to Chinese magazines – everything from car magazines to fashion periodicals – to keep the settlers happy. The news is all from China, and thus all screened. There is a media blackout in Tibet – you cannot find any foreign magazines at all. And despite the great advances the Chinese say they have made in Tibet, there is not a single Tibetan newspaper to be found for sale on the streets of Lhasa.

Fax and phone
There's a long-distance calling office next door to the main post office (calls are most likely routed through Beijing); the same office will allow you to send faxes. A second telecom office is located at the Mountaineers-on-Everest roundabout. Faxes can also be sent at Lhasa Hotel's business centre, but they're more expensive. International phone calls can be placed through hotels, even at the budget hotels. It's cheaper to use a pre-paid card with a yellow phone (these phones are sometimes found in hotel lobbies, and sometimes on the street). The country code (China) is 86; the Lhasa area code is 0891 (for calls within China) or 891 (for incoming international calls).

them. There are several carpet factories in town, including one to the southeast side of Lhasa and another out near Drepung. Potala Carpet Factory, 300m past the turn-off for Drepung, welcomes visitors – you can see women weaving and singing here as they work on complex patterns. There is an exhibition and retail room on the premises. Check out the various designs: a Tibetan dragon has four claws, the Chinese imperial dragon has five claws. A German joint-venture outfit displays yak-leather products at a showroom under the Pentoc Guesthouse – items include wallets and yak-wool sweaters (and some pretty heavy socks). Nearly opposite the Pentoc is Tibet Yekyl Tour Shop, a Tibetan-run place stocking a small but good-quality range of Tibetan handicrafts.

WHAT TO SEE
Orienting yourself
To get a better idea of the layout of Lhasa, there are a number of places that offer expansive views. The highest place is, of course, the Potala rooftop. The Jokhang rooftop has stunning views, too. Some hotels like the Yak, Mandala and Kecho offer rooftop views over the Barkor area.

Traditionally, Tibetan pilgrims approaching the holy city embarked on three sacred circuits: the inner circuit of the Jokhang Temple (called the Nangkor), the 20-minute outer circuit of the same temple (around the Barkor), and a 90-minute circuit around Lhasa itself, called the Lingkor. The first two are eminently possible, but the Lingkor is no longer easy to follow – it has been disrupted by modern Chinese building. The description of sights that follows is based on clockwise circuits of the Nangkor, Barkor and Lingkor – that is, starting at the Jokhang Temple, and spiralling outwards around Lhasa. On the outskirts of Lhasa lie the great monastic citadels of Sera and Drepung. You have to read between the lines in Lhasa when it comes to the sacred and the secret. There's been so much upheaval in the Holy City that half the time you don't know if what you're looking at is sacred or not – whether the statuary at the Jokhang is real or not, whether the West Gate is original or reconstructed.

Entry fees
It all starts to add up when you are charged Y70 to enter the Potala, Y30 for Tibet Museum, Y35 for the Jokhang, and other temples ranging from Y15 up. These tabs are not paid by some tour operators – notably the ones packaging three-day sorties from Chengdu.

Barkor area
There are two areas left in Lhasa where the Tibetan pulse can still be felt: at the Potala (a faint museum pulse) and Barkor Bazaar (throbbing pilgrim pulse). Other than that you're looking at Chinatown. It seems absurd to put it this way, but you really have to visit the 'Tibetan Quarter' – the quarter around the Jokhang Temple and the Barkor – to catch any Tibetans in action. Sadly, this quarter only comprises a small fraction of Lhasa's land area.

The Jokhang
The Jokhang or Tsug Lakhang (central cathedral) is Tibet's most sacred temple – the heart of Tibet – with streams of pilgrims coursing through. The temple was built in the 7th century by King Songtsen Gampo when he moved his capital to Lhasa. Apart from his three Tibetan wives, the powerful Songtsen Gampo had two wives offered by neighbouring nations – Nepalese Queen Tritsun and Chinese Queen Wencheng. The Jokhang was originally designed

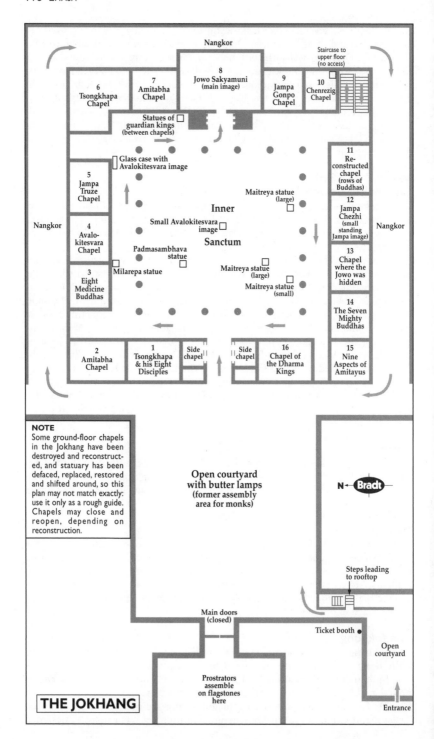

Nangkor

Staircase to upper floor (no access)

6 Tsongkhapa Chapel

7 Amitabha Chapel

8 Jowo Sakyamuni (main image)

9 Jampa Gonpo Chapel

10 Chenrezig Chapel

Statues of guardian kings (between chapels)

Glass case with Avalokitesvara image

5 Jampa Truze Chapel

Inner

Maitreya statue (large)

4 Avalo-kitesvara Chapel

Small Avalokitesvara image

Nangkor

Sanctum

Padmasambhava statue

Milarepa statue

3 Eight Medicine Buddhas

Maitreya statue (large)

Maitreya statue (small)

Nangkor

11 Re-constructed chapel (rows of Buddhas)

12 Jampa Chezhi (small standing Jampa image)

13 Chapel where the Jowo was hidden

14 The Seven Mighty Buddhas

2 Amitabha Chapel

1 Tsongkhapa & his Eight Disciples

Side chapel

Side chapel

16 Chapel of the Dharma Kings

15 Nine Aspects of Amitayus

NOTE
Some ground-floor chapels in the Jokhang have been destroyed and reconstruct-ed, and statuary has been defaced, replaced, restored and shifted around, so this plan may not match exactly: use it only as a rough guide. Chapels may close and reopen, depending on reconstruction.

Open courtyard with butter lamps (former assembly area for monks)

N Bradt

Steps leading to rooftop

Main doors (closed)

Ticket booth

Open courtyard

Prostrators assemble on flagstones here

THE JOKHANG

Entrance

by Nepalese craftsmen to house a Buddha image brought by the Nepalese queen. Upon Songtsen Gampo's death, Queen Wencheng switched the statue she had brought (the Jowo Sakyamuni) from the Ramoche Temple to the Jokhang, apparently to hide it from Chinese troops. That's why one part of the Jokhang (Chapel 13) is called the Chapel where the Jowo was Hidden. In time, the Jowo Sakyamuni statue became the chief object of veneration. The Jokhang was enlarged and embellished by subsequent rulers and Dalai Lamas. Although the building is as old as Lhasa, much of the statuary is quite new. During the Cultural Revolution, the temple was used as a military barracks and a slaughterhouse; later it was used as a hotel for Chinese officials. Much of the statuary was lost, destroyed or damaged, so it has been replaced with newer copies of the originals.

In 2000, the Jokhang was inscribed on the UNESCO World Heritage List as an addition to the Potala Palace, which is good news because it may bolster protection of the buildings in the immediate vicinity.

Outside the Jokhang

Fronting the Jokhang are flagstones where Tibetans gather to prostrate before the temple. A bit further back are two small walled enclosures with obelisks inside. One enclosure shelters two stone obelisks with an edict in Chinese about curing smallpox – the edict, from 1794, is largely illegible because Tibetans gouged pieces out of it, supposing that the stone itself had curative properties. The second enclosure, with a tall thin obelisk, bears a bilingual inscription about a peace treaty between Tibetan king Ralpachen and Chinese emperor Wangti, concluded in AD823, delineating the borders between the nations of China and Tibet. The brick enclosures around the obelisks were put up when Barkor Square was created in 1985.

Access

Exit and entry are by a side-door off the Barkor: an entry fee of Y35 is charged. However, if you go straight to the Jokhang rooftop, you can skip the entry fee. It's best to visit the Jokhang in the mornings, from 08.30 to noon. The Jokhang may be closed on Mondays. Entering the inner sanctum of the ground floor chapels may be difficult for Tibetan pilgrims. As a tourist, you are privileged to be allowed in. Photography is allowed in certain parts of the Jokhang – if in doubt, ask first. Second floor chapels may be closed off and only accessible to monks residing at the Jokhang – you should respect this limitation. It should be all right to access the rooftop, however, and you might be able to visit the rooftop at times when the ground-floor chapels are closed.

The rooftop

You can take a staircase near the ticket booth at the front straight up to the golden rooftop of the Jokhang, with excellent views over Lhasa rooftops and the Potala in the distance. In the summer months there is a tented teahouse up on the Jokhang rooftop, run by the monks. Visiting the rooftop seems to be a privilege reserved for tourists – both Western and Chinese – as you don't see Tibetan pilgrims up here. The monks at the teahouse do a roaring trade with Chinese tour-groups, selling Jokhang talismans and postcards, and T-shirts, books and souvenirs, plus drinks. Chinese tourists excitedly chatter on their mobile phones to callers across China (they even talk on cellphones when visiting the shrines in the Jokhang – including the Jowo shrine). Although it can, at times, turn into a Chinese photo-taking zoo, the rooftop is a bright, peaceful spot – a refreshing place after the dark, smoky chapels of the Jokhang interior. There are beautiful ornaments hanging from the eaves of the gilded sloping roofs, some in the shape of dragons, others in the shape of mythical birds.

Ground-floor icons

Walking through the dark corridors and chapels of the Jokhang, you enter another world – dim light is provided by a galaxy of butter lamps; the air is thick with the odour of yak-butter and incense; echoing through the halls is the sound of murmuring, from throngs of Tibetan pilgrims. If your timing is right, the inner sanctum may reverberate with the sound of deep, hypnotic chanting of monks at prayer. About 100 monks live at the Jokhang, residing on the upper levels.

Some of the chapels in the Jokhang have been destroyed and reconstructed, and statuary has been defaced, replaced, restored and shifted around, so the plan on page 118 may not match exactly with what is on the ground. Chapels may close and reopen, depending on reconstruction. With this jumble of old and new, it is also debatable which statuary is original and which is copied.

The world you enter seems quite complex and confusing, withno point of reference, no rhyme or reason. However, that may be a matter of familiarising yourself with the icons of Tibetan Buddhism – which, admittedly, are bewildering in their scope and number. If you want to explore Tibetan temple iconography, the Jokhang has the lot – a virtual Who's Who of the Tibetan Buddhist pantheon. Using the plan of the Jokhang in this section, you can identify which images are Avalokitesvara, Sakyamuni, King Songtsen Gampo and so on. The same icons pop up in many other temples in Tibet, and are referred to in other parts of this book. Only some of the ground-floor chapels are described here: the emphasis is on the icons.

Unlike most temples, the Jokhang is not identified with a particular sect. Leaders and teachers from the different sects are shown in statuary and murals. **Tsongkhapa** (Chapel 1) is the founder of the Geluk (Yellow Hat) sect. There's a finer image of him in Chapel 6, wearing monk's robes and a pointed yellow cap; he lived from 1357 to 1419. Between Chapel 3 and Chapel 4 is an image of the great poet-saint **Milarepa** (1040–1123), with his hand cocked to one ear so that he can better hear the music of the spheres and the voice of teachings. The sage appears with skin of a greenish hue – a case of nettle anaemia (he dined solely on nettle soup for a number of years). Milarepa was a founding member of the Kagyu sect. Another historical figure seen in chapels and in larger statues at the inner sanctum is **Padmasambhava**, the 8th-century tantric Indian master who is credited with establishing Buddhism in Tibet. He is the founder of the Nyingma sect, and is shown with a stern expression and a curled moustache, wearing a folded red hat.

In the Tibetan pantheon are many Buddhas and bodhisattvas. A bodhisattva is a being on the way to becoming a Buddha, but one who has decided to delay the pursuit of nirvana and devote himself or herself to the welfare of others. The Dalai Lama is thought to be an emanation of **Avalokitesvara**, the bodhisattva of Compassion (Chenrezig in Tibetan). Often shown in a standing statue, Avalokitesvara has 11 heads (one of which is wrathful) and multiple arms, and may be encircled by a thousand hands. The many heads are said to have burst from the original head as a result of contemplating the suffering of living beings.

The figure of Avalokitesvara is found in several parts of the ground floor – in Chapel 4, outside Chapel 5 in a glass case, in Chapel 10, and right at the centre of the inner sanctum. The image in Chapel 4 has a long story behind it: some parts of the statue are original, some are copies. The image was commissioned by

Barkor Bazaar

Barkor Bazaar is a lively combination of market-place, pilgrim circuit and ethnic melting-pot. The 20-minute hexagonal circuit, running clockwise around the Jokhang and other structures, is always busy, especially at dawn and dusk. Join the pilgrims for a few circuits – it's good for exercise and good for people watching.

At the front of the Jokhang, the flagstones are worn smooth – polished from many years of pilgrims performing prostrations. Two-metre-high conical incense-burners billow clouds of smoke, and the smell of juniper fills the air. Vendors – mostly Chinese making a buck off Buddhism – sell *kata* scarves (see *Glossary*, page 271), prayer flags and prayer-wheels to the pilgrims. Arriving on pilgrimage from far-flung regions – such as the Kham or Golok areas – pilgrims mutter mantras as they circumambulate. You might see nomad women from eastern Tibet, their long tresses smeared with yak-butter; or an old woman leading her favourite sheep around the circuit; or a proud Khampa from eastern Tibet with tassels of red yarn braided through his hair, and a dagger on his belt (not entirely decorative); or a hardy prostrator with rubber apron and padded gloves flinging himself forward on the ground, completing the circuit on his stomach.

The Barkor is a magnet for beggars seeking alms, and for pilgrims seeking funds for their return home (and to support themselves in Lhasa in the meantime). More sophisticated are sutra-chanters: for a small sum, they will recite from sacred texts. And finally, there is the bazaar itself – shops and businesses line the entire circuit. Competing with these are open-air stalls laden with souvenirs and household goods; and there are roving vendors with bags of Tibetan music cassettes or other items. Since 1987, Barkor Bazaar has assumed another role – as the focus of protesters who encircle the Barkor when demonstrating against the Chinese occupation of Tibet. This explains the presence of police and security personnel in the area, ready to intercept any demonstrators.

Barkor Square

Officially, Barkor Square was completed in 1985 to mark the 20th year of the creation of the TAR. Unofficially, it was built to provide full military access to the troublesome Tibetan quarter and the maze of alleyways in the Barkor beyond. In the process, the Jokhang – previously hidden from view – has been exposed by a large plaza. There used to be a small square in front of the Jokhang – used as a marketplace – but nothing on the scale of the present plaza. This architectural approach might suit a grand European cathedral, but it is a travesty when applied to an intimate corner like the Jokhang.

Barkor Square is lined with shops and eateries, but it is also an elaborate parking lot for army trucks should trouble arise. A lot of older housing was ripped up and then replaced with mock-Tibetan-style shops, but these do not quite look the same. For one thing, the outer walls of these newer buildings are vertical, not bevelled as in old Lhasa. Old Lhasan housing is conservative in style, with an 'extraordinary biblical severity ... preserving for us living architectural forms of ancient civilisations', as one writer noted. Typical housing consisted of flat-roofed two- or three-storey structures made of stone or sun-baked brick. Some buildings in the Barkor area date back to the 17th century and have withstood the test of time. Like the great masons of ancient Egypt or the Inca empire, Tibetans used no nails or cement: they fitted large blocks of stone closely together and relied on gravity, which meant inward-sloping walls were constructed.

In the PRC, squares like this are used for mass shows of solidarity with the Party, but occasionally (as at Tiananmen Square in 1989) they can be used for mass demonstrations against the Party. In Barkor Square, if 20 or so Tibetans

Songtsen Gampo in the 7th century. During the Cultural Revolution, this image and others were tossed into the streets. Tibetans managed to salvage a wrathful and a peaceful aspect of the faces of Avalokitesvara – the images were smuggled out via Nepal to India. The faces were eventually made into a new image of Avalokitesvara at the Tsug Lakhang in Dharamsala.

Tara (Drolma in Tibetan) is said to be the spiritual consort of Avalokitesvara, and possesses more than 20 forms. **White Tara** is identified with Queen Wencheng and the fertile aspect of compassion, while **Green Tara** is identified with Queen Tritsun and the motherly aspect of compassion. Green Tara is the patron female saint of Tibet; she sits with her right leg extended slightly, resting on a lotus blossom. White Tara sits cross-legged upon a lotus flower – she is easily recognised by the eyes depicted in the palms of her hands: she is believed to have sprung from a tear of compassion falling from the eye of Avalokitesvara. While there is little statuary of Tara in the ground-floor chapels, her image appears in a number of murals – a Tara fresco is shown on a wall recessed at the back of Chapel 16.

Tibetans believe that the historical Buddha (Sakyamuni) is the Buddha of the present era, but only one of the many Buddhas to appear – past, present and future. The Buddha is 'he who is fully awake' – an enlightened being. **Amitabha**, appearing in Chapel 2, is the Buddha of Infinite Light (*Opame* in Tibetan) – usually depicted in a red colour, with hands clasping an alms-bowl. The Panchen Lama is thought to be an incarnation of Amitabha. A row of eight **Medicine Buddhas** is shown in Chapel 3 – these are the Buddhas of healing, and caring for the sick. **Jampa** is the Buddha of the Future, also known as Champa or the Maitreya Buddha. This Buddha is not usually shown cross-legged, but seated conventionally on a throne. The Jampa statue shown in Chapel 5 is a copy of one brought to Tibet from Nepal by Queen Tritsun. In Chapel 9 is an image of Jampa (brought in from Drepung to replace a destroyed image); this statue was once paraded around the Barkor at Monlam. In the inner sanctum are two Jampa images.

The centrepiece of the Jokhang is a 1.5m-high gilded statue of **Jowo Sakyamuni**, the Buddha of the Present, born in 543BC in Nepal. The image was brought to Tibet by Queen Wencheng. It depicts the Sakyamuni Buddha at the age of 12: features such as long earlobes and a cranial bump are special marks of the Buddha. The highly revered statue bears an elaborate headdress and is encrusted with jewels; pilgrims crowd in to make offerings, and to walk around the statue.

Revered as deities are the early religious kings of Tibet, who converted to Buddhism. Easily identified in the ground-floor chapels is **King Songtsen Gampo** (circa 608–650), the first of the great religious kings, considered to be a manifestation of Avalokitesvara. He wears a high orange or gold turban; his Chinese wife, **Queen Wencheng**, is on the viewer's right; his Nepalese wife, **Queen Tritsun**, on the viewer's left. This is the arrangement for a group to the left of the Jowo Sakyamuni image. The three great religious kings of Tibet are found in the Chapel of the Dharma Kings (Chapel 16) – the central figure being Songtsen Gampo; to the viewer's right, **Trisong Detsen** (the second religious king, who ruled from 755–797); and to the viewer's left, **Tri Ralpachen** (who ruled from 815–838). On the way out of the area, take a closer look at the two **side chapels** by the entrance: these contain guardian deities, designed to ward off evil forces.

Entering or exiting the inner Jokhang sanctuary, you pass two side chapels. The side chapel to the left (on the north side) contains a statue of Palden Lhamo, the main protective deity of the Jokhang, as well as fierce guardian deities. To the right, on the south side, are three Naga deity statues, also with a protective role.